MAYBERRY 101

BEHIND THE SCENES
OF A TV CLASSIC

JOHN F. BLAIR, PUBLISHER

WINSTON-SALEM, NORTH CAROLINA

MAYBERRY 101

BEHIND THE SCENES
OF A TV CLASSIC

by Neal Brower

DESIGN BY DEBRA LONG HAMPTON
COVER DESIGN BY LIZA LANGRALL
PRINTED AND BOUND BY R. R. DONNELLEY & SONS

*The paper in this book meets the guidelines for permanence
and durability of the Committee on Production Guidelines
for Book Longevity of the Council on Library Resources.*

Library of Congress Cataloging-in-Publication Data
Brower, Neal, 1954–
    Mayberry 101 : behind the scenes of a TV classic / by Neal Brower.
        p.   cm.
    Includes index.
    ISBN 0-89587-218-8
    1. Andy Griffith show (Television program)   I. Title.
PN1992.77.A573B76   1998
791.45'72—dc21   98–28733

For Toni and Keaton

May our lives together be full of
days as happy as time spent in Mayberry
and nights as serene as
an evening on Andy's front porch.

CONTENTS

Foreword

Barney Fife had it right. "It's big!"

After spending every season in the Nielsen's Top Ten, *The Andy Griffith Show* was the Number One show in prime-time television when Andy Griffith decided that eight years was enough in 1968.

But eight wasn't enough for the rest of us. By the millions, we have continued to watch this wonderful show every week in reruns. (O.K., for many of us, it's often several times every day, but I didn't want you to think I was some kind of a "compelsion nut.") I wonder what causes that?

Indeed, what *does* cause that? As Presiding Goober of *The Andy Griffith Show* Rerun Watchers Club (TAGSRWC) for nearly two decades, I've participated in many discussions and received thousands of letters from fans about why *The Andy Griffith Show* remains so popular.

Some folks speculate that it's the show's nostalgia—that people yearn for a simpler time that maybe never was. Mayberry provides a happy, thirty-minute escape from the difficulties of the "real" world, they say.

Others say that they think the show's appeal is its wholesomeness— that it's a show the entire family can watch together without being concerned about inappropriate language, violence, or sexual situations. (Parents often tell me that when they encounter a challenging parenting situation, they ask themselves, "What would Andy do?")

I agree that the show's warm nostalgia and gentle wholesomeness are parts of its allure. But we wouldn't be watching the same episodes over and over if they were just nostalgic and merely wholesome. There's something else at work.

I believe what has made *The Andy Griffith Show* an evergreen of popularity in reruns is that it is truly outstanding storytelling. The high quality of all aspects of the show's production rarely has been equaled (and, to my mind, never surpassed) in all of television. It is that superior craftsmanship that has allowed the show to stand the test of time through generations.

I've never watched a finer ensemble of actors. Just think of all of those fabulous characters. Why, they're so real that they could be our neighbors and best friends. And behind every one of those characters was a marvelous actor at work. You'll find similar genius in the show's music and its artful direction. The entire production, quite simply, was done with extraordinary skill.

We should salute executive producer Sheldon Leonard for putting together the winning creative team behind it all. With writer/producer Aaron Ruben (and later Bob Ross) as the head coach, the writers seldom came up with a play that didn't work. And with Andy Griffith as the star quarterback, the talented team rarely fumbled.

Whenever I watch episodes of *The Andy Griffith Show*, I am awestruck by the utter brilliance of the writing. I would consider my career as a writer to be a success if I were to come up with just one turn of phrase as good as any line in Harvey Bullock's "The Pickle Story" or Everett Greenbaum and Jim Fritzell's "Convicts at Large" or Bill Idelson and Sam Bobrick's "The Shoplifters." (One need only look at how many of the names of the thousand-plus chapters of TAGSRWC are inspired by references and dialogue from just these three episodes to know that many other fans share this enchantment.)

And so it is that Neal Brower has prudently organized this book's discussion around the writers. By doing so, he gives the reader an unprecedented, behind-the-scenes look at the creation of each of the episodes written by three of the best writing teams in the history of. . .well, in history.

Just as scientists use the Hubble Telescope to see back to the birth of the universe, *Mayberry 101* is our humble time machine for catching a glimpse of each episode's own "Big Bang" (and no, that's not just the sound that inevitably occurs when Barney fails to keep his bullet in his left shirt pocket).

On just about every page of this book, you'll learn about fascinating things that you've never noticed before—even if you've seen a particular episode fifty or a hundred times. (It's O.K. to admit that you've seen episodes that many times. You're among fellow Goobers now.) Neal's thoughtful examinations of each episode will bring new depth and perspective to how you watch an episode. You're guaranteed to have a better understanding of how the episodes were conceived and produced.

Whether you've watched *The Andy Griffith Show* all of your life or are just starting to watch it, the information and insights in this book are sure to enrich your enjoyment and appreciation of watching the show.

Mayberry 101 is a dream come true for those of us who, since 1991, have enjoyed Neal's regular column for *The Bullet* (that's the official newsletter of TAGSRWC) or who have had the pleasure of attending sessions of his 10-week continuing education course on the show. And even if this is your first exposure to Neal's discussions of Mayberry, you'll find that his deep passion for *The Andy Griffith Show* is highly contagious! (It's what you might call Mayberry Fever, and if you've read this far, you've probably already got it.)

We're all entertained by *The Andy Griffith Show*. We know why it's enjoyable to watch. We know why it's funny. Now we have *Mayberry 101* to help us discover some of the mysteries and mechanics of *how* it was that *The Andy Griffith Show* became what many of us consider to be the greatest show on earth.

If only all homework was this much fun!

Jim Clark

The address for *The Andy Griffith Show* Rerun Watchers Club is:
9 Music Square South
Suite 146
Nashville, Tennessee 37203-3203

Acknowledgments

My thanks go out to everyone who helped make this book possible: Jeanne Swanner Robertson for giving me the pep talk that finally convinced me I should and could write this book; Jim Clark for helping me make contacts, providing pictures, writing the foreword, and allowing me to share my interest in *The Andy Griffith Show* with other fans through my column in *The Bullet*; Jim Ballance, who was my traveling companion to California and prepared the book's index; Don Teague, who provided a listening ear throughout the writing process; and The Barney Chapter of *The Andy Griffith Show* Rerun Watchers Club for their friendship and mutual love of Mayberry.

Thanks to John F. Blair, Publisher, for taking an interest in this project. A special thank you is due Carolyn Sakowski. She was my editor. Her comments were gentle and wise and made the book better.

I thank the late Jack Dodson, Hoke Howell, Jack Prince, and Hal Smith. Their kindness and cooperation are not forgotten.

And thanks to all the cast, directors, producers, and friends whose voices told the story: Courtney Bullock, Jean Carson, Bernard Fox, Jeffrey Hayden, Rance and Jean Howard, Mitch Jayne, George Lindsey, Richard O. Linke, Betty Lynn, Howard Morris, Aaron Ruben, Jay Sandrich, and Amzie Strickland.

Thanks to writers Sam Bobrick and Bill Idelson for sharing their memories.

A special word of thanks to Everett Greenbaum and Harvey Bullock. Everett felt "it was important to keep the memories alive" and faithfully answered my questions. Harvey's answers were unparalleled in detail and length. He touched my heart and became my friend.

Introduction

Mayberry is my passion. I love *The Andy Griffith Show*. I grew up watching *The Andy Griffith Show*. It was on television throughout my teenage and young adult life. In 1985 the Mayberry bug bit me. It was then that I purchased a copy of *The Andy Griffith Show* by Dr. Richard Kelly. In the back of the book, there was a listing of all 249 episodes. I was now a man with a mission. I would tape all 249 episodes.

I eventually accomplished my mission. While doing so, I got caught up in the lives of Mayberry's residents and the loving spirit of their town.

In his book, Dr. Kelly included the address of *The Andy Griffith Show* Rerun Watchers Club. Wanting to know more about the show, I wrote to the club. The club's Presiding Goober, Jim Clark, enrolled me and sent a copy of the club's newsletter, *The Bullet*.

From *The Bullet*, I learned there were other fans who shared my love for Mayberry.

I began corresponding with Mike Tobkes, a fan in New York. Mike exposed me to a whole new world—the world of *The Andy Griffith Show* research. Mike had searched the New York City libraries for magazines, newspapers, etc. that contained articles related to the show. He shared the information with me, and I too began looking for anything that was related to Mayberry.

Over the next several years, I accumulated a wealth of material about the show. The question became: Now, what do I do with it?

I was looking through a listing of course offerings at an area community college. When I saw an offering for a *Star Trek* course, it gave me an idea.

If a community college would approve a course about *Star Trek*, I was sure they would approve a course on *The Andy Griffith Show*, especially a North Carolina community college.

I compiled my Mayberry materials into a lecture format and presented the results to Central Piedmont Community College in Charlotte, North

Carolina. Thus, "*The Andy Griffith Show*: An In-Depth Study" was approved. Since 1988 I have taught the course over twenty times at six different community colleges.

I also wanted to share my interest and knowledge with fans who were unable to attend one of my classes. *The Bullet* provided that opportunity. In 1991 I wrote the first "Professor Brower's Class" column for the newsletter. The column offered a behind-the-scenes look at one of the episodes from the series.

The first few columns consisted of my personal observations and comments about the episode. Then I had an idea. I decided to try to include comments from the writers. Where did they get the ideas for their stories? Where did they get ideas for the details in the stories? For instance, why did Thelma Lou serve Opie brownies and homemade peach ice cream instead of chocolate cake and vanilla ice cream?

Harvey Bullock, the first writer I contacted, graciously agreed to answer my questions. This opened up another world. Now I not only wanted the writers' observations when writing my column, I wanted the producers' and actors' input as well.

I gradually contacted many of these people, and my columns began to center primarily on their telling of the Mayberry story. As time went on, I realized it was a wonderful story that needed to be told.

The Bullet comes out three times a year. Offering only three columns a year was too slow a process. The stories needed to be told before the memories faded.

This book is the end result of the need to tell the story in a more timely format.

In one of his letters, writer Everett Greenbaum wrote, "Neal, I will be glad to answer your questions because I feel it is important to keep the memories alive."

Thanks to Everett and all who were willing to share their time and comments, another part of the Mayberry story has now been preserved. In this book their stories are told—the memories live on.

1960·61

Quiet Sam

EPISODE #29

FIRST BROADCAST ON MAY 1, 1961

WRITTEN BY JIM FRITZELL AND
EVERETT GREENBAUM

DIRECTED BY BOB SWEENEY

WILLIAM SCHALLERT GUEST STARS
AS SAM BECKER

"I had no idea when we wrote 'Quiet Sam' that it was the beginning of a lifetime association with Mayberry."

Everett Greenbaum

"I guess Jim Fritzell and I wound up with TAGS [*The Andy Griffith Show*] as a result of our knack for writing Americana," says writer Everett Greenbaum. "Aaron Ruben and TAGS executive producer Sheldon Leonard were familiar with our writing from *Mr. Peepers* and *The Real McCoys*.

"But there was another thing. Bob Sweeney (who directed most of the shows in the early years) went to high school in San Francisco with Jim Fritzell. A year ahead of Jim in high school, Bob was Jim's idol, because he had been head of debate and was later a success in show business. Bob helped Jim get started in Hollywood and may have encouraged Aaron to give us a try.

"At the time, Jim and I didn't have any trouble finding writing assignments, and I wasn't overly thrilled about being hired to write a TAGS script because what I really wanted to do was write movies. I had only watched the show a couple of times. But, I had loved Andy in *No Time For Sergeants* as well as his record, 'What It Was, Was Football'."

Everett and Jim's finished script opens with Barney and Floyd standing in front of the barbershop. Barney sees a truck parked close to a fire hydrant and suspects a violation of "Code 8, Section B." The truck belongs to Sam Becker, "a strange duck" who "doesn't say word one."

"We kind of borrowed the code dialogue from Jack Webb's *Dragnet* show, which was number one in the ratings in those days," says Everett.

Barney tries to get Sam to talk but is unsuccessful. After Sam drives

IN THE BEGINNING

"When *The Andy Griffith Show* [TAGS] was being put together by Danny Thomas and Sheldon Leonard in Los Angeles, Andy and I were in New York City," says TAGS associate producer Richard O. Linke. "The four of us would go back and forth by phone, and Sheldon flew in a couple of times. When it came time to hire the line producer, who is usually the head writer and the day-to-day guy in charge of what happens, we thought Sheldon was going to hire a man by the name of Fred DeCordova. DeCordova was a big, big movie and television director in Hollywood. I said, 'Man, that's great.' But it turned out that DeCordova wasn't available.

"So Sheldon sent us a list of names of other possible candidates. It's funny because all the persons that were recommended were both New York-bred and Jewish. At first, I said to myself, 'This sounds a bit funny. How would they know about an Andy Griffith and the South?'

"The list was narrowed down to Aaron Ruben and Marvin Marks, who was the head writer for *The Jackie Gleason Show*. I had heard about Aaron Ruben, but I didn't know too much about his work. Andy and I talked to both candidates and were sort of confused about who to hire.

"I remember my office was a two-room suite at the Park Sheraton away, Andy walks up, and Barney tells him that Sam has all the characteristics of a criminal. Barney asks, "Doesn't it bother you the way he won't look you in the eye? The way he's always in a hurry. The busiest man in the world has five minutes to pass the time of day."

"Sam Becker had to have a quality of shyness and mystery in the beginning, and William Schallert, who was cast in the role, fit my image of the character very well," says Everett. "When writing a script, I used names I knew rather than stopping to make one up. The Becker family lived across the street from us in Buffalo."

Another example of Everett's method for selecting names was the naming of Nate Pike, Opie's wise four-year-old acquaintance. Opie

Hotel, and Andy used to come over there for meetings. He was doing *Destry Rides Again* on Broadway at the time. So Andy said, 'What do you think?' And I said, 'Jees, I don't know.' It was almost a flip of the coin at that stage. Finally we said, and I don't remember if Andy said it to me or I said it to Andy, 'Let's go with Aaron Ruben.'

"Our decision was not based on any big knowledge or document. But, it was probably the luckiest and the best decision we ever made because Aaron turned out to be a really top, top writer-producer and a very brilliant guy in his own field. And that was it. We called Sheldon with our decision, and the William Morris Agency, who put the TAGS package together, did the actual hiring."

"As the producer of the series, my main responsibility was to be sure we had a good, workable script on that first day of shooting," says Aaron Ruben. "If necessary, I would do a re-write and make certain all of us—Andy, the director, the executive producer, and I—were agreed we were ready for the camera. The other responsibilities I had to attend to were casting, conferring with the editor, the composer, the wardrobe people, and the writers."

mentions Nate as a thunderstorm begins. Opie asks Andy if he thinks lightning will hit the backyard and requests a penny. Andy questions Opie about the request and is told Nate Pike said "a penny hit by lightning is worth six cents."

"Nate Pike was a great, big bully who used to beat me up in school," recalls Everett. "Nate's theory about a penny hit by lightning grew out of a childhood memory. As kids, we thought a penny run over by a train was lucky, so we extended it to lightning strikes."

Barney stops by the Taylors' to report on the "Becker case." Barney has checked the sales records at the drugstore and found that Sam has purchased large amounts of absorbent cotton, antiseptics, vitamins, tranquilizers, and swab sticks. Barney thinks Sam is harboring someone with a bullet in him and convinces Andy that they should go look around.

Andy and Barney park at a distance when they arrive at Sam's house. They watch as Sam plows his field in the middle of the night. Barney suggests that Sam's strange behavior may be due to the fact that Sam is growing marijuana.

This is somewhat surprising dialogue for 1961, especially in a small Southern town. "I think we wrote the script about the same time marijuana was in the news because Robert Mitchum had been arrested for possession," explains Everett. "Barney's comment was inspired by the extensive news coverage of the incident."

Soon after Andy and Barney return to Mayberry, Andy receives a call that there is trouble at the Becker place. Andy leaves word for Barney, who is out checking door knobs, that he is returning to the Becker place.

As Andy arrives at Sam's home, a thunderstorm occurs. The on-screen lightning storm visually communicates the feeling of mystery initially created by the suspicious behavior of Sam Becker. The TAGS production crew realistically created the storm through the use of wind machines, sound effects, variations in lighting, simulation of pouring rain, and the addition during the editing process of actual footage of lightning flashing across the sky.

Soon after arriving at Sam's house, Andy learns the real reason for Sam's suspicious behavior—he and his wife are expecting a baby.

Meanwhile, Barney gets the message about Andy's whereabouts and jumps to the conclusion that Andy is in serious trouble. Barney telephones Floyd and instructs him to round up anyone he can find to help rescue Andy.

The careful attention given to detail on TAGS is evident in the brief telephone-conversation scene between Floyd and Barney. Pouring rain can be seen through the window behind Floyd. Such detail enabled Mayberry to come alive as a real and believable place.

When Barney arrives at the Becker place, he learns that the birth is going to happen at any time. Barney becomes nervous when he learns that the inexperienced Andy is going to perform the delivery. Barney reminds Andy that he flunked "Miss Webster's biology class in the spring of 1938."

"Biology class dissection jokes have always been grist for the comedy mill, so we had Barney remind Andy about flunking Miss Webster's biology class—while dissecting a grasshopper, he froze," says Everett.

Andy tells Barney and Sam that they need to get their minds on something other than babies. Andy diverts the conversation by bringing up Barney's army service. Barney shares his memories about his experience "across the big pond" in Staten Island's 3,000-book PX library. Sam tell of his service in Korea. As the two talk, Andy quietly leaves to deliver the baby.

After "army story number seventeen" has been told, Andy returns with Sam's baby boy. Sam takes his son but soon calls upon the sheriff to help the baby "Andy" stop crying.

Everett comments, "Jim and I liked the humor of Barney's army experience so well that several years later we used it a second time in the Don Knotts movie *The Reluctant Astronaut*. Becker naming the baby 'Andy' ended the second act on a sentimental note and was a sure-fire crowd-pleaser, like waving a flag in vaudeville."

"Quiet Sam" concludes with a group of Mayberry residents celebrating

Andy's birth. The celebration includes a forty-second performance of "She'll Be Comin' 'Round the Mountain."

"There was no musical performance in our script," says Everett. "I imagine the filmed script was too short, and the music was added to fill in the remaining time."

1961-62.

Opie's Hobo Friend

EPISODE #40

FIRST BROADCAST ON NOVEMBER 13, 1961

WRITTEN BY HARVEY BULLOCK

DIRECTED BY BOB SWEENEY

BUDDY EBSEN GUEST STARS
AS DAVID BROWNE, THE HOBO

"In my brief career, I had never written alone before, or for any of the Hollywood studios or producers. I knew nobody in town. I had no contacts. The only familiar thing in sight was my battered, old, Royal manual typewriter."

Harvey Bullock

"There was always a special joy in doing an 'Opie' story," says producer Aaron Ruben. "We always tried to open the new season with an 'Opie' script because they had such enormous appeal, and we felt it was a smart way to hook an audience for the start of the new season. 'Opie's Hobo Friend' was a wonderful story, and just the kind that Harvey Bullock was so capable of writing—lots of heart, warmth, a solid moral lesson, and always the meaningful relationship between Andy and Opie."

" 'Opie's Hobo Friend' has a very special meaning for me," says Harvey Bullock. "It was the first one I wrote for the series. I was new in town, having left my wife and three infant daughters back in New York while I sought employment in the booming sitcom business in Hollywood.

"I was living in a run-down motel and driving a rent-a-wreck when my agent managed to get me a meeting with Aaron Ruben. This was my big chance. The Griffith Show was the absolute Tiffany of all comedies. A writing assignment on that highly respected show would almost guarantee assignments on any other show in town.

"The thought of the meeting made me very nervous. But being from a small town, I felt comfortable with the Mayberry style. I also recognized the obvious—their stories were emotional and character driven, not physical farce.

"I have always delighted in older, colorful characters who were not the stuff of convention. The bare bones of the story I had in mind featured an irresponsible vagrant who seemed to live in glorious freedom and would thus be appealing to a youngster who didn't recognize the pitfalls. But it was important the vagrant be somewhat glib, educated, articulate, even likable—all of which made him an even more effectively tempting role model.

"I went in to meet Aaron with all fingers, toes, arms, legs, and, certainly, stomach crossed. To my immense relief, he turned out to be the most friendly, understanding, and helpful producer I have ever met. I think he sensed I was nervous and went out of his way to relax me. He prodded, added, spent time, and gradually the 'Hobo' evolved. 'Go home and get started on it,' I remember Aaron saying. 'It'll be a good one.' After the meeting, I drove my old rented wreck of a car out the studio gate—and the wheels never touched the ground."

Harvey's finished script came alive through the wonderful acting abilities of TAGS cast and guest star Buddy Ebsen. "Buddy Ebsen was cast as the hobo because he is a fine actor, and he had that easy-going, happy-go-lucky look one might associate with a guy who has dropped out of the competitive world and embarked on an aimless, wandering existence," says Aaron Ruben. "The process of hiring guest stars begins with hiring a good casting director. Having been told by the producer what the part calls for, he or she will then go through their file on the actors they are familiar with and decide which would be most suitable for the role. They will submit a short list of possibilities to the producer, and, thus, spare him the lengthy process of having to audition an endless parade of candidates."

Harvey drew upon his past during the writing of the episode. "I actually had a friend whose name was Dave Browne," says Harvey. "It came up accidently that he had an *e* [on the end of his last name] and we teased him mercilessly. It [the name Browne] seemed to fit the hobo character, who used that little touch as a subtle claim to class."

Harvey introduces Dave Browne in the episode's opening scene. Andy and Opie meet Mr. Browne as they arrive at a lake for a morning of fishing. After Andy and Opie are out of sight, Mr. Browne helps himself to a sandwich from the lunch bag in the back seat of the squad car.

Later that afternoon, Barney brings Mr. Browne in on a vagrancy charge. After Andy and Opie return from fishing, Barney tells Andy that Mr. Browne doesn't have a cent on him. When Mr. Browne asks for a coin, he explains that money disappears whenever he has it, and when he needs more it reappears. Mr. Browne illustrates this by making the coin magically disappear and reappear from Opie's ear. Andy dismisses the vagrancy charge, and Mr. Browne leaves.

Barney objects to Andy's release of Mr. Browne. Not wanting Opie to hear Barney's objections, Andy gives Opie a penny for the gumball machine down the street. Barney feels Browne "is no ordinary hobo" and vows to keep "his baby blues" on him.

When Opie encounters Mr. Browne at the gumball machine, Mr. Browne tells Opie he doesn't need money as long as he has "the magic touch and knows the magic word." Mr. Browne demonstrates by saying "Tuscarora," as he taps the stop of the gumball machine. Although he retrieves a gumball using his magic touch, he is actually reaching behind the machine and jimmying the machine with a pick.

"I grew up in Binghamton, New York, a town about halfway between New York City and Buffalo, near the Pennsylvania border. My parents would sometimes take my sister and me on car trips in our vintage Plymouth. Often we would return to Binghamton on Route 17, and near Deposit, New York, the road went near the top of Tuscarora Mountain and then descended in a very long stretch of highway. My father would say the magic word, 'Tuscarora,' and to our squeals of delight, he would turn off the motor, and we coasted down in the quiet for miles.

"I had completely forgotten about it. Then thirty years after, as an ink-stained wretch laboring over my typewriter in the small hours, doing a story about a roguish hobo, the word jumped out of my subconscious, slid through my fingertips and onto the paper. And it somehow seemed exactly right."

One of the strengths of TAGS was its realism. An excellent example of detailed realism is present in the Tuscarora scene. Mr. Dave and Opie are standing in front of a store window. A pedestrian walking on the sidewalk on the other side of the street can be seen in the window's reflection.

"The assistant director on 'Opie's Hobo Friend' was Bruce Bilson," says Harvey, "and one of his duties as A.D. was to set up background happenings, extras crossing the street, etc., so the director could concentrate on the main action with the principle players. I could always tell when Bruce was the A.D. He would have layers of happenings to give flavor to the film. Most importantly, they were always muted enough so they did not distract. I used to kid him about his great eye and inventiveness for detail, how he would have a man mowing his lawn in the background three blocks away!"

Later in the episode, Barney arrests Mr. Browne for loitering. Not wanting to imprison Mr. Browne, Andy gives him a job trimming hedges. Before he begins the job, Mr. Brown discusses the job with Opie and reaches the conclusion that he will cut the hedges tomorrow—"the perfect day to start any job."

Mr. Browne's philosophy makes an impression on Opie. The next morning Opie decides to "wait until tomorrow" to pick up his room. After breakfast, Opie leaves for school and encounters Mr. Browne. Mr. Browne tells Opie he can hear the fish jumping at the lake and shows him a homemade fishing lure he calls the "Gollywobbler Super Fish Catcher."

"The name of Mr. Dave's homemade fishing lure just jumped out. Gollywobbler was a word used for a stomach disorder. It always intrigued me, so I bent it around to embellish a homemade fish hook," says Harvey.

Influenced by Mr. Browne again, Opie decides to play hooky from school and go fishing. Barney catches Opie and takes him home.

Andy decides it is time to pay Mr. Browne a visit. He explains to Browne that Opie is having trouble being able to tell the difference between right and wrong. Andy decides that Mr. Browne is not a good role model and invites him to leave town. Andy explains to Mr. Browne that he has a lot of "unscrambling to do" to straighten Opie out.

Shortly after this exchange, Barney brings Mr. Browne in a third time. This time he is arrested for purse snatching. The purse found on Mr. Browne has Aunt Bee's name inside it. Opie enters the courthouse and overhears the charge. He questions Mr. Browne about the theft. Mr. Browne offers no explanation. Opie turns to leave but stops. He takes the Gollywobbler from his pocket, hangs it on a bar of Mr. Browne's cell and departs.

After Barney and Opie leave, Andy walks over to the cell and tells Mr. Browne that he knows the pocketbook is one Aunt Bee had thrown in the trash. A train whistle is heard blowing in the distance. Andy opens the cell and says, "Mr. Dave, I'd say you got a train to catch."

"Several weeks after completing 'Hobo' I was on my way out of the studio when Sheldon Leonard, the king himself, intercepted me," Harvey recalls. "He had gone out of his way to find me and tell me how much he enjoyed the script of 'Hobo.' His final words were, 'I find your writing very literate.' I rushed home to read the script again. What part was he referring to? I never did know exactly, but I revelled in having pleased that man and was thrilled at having the chance to contribute to such a class show. Happily, the episode worked well. That opened the door for me, and I went on to do some thirty-odd more. But the 'Hobo' will always be the most meaningful."

The Pickle Story

EPISODE #43

FIRST BROADCAST ON DECEMBER 18, 1961

WRITTEN BY HARVEY BULLOCK

DIRECTED BY BOB SWEENEY

"I have fond memories of almost every aspect of working for Sheldon, Aaron, and Andy during those halcyon days."

Harvey Bullock

"The story line for 'The Pickle Story' evolved from one of the legendary writers' seminars conducted by TAGS executive producer Sheldon Leonard," says writer Harvey Bullock. "Sheldon and producer Aaron Ruben would invite a half-dozen writers to a 'spitball' session wherein everyone would toss ideas in the air. It was a wide-open, invigorating exercise with all those active minds spinning at once.

"At the time, I had just come to Hollywood and had written only one TAGS episode, 'Opie's Hobo Friend,' which turned out extremely well. I was very flattered to be invited to the seminar based on one credit and was totally in awe of the veteran writers I was privileged to mingle with.

"In the seminar, the bare bones of 'The Pickle Story' emerged. Among the writers attending that day was the team of Fred Fox and Izzy Ellinson.

Fred, one of the most affable, popular, and talented guys in the business, had an extreme stammer which he (and we) all joked about.

"At the end of the seminar, Sheldon doled out each story to whichever writer he thought might be best suited for it. Evidently, Fred coveted 'The Pickle Story' because when Sheldon came to that one, Freddy raised his hand but was so excited his stammering overcame him. He struggled to get the words out, unnoticed by Sheldon. In desperation, Fred tugged at his partner's arm. But Izzy was busy making notes about a previous story allotted to them.

"Poor Freddy was apoplectic, but sadly, also still speechless. Hardly looking up from his notes, Sheldon finally decreed: "'Okay Harve, you take that one.' At that point, but too late, Freddy finally found his voice and bemoaned loudly, 'F-F-F-F-F-For P-P-P-P-P-Pete's sake, Izzy, you just b-b-b-b-b-blew "The Pickle Story".' Nobody else requested it, and to be honest, I didn't have strong feelings about it myself. I was just wildly anxious to get an assignment—any story at all would do. By the way, Freddy later got another story he liked equally as well."

Harvey developed the assigned story into a wonderful comedic script that begins with Clara Johnson and Aunt Bee in the kitchen. Clara has brought over a jar of her homemade pickles. Aunt Bee has recently made pickles as well, and the two comment on the pickle contest they have entered for the past eleven years. Clara and Aunt Bee sample the pickles. Clara's pickles are "simply delicious." According to Clara, Aunt Bee's pickles are "very nice" and need only a few changes.

This opening scene has some inconsistencies with previous TAGS episodes. Although Aunt Bee has entered and lost the pickle contest for eleven years, at this point in the series she had only been in Mayberry one or two years. Aunt Bee is also known as an excellent cook, yet she cannot make good pickles.

"The time inconsistency never seemed to bother any of us," says Harvey. "It never came up in the comprehensive review each script underwent. I think we never equated the two years the series was on the air as necessarily two years passing in Mayberry—the stories didn't purport to happen a week apart. It was not a contemporary show, so time was malleable. Furthermore, when a character became a series regular, they seemed to be granted an endless past.

"Aunt Bee's inability to prepare edible pickles posed absolutely no problem to me. It's believable (and even endearing) that a master of anything can have a drastic weak point or two."

The first courthouse scene begins with Andy and Barney singing "Tell My Darling Mother I'll Be There." "My copy of the script has the courthouse scene opening with Barney whispering to a passed-out Otis in his cell," says Harvey. "Barney is trying to probe Otis's subconscious mind into revealing where his whiskey still is operating. The replacement of this with the singing could have been the decision of Andy or Aaron Ruben."

Harvey's idea, however, was too good to discard. It was renamed "The Barney Fife Subconscious Prober Primer" and used one week later in the episode, "Sheriff Barney" (Episode #44), written by Leo Solomon and Ben Gershman.

At this point in the episode, Aunt Bee brings lunch, including a jar of her homemade pickles, to the courthouse. Andy and Barney are hesitant to try the pickles but do so to satisfy Aunt Bee. After she departs, they decide to dispose of the whole batch of homemade pickles and replace them with good "store" pickles.

After the switch is made, Aunt Bee notices that Andy, Barney, and Opie really seem to like her pickles. Encouraged by this, she decides to enter the pickles in the contest again.

Andy and Barney are faced with a dilemma. Aunt Bee might win the contest with the store pickles. Andy realizes the severity of the situation after Clara Johnson brings a jar of her pickles and a scrapbook containing her blue ribbons to the courthouse. The contest means alot to Clara, and Andy wouldn't be able to forgive himself if she "got nosed out by a store pickle."

Andy tells Barney they have to eat up all the store pickles so Aunt Bee will make more to enter in the contest. Barney can't believe that Andy wants Aunt Bee to make another batch of "those kerosene cucumbers."

"Annabelle Folker, my late mother-in-law, was a feisty, outspoken delight," recalls Harvey. "She had a wondrous vocabulary and sure called 'em as she saw them. One time my wife Betty made some new salad dressing. Belle took one taste and immediately pronounced it 'kerosene.' I thought it was uproariously funny and stuck it in my mind for future use."

TAGS musical director Earle Hagen's talents are highlighted in the fifty-second scene showing Andy, Barney, and Opie eating up the store pickles. Earl reinforces the on-screen action with variations of the TAGS theme song that fit the scene perfectly. For example, he slows the music's tempo to audibly communicate the characters' feelings of being stuffed.

Andy, Barney, and Opie eventually consume the store pickles and encourage Aunt Bee to make another batch. Aunt Bee "has to hurry some," but the pickles are prepared and entered in the contest.

The pickle-judging scene that concludes the second act includes an interesting and beautifully photographed fifteen-second segment in which the camera is positioned behind the seated Clara Johnson. The camera fluidly pans right, around the end of the aisle where Clara is seated, and stops directly in front of her.

The scene likewise uses silence to heighten its dramatic impact. The carousel music playing in the background stops as the judges taste Aunt Bee's pickles. The music resumes after the judges react negatively to the kerosene cucumbers.

Once again, Clara's pickles win the blue ribbon. After the winner is announced, Opie is seen standing on a chair behind Aunt Bee. He affectionately reaches out and places his hand on her shoulder. This small gesture is a wonderful expression of love.

Andy comforts Aunt Bee by telling her she may win next year. Aunt Bee replies that as long as her family likes her pickles "that's blue ribbon enough for me." She then announces that the boys are still going to be winners because she's made a new batch of pickles for them. She noticed that they liked them so much, she's made sixteen jars this time.

The epilogue ends the episode on a comic high note. Barney drops by during breakfast. Andy asks him to have some toast and jelly. The two become aware of an unidentifiable odor. Barney discovers the odor's source when he opens the lid on the jelly container. Aunt Bee has been making marmalade!

"The idea for the bad marmalade came out of the blue," says Harvey. "I usually did not write an epilogue until after the script was complete. By then I had a better sense of which story elements had worked best, what loose ends there were, and a general feeling of the story's momentum.

"The popularity of 'The Pickle Story' [It ranked second in 1994 when *The Andy Griffith Show* Rerun Watchers Club (TAGSRWC), the show's fan club, published a poll of club members' favorite episodes] has a certain sweet irony to me. Years after the series, someone told me when the 'pickle' script was first read by the actors there was a deadly silence. Consensus seemed to be that the script just somehow did not work. They all wondered if my previous success with the 'Hobo Friend' story had been a fluke. But they had no time to replace it, so they proceeded to give it their best shot."

"I don't recall a deadly silence at the first reading of the 'pickle' script," says producer Aaron Ruben. "If there was no enthusiastic response, it was because the story was a rather light one and did not have the weightier subject matter that episodes like 'Opie's Hobo Friend' had. In the end, it was fun doing it and a most enjoyable show."

Jailbreak

EPISODE #50

FIRST BROADCAST ON FEBRUARY 5, 1962

WRITTEN BY HARVEY BULLOCK

DIRECTED BY BOB SWEENEY

ALLAN MELVIN GUEST STARS AS
CLARENCE "DOC" MALLOY

"We were all hungry, freelance writers, pitching story ideas to as many different shows as we could but happiest when it was The Andy Griffith Show. *Every writer in town wanted an assignment there, knowing the performers were magic and the production / direction was flawless. The friendly atmosphere on the set gave it the sweet smell of success."*

Harvey Bullock

"'Jailbreak' was my first 'Barney' show," says Harvey Bullock. [Harvey's two previous TAGS scripts, 'Opie's Hobo Friend' and 'The Pickle Story' had not featured Barney prominently.] My reaction to getting the assignment? Pure joy. I had, of course, watched Don Knotts perform other scripts and marveled at his magic. That gifted man was a writer's very best friend; he made us look good.

"'Jailbreak's' story line developed from inevitable chuckles while watching Don do other episodes. It also involved long hours of staring at the ceiling, making false starts, then finally getting a few notions in good enough shape to present them verbally to TAGS producer Aaron

Ruben. To me, getting a story idea was by far the hardest part of writing. But, when you finally molded and shaped the idea, and the outline worked, then it became interesting, and the fun began. I couldn't wait to give Barney some transparent tough-guy lines and all the other business at which Don was so masterful."

The filmed episode begins with Barney reading a book out loud to himself. The word "silenc-er" is separated by the turning of a page. "The title of Barney's book, *Penitentiary*, was named in my script," says Harvey. "The page-divider joke was not. It may have been added from Andy's recollections of the opening scene from *No Time For Sergeants* in which Will Stockdale reads a page-divided word."

Barney's reading is interrupted by the arrival of State Inspector Horton. Horton, who is looking for the sheriff, refuses to explain the reason for his visit to Barney. Hoping to impress the inspector, Barney stands in front of a framed newspaper clipping that reports one of his arrests. Barney asks Horton if the frame is straight. The headline of the clipping reads, "Deputy Sheriff Barney Fife Cracks Walker Case."

"In my script the headline reads, 'Barney Fife Makes Heroic Capture' and underneath, 'Commended For Excellent Police Work'," says Harvey. "The script directions were, 'framed, large headlines, large clear picture of Barney'."

By referring to a previous crime from a first-season episode ["Andy the Matchmaker"], this minor change adds realism to the episode and establishes a sense of continuity with Mayberry's "on-screen" past.

Barney gets a call from the grocery store while Horton is waiting for Andy. The grocer tells Barney he has captured "Sam," a dog belonging to Floyd "that's been barking every morning and waking up the whole neighborhood." Again hoping to impress Horton, Barney says he'll "take the big brute single-handed." Horton still refuses to explain the reason for his visit. Instead he asks directions to Andy's house.

Harvey's guidelines for Sam's physical appearance were given primarily through a joke omitted in the filmed episode. Barney was originally supposed to say, "Looking at him, you'd never guess he belonged

to a barber, would you?" The line was followed by the script instructions, "Close on dog—featuring long hair over eyes."

The inclusion of a grocery-store scene required the hiring of an additional actor and the decorating of a grocery-store set. Both increased
the total production cost of the episode. Although it was easier and
cheaper to simply show Barney taking the call in the courthouse, Harvey
explains why the short scene was necessary: "The grocery set was very
small, what is called a 'fragment.' It was vital that the grocer set all the
lines for Barney's listening, and the 'feed' lines from the grocer had to
be clear. If Barney was just listening, it would bog down and any words
from the grocer that Barney heard might also be overheard by State
Police Inspector Horton. Yes, the inclusion of the scene was a small
decision, but a very good one."

When Horton finds Andy, he tells Andy that one of the fellows who
robbed the furniture-factory payroll, Clarence "Doc" Malloy, is in
Mayberry. Horton feels that Malloy will eventually lead him to Malloy's
partner and the stolen payroll. Horton wants Andy's agreement to stay
clear of the operation.

Soon afterwards, Malloy gets "wise" and "makes a break for it." Horton
arrests Malloy and brings him to the courthouse to be locked up. Malloy
is locked in the cell where Barney has been holding Floyd's dog Sam.
Sam has been shedding, so the cell's cot is covered with dog hair.

Barney gets excited when he learns that Malloy is in the Mayberry
jail. Barney feels this is a "golden opportunity to interrogate this bird."

The comic spotlight shines brightly on Barney as he prepares to
be "planted" as a stool pigeon in Malloy's cell. Don Knotts brings
Harvey's directions for the scene magically to life. The directions
were as follows:

> Barney appears from the back room. He has changed into
> his street clothes, suit, and tie. Barney walks over to the
> mirror to check his appearance. Not too happy, he loosens
> his tie, that's better—still not right. He musses his hair a

little—better and better. Now he tries a hard, bitter expression, checks it full face and profile—adds a bit of a meaner leer and goes into the cell.

The sleeping Malloy is awakened when Barney enters the cell. Playing the role of a fellow prisoner, Barney tells Malloy that he's going to "pick the lock, get that 'gat' (the gun hanging on a rack beside the framed newspaper clipping), and bust out."

When Malloy looks at the gun, he sees Barney's picture in the framed clipping. Malloy asks Barney, "Who are you?" Barney replies, "Puddingtame." Playing along, Malloy questions Barney about his ability to "spring out of here." Barney answers, "They don't call me 'Fingers' for nothing."

Barney tells Malloy that after they break out they'll need some "dough for a hideout until we cool off." Barney asks Malloy if he has a partner or any money. Malloy says he is hesitant to answer because he feels Barney may "tell the cops." Barney assures Malloy that he "has been called plenty, everything from 'Chopper' to 'Mad Dog.' One name they never call me is 'Tattletale.'"

After Barney picks the lock and opens the door, he and Malloy say in unison, "So far, so good." Barney insists that they lock little fingers and say, "needles/pins." While Barney's back is turned, Malloy gets the gun. He then locks Barney in the cell and escapes.

"Barney's progression of nicknames ('Fingers, Chopper to Mad Dog, but never Tattletale') helps set up his lock picking," says Harvey. "They were just a mishmash in Barney's style. 'Puddingtame' is an old wheeze, funny when used by an adult. 'Needles/pins' is an example of another child's routine from a desperate adult."

Horton is upset when he learns of Malloy's escape. He again orders Andy "to stay out of this." Andy feels otherwise. However, Barney has no desire to get involved further. Instead, he plans to take the suit he wore while in the cell with Malloy to the cleaners. The suit is "just full of dog hairs."

While stopping by the dry cleaners to drop off Barney's suit, Andy and Barney learn from dry-cleaner H. Goss that "this is the second suit in a row to come in here with dog hairs." Goss's comment captures Andy's attention. Andy questions Goss further and learns a lady brought the suit in. Goss points out the lady's car, which is still parked across the street. The car has a trailer hitch on the back bumper. From this, Andy figures out that Malloy is hiding at the trailer camp.

"I don't know where I got the name 'Goss'," says Harvey, "but for once I did have a source for the character. When I lived in New York City, my hearing was getting bad, and my family doctor sent me to an ear doctor, evidently a very unfashionable, but very talented, older man. I went to his office in a stuffy, crammed house, and he pulled up a stool to put the 'flashlight' in my ears. His vest was covered with cigarette ashes, and he was smoking the whole time I was there, seemingly unaware of his ash-tray vest and the constant fresh ash dropping."

After going to the trailer camp, Andy and Barney split up. While searching for Malloy, Barney comes across a trailer with a "Just Married" sign. He sees the sign, walks away but goes back for a look. The newlywed couple, the Franklins, sensing Barney's presence, stop kissing and look up. Harvey explains the thinking behind Barney's actions, "Barney's instructions were to search every vehicle, and the sign could have been a ruse. He decided that he must check them all and, with some apprehension and embarrassment, looked in the Franklins' window."

Andy and Barney reunite and spot the car Malloy's partner was driving. Barney looks inside the attached trailer and sees Malloy, his partner, and Horton, who is being held prisoner. After Andy goes to get some help, Malloy decides to leave. While Malloy is inside the trailer, Barney jumps in the car and drives away. Pulling the trailer, Barney drives the car to the courthouse, where the shaken Malloy is recaptured.

As Malloy exits the trailer, Barney points to his gun and says, "This baby's loaded with six bullets this time."

There is no previous mention in the episode that Malloy was aware of only one bullet or that the one bullet was a factor in his escape, so the line seems unnecessary.

"Yes, Malloy was never told about Barney's single bullet," says Harvey. "It is not important to the story that Malloy knows what Barney means. It is just Barney being excitable and delighted with the extra artillery and telling the world—and Andy."

In the epilogue, Andy, Barney, and Opie are looking at the disguises in a toy detective set. The Franklins stop by the courthouse to report a peeping Tom at the trailer camp. The complaint is given to Andy. Barney turns his back to the couple. Andy asks Barney if he will take down the information about this peeping Tom. When Barney turns around, he is wearing a fake nose and glasses from the toy detective set. He gives an excuse (which is unclear because of the laugh track) and makes a hasty departure.

"I don't think I introduced the Franklins earlier in the episode just to set up the epilogue," says Harvey. "I concentrated on the main story, then when that was finished, I looked for some loose ends or a funny set-up—and bringing back the Franklins seemed to do it."

"On my script, Barney's last line reads, 'I can't now, Andy, Opie and I are going out for a soda'," says Harvey. "I guess the laugh at his disguise covered the line, but it wasn't a gag line. It was just a production line. A gag line together with the disguise would have been trying for a 'double' joke, which can be tricky and confusing."

Harvey adds, "I was told that the crew seemed to enjoy shooting 'Jailbreak.' This is oddly pleasing to a writer. That millions would view it with approval was a fuzzy distant possibility, but if two-score working professionals—who had seen it all—if they approved, then the long hours of ceiling-staring were all worthwhile."

Andy and Barney in the Big City

EPISODE #57

FIRST BROADCAST ON MARCH 26, 1962

WRITTEN BY HARVEY BULLOCK

DIRECTED BY BOB SWEENEY

ALLAN MELVIN GUEST STARS AS
DETECTIVE BARDOLI

*"The 'Barney Fife, M.D.' [Mayberry Deputy]
bit was written for this script. I don't recall
any other episodes in which Barney used it.
Perhaps it was best as a one shot."*

Harvey Bullock

"I cannot remember whether Aaron Ruben suggested the idea for the script, or whether I brought the notion in," says writer Harvey Bullock. "It probably just accumulated slowly in our minds that a trip to the big city might be interesting because it would give the show a different look in set and wardrobe."

Though primarily set in the "big city," Harvey's finished script begins in the familiar Taylor home. Andy is departing on a two-day business trip. Barney arrives and notices Opie's front tooth is missing. Barney has Opie repeat a tongue-twister to test how the missing tooth affects his pronunciation. Aunt Bee packs Andy and Barney "a brown paper sack full of sandwiches to eat on the bus" and reminds the two "to step out with your right foot, so all will go well."

"I had no idea Ronny had a missing tooth," says Harvey. "Once I dropped off the second draft of a script I did not hang around the set. I guess Ronny showed up with a missing tooth, and Aaron reshaped the script to use it. Andy and Barney's 'stepping out on your right foot' was also not in my script and is another example of an addition by either Aaron or Andy.

"Aunt Bee's preparation of 'a sack of sandwiches' was my idea and grew out of my understanding of the character. Aunt Bee's response to almost any happening is to cater it. She's totally convinced that 'you are what you eat,' and the more the better. If a twister hit Mayberry, Aunt Bee would immediately start handing out slices of pie, and Andy's trip definitely called for a movable feast."

After arriving in "Capital City," Andy and Barney check into their hotel. While standing in the lobby, Barney notices a lady claiming her emeralds from the hotel's safe. While the lady places the jewels in her pocketbook, Barney observes that she is being watched very carefully by a man.

Later that day, Andy and Barney visit the state commissioner with a request for new equipment. The commissioner is not optimistic about the request. He feels there have not been enough arrests in Mayberry to justify new equipment. Barney believes "that one good felony" would get them everything they want. Andy suggests they go back to the hotel, eat supper, and "forget about our problems."

Andy and Barney have supper in the hotel's French restaurant. The menu is printed in French, which neither Andy nor Barney can read. Andy asks the waiter for a steak. Not wanting to appear to be a hick, Barney points randomly to items on the menu, which turn out to be snails and brains.

"What we have here is a variation on the so-called 'Fish Out of Water' sketch," says Harvey. "Ordering fanciful food by mistake is a basic comic staple. It's a minor tweak, but in my script, Barney ordered frog legs and snails."

Barney sees the "emerald" lady leaving the restaurant. The man Barney observed earlier departs immediately afterwards. The suspected "crook" makes a telephone call in the lobby and identifies himself during the conversation as Bardoli, the hotel detective.

"Allan Melvin, who played Bardoli, was a wonderfully versatile type and a 'great face,'" says Harvey. "He was a close friend of Aaron's from the early *Sergeant Bilko/The Phil Silvers Show* days. But there was no favoritism here. Allan was a scrupulous professional and totally reliable. It didn't matter that Allan was cast as Bardoli after portraying 'Doc' Malloy in 'Jailbreak' [Episode #50]. Television audiences are most amenable. They can absorb all kinds of cast changes without being disturbed, as long as the laughs keep coming."

"We came up with the last name for the hotel detective, Bardoli, after putting together a few syllables which sounded Italian. Aaron may have suggested it. He was a giant Italophile. He even took lessons in Italian from TAGS director Peter Baldwin and got pretty good before Peter left and there were no others to practice his new language on."

The next day, Andy tells Barney he is "going down to police headquarters and browse around." Barney decides to stay at the hotel and watch "his man." On his way out of the lobby, Andy bumps into a man. Bardoli suspects that the man, C. J. Huffman, is a thief. After Andy leaves, Bardoli tells Huffman to "keep his hands in his own pockets."

"Writers were not consulted on casting but occasionally would suggest the type of performer needed," says Harvey. "My scripted description for C. J. Huffman was 'a pleasant Rotarian type.' Actually this doesn't fit Les Treymayne [who was cast in the role], but the character wasn't written finitely, so many different types could play it equally well. Les, by the way, was great in the role."

Huffman takes a seat in the lobby and is joined by Barney. Barney warns him to be careful about talking to strangers. Barney then informs Huffman that Bardoli is a jewel thief. Barney also tells Huffman about the "emerald lady." Huffman identifies himself as the owner of a newspaper and agrees to help Barney catch the jewel thief.

Barney and Huffman follow Bardoli upstairs to the emerald lady's room. Bardoli checks to see if the door is locked and departs. Huffman and Barney decide to see if Bardoli has already stolen the jewels. After Huffman pries open the door, he and Barney search the room. Barney searches the outer room while Huffman looks in the bedroom. Huffman finds the jewels and places them in his pocket. Bardoli returns while Barney and Huffman are in the room. When Bardoli enters the room, Barney pushes him into a closet and locks the closet door.

Meanwhile, Andy's visit to police headquarters included a look around the file room. While thumbing through a book of mug shots, Andy spots a picture of the man he bumped into in the hotel lobby.

Accompanied by a policeman, Andy returns to the hotel. He sees Bardoli in the lobby and is told by the policeman that Bardoli is the hotel detective.

Harvey's carefully constructed story enables the audience to view the episode from an informed viewpoint. Part of the viewer's satisfaction is gained from knowing the truth about Bardoli and C.J. Huffman while Barney does not. Harvey lets the audience in on the deception/joke.

"There are two main types of drama, the 'open' and the 'closed'," explains Harvey. "The open lets the audience in on 'who done it.' In a closed format the guilty party is not revealed until the end, and both the audience and 'good guys' have to work to figure it out. Would the story benefit from being open or closed? That is a difficult decision to make when fashioning a story. You run the story through your head endlessly, both open and closed. Sometimes it seems to work both ways equally well—and sometimes it doesn't seem to work either way!"

Barney and Huffman encounter Andy in the hotel lobby. Barney tells Andy the "fellow I spotted took the emeralds, and C.J. and I locked him in a closet." Andy immediately recognizes Huffman "from his likeness at police headquarters," and Huffman is arrested.

Following the arrest, Andy explains the situation to the baffled Barney. The explanation and Barney's reaction to it are presented in pantomime. An audible explanation would have been somewhat repetitious, since Harvey has already let the audience in on "who done it." Barney's exaggerated reaction, accompanied solely by TAGS musical director Earle Hagen's musical sound effects, is more comical and satisfying.

The episode concludes with Detective Bardoli asking for Barney in order to commend him for his arrest of Huffman. Mistaking Bardoli's intentions, Barney hides in a closet in his hotel room. By taking an earlier situation and reversing the circumstances, Harvey cleverly creates a comic ending.

Wedding Bells for Aunt Bee

EPISODE #58

FIRST BROADCAST ON APRIL 2, 1963

WRITTEN BY HARVEY BULLOCK

DIRECTED BY BOB SWEENEY

> *"I remember as a child, slipping out to the shed behind our house, crawling up on top of a table, and falling asleep to the tapping of my father's manual typewriter. I still love to hear that sound."*
>
> Courtney Bullock

"The 'Wedding Bell' story line began where most of the story lines originated, my office ceiling where I did my major heavy-duty staring," recalls writer Harvey Bullock. "The office was actually a shed behind our home. I would stare at the ceiling, juggling half notions, seeking to find a story problem. That was the magic word which helped me get started—the problem. Who could handle it? What was its progression? What was at stake, and what is the solution? I'd have a constant circus of thoughts dancing through my head, but I didn't always come up with anything.

"So I'd give up and go in the house to raid the fridge. Often nothing worked until after nightfall when there were no distractions. My wife would tell our three, small daughters, 'Don't disturb Daddy, he's thinking.' And I'm out in the shed, praying for an interruption.

"Aaron Ruben tried to rotate scripts to give each cast member a prominent role in upcoming episodes. Oddly enough, the one character most difficult to find stories for was Andy himself. The reason for this was that he had no pesky little foibles. So when it came time for an Andy story, we found it could be someone else's problem that he is dragged into."

Harvey's "Wedding Bell" script begins with Aunt Bee, Clara Johnson, and Otis Campbell in the dry cleaners. Aunt Bee has stopped by to pick up Andy's suit. When the owner of the dry cleaners, H. Fred Goss, invites Aunt Bee to attend a dance with him, she declines the invitation.

H. Fred Goss first appeared in "Jailbreak" (Episode #50). "I can't recall the exact circumstances of selecting Goss again," admits Harvey. "It might have been that Aaron and I, knowing what we wanted, mutually made suggestions during the early discussions of the story. The character we had in mind had to be a contemporary of Aunt Bee's and a solid citizen who was a known commodity in Mayberry, so viewers wouldn't suspect an outsider was working a scam. Fred Goss fit both these requirements and, moreover, could do the boring speeches on his sole interest in life—the honorable cleaning profession."

After leaving the dry cleaners, Otis stops by the courthouse to leave his suit in case he "gets out in time to go to church on Sunday." While at the courthouse, Otis tells Andy about Goss sweet-talking Aunt Bee. As the two talk, a rare thing happens—Otis and Andy become equals, two adults. (Otis is usually childlike in relation to Andy.)

"Otis's scene in the courthouse was written straight, adult-to-adult," says Harvey. "I knew Otis had to be dead sober to give credence to his observation that Goss was sweet-talking Aunt Bee."

Aunt Bee and Clara return to the Taylor home after leaving the dry cleaners. As the two put up groceries, Clara tells Aunt Bee that she shouldn't be so quick to turn down Mr. Goss. Clara feels Andy needs to be married, but he "can't bring a wife home" with Aunt Bee living in the house.

While conversing at the kitchen table, Clara confidently helps herself to a cookie from a jar on the table. Clara's behavior visually reinforces the character's boldness and authority.

"This bit of business was not in the script," says Harvey. "Clara's behavior was probably one of the many suggestions offered by Bob Sweeney, the director, to make the scene flow. Clara is an authoritative character without props, but I think the 'cookie' thing was a very nice corroborative touch."

Andy and Opie enter the kitchen while Aunt Bee and Clara are talking. Aunt Bee asks Andy who he's taking to the dance. She names several possibilities. Andy answers that he's not going to the dance. He thinks he'll just spend "a nice, quiet evening at home."

"Near the end of the kitchen scene, Aunt Bee is eagerly asking Andy if he's going to the dance," says Harvey. "She asks who he's taking and volunteers a few names. Well, I just typed in whatever names and then the name of a girl I had worked with on the *Today Show* popped into my mind, and I routinely added it to the list. The lady in question, Estelle Parsons, went into performing and did that marvelous role in *Bonnie and Clyde*."

Acting on Clara's advice, Aunt Bee invites Goss over for dinner. As a result, Andy postpones taking the family to Mt. Pilot for a Chinese dinner.

"This idea grew out of a childhood memory," recalls Harvey. "As kids, we loved going to The Grotto, a Chinese restaurant where it was all spooky, like a darkened cave. Dinners were 89 cents, and little paper parasols came with the rice."

Mr. Goss accepts Aunt Bee's invitation and joins the Taylors for dinner. During the meal, Goss talks about cleaning chemicals and the hardships of removing spots and stains.

"I went to the local cleaner and found out some cleaning tips and vexations of the cleaning business when working up the character of Fred Goss," says Harvey. "It was worth all the effort just to find the word 'perchloroethylene'."

Aunt Bee dislikes Mr. Goss but continues to see him for Andy's sake. Thinking Aunt Bee is interested in Goss, Andy encourages the relationship.

After Aunt Bee and Goss leave for a picture show, Andy goes to check on Opie. Opie is exiting the bathroom as Andy enters the upstairs hallway. Andy asks if Opie's brushed his teeth. Opie replies, "Just feel how wet the toothbrush is." Andy tells Opie the story of a boy who thought it was funny to wet his toothbrush instead of brushing his teeth. Andy says, "To him, it was a right-funny joke. Every time he thought about it, he'd smile. And then one day, he quit smiling, never smiled again the rest of his days—he couldn't, he didn't have any teeth." Upon hearing this, Opie immediately goes back into the bathroom to brush his teeth.

"In general, it is nice to open an Opie scene with a light touch before getting into the more serious stuff," says Harvey. "The wet-toothbrush scene affirmed the warm, fun relationship between father and son, so Andy wasn't just into preachments. I tried to use the phoney, wet-toothbrush evidence when I was a child, and I think Andy's story about the 'boy who quit smiling' was original."

As Opie brushes his teeth, Andy tells him, "It looks like Aunt Bee might be getting married pretty soon." Hearing this, Opie asks, "Why do people get married, Pa?"

Andy's explanation is photographed in three separate sequences. The first is filmed with the camera positioned in the hallway, looking past Andy into the bathroom where Opie is standing in front of the sink. In the scene's master shot, the wall with the mirror has been removed. The camera is positioned behind the sink, looking past Opie at Andy. The third camera position photographs Andy's closeups. The three sequences, which are edited expertly in the finished film, flow together flawlessly.

After Opie brushes his teeth, he continues to question Andy about love as the two enter Opie's bedroom. Andy explains "the marrying kind of love" as he tucks Opie into bed. The dialogue reflects the serious side of childhood and is very special.

> OPIE: Did you and Mom have that deep-down kind?
> ANDY: Yes, son, we did.
> OPIE: And does Aunt Bee have that kind now?
> ANDY: Yes, she does.
> OPIE: Then, it's alright, ain't it?
> ANDY: Yes, son, I s'pect it is.

"I didn't realize at the time that this was the first, and last refer-ence, to Opie's mother in the series," says Harvey. "I'm uncertain why she wasn't referred to again. It might have been that Aaron preferred to emphasize Andy as the eligible bachelor rather than as the grieving widower."

Aunt Bee returns from her date later in the evening. Opie wakes up and comes downstairs. Andy invites Opie to join him and Aunt Bee on the porch for a piece of "berry" pie.

After the pie is finished, Andy and Aunt Bee discuss the advantages of her marrying Mr. Goss. Andy says, "all in all, I'd say there's every rea-son in the world for you to get married." Opie has been listening care-fully to what has been said and comments, "Pa, you left out one of the reasons—that Aunt Bee's getting married because she's got that special deep-down type of feeling."

Reflecting on Opie's comment, Andy realizes that Aunt Bee doesn't have the marrying-kind-of-love for Mr. Goss. Andy explains to Aunt Bee that "among folks that love each other, like we do, nothing can be best for us unless it's best for you."

The impact of the scene lies in the audience's identification with what Andy is saying. Andy's dialogue expresses concisely and beautifully the universal appeal of giving love to someone else.

Aunt Bee decides to end her relationship with Mr. Goss immedi-ately. The next day, Andy breaks the news to Mr. Goss. The Taylor fam-ily, free of the dry cleaner, happily heads to Mt. Pilot for a Chinese dinner.

The Bookie Barber

EPISODE #60

FIRST BROADCAST ON APRIL 16, 1962

WRITTEN BY RAY SAFFIAN ALLEN AND
HARVEY BULLOCK

DIRECTED BY BOB SWEENEY

HOWARD MCNEAR IS FEATURED
AS FLOYD THE BARBER

"The Bookie Barber," Scene 4, INT Floyd's Barber-shop. Andy is encouraging Floyd to hire a second barber, telling Floyd he could put a sign in the window—'Two-Chair Shop—No Waiting.' Floyd nods, wide-eyed in thought, and delivers his all-time classic line: 'Uh-huh—and I got enough magazines to swing it'.

"The late Ray Saffian Allen hired me for my first, true writing job at CBS, where he was head writer for a daily variety show," says writer Harvey Bullock. "Ray had other writers who did most of the work, giving me a chance to fail and fail—which meant learn and learn. After a year of that, a friend of Ray's asked him to come to London to write a sitcom [*Dick and the Duchess*]. Ray asked if I would like to go with him as his partner, and I jumped at the chance.

"After completing the sitcom, I wanted to return to the states, but Ray wanted to stay in London and develop some ideas there. So we agreed that we would each do what we wished, and we could reunite at the first opportunity.

"I worked solo in New York (*The Johnny Carson Show*) and then went

Floyd gives Andy a haircut.

TAGSRWC Archives

to Hollywood, where I got jobs as a freelancer on various shows. The time on my own proved very valuable. Hitherto, I wasn't sure if I was depending too much on Ray. After I had worked alone and was reasonably successful, I had total confidence, but I knew I preferred working with Ray.

"Ray eventually returned to the states and came west. By this time, I had written for TAGS, and Aaron gave me the supreme vote of confidence—a twelve-story commitment. Ray and I starting working on them, 'The Bookie Barber' being the first. I did the bulk of the writing, and Ray assisted."

In the opening scene of the completed script, Opie is trying to talk his way out of a haircut. Opie feels he doesn't need a haircut because "he can still see." He dreads "the little hairs that itch your back." In response to Andy's suggestion that he can get rid of the hairs by taking a bath, Opie replies, "A bath too! This is turning out worse than I thought."

"My children (I have four) all think of me as a 'kid' person," admits Harvey. "I've always enjoyed the honesty of the small ones, before terminal sophistication sets in. In my younger days, I worked summers as a leader at a YMCA camp. My charges were eight years old. Spending two months in the same little cottage with seven of them, you get a hint of how their minds work."

Andy accompanies Opie to the barbershop. To photograph this scene, the mirrored wall in the shop has been removed, and the camera is positioned in its place. The camera films past the freestanding sink. Barney is also in the barbershop, getting a haircut. The shop is full of customers, and Floyd is rushing to finish.

When his haircut is finished, Barney walks over to the camera. A closeup shows Barney carefully scrutinizing his sideburns. Barney comments that just once he'd like "them sideburns to come out even."

"Barney's complaining about his sideburns was inspired by a personal observation I have made," says Harvey. "Somehow, customers never pass up a chance to air disapproval of their haircuts. The easiest target to disapprove is the sideburns. They are a true index, used by the knowledgeable, as to the value of the haircut. Sideburns are never even, because if they are, a tilt of your head, and they're out of alignment. Barney has been having his sideburns adjusted regularly for years. They're still not exactly right and never will be."

Andy leaves Opie at the barbershop. Bill Medwin enters as Floyd is finishing Opie's haircut. Medwin introduces himself and says he too is a barber. He then asks Floyd if he would be interested in "taking on another man."

When Andy returns to pick up Opie, he meets Medwin. Andy encourages Floyd to take on the new man. Andy reminds Floyd that a two-chair shop is something he has always wanted. Andy tells Floyd that he could put a sign in the window saying "Two-Chair Shop—No Waiting."

The possibility of owning a two-chair shop with no waiting has a dramatic effect on Floyd. He begins speaking in unfinished sentences and anxiously fumbles with a comb as he thinks the situation through out loud. At one point, he gets so flustered that he sits on Opie, who is seated in the barber's chair.

"Floyd's animated behavior was not caused by nervousness," explains Harvey. "He has decided to take on the other barber, and the idea of having a two-chair shop is so delicious, he backs onto the chair (and Opie) in sheer wonderment."

The new barber immediately attracts customers. The new customers are a "smart-looking" clientele. They all seem to be well dressed and stern faced.

"We didn't include a detailed description of the new barber's clientele because there were really no hard specifics needed," says Harvey. "They were described in the script simply as 'mug-like customers.' Aaron

HARVEY BULLOCK TALKS ABOUT HOWARD MCNEAR

"I never met Howard McNear. Writers seldom visited the shooting set. We just plain weren't needed. We had already done our part, the rewrite completed and slid under the producer's door. Any small fix-ups could easily be done by the director or actors. And the economics would not let us indulge. We had to be constantly beating the bushes, trying to sell stories.

So, I never met Howard McNear. But, we share a very special, mutual friend. That fey and wispy, wide-eyed barber of Mayberry, Floyd Lawson.

Howard/Floyd was a magician. His signature 'oohs and ahs' lent his lines a whimsical touch which defies analysis. He would suddenly switch to sing-song, then to an unconvincing, stern authority, then whispered amazement—all the time, wheezing, worked ahead on all scripts, and he knew what type of cast was needed. In this case, an easy cast, just three rough-looking guys."

The mug-like customers' frequent patronage of the barbershop arouses Andy's suspicions. His suspicions are confirmed as it becomes evident that Floyd's barbershop has become a front for a booking operation.

Andy shares the information with Barney. Barney wants to make an immediate arrest. Andy tells him that a hasty arrest won't work because the bookie would just "hide the evidence and play innocent." Andy suggests they use a plant to place a bet. When the bookie takes the bet, they can then make an arrest. Barney thinks a sweet little old lady like Emma Watson would be the perfect plant. Andy disagrees because he feels the situation is too dangerous to involve a private citizen.

Andy leaves to attend to other business. Before departing, he tells Barney that they'll think of something when he gets back. Barney, however, cannot resist the opportunity. He decides to become a plant himself and dons the disguise of a little old lady.

gasping and rolling his eyes. All of which, busied him so he never got to finish a sentence. It was very funny, and viewers never thought he was acting!

When we wrote for Floyd, we couldn't wait until that episode was shown to see how he had immeasurably improved the dialogue with his stop-and-go delivery, his breathlessness, his awe, and his pained disapproval.

TAGS cast members were very close to Howard. When his health worsened, you could sense a palpable sadness on the set. Scenes were re-staged so he could do his lines seated in his barber's chair. And he did them as fresh and funny as ever.

When the end came, he was mourned on every sound stage in Hollywood where he had done his quiet, wondrous wizardry.

Yes, I sure wish I had met Howard. But at least, I knew Floyd. And now, up in that 'Great Barbershop in the Sky,' perhaps Floyd is finally speaking complete sentences—but I hope not."

The scripted directions for the scene in which Barney first appears in disguise were as follows:

> HOLD ON DOOR a moment, then door slowly opens, and Barney peers outside. Door opens wider, and Barney steps out into the street, looking furtively. He is dressed something like Emma Watson.

The directions were expertly photographed and edited to heighten the scene's comedy. The forty-five-second scene is visually presented on-screen in the following manner: The courthouse door cracks open. Barney is shown in extreme closeup. As the door opens further, the camera pans backward for a heightened shot, revealing a woman's hat on Barney's head. As Barney steps out to the sidewalk, the camera pans backward for a medium shot, which shows Barney putting on gloves before proceeding toward the barbershop.

Medwin and his clients are stunned by Barney's appearance. They become suspicious when Barney talks about a daughter-in-law who disapproves of his gambling and his need to place a quick bet. Barney then spots a black bag on the floor that contains "the names of the horses and things." He, Medwin, and the other clients all dive for the bag at the same time.

Meanwhile, Andy has returned. Opie tells him that Barney "looks like a little old lady." Suspecting what Barney is up to, Andy rushes to the barbershop. He arrives just in time to break up the scuffle over the bag. The needed evidence is scattered on the floor, and Medwin is caught red-handed.

In the episode's epilogue, Floyd is unaware of Medwin's arrest. He believes the barber has been receiving calls from numerous girlfriends and had to leave because of a romantic conflict. The problem has thus been resolved without Floyd ever "having to know the awful truth." This reaffirms a basic TAGS premise—bookie barbers and other problem-causers may invade Mayberry, but the town and its residents are never permanently threatened or changed.

1962-63

Andy and Opie, Bachelors

EPISODE #65

FIRST BROADCAST ON OCTOBER 22, 1962

WRITTEN BY JIM FRITZELL AND
EVERETT GREENBAUM

DIRECTED BY BOB SWEENEY

JOANNA MOORE APPEARS AS
PEGGY McMILLAN

*"Even though Jim died seventeen years ago,
I still dream that we are meeting at the
typewriter every morning to get on with
an overdue script."*

Everett Greenbaum

"**I**'m amazed at the length of time between 'Quiet Sam,' our first TAGS script, and this one," says writer Everett Greenbaum. "After nearly forty years, which is half of my lifetime, I can't remember why there was such a long period between our first and second TAGS scripts.

"My reaction to seeing our names as writers in the 'Bachelor' episode's closing credits is to say to myself, 'Jim and I never wrote that one.' But sure enough, I found it in one of the bound volumes of my past scripts.

"I think the reason I can remember so little about this one is because it was likely my least favorite of the twenty-nine TAGS scripts we wrote. Joanna Moore didn't seem to me to belong in a small town and didn't bring with her an inborn sense of comedy like so many of our cast.

Also, the story didn't provide enough 'meat' to fill a half-hour. It seems to me that we did a lot of padding to stretch out its length."

"Joanna Moore was cast as Peggy McMillan after the script was written," says producer Aaron Ruben. "The script called for an attractive woman, and Joanna was certainly that. The relationship between Andy and Peggy, however, didn't seem to gel. We wanted to get the right actress for the role, so Joanna appeared in only four episodes."

Jim and Everett's "forgotten" script begins at the Mayberry sidewalk bus stop. Andy, Opie, and Aunt Bee are preparing for Aunt Bee's departure to visit her Aunt Louise for three or four days. As they await the bus's departure, Peggy McMillan walks up. Aunt Bee asks Peggy if she will look in on "these two helpless creatures" while she's gone.

After boarding the bus, Aunt Bee tells Andy and Opie to be sure to change their underwear. "Opie's bottom is ripped." She also wants the two to be "clean on the inside and the out." Andy is embarrassed by Aunt Bee's instructions because Peggy overhears them. Aunt Bee also reminds Andy to take Opie for a haircut on Friday and to make sure that Floyd does not "cut him so naked at the back of his neck. Last time, he looked like a baby bird." These instructions are excellent examples of comedy presented through everyday conversation.

After the bus departs, Andy, Peggy, and Opie walk towards Floyd's barbershop. At this point, Peggy offers to help out while Aunt Bee is gone.

Floyd overhears Peggy's offer. After she leaves, he compliments Andy "on the pretty little housekeeper who is coming in to take over for Aunt Bee." Floyd explains that "it starts here and ends with your mailbox." He predicts that Peggy "will want to come over to the house to make supper. Then she'll kind of hint around that she wants to do this all the time. And then it happens. You'll be out changing the card on your mailbox to read, 'Mr. and Mrs. Andy Taylor'."

Later that evening, Opie asks Andy what they're having for supper. Opie suggests they "chew tar." Opie says that his friend, Johnny Paul Jason, says that "chewing tar is real good for the teeth."

When Andy puts a chicken in the oven, Opie gives him a pencil, so he can figure out what time to take the chicken out. Opie warns Andy "to be sure and not lick the point—it's an indelible pencil." Johnny Paul has told Opie that "if you lick indelible pencil lead, you die in a minute and a half." Opie tells Andy that Johnny Paul learns his facts from "reading in bed with a flashlight."

The wisdom of Johnny Paul Jason is introduced in this episode. Jim and Everett drew upon past memories when writing Johnny Paul's sayings. "Johnny Paul's words of wisdom were based on folklore from my childhood, and Jim recognized it as part of his," says Everett. "Opie's telling Andy that Johnny Paul knows so much because 'he reads in bed with a flashlight' came from another childhood memory. Reading under the covers with a flashlight, preferably Tom Swift books, was something the two of us had done as children."

Despite their best efforts, Andy burns the supper. Arriving just as Andy examines the charred chicken, Peggy offers to "fix something." She prepares an elegant table setting and serves a delicious meal that is "pure gala."

After the meal, Andy, Peggy, and Opie sit on the front porch. Andy plays his guitar as he and Peggy sing "Down in the Valley." The simple and harmonious singing, the set's shadowy lighting, and the peaceful sound of chirping crickets combine to create a serene Mayberry evening. The realistic squeaking of the screen door, as Opie enters the house, ends the scene on a perfect note.

"We didn't include the song to highlight Joanna Moore's singing talents," says Aaron. "The song simply seemed to fit the scene, so we used it."

The next day, Opie asks Andy when Barney will be coming home from his vacation in Raleigh. Opie's questions lead into Andy's hilarious description of Barney's idea of a good time in the big city.

"Andy's telling Opie about Barney's life at the Raleigh YMCA—wearing a Pongee shirt, seeing a movie or hearing a lecture on cleanliness, and concluding his evening with tapioca pudding and a cup of hot chocolate—is typical Fritzell and Greenbaum," says Everett. "It was the sort of thing we wrote together that we couldn't write apart.

"What one missed, the other one could provide. I knew nothing about sports, or cared. Sports was one of the main concerns of Jim's life. While I knew all about science, machinery, flying planes, literature, and music, Jim knew how to play cards, what people drank, and the slang of fighters, jazz players, and factory workers."

Meanwhile, back at the courthouse, Peggy brings lunch. After she leaves, Opie asks Andy if "Miss Peggy is practicing for when you and she might get married."

When Peggy offers to come over that evening, Andy rejects her offer. Instead, he prepares burnt weenies and beans. After the meal, he and Opie sit on the front porch. When Opie suggests that they talk, neither can think of anything to say. Opie asks Andy to play his guitar, but Andy says he doesn't "feel much like playing."

Peggy stops by while Andy is washing dishes. Opie tells her that they had a "terrible supper," and Peggy offers to cook. At this point, Andy asks her quite frankly why she is doing all of this. Peggy answers that she just feels sorry for "two helpless bachelors. Besides, I enjoy it."

Andy accepts the sincerity of Peggy's reply, and the joyous atmosphere created when good friends get together is instantly restored.

Opie is puzzled about what has happened and asks Andy for an explanation. Andy simply replies, "There's a woman in the house. We're just going to have fun, and that's all there is to it."

Jim and Everett humorously conclude the scene with a final reference to Opie's wise friend. "That's all there is to it," Opie ponders aloud. "I'll have to ask Johnny Paul about that."

Mr. McBeevee

EPISODE #66

FIRST BROADCAST ON OCTOBER 1, 1962

WRITTEN BY RAY SAFFIAN ALLEN
AND HARVEY BULLOCK

DIRECTED BY BOB SWEENEY

KARL SWEENSON GUEST STARS
AS MR. MCBEEVEE

"Yes, the 'bedroom' scene is one I am proud of."

Harvey Bullock

"I vividly remember the story-line origination for this script," says writer Harvey Bullock. "Ray Saffian Allen and I were attending one of TAGS executive producer Sheldon Leonard's legendary two-day story seminars, along with some other writers, plus Andy and Aaron Ruben. We tossed notions haphazardly in the air, and often someone would grab one and suggest an embellishment.

"Someone tossed up a notion about Opie having an imaginary friend. Another writer suggested that Opie might thus be having trouble separating the real from the fanciful. Then Sheldon offered, 'And Andy has to lecture Opie sternly about telling the truth.'

"At that moment, I got a quick, urgent flash like nothing I had ever experienced," says Harvey. "As Sheldon was trying to figure out whether to proceed with the story, I stood up and said, 'There's a better way.' Already this was strange, because no one ever stood up at those meetings. But I suddenly had a picture in my mind of Andy and Opie in the bedroom. I continued, slowly, feeling my way, still under some unreal impetus. 'After Opie makes seemingly outrageous statements, Andy does go to punish him, as you suggested. But Andy then realizes Opie wouldn't lie, and preposterous as the statements were, he owes it to Opie to believe the boy, since so many times Opie has blindly believed him.' Sheldon loved it immediately. 'Yes, that's the story! Go write it!'

"The episode was originally named 'Mr. McTeevee,' but we were later told this title was not available—I presume for legal reasons. So Aaron changed it to 'Mr. McBeevee.' The role was played by veteran actor, Karl Sweenson, a most able and versatile performer. Aaron thought so much of Karl he even hired a double (Thurston Holmes) to do the scenes of climbing down from trees or poles. The 'climb downs' were pretty tame. Karl always said he could have done them himself, but I suspect he was happy to have a stunt-double take over."

Early in the episode, Opie delivers mail to the courthouse that was wrongly delivered to the house. When Andy asks Opie to take out the trash, Opie says he can't because he told Mr. McBeevee he'd be right back. Opie tells Andy and Barney that Mr. McBeevee is "new around here." Opie says he met Mr. McBeevee in the woods and describes him as a man who "walks around in the treetops and wears a great, big, shiny, silver hat."

Later that day, Opie returns home with an unsharpened hatchet. Opie says the hatchet is a gift from Mr. McBeevee. At this point, Andy thinks Mr. McBeevee exists only in Opie's mind. Andy explains to Opie that somebody probably left the hatchet in the woods, which means he'll be coming back to pick it up. Andy tells Opie to return the hatchet to the place where he found it.

As instructed, Opie returns the hatchet to Mr. McBeevee. At this point, the audience sees that Mr. McBeevee is actually a lineman for the telephone company. Upon the return of the hatchet, Mr. McBeevee agrees that "perhaps it is too dangerous." He cheers Opie by showing him how the "heathen cannibals" taught him how "to make smoke come out of me ears." In place of the hatchet, McBeevee gives Opie "an old,

old quarter that's just begging to be turned into gum and ice cream."

"The 'smoke from the ears . . . learned from heathen cannibals' idea came from a childhood memory of a favorite black-sheep uncle who used to visit my family," says Harvey. "He did the smoke-from-the-ears trick over and over. We were enchanted, and he appreciated our enthusiastic reception because it was his only trick. I decided to include an on-screen performance of the trick without hesitation. I figured if my beloved, but inept, uncle could do the trick, any good actor could too."

After carefully thinking the matter through, Barney believes there really is a Mr. McBeevee. He decides that an eyewitness identification by Opie will confirm his belief.

"We wanted a casual device, which would justify Opie giving lots of answers, so we could get maximum mileage out of his seemingly fanciful description," says Harvey. "We felt we could have more fun with a relaxed boy helping Barney out than with Opie, a suspected faker, being sternly admonished by his father, so we came up with the idea of Barney's eyewitness identification test."

When Opie returns to the courthouse, Barney casually talks him into identifying Mr. McBeevee. Opie answers questions about McBeevee's height, weight, eye color, and hair color. Barney is pleased with Opie's answers until Opie tells him that Mr. McBeevee "sort of jingles" when he walks. Opie then adds that the jingling comes from the "twelve extra hands that hang from his belt." Opie also mentions that Mr. McBeevee can make smoke come out of his ears. Opie ends his description by saying, "And, he's a real nice man. He even gave me this quarter."

"Opie's description of McBeevee was fashioned by staring at that spot on the ceiling in contemplation and testing and re-testing mentally crazy things that described McBeevee and also had a second solidly sane meaning," says Harvey. "I visualized all the tools, and how colorful McBeevee would describe them, which led to his 'twelve hands,' etc."

After Opie shows the quarter, Andy asks him where he got it. Given the description that Andy has just heard, Andy does not think Mr.

McBeevee is the source for the quarter. To settle the issue, Opie suggests they go and ask Mr. McBeevee about it.

When Andy and Opie arrive at the woods, Opie calls to Mr. McBeevee, but his calls are not answered. Unbeknownst to either Andy or Opie, Mr. McBeevee has left the site to pick up another worker.

Andy then takes Opie home and sends him up to his bedroom. Andy believes Opie has gotten in the habit of "stretching the truth a little out of shape" and thinks it's time "for a whipping."

Ray and Harvey's script directions for the next scene were quite simple. They read: "INT. OPIE'S BEDROOM—DAY Opie is sitting in the window seat. Andy enters, sits next to him."

Director Bob Sweeny followed those script directions exactly. Andy and Opie are seated by the window, but instead of photographing the scene from inside the house, the scene is photographed looking into the bedroom from outside. The window effectively frames the scene, and the simulated sunlight filtering through the trees dramatically lights the set.

At this point, Andy wants the truth. He expects Opie to admit that Mr. McBeevee is just make-believe.

The scene's climax was scripted as follows:

> Opie makes a decision. He shrugs, speaks in a weary
>   monotone.
> OPIE: Mr. McBeevee. . .is only make-. . .
> ANDY: Say it.
> Opie makes a difficult decision.
> OPIE: I can't, Paw. Mr. McBeevee isn't make-believe. He's
>   real.
> Andy looks at the boy's upturned face. Now comes the
>   fateful question.
> OPIE: (continuing) Don't you believe me?
> Andy pauses. He wants to postpone facing the all-important
>   question.
> OPIE: Don't you, Paw?

It's the moment of decision. Andy is troubled. He looks at
the earnest face. Then the answer is there. Andy's
sternness relaxes. He finds a strange peace within him as
he reaches out to take Opie's hand.
ANDY: I believe you.

"Ronny's picking at the window sill, his trembling lower lip, and the cue for the tears in his eyes were carefully worked out during rehearsals," says Rance Howard, Ronny's father. "Nothing you see on screen was improvised. Andy and Ronny knew exactly what they were going to do before the cameras started filming."

"Ronny and his father went over the lines repeatedly," says producer Aaron Ruben. "Ronny's attitude in the scene was established by the director and Andy."

After leaving the bedroom, Barney questions Andy about what happened upstairs. In response to Barney's question about whether Andy believes in Mr. McBeevee, Andy replies, "No, no, but I do believe in Opie."

"Earlier in our careers, Ray and I worked in New York for a daily variety show," says Harvey. "At Christmas one year, we wrote a 'Santa interview' bit. We ended the interview with Santa saying sadly, 'I don't know why people don't believe in me. I believe in them.' I remembered that line while working on the McBeevee script, changed it some, and gave it to Andy."

Harvey continues, "One of the decisions a writer always makes is whether to write a show open or closed. This episode is half-closed, half-open. It is closed right up to the end of act one, where McBeevee is first seen by the audience. The second act is open—the audience now knows Opie isn't faking it—and the scene where Andy believes him is made even more solid."

After his talk with Opie, Andy drives to the woods. He calls out, "Mr. McBeevee." A voice answers, "Hello, somebody call?" At that point, Andy realizes Mr. McBeevee is real and is overjoyed!

Andy returns to the courthouse and tells Barney he just met Mr. McBeevee. Barney feels Andy has been working too hard and needs to let his "mind go blank." When the telephone rings, Barney answers. It is Mr. McBeevee calling to confirm a supper date at the Taylors. This leaves Barney speechless.

"By the episode's end, the only principal player not knowing McBeevee actually exists is Barney," says Harvey. "So we felt we could continue the double entendre one more time in the epilogue. We tried to make the scene believable by Andy initially trying to tell the truth, but Barney just overrides him. So Andy, as he so often does, goes along with it a bit and lets him run on."

Andy's Rich Girlfriend

EPISODE #67

FIRST BROADCAST ON OCTOBER 8, 1962

WRITTEN BY JIM FRITZELL AND
    EVERETT GREENBAUM

DIRECTED BY BOB SWEENEY

JOANNA MOORE RETURNS AS
PEGGY McMILLAN

"I loved Barney's speech about how rich people grow up. I recall how Jim and I laughed as we wrote it."

Everett Greenbaum

In the opening scene of Jim and Everett's third TAGS script, Andy, Peggy, Barney, and Thelma Lou are out on a date. After eating at Mom's Diner, the foursome decides to go for a ride. Barney takes Andy aside and asks him to drive. Barney plans to sit in the back seat with Thelma Lou. In an effort to accommodate Barney, Andy rushes everybody into the car. In the confusion, Barney ends up in the front seat with Andy.

"Barney's scheme about how to get together with his date in a car without mentioning anything about it goes back to the puritanical mores my generation grew up with," says writer Everett Greenbaum.

As the episode continues, Andy drives the group to a beautiful lake. Andy and Peggy walk toward the lake shore. Barney and Thelma Lou remain in the back seat, kissing.

As Andy and Peggy walk, a hawk calls out. Andy asks Peggy if she'd like to hear him "talk" to the hawk. Andy places a blade of grass between his thumbs and blows.

"Jim and I always loved writing one-way dialogue between a character and an animal," says Everett. "In one of the shows we had written for, *Mr. Peepers*, Wally Cox's character talked to small creatures, crustaceans, and even microbes numerous times. So, we decided Andy would talk to the hawk, making the noise with a blade of grass just as we had done in our childhoods."

Thelma Lou and Barney eventually join Andy and Peggy. Thelma Lou suggests they take off their shoes and go wading. Barney is reluctant. He doesn't want to take his shoes and socks off in front of the girls.

"The concept that Barney would not want to appear barefoot in front of the girls also harks back to my puritanical early years," says Everett.

Andy and Peggy skip stones across the water and have a wonderful time. At the date's conclusion, Andy walks Peggy to her door and asks for another date the next night. Peggy tells him that she is on duty at the hospital the next night, but she will be available the night after. With the next date set, Andy kisses Peggy good night.

The next morning, Andy stops by Peggy's house to return a compact that she left in the squad car. Andy notices a new car parked in front of Peggy's house and asks about the car. Andy learns that the car is a gift from Peggy's father, who owns the R and M Grain Elevators in Raleigh.

"In my hometown of Buffalo, New York, grain elevators were a common sight," says Everett. "Tall cylinders of concrete were all along the lakes, getting grain from the ships. When we were thinking of a business for Peggy's father, the Buffalo grain elevators came to mind."

Andy tells Barney about Peggy's new car and her father's wealth. Barney then tells Andy that his relationship with Peggy won't work. Barney explains that Peggy is "one of the rich, and they are different." He advises Andy to "give Peggy up. Nip it in the bud."

"I started using Barney's trademark phrase after I got married," says

Everett. "My wife Deane (a girl who grew up in a cabin in Arkansas) was not at all familiar with machinery, especially cars. I remember the two of us were out driving, and I had put my new Thunderbird into low gear as we went down a steep hill. It produced a high whining noise. At the bottom of the hill, I shifted back into drive. When the sound stopped, Deane said, 'Well, you sure nipped that in the bud.' By the way, my Thunderbird was the same model as Peggy's."

Barney then "spells out" the ways of the rich for Andy—"they are born with a silver spoon in their hand," a rich kid's bike is "solid chromium with six or seven reflectors," and after the bicycle age they go off to a "refinishing school."

Barney's two-minute-fifty-second description of the wealthy is filmed in one long, sustained shot. Two reaction closeups of Andy were edited in later. The scene ends when Andy stands and walks out of the back room. The next shot is photographed with the camera positioned outside the courthouse. Both courthouse doors are propped open, and Andy is seen exiting out the door towards the camera.

The next day at the courthouse, Andy makes final preparations for his date with Peggy. Barney advises Andy to cancel his out-of-town date. Barney reminds Andy of their shared experiences, "We made second-class scout the same month," and "I was second to your first in the county penmanship contest." Barney then warns Andy, "Don't get hurt."

"The scouting remark and the penmanship award were Barney's way of showing Andy how close and intertwined their lives were," explains Everett. "Hence, his advice to give up Peggy was given out of concern for Andy's well-being."

On their date, Andy takes Peggy to a fancy restaurant in Raleigh. Peggy orders a "New Orleans" drink and asks Andy if he has ever been to New Orleans.

Andy tells Peggy that he and Barney once drove to New Orleans in a Model T and wound up selling the broken-down car for twelve dollars.

"Andy's story about the car breaking down was based upon something that actually happened to my cousin Calvin and me," says Everett. "The two of us were driving to New York City in a 1934 Pontiac. The car broke down, and a junkman took the car as compensation. We completed the trip by bus."

During the course of the evening, Peggy orders escargot for herself and Andy, mentions a trip that she made to Paris when she finished high school, and asks Andy to dance. In declining the invitation to dance, Andy says he can "two-step a little, but when they start in on the cha-cha, I generally sit down." In general, Andy has a miserable time on his date.

The next day, Andy avoids Peggy when she drops by the courthouse. He also refuses to take her calls when she telephones his house.

Eventually, Peggy finds Andy in the courthouse and asks him what is going on. Andy denies Peggy's accusation that he is avoiding her, but he immediately cancels a future date the two had planned.

Andy and Peggy's reconciliation occurs when both discover each other later that night skipping stones at the lake. Peggy tells Andy that he is a snob. She says, "Just because my father's rich, you're snubbing me. I want to go out with you, but you don't want to go out with me. You think that nothing can ever measure up to Paris, New Orleans, wherever. The other night when we came out here with Thelma Lou and Barney, that was one of the nicest evenings I've had in a long time."

Andy realizes that Peggy is sincere. He picks up a stone and skips it across the lake before the two walk off arm-in-arm.

"We always had to balance believability with a quick resolution to the problem," says Everett. "Sometimes, as in this episode, the solution comes too easily to be credible, but we were writing a half-hour show which didn't allow the luxury of fully developing a solution. Our attention was always focused foremost upon the comedy."

Andy and the New Mayor

EPISODE #69

FIRST BROADCAST ON OCTOBER 15, 1962

WRITTEN BY RAY SAFFIAN ALLEN
AND HARVEY BULLOCK

DIRECTED BY BOB SWEENEY

PARLEY BAER APPEARS AS
MAYOR ROY STONER

"Capture the fragrance of Riviera rose petals and the passion of the Mediterranean moon in a rugged he-man scent. Caution: User should wear gloves."

Nuit de Paris (Paris Night) bottle label

Ray and Harvey set the opening scene of their "New Mayor" script in the courthouse. Barney is calling Juanita, who is working the breakfast shift at the diner. Barney explains his morning call by saying that he wanted to call to ask for a date that night. He then adds that "the early bird gets the worm." Realizing what he's said, he adds, "No, I didn't mean it that way—honest."

"Barney just bulges with common sayings and laces his talk with them," says writer Harvey Bullock. "Barney perceives himself as a smooth conversationalist. He loves a reassuring phrase, but he can also foul them up mightily. In this instance, he has to undo an embarrassment, 'No, I didn't mean worm'.

Parley Baer played Mayor Roy Stoner

TAGSRWC Archives

"In the early going, it was tempting to cast Juanita in a script. But TAGS producer Aaron Ruben realized that Mayberry was already well populated and having a character talked about but never seen would stimulate the audience's imagination. Everyone could fashion their own version of Juanita however they liked. As long as the character remained unseen, no one could prove their 'Juanita' was incorrect."

Barney tells Juanita he would like to bring a new Ted Weems record over to her place for a late-night listen. When describing Ted Weems's music, Barney says, "It soothes the savage in me."

"Ted Weems was a band leader in the thirties," says Harvey. "He was popular but very unexciting. His appeal was his dreamy style, which was perfect for slow dancing. It's easy to see why Weems was one of Barney's favorites. You could 'dip' to his music, which was Barney's favorite dance-floor maneuver."

In anticipation of his upcoming date with Juanita, Barney picks up a bottle of "Paris Night" shaving lotion. When Andy enters the courthouse, he stops and asks Barney if he's been painting. The fact that the fragrance of Barney's aftershave smells like paint is a running gag throughout the episode's first act.

"The idea for and the name of Barney's lotion originated from a childhood memory," says Harvey. "Way back when I was just a little older than Opie, I went downtown to buy my mother her Christmas present. I always bought her the same thing, a tiny bottle of 'perfume' called 'Evening in Paris,' which I had heard advertised on the radio. It cost thirty-five cents. My mother would enthuse mightily over it, and I would boast importantly, 'They talk about it on the radio'."

Later in the episode, the newly elected mayor, Roy Stoner, has arranged to meet with Andy. Andy is late for the meeting because he has taken Opie fishing and "it got late on us." At the meeting, the mayor makes recommendations for improvements in the sheriff's department.

When the new mayor complains that Andy does not carry a gun, Andy responds that "over in the old country, in London, England, policemen carry sticks."

The old-country reference sounds like a line from one of Andy Griffith's early comedy monologues. "The old-country line does not appear in my script," says Harvey. "I think Andy did contribute that.

"The events surrounding the creation of the new mayor are difficult to remember. I can't recall whether Parley Baer was in place, and we wrote with him in mind, or if we wrote just for a generic, fussy bureaucratic type."

Andy and the mayor conclude their meeting with a look around the courthouse. While the mayor is looking around, Mrs. Morgan stops by to pick up her husband Jess. Andy is holding Jess for moonshining. Jess has not served his full sentence, but Andy allows him to split his sentence so he can harvest his crops before they spoil.

"I know Andy contributed the idea to let the prisoner, Jess Morgan, out of jail for three days so he could bring in his crops," says Harvey.

"While Andy did not actually write a complete script, his comments and suggestions were invaluable," says TAGS producer Aaron Ruben. "Andy would not leave the table where we would be doing a final rewrite until he was satisfied that not just his lines were exactly right, but that of every other character in the script as well. I honestly don't know how successful the series would have been without his input and the authenticity he brought to it."

The mayor tells Andy he wants the prisoner to serve his "full time." After the mayor departs, Andy releases Jess. Jess gives Andy his word that he will return in three days.

On the morning of the third day, Barney encourages Andy to go pick up Jess. Andy refuses. He told Jess he had until five o'clock. Andy explains to Barney that "if we go running out there ahead of time, it'll show that we don't think Jess's word means a thing. A guy like Jess Morgan ain't got too much more than his word. Take that away from him, and he's really got nothing."

Andy's desire not to take away Jess's word is very "noble" and a wonderful example of how the show taught some of "life's little lessons."

"TAGS was a show which liked to point out life's little lessons," says

Harvey. "We were constantly seeking comedy story ideas with implied or explicit morals. It was always a challenge. Comedy was central, and overdone moralizing can be worse than none at all."

The mayor stops by the courthouse while Andy is at home eating lunch. Barney is lying on the jail cot with a blanket pulled over his head. The mayor thinks Barney is the unguarded prisoner. The mayor immediately drives to Andy's home and confronts him about leaving prisoners alone. Unaware of the mistaken identity, Andy explains that nobody is at the jail because "the best interest could be served by letting Jess go home for three days."

The mayor then orders Andy to "go get Morgan." The mayor threatens Andy by saying, "After this, somebody else may be wearing that badge." The mayor then angrily taps Andy's badge with his keys to make his point.

"Yes, the mayor flicking Andy's badge was scripted," says Harvey. "Sometimes these touches were included if we felt strongly about them—which we did in this case. Otherwise, the directors added 'business' where needed."

Andy refuses to pick Jess up early. Andy, Barney, and the mayor wait for Jess's return until twenty-five minutes after five. Andy tells the mayor that something must have happened to keep Jess from keeping his word and suggests that they drive out to Jess's house together.

After Andy parks the squad car by the road, he suggests they take a shortcut through the woods. When Barney spots Jess up in a tree, the mayor believes Jess heard them coming and "crawled up in that tree to hide." When Andy orders Jess to come down, he refuses. The mayor then decides to go up and get him.

As the mayor approaches the tree, the camera reveals a bear sitting at the bottom of the tree that Jess has climbed. The bear then attacks the mayor. Although his clothes are torn, the mayor is not hurt. When the mayor joins Jess in the tree, the bear turns its attention on Andy and Barney. Andy and Barney seek refuge on top of the squad car, and the bear climbs into the car's back seat.

"We never thought the bear would be difficult or dangerous to work with when we were writing the ending," admits Harvey. "But the particular bear doing this show was a real ornery cuss. We were told it chased Don Knotts all the way back to the squad car, where the gasping Don actually climbed up on the car roof!"

Harvey adds, "Sometimes we teased production chief, affable Frank Myers, by sneaking a page into a script he was analyzing for location, props needed, etc. Our insert would call for an elephant stampede or a bridge collapsing, and we could hear poor Frank scream from way down the hall."

The episode concludes with Jess in his cell. Barney is in the courthouse making his final preparations for his date with Juanita. Andy enters and tells Barney the mayor wants "no parking" signs put up at the duck pond because the site has turned into a "regular lover's lane." Andy gives the assignment to Barney.

Barney had planned to take Juanita to the duck pond himself, so he takes the signs from Andy, places them under his arm, and angrily storms out.

The Cow Thief

EPISODE #70

FIRST BROADCAST ON
OCTOBER 29, 1962

WRITTEN BY RAY SAFFIAN ALLEN
AND HARVEY BULLOCK

DIRECTED BY BOB SWEENEY

MALCOLM ATTERBURY GUEST STARS
AS LUKE JENSON, RALPH BELL AS
WILLIAM UPCHURCH, AND
PARLEY BAER AS MAYOR ROY STONER

"This script was a good detective story."
Aaron Ruben

"**F**or once I know with absolute certainty where a story came from," says writer Harvey Bullock. "During one of Sheldon Leonard's seminars, Andy mentioned that back home a fellow once stole some cows by putting shoes on them. The thief was then able to lead the cows away without leaving hoofprints for the owner to follow. All the writers present shouted their appreciation. Andy's recollection was a guaranteed good story.

"At the close of the seminar, Sheldon assigned the various story notions we had worked on, and I got the 'Cow Thief.' I was very pleased. An episode with a strong plot element is often easier to make funny. But Andy's notion was also a bit wacky, so it had to be made credible."

Ray and Harvey's completed script quickly introduces the mystery—

someone is stealing cows. In its opening scene, Farmer Tate "Fletch" Fletcher tells Andy that his cow has been stolen—just like Weddie Huff's cow.

As Andy talks with Fletch, Barney examines the fence beside the barn. Fletch warns Barney to keep away from the gate because "I just put my big bull in there. Since the police ain't giving me no protection, maybe he can."

"I named one of the farmers whose cow was stolen Weddie Huffman," says Harvey. "Weddie was a North Carolina classmate of mine at Duke University—actually just a nodding acquaintance, but a neat guy. His name just popped up when I was writing the script. I thought Weddie was a good Southern name. How his named popped into my typewriter I'm not quite sure, and quite possibly he has never known about it either. Somehow in making the episode, Weddie's last name shrank to just 'Huff.' It's a total mystery why, but somehow a 'man' is missing."

The mayor arrives to console Fletch on his loss. The mayor assures Fletch that his administration will see that Fletch gets "proper protection." Because the mayor feels Andy isn't doing enough, he plans to "phone down to the capital and have them send up a man who really knows something about solving crimes."

This is the second consecutive TAGS episode that uses Mayor Stoner as an antagonist. (The character's first appearance was in Episode #69, "Andy and the New Mayor.")

"Scripts were processed by the producer and then scheduled for shooting, but incoming scripts were not necessarily shot in the order received," explains Harvey. "Aaron would juggle the scripts to give each of the top performers an episode in which they were a dominant part. Mayor Stoner may have appeared in two consecutive scripts, written by two different writers, at two different times, which happened to be juxtaposed and filmed one after the other."

After returning to the courthouse, Barney tells Andy that they can handle this case without "any nosey parker coming up here from the state capital." Barney feels they should make it clear to the outsider that he is not needed. He proposes that they "stand together and turn on the big freeze."

While Barney is talking, Andy looks out the window and sees Luke Jenson, who has a reputation of being a "bad penny," crossing the street to the hardware store.

Ray and Harvey's script directions for the character's initial appearance were as follows:

> Display tables have been set up outside the store, stocked with hardware miscellany, tools, kerosene lanterns, hangs of rope, paint cans. One table has various sizes of cast-iron skillets, cheap tableware, etc. A hand-lettered sign over the items says, 'SERVE YOURSELF.' Luke Jenson wanders by and stops. He is shabby, grim, withdrawn. He is nearsighted and squints continually. His mongrel hound stays close by his side. Luke surveys the street, squints toward store to see if he is being watched. Then he casually picks up a skillet and inspects it.

"Luke's glasses were not in the original script," says Harvey. "Instead Luke's nearsightedness was, hopefully, brought to the audience's attention by his constant squinting. It may be that Aaron wanted to make sure Luke's poor vision was remembered by the audience, so he brought in the glasses."

Malcolm Atterbury, the actor who portrays Luke Jenson, fit the role well, but a mistake was made in the selection of Luke's dog Mac. The dog is too clean and polished looking—not at all the stray mutt that Jenson would have.

"I haven't seen this episode for thirty years and don't remember my reaction to the dog's appearance," says Harvey. "We just wrote his description as 'a mongrel hound.' If indeed a clean and polished dog was cast, it was a goof."

Luke Jenson's menacing presence is heightened audibly by TAGS musical director Earle Hagen's score. The character's on-screen appearance is accompanied by deep bass notes, which signify evil.

"We never had to suggest music," says Harvey. "Earle Hagen was a resident genius, and all could be left to him. Occasionally, a comedy bit might require a definite piece of music, and we would so specify in the script. But mostly, we just sat back and enjoyed Earle whistling away."

Andy walks over to the store and greets Luke. He advises Luke not to take the "serve yourself" sign too seriously. After Andy walks away, Luke turns to Mac and says, "Everybody knows poor, old Luke ain't got any money." At that point, Luke takes a wad of bills out of his shirt pocket and continues his conversation with the dog by saying, "Everybody but you and me."

William Upchurch, the crime expert, arrives from the capital that afternoon. At first, he mistakes Barney for the sheriff. He tells Barney that he remembers when Barney made a special report about safety procedures on country roads. Upchurch especially remembered the jingle Barney used: "Walk on the left side after dark, or you'll wind up playing a harp."

Upchurch wins Barney over immediately, and Barney forgets all about the "big freeze."

"The special-investigator character, William Upchurch, was named after an administrator at Duke University," says Harvey. "He was a small man, ever neat, and totally in command. I liked the sound of 'Upchurch' and brazenly appropriated it. Oddly enough, the real Mr. Upchurch always wore a bow tie. Although we had not requested it in any way, Ralph Bell, the actor cast as Upchurch, turned up with a bow tie."

Andy, Barney, Upchurch, and the mayor visit the Fletcher farm so Upchurch can begin his investigation. Upchurch notices footprints on the ground and asks Andy if he made a moulage (a plaster cast of the prints).

Upchurch joins Barney by the footprints and says, "The sheriff tells me you've decided not to make a moulage." Barney responds, "That's right, we decided not to make a moulage. We told a few people, but we decided it didn't make any sense upsetting folks—running around blabbing, making a big moulage out of it."

"I am uncertain where I heard about moulage. Obviously, it had stayed for years in the dusty files of my mind. Somehow, when I was writing the script, the word just popped up, and I knew instantly it was right for Barney. The word *moulage* was a godsend. The perfect bit of exotica for Barney to at first misunderstand and then revel in using."

Upchurch speculates that the footprints were made by a gang of three fellows. The mayor feels they are finally getting somewhere and rushes the group off to find the culprits.

After they depart, the barn door creaks open slowly. Luke Jenson emerges with a cow in tow. The cow has a shoe on each foot.

When Andy, Barney, and Upchurch return to the farm to make a moulage, Andy becomes suspicious about the way the footprints line up. He notices that "number two walked right through a mudhole."

The three return to town and set the plaster prints up in the courthouse for "extended data analysis." As Upchurch explains his investigation to the mayor, Andy looks out the window. When he sees Luke Jenson, Andy comes up with a plan.

Acting on Andy's instructions, Fletch brings a prize cow to town in his truck. As Luke walks by, he sees the prize cow and overhears Andy telling Fletch he will be working late in the office that night. After Fletch leaves with his cow, Luke decides that night will be an appropriate time for the cow thieves to pay Fletch's farm another visit.

That night at the farm, Andy presents his theory to the others. He has figured out what Luke is doing because there were not any footprints for the stolen cow. Since he believes Luke or his dog would spot them outside, Andy suggests they hide inside Fletch's house until they can catch Luke with the evidence.

The mayor feels Andy's theory is implausible, so he, Upchurch, and Barney depart.

A short time later, Barney returns to stand watch with Andy and says, "I was almost out in the car, and I remembered another time a few years back when another mayor of our town accused you of having a hair-brained idea—when you had the idea of making me your deputy."

"Whenever a story gave an opening for a touching, heartfelt scene, we tried to fulfill it," says Harvey. "The 'Andy and Barney' scene fit in nicely and reminded the audience of the true strength of the show, which was the caring that existed between the leading characters."

As Andy and Barney wait inside the house, they hear Luke Jenson yelling, "Help, get away!" They rush outside and capture Luke with shoes in hand. Andy explains that Luke got more than he bargained for when "a nearsighted man tries to put shoes on an ornery old bull."

In the epilogue, Andy and Opie are taking items to the street that Aunt Bee has cleaned out of the attic. When Opie finds a discarded elephant-foot umbrella stand, he asks if he can play with it. When Barney arrives, he sees the hoofprints that Opie has made with the stand and jumps to the conclusion that an elephant is loose in Mayberry.

"The elephant-hoofprint hoax was actually pulled off by students at Colgate University," says Harvey. "It was after a deep snow, so the prints made four at a time were deep and clear. But just because something really happened doesn't mean it is a good story. I have always preferred to make up my own stories. I believe truth isn't important as long as you can make the false plausible."

The Mayberry Band

EPISODE #72

FIRST BROADCAST ON
NOVEMBER 19, 1962

WRITTEN BY JIM FRITZELL AND
EVERETT GREENBAUM

DIRECTED BY BOB SWEENEY

PARLEY BAER GUEST STARS AS
MAYOR ROY STONER

"My favorite memory of this episode is the be-atific smile on Floyd's face as he marched."
Aaron Ruben

"Andy Griffith played the sousaphone and the guitar and always loved it when an episode included a musical sequence," says TAGS producer Aaron Ruben. "This may have given Jim and Everett the idea to write an episode featuring the Mayberry Band."

As the episode opens, Andy is getting a haircut. The barbershop is full of members of the town band because all of the band members need haircuts for their annual trip to the band festival.

Barney rushes into the barbershop to tell Andy he's got something at the courthouse to show Andy. Andy joins Barney outside, and the two see that Freddy Fleet's band is in town. Freddy introduces Andy and Barney to Phil Sunkel, "his new horn."

The same band made its initial TAGS appearance in "The Guitar Player"

(Episode #3), but that band was led by Bobby Fleet, not Freddy Fleet.

"At the time we wrote this script, Jim and I were just trying to make a living," says writer Everett Greenbaum. "We didn't know we were making history and never dreamed the episodes we wrote would be watched and analyzed for years to come. If we had, we would have looked at old scripts once in a while to verify a name or two.

"Aneta Corsaut, who would be cast later as Helen Crump, was a good friend of ours. Aneta had a musician friend in New York and wanted to give him a thrill by having us use his name in the script. So, we named Fleet's 'new horn' Phil Sunkel. The real Phil Sunkel sued us for twenty thousand dollars. Aneta was devastated and made many long-distance phone calls trying to get Sunkel to 'call off the dogs.' The show finally got him to settle for five thousand dollars."

Freddy Fleet asks Andy's permission to leave his bus parked on the street for an hour while he goes into the diner "to make the food scene." Andy and Barney proceed to the courthouse.

Caught up in the excitement of the Mayberry band's annual trip to the capital, Barney purchases a pair of Andre Kostelanetz marching cymbals, which are pure brass with leather straps. Barney asks Andy to "sit there with your back to me" while he auditions for a position in the band. Barney then quietly walks up behind Andy and presents a loud audition. After this performance, Andy agrees that Barney can be a "stand-by cymbalist."

"Andre Kostelanetz was a big conductor of concert music," says Everett. "There were no cymbals of that name. It just sounded comical."

Following Barney's audition, Andy meets with the town council. Andy requests the approval of funds to "send the town band to the capital." Mayor Roy Stoner refuses to give his approval because he feels "we have the worst town band in the entire state. The band is a disgrace to the town of Mayberry. There will be no trip this year."

"We had seen Parley Baer's two previous TAGS appearances and

*"Andy Griffith played the sousaphone
and the guitar and always loved it when an
episode included a musical sequence."*

Aaron Ruben

TAGSRWC Archives

thought he was very, very good as the mayor," says Everett. "He was a grouchy-type of character and the perfect antagonist, so we decided to use him."

Andy pleads with the mayor to hear the band one more time before making a decision. After Andy promises "to rehearse the boys real good and real hard," the mayor reluctantly agrees.

When Andy gathers the band for rehearsal, Barney calls the group to attention with a cymbal crash. He orders the band to "Cool it! Let Andy make the scene." Floyd explains to Andy that Barney got his new slang from Phil Sunkel.

"Jim adored baseball players and swing musicians to distraction," says Everett. "He picked up their speech easily. The musician's slang used throughout the script, such as Barney's, 'Cool it! Let Andy make the scene,' was written by Jim."

When the mayor arrives, Andy instructs the band to turn to "number twelve in the brown book and play it like you never played it before." The band's performance is terrible! Despite this performance, the mayor admits, "They sound better than they did last year, but they are still the most disgusting band I have ever heard in my life—no trip."

"Because the story line involved music, TAGS musical director Earle Hagen played a prominent behind-the-scenes role in the episode," says TAGS producer Aaron Ruben. "Earle scored the episode and worked out all the arrangements for the musical performances. He even wrote in and carefully arranged the town band's sour notes."

Later in the afternoon, Andy has an idea. He wants Freddy Fleet's boys to play with the town band. Fleet refuses because he's "got to get going." Andy then threatens to hold Fleet's bus for an interstate pest-control inspection because it is bug month. In order to avoid the inspection, Fleet agrees to go along with Andy's plan.

Andy asks the mayor to listen to the band "while we're marching." Andy explains that the band didn't sound good during the previous performance because they were sitting down. He explains that they are a marching band, so they need to keep moving. The mayor agrees to listen one more time.

Andy has the band members change uniforms with Freddy Fleet's boys. After the exchange, the band consists of Freddy Fleet's boys and a few members of the original Mayberry band. Andy instructs the Mayberry band members not to play their instruments.

"Two of the episode's best visual gags came from director Bob Sweeney," says Everett. "Bob came up with the idea to have a giant piccolo player exchange band uniforms with a very short man. During the marching scene, the second gag includes a wonderful closeup of Floyd playing his horn in a comical manner."

"Bob Sweeney was also involved in all areas of pre-production planning," says Aaron Ruben. "The first meeting of the week was the production meeting in which Bob met with the heads of all departments. During the meeting it was decided what was needed in the way of sets, props, wardrobe, etc., for that week's episode. Bob would also lay out the schedule for the week's shooting, which actor he would need and for how long, and how much time was needed for getting the seven or eight pages of script shot that day. It was an early morning call, but when the production meeting was over everyone knew his or her task for the week, and the week's work was properly organized."

As the episode continues, the town band marches down the street and plays a rousing rendition of "Stars and Strips Forever." The mayor can't believe how good they sound. He agrees to allow the band to go to the capital.

After Andy announces that they can go, he pats the mayor on the shoulder and says, "Much obliged, mayor. You won't regret this." This dialogue, photographed with the camera facing the actors, is immediately followed with a shot photographed behind Andy and the mayor. Andy repeats the two lines of dialogue a second time and pats the mayor's shoulder again.

"I don't think the repetition of Andy's dialogue was in our script," says Everett. "Most likely what happened was that the 'much obliged' line and the shoulder patting were used as a starting point for photographing the scene from a different angle and should have been edited out in post-production. It was a small mistake that was overlooked."

Convicts at Large

EPISODE #74

FIRST BROADCAST ON DECEMBER 10, 1962

WRITTEN BY JIM FRITZELL AND
EVERETT GREENBAUM

DIRECTED BY BOB SWEENEY

RETA SHAW, JEAN CARSON,
AND JANE DULO GUEST STAR
AS THE ESCAPED CONVICTS

"I loved writing this episode, and it has always been one of my favorites to watch."

Everett Greenbaum

"'Convicts at Large' was an attempt to do a satire on a popular movie, *The Desperate Hours*," says writer Everett Greenbaum. "Before the movie was made, *The Desperate Hours* was a Broadway play based on the kidnapping of the Hill family in Philadelphia. We got the idea for our script from the play and movie and turned the kidnappers into women, which seemed funny.

"Our idea got Jim and me into a lawsuit. Another writer sued, claiming that he had submitted a similar idea to Jim Fritzell's agent. TAGS finally agreed to pay this guy some small fee, which was cheaper than going to court."

The "convicts" script begins with a prison escape. Searchlights scan the prison walls, and sirens sound the alert that an escape has occurred.

Three women convicts are shown emerging from heavy underbrush. The three are looking for a hideout.

Andy hears a news bulletin about the escape on the courthouse radio. The alert warns that the women are unarmed but possibly dangerous. The leader of the group is named Big Maude Tyler. She is accompanied by Naomi Conners and Sally (no last name is given).

"We created Big Maude Tyler with Reta Shaw in mind," admits Everett. "Jim and I had previously written for Reta on *Mr. Peepers*, and we knew what we would get out of her. She was a wonderful actress and a personal friend of my family."

"I assume that TAGS producer Aaron Ruben knew our work from

As instructed by the convicts, Barney phones the courthouse to tell Andy that he and Floyd are at O'Malley's house.

TAGSRWC Archives

New York theater and live television," says Jean Carson, who portrayed escaped convict Naomi Conners. "I had known Reta for years in New York and always wanted to work with her. She was a brilliant actress. I had seen Jane work as a stand-up comic several times in New York supper clubs."

As Barney and Floyd return from a fishing trip, they discover Floyd's car is out of gas. The two decide to go to the O'Malley cabin to borrow some gas. They do not know the convicts are hiding there while Mr. O'Malley is in Detroit. As they approach the house, Barney notices smoke coming from the chimney and calls out. Barney explains that they would like to borrow some of Mr. O'Malley's gas for their car.

Big Maude invites Barney and Floyd inside. Barney quickly realizes from the prison uniforms that the women are "cons." The convicts grab Barney and Floyd, steal Barney's gun, and take the two prisoner.

"You can't work with better actors than Andy Griffith, Don Knotts, and Howard McNear," says Jean. "They were total professionals. The only problem I had was breaking up on camera. I wanted to laugh anytime I had to look Howard or Don in the face. TAGS was ensemble work all the way. It was a marvelous experience working with all that talent and, most of all, niceness."

Barney reminds Sally of "Al at the old Cascade Club in Toledo." Barney has "that same dumb face, weak chin, and round shoulders." Sally begins calling Barney "Al," and the bit becomes a running gag throughout the episode.

"The 'Al' gag was inspired by a line from Al Jolsen's 'Buddy, Can You Spare a Dime' song," says Everett. "The line was 'Call me, Al.' To my knowledge, there is no Cascade Club in Toledo."

As instructed by the convicts, Barney phones the courthouse to tell Andy that he and Floyd are at O'Malley's house. He tells Andy that they are tired and plan to spend the night.

The convicts grow bored waiting for a chance to escape. The cabin has a record player, so Big Maude tells Sally to put on some music. The song on the record player reminds Sally of "that old Cascade Club," so she asks Al to dance. Barney refuses but is told by Big Maude, "If Sally wants to dance, you dance."

"We figured that one of the great differences between male and female convicts is that the female convicts would want to dance," says Everett. "It was a funny idea that had great potential."

Sally decides "to play something dreamier," so she changes the record. Naomi has a strong reaction to the new music and breaks a vase over Floyd's head. Big Maude explains Naomi's behavior by saying, "Naomi and her husband—that was their song."

"At that time, I had been involved in several mishaps in live television, such as a gun misfiring and the bullet flying into my face and hitting an actor with a break-away bottle that didn't break," says Jean. "I was petrified that I might hurt Howard McNear. I checked and double checked to make sure he had good protection under his hat but was still very uneasy about hitting him with the vase."

As the episode continues, Big Maude sends Floyd and Sally to town for supplies. Floyd is told if he "tries any funny business, Big Maude will let Al have it."

When Andy spots Floyd in Mayberry, he notices Sally sitting in Floyd's car and thinks "O'Malley is having a little party up there." Floyd and Sally quickly depart.

Andy sees the bus arriving soon after Sally and Floyd drive away. When Mr. O'Malley greets Andy as he gets off the bus, Andy realizes "something sure is fishy somewhere" and offers to drive O'Malley out to his place.

After Floyd and Sally return to the cabin, Big Maude sends Sally "out for some water" and tells Naomi "to cook." Naomi constantly scratches as she fries hamburgers.

"Naomi's constant scratching was my idea," says Jean. "Naomi was a nasty, mean little character, and I somehow thought that the scratching would imply a nasty habit for a woman. The intention was to indicate that she might have lice. The scratching ended up creating a lot of extraneous movement. Every time I see it, I cringe. In defense of director Bob Sweeney, you must remember it was Floyd's show, and I'm sure a lot of Sweeney's focus was on Floyd's character. Then in the women's scenes, the focus was definitely on Big Maude. I've always suspected Sweeney's failure to point out the distracting scratching was an oversight, because nobody knew more about what was right—what worked and what didn't work—than Sweeney."

When Andy and O'Malley arrive at the cabin, Andy sneaks up to an open kitchen window and looks in. When Naomi turns away, Andy reaches through the window and pours the bucket of water that Sally had placed on the counter down the sink.

Naomi discovers the empty bucket and decides to get the water herself. She steps outside to the pump and is captured by Andy and O'Malley. When Big Maude sends Sally outside "to see what's keeping Naomi," she too is captured.

Big Maude orders Barney into the kitchen to tend to the hamburgers. Andy gets Barney's attention through the open window and tells him to "get the big one to come outside."

Barney asks Big Maude to go outside with him to get some water. Big Maude refuses. Instead, she puts on a record. The music gives Barney an idea. He looks at Big Maude with steely passion and says, "Let's you and me dance—you're beginning to get to me."

Barney dances over to the door and opens it. He explains that he "can't stand crowded ballrooms." As Barney and Big Maude dance back and forth across the room, Andy, who is out of view, swipes at Big Maude's wrist with a pair of handcuffs each time Barney leads her through the doorway. On the third pass, Andy cuffs Big Maude. After a struggle, she is apprehended.

Oblivious to the capture, Floyd runs to the door and shouts, "Maude, Al, if those hamburgers are ruined, I won't be responsible!"

"The physical action in the capture was suggested in great detail in our script and executed brilliantly on the set," says Everett. "When I first saw the scene on the air I fell apart. Reta and Don played the scene even funnier than I had imagined it would be.

"The idea that kidnap victims may eventually identify themselves with the kidnappers seemed funny with Floyd. We used that idea throughout the episode and, especially, in the end when Floyd is more concerned about burning the hamburgers than anything else."

The epilogue is set in the courthouse. Barney recalls the experience with the convicts and tells Andy that Floyd was "helpless in the face of grave danger." When a knock is heard at the door, Barney opens the door and retrieves the newspaper. He looks at the front-page headline and yells, "For crying out loud!" The headline reads: "LOCAL BARBER CAPTURES ESCAPED CONVICTS."

"Shortly after the completion of 'Convicts at Large,' Howard McNear suffered a stroke," says producer Aaron Ruben. "We were all devastated by the news. The stroke was obviously not a minor one, but Howard's spirits never flagged, and he triumphantly returned to work with us again fifteen months later."

The Bed Jacket

EPISODE #75

FIRST BROADCAST ON DECEMBER 17, 1962

WRITTEN BY RAY SAFFIAN ALLEN AND
   HARVEY BULLOCK

DIRECTED BY BOB SWEENEY

PARLEY BAER GUEST STARS AS
   MAYOR ROY STONER

"'The Bed Jacket' has always been one of my favorites."

Harvey Bullock

"A writer gains an appointment to pitch brief story ideas to the producer," explains writer Harvey Bullock. "If an idea captures the producer's fancy, the writer is given the green light to write a very detailed outline of the projected episode. Fashioning the outline was time consuming and exhausting but, without question, the most vital step in writing the episode.

"I made a long, complete road map of every story before writing one word of dialogue. My endings were always totally worked out before I started—as was the middle break, etc. This was hard labor, but I was very dependent on a thorough outline, and it made fleshing out with dialogue more relaxing—more attention could be focused on the fun words when you didn't have to worry about writing yourself into a corner.

"Upon completion, the outline was sent to the producer who studied it carefully, then summoned the writer to discuss changes. This was the crucial moment when all snags and problems had to be perceived and resolved before the actual script was written. Sometimes the story was changed completely, sometimes the outline was accepted almost 'as is'."

Producer Aaron Ruben is listed as story consultant in the closing credits of "The Bed Jacket." "The story-consultant title was part of my duty as the producer of the show," explains Aaron. "I believe it was done to give me credit as a Writers Guild member and, therefore, as a writer. As story consultant, I did just that. I was consulted as to the theme of the play, how it was to be constructed, what the act break would be, the conclusion, etc."

"The Bed Jacket" opens with Andy and Opie fishing. Opie says to Andy, "We sure are catching them today, huh, Pa?" Andy replies that his fishing rod, "Eagle-Eye Annie," is "doing herself proud."

At this point, Mayor Stoner walks up. He tells Andy "they're not biting today—fishing is a waste of time." Andy casts his rod and immediately catches a fish. Andy asks the mayor if he would like to try Eagle-Eye Annie. The mayor takes the rod and catches "a fish that is a fish." The mayor then offers to buy Annie, but Andy refuses.

"The location lake-shoots were not difficult to set up," says Aaron. "However, if it was an overcast morning, we would often have to wait for the sun. And, of course, rain cancelled it all.

"Whenever we had an episode dealing with an animal—whether it was a dog, a bird, or a fish—we had an animal trainer who would come in with the species called for. In this episode, the trainer brought a bucket of live fish. Just before the scene was to be shot he hooked a fish on the line. We then went to a closeup of Opie and Andy, showing their reaction as we went to a wider shot, showing the line tightening as the fish was flapping around."

Mayor Stoner was a one-dimensional character and served primarily as a problem-causer. "This did not make the character difficult to write for," says Harvey. "His was, I suppose, a clichéd role. It would be nice to give all characters full dimension, but ofttimes we just needed a single note from them and couldn't indulge in filling them out at the expense of air time more usefully spent filling out roles for major characters. Making the lesser characters more dimensional would be distracting and disproportionate to their story importance."

After the mayor leaves, Andy tells Opie they need "to scoot on home—we got to do some shopping for Aunt Bee's birthday."

Andy and Opie take Aunt Bee with them when they drive into town to do their shopping. Aunt Bee tells Andy she is going to be very upset if he does anything foolish about her birthday. She makes him promise to be "sensible."

Andy parks the squad car in front of Lukens' Style Shop. When Andy and Opie leave to shop for Aunt Bee's present, Aunt Bee stays behind. When she looks in Lukens' front window, she sees a beautiful bed jacket on display.

When Aunt Bee looks at the jacket, the camera is positioned on the sidewalk, looking in through the store window. In contrast, the closeups of Aunt Bee are filmed with the camera placed inside the store, looking outward. After entering the store, there is no audible dialogue between the sales clerk and Bee, just background music.

"The no-dialogue scene was the writers' idea," says Aaron. "We know exactly what Aunt Bee has gone into the store for, and it would have been somewhat dull to hear what we can guess by the pantomime. It also seemed to be dramatically more interesting. The camera angles used were included in the writers' script directions."

The script directions for the scene were as follows:

> Aunt Bee stands transfixed, her eyes wide with appreciation. Slowly, she leans a little to one side to get another angle. Then she leans the other way for a different perspective. She stares again and sighs. Determined, she breaks the spell and averts her gaze and starts walking briskly away, but her steps gradually slow until she stops. She turns and

goes back and looks again in the window. She repeats by turning and walking away. As she passes the shop door, her steps falter. She stops, gives up, and goes in. The CAMERA MOVES OVER to the window. In a second, a saleslady picks up the jacket carefully. She holds it up near Aunt Bee and nods approvingly at the size. The saleslady asks another question; Aunt Bee shakes her head. The bed jacket is replaced in the window. The saleslady leaves. CAMERA MOVES IN as Aunt Bee reaches over and fingers the jacket lovingly.

Meanwhile, Andy has decided to buy Aunt Bee two dozen glass preserving jars. Opie selects salt-and-pepper shakers.

After making the purchases, Andy joins Aunt Bee in front of Lukens' Style Shop. Aunt Bee hints that the store has "some awfully nice things" in their front window and remarks that "they're so nicely displayed." Andy looks at the window and sees the mayor inside the shop making a purchase. Andy is reminded that he is supposed to have some papers ready for the mayor, so he rushes off to the courthouse.

The mayor comes out of the shop and explains to Aunt Bee that his wife has been away visiting her sister for a month, so he was purchasing some guest towels for a coming-home present. Knowing that the mayor will be talking with Andy, Aunt Bee points out the bed jacket and remarks that it would make "an ideal gift for almost any occasion."

After the mayor checks Andy's reports, he tells Andy he has another meeting in his office in five minutes. Before leaving, the mayor asks Andy to do him a favor. The mayor wants Andy to exchange the guest towels for the bed jacket.

Aunt Bee and Clara Johnson are standing across the street from Lukens' store, so they see Andy making the exchange. Aunt Bee tells Clara, "Tomorrow I'm going to have a birthday I'll never forget."

The next morning, Andy and Opie give Aunt Bee her presents. Aunt Bee's hands shake as she opens Andy's present. She removes the wrapping paper and discovers preserve jars. She thanks Andy and goes upstairs to hide her disappointment.

The doorbell rings. It is Clara Johnson. She couldn't "wait another second to see how Bee liked her birthday present. How'd it look on her? I was with her yesterday when she saw you take the bed jacket out of Miss Lukens' window."

Andy then realizes his mistake. He goes to Lukens' shop to buy another bed jacket, but there are no more in stock.

Andy goes to the mayor's house, wakes him up, and asks to buy the bed jacket. Andy explains that "Aunt Bee's got her heart set on it." The mayor thinks "perhaps we can work something out. You sell something to me, and I'll sell something to you. You want the bed jacket. I want your fishing rod."

Andy returns home and tells Aunt Bee she needs "to finish opening up her presents." Aunt Bee opens present "number three" and finds the bed jacket.

Aunt Bee calls Clara to tell her about her present. While Aunt Bee is on the telephone, Opie enters the room and tells Andy, "If we're going fishing, Pa, we better hurry." Opie reaches for his fishing rod and notices Eagle-Eye Annie is missing from her usual place.

Andy explains to Opie why he sold Annie. Andy's explanation, which is beautifully written, reads as follows:

> OPIE: You sold it! But, you said you'd never sell it.
> Aunt Bee can be heard in the background talking excitedly
> on the phone.
> ANDY: No, not quite. I said I kept it because it gave me so
> much enjoyment and that I wouldn't sell it for money.
> And, I didn't sell it for money. I kind of swapped it for a
> different kind of enjoyment. So old Eagle-Eye Annie's
> doing just what she did before. Even right now she's
> giving me pleasure—real, heart-warming pleasure.

"I don't recollect this scene being difficult to write," says Harvey. "The whole thrust of the story fostered this revelation of feelings involved and discovered."

In the epilogue, Andy and Opie watch Aunt Bee blow out the candles on her birthday cake. After successfully blowing the candles out, Aunt Bee victoriously shakes hands with Opie.

"The handshake was not scripted," says Harvey. "It was either the suggestion of the director, or Frances Bavier came up with it."

The doorbell then rings. It is the mayor, who is desperate. His wife was in Lukens' store and found out that he bought a bed jacket. She thinks he gave it to some other woman while she was away. The mayor wants Andy to call his wife and explain things.

Andy thinks the situation over and says, "Perhaps we can work something out." Andy agrees to straighten things out if the mayor will sell him Annie. The mayor agrees.

"Most episodes were written with the plot all wrapped up at the end of the second act," says Harvey. "Being unnecessary to the story, the epilogue was just an added fun decoration. However, this story is different from most. I feel this epilogue is vital. The difference is that there are actually two stories in the episode. One, 'The Gift For Aunt Bee,' the second, 'The Fishing-Rod Finagle' or 'Getting Even With the Mean Ol' Mayor.' However, I could not work the fishing-rod denouement at the end of the second act, because Aunt Bee's-gift story was primary, and it would be anticlimactic at that point to continue and add the fishing-rod climax. So, I had to take a chance, give the gift ending the full treatment—and hope the epilogue would always be included.

"After we completed the 'Bed Jacket' script, Ray admitted he would rather not do any more. He just didn't have the feel for small-town life, and Aunt Bee was a total mystery to him. Ray was a supremely gifted big-joke writer and did well on other sitcom stories, but he felt unable to contribute to Mayberry stories. So I went to Aaron to say we wouldn't be doing more TAGS scripts.

"Aaron stunned me. He said, 'Why don't you do them yourself?' I suddenly realized I wanted very much to stay with TAGS. I told Ray about Aaron's suggestion, and he said I should do whatever pleased me.

There was never a better understanding between two men than there was between us. So I used nights and weekends to do TAGS and collaborated with Ray during the day on all other mutual projects. Ray never gave it a second thought. We were together thirty-one years. I miss him."

Man in a Hurry

EPISODE #77

FIRST BROADCAST ON JANUARY 14, 1963

WRITTEN BY JIM FRITZELL AND
EVERETT GREENBAUM

DIRECTED BY BOB SWEENEY

ROBERT EMHARDT GUEST STARS
AS MALCOLM TUCKER,
THE MAN IN A HURRY

NOTE: THIS EPISODE WAS ACTUALLY
WRITTEN AFTER EPISODES #78
AND #79, BUT IT WAS AIRED
BEFORE THEM.

"This is one of Andy's favorites."
Everett Greenbaum

The story line for "Man in a Hurry" is a variation of the theme in which an outsider gets "stuck" in Mayberry and is transformed by the experience. This theme was also used in the earlier episodes, "Andy and the Woman Speeder" (Episode #35) and "Bailey's Bad Boy" (Episode #47).

"The story line for the episode came out of a meeting between Aaron Ruben, Jim Fritzell, and me," says writer Everett Greenbaum. "I don't think the 'stranger stuck in Mayberry' theme was consciously repeated."

"We were never concerned that a theme had been repeated if it had a variation," says producer Aaron Ruben. "Each episode stood on its own, and each new character had his or her own tale of woe."

Jim and Everett's script begins with Malcolm Tucker, a businessman, driving through the outskirts of Mayberry on a Sunday morning. After

Tucker experiences car trouble, he parks his car and walks into town to find help. Tucker has urgent business in Charlotte, so he must get the car fixed.

"Tucker was the typical, well-fed, no-nonsense, impatient, successful businessman," says Aaron. "He was probably a workaholic with no time for the civilities and pleasantries that make life more bearable. Robert Emhardt was perfect casting for the role."

Mr. Tucker arrives in Mayberry just as the congregation is leaving the Sunday morning worship service. Andy, Barney, Aunt Bee, and Opie are among the worshippers. Opie meets his friend Johnny Paul in the churchyard and trades a horsehair from the lapel of his suit for a penny that's been run over by a train. According to Johnny Paul, if you put a horse hair in stagnant water it'll turn into a snake.

"When I was a kid, we used to observe long, slender worms in stagnant pools," recalls Everett. "The popular belief was that they were horse hairs come to life. We also believed that a penny flattened on the train track would become magical and bring you luck."

Mr. Tucker asks Andy for help. Andy tells Tucker he will drop the family off and take him to Wally's filling station. Andy warns Mr. Tucker that the station is just barely open because Gomer Pyle's in charge.

Told of Mr. Tucker's car problem, Gomer offers to fill his car with gas. Andy explains that Gomer is not a mechanic and that Wally, the owner of the station, "is the man you're gonna have to see." Andy suggests that Tucker plan to stay in town overnight because "it's nigh impossible to get anything done here on Sunday."

"Jim and I created Gomer Pyle for this script," says Everett. "The character was inspired by an actual experience. I was having car trouble, and the guy at the service station could think of no cure except to put more gas in the tank. I never dreamed at the time that such an incompetent would provide the inspiration for a character that would eventually find his way into the dictionary."

Andy agrees to drive Mr. Tucker over to see Wally. As the two are leaving the filling station, Mr. Tucker refers to Gomer and asks why "they leave a boy like that in charge?" Andy responds, "It's just a part-time job. He's saving up to become a doctor."

"Andy's response to Mr. Tucker's question is typical of Jim Fritzell's humor and was inspired by the Miss America beauty contest," says Everett. "Jim was always amused at the Miss America contestants who were going to be brain surgeons or bring peace to the world and gave a similar aspiration to Gomer."

Wally tells Mr. Tucker that he will repair his car in the morning. Frustrated by the delay, Mr. Tucker returns to the filling station to ask Gomer who else might be able to fix his car. Gomer suggests that his cousin Goober might be able to because he knows about motors. Gomer relates that Goober "hopped-up an old V-8 engine and put it on his rowboat. That thing'll do eighty, that's fast on water." Gomer then tells Mr. Tucker that Goober is not available on Sundays because "he's always out on his boat."

"As teenagers, my gang was not into parties or dates," says Everett. "We bought old motorcycles or cars for a few bucks and tried to get them running. We always talked about putting a V-8 engine in a boat. You'd say, 'She'll probably do thirty. That's fast on water!'"

Mr. Tucker is so desperate that he jumps in Wally's truck and drives away while Gomer is helping a customer. Andy catches up with Tucker and suggests that he "come on home with me 'fore you get in any more trouble." Mr. Tucker reluctantly agrees.

Mr. Tucker then tries to use Andy's telephone, but he is unable to place a call because the line is tied up by Maude and Cora Mendlebright. The sisters visit by phone for three or four hours every Sunday afternoon. When Mr. Tucker overhears the sisters talking about "their feet falling to sleep," he wants to know how "a public utility would be tied up with such drivel."

"The script included two memorable off-screen characters, the Mendlebright sisters," says Everett. "We wanted two elderly sisters to talk endlessly about the most boring thing we could think of—why their feet hurt."

That evening, Barney joins the Taylors for supper. He and Andy are still dressed in their Sunday-morning white shirts and ties.

"I was raised in the reformed temple of the Jewish religion," says Everett. "They believe the Sabbath was Sunday, not Saturday. I had to go to Sunday school wearing my Sunday suit. Then for the rest of the day, I was in tie and white shirt, having doffed the jacket. There were a lot of horse hairs on the lapels of that jacket, by the way."

After supper, Andy and Barney retire to the front porch. Andy plays his guitar as he and Barney sing "Church in the Wildwood." Mr. Tucker steps out on the porch and is momentarily transformed by the singing. For the first time that day, he is at peace.

"The front-porch shadows were carefully set up for maximum effect," says Aaron. "The singing scene was lengthy [three minutes, thirty seconds] because we knew it would hold, plus the fact that there were two dramatically arresting things going on—the lovely singing of Andy and Barney and the noticeable effect it was having on Tucker."

"I'm sure Andy chose whatever hymn they sang," says Aaron. "He is a great gospel fan." Everett concurs, "Andy knows every hymn ever written. He picked 'Church in the Wildwood.'"

At this point in the episode, Gomer rushes up and breaks Mr. Tucker's serenity. It turns out that Goober is back, and he's going to fix the car.

As Mr. Tucker paces back and forth across the porch, Barney shares with Andy what he's going to do—"Go home, take a nap, then go over to Thelma Lou's for TV. That's the plan." Barney repeats the "plan" three times. Exasperated by the repetition, Mr. Tucker tells Barney, "For the love of Mike, do it!"

"I may have been responsible for the repetitive 'that's the plan' dialogue by Barney," says Aaron. "To me it is typical of a person who is stalling for time, not ready to give up the comfort of just sitting, and trying to convince one's self that leaving is the thing to do. It may be boring, but it's funny."

After Barney leaves, Mr. Tucker waits with Andy and Aunt Bee on the front porch. Andy peels an apple without breaking the peeling and proudly holds the peeling up for Mr. Tucker to see.

Gomer returns with Mr. Tucker's car and says, "We just blowed out the fuel lines, and she runs as good as new. Goober deemed it a real honor to get under that fine a machine, so there's no charge."

Aunt Bee comes to the screen door and asks Andy if he would give her a hand. She was planning to make ice cream and is disappointed when she learns Mr. Tucker is leaving.

Opie runs up as Mr. Tucker is getting into his car. He too is disappointed that Mr. Tucker is leaving. Opie says, "Oh rats, if you was staying I was going to get to sleep on the ironing board between two chairs—that's adventure sleeping."

"The idea for Opie's adventure sleeping came from Jim," says Everett. "Jim was Swedish and half Norwegian. I guess Scandinavians don't give warnings before they come to visit. Jim spent many nights sleeping in bathtubs and, he claimed, on ironing boards."

Aunt Bee prepares chicken legs and cake for Mr. Tucker to eat on the road. Opie gives Mr. Tucker his lucky penny that was run over by a train. After Mr. Tucker starts the car, he hesitates as he contemplates what he is leaving behind.

Mr. Tucker jumps out of the car and says, "Listen to that motor. Sounds like it's falling apart. Don't you think I should wait until morning and let Wally look at it?" Andy agrees.

The epilogue is set late in the evening. Barney has returned, and he, Andy, and Mr. Tucker are seated on the front porch. Andy suggests to Barney that they all "go uptown and get a bottle of pop." Andy asks Mr. Tucker if he'd like to go along. There is no answer. Mr. Tucker is asleep—in his hand is an apple with a long peeling hanging down.

"Andy came up with the apple peeling," says Aaron. "It was very homey and just the sort of bit that Andy was so fond of—what he refers to as the 'humanity.' The closing zoom on the apple had to be the director's choice, since the script direction calls for a dolly in on Tucker asleep.

"I am not at all surprised that 'Man in a Hurry' was voted the favorite episode by TAGSRWC [*The Andy Griffith Show* Rerun

Watchers Club—the show's fan club] members. More than any other episode, it symbolizes what the show was all about and why it endures to this day. *The Andy Griffith Show* is every grownup's Oz. Imagine a town where one could live peacefully, securely, and happily with one's family and neighbors. No drugs, no gangs, no violent crimes. If this was a dream back in the sixties, think what a longed-for dream it is in today's world."

SING ALONG WITH "BARN"

I am often asked to do programs about TAGS for church groups. Several years ago, I did a program for a United Methodist Church in Charlotte. The program was held in the sanctuary, and I showed "Man in a Hurry." The lights were turned off, and during the front-porch scene a wonderful thing happened. As Andy and Barney were singing, I noticed a few voices, confident in the anonymity of the darkness, joining them. The singing was very reverent and sincere. Gradually, as the scene progressed, more and more of the audience joined in—just like Malcolm Tucker—until everyone was singing.

Neal Brower

The Bank Job

EPISODE #78

FIRST BROADCAST ON DECEMBER 24, 1962

WRITTEN BY JIM FRITZELL AND
EVERETT GREENBAUM

DIRECTED BY BOB SWEENEY

"Bank Hold-Up Foiled Here."
    Mayberry Gazette headline

The opening scene of Jim and Everett's "Bank Job" script is set in the courthouse. Barney is reading a newspaper and sharing with Andy the details about several robberies that have taken place in nearby Marshal County.

"We made up the names of places as needed," says writer Everett Greenbaum. "Sometimes we used names of towns in Arkansas, my wife Deane's home state, or upstate New York, where I was raised. Our scripted names were sometimes changed by Aaron Ruben when he wanted to match up a town or county with a name used in an earlier show."

Barney grows concerned about the crime wave and tells Andy,

"Today it's happening over in Marshal County, tomorrow it's us. This town is a piece of cake. A crook could come in here and walk off with the place. Why? There's no security."

Andy tells Barney he is "awful police this morning." After questioning Barney about his date with Thelma Lou the previous night, Andy learns that the two saw the Glenn Ford movie, *G Men*.

"There was no actual movie *G Men* with Glenn Ford," admits Everett. "Barney was the type who could get all worked up after seeing a B-grade police picture and *G Men* sounded like the typical title given that type of film."

Inspired by the movie, Barney decides to do a security check of the Mayberry bank. Barney finds the security guard, Asa Breeney, asleep with a cash drawer and the vault open and Asa's gun in need of repair.

Barney is convinced that the bank is a "cracker box." When Andy enters, Barney reports his finding. Andy tells Barney that he's "getting all steamed up over this." In an attempt to calm him down, Andy suggests that Barney "take a walk over to the Grand and watch them change the marquee. Then, go over to the drugstore for lunch and order the businessman's special."

"In my hometown, the Grenada theater was next door to Woolworth's," says Everett. "When I was a child, my friends and I used to enjoy watching the guy climb a ladder to change the signs on the movie marquee. This was a regular ritual, and afterwards we would go into Woolworth's for a soda. That's how I remembered the drugstore's lunch specials. It was a leisurely way to pass a hour and inspired Andy's advice to Barney."

Barney complains to Andy that for four years Asa has been walking around "without any screws in his gun." In response, Andy shares a fond childhood memory he has of putting Asa's gun in his belt. The gun slipped through the belt, tearing the buckle off his knickers.

"Andy's story about Asa's gun was the result of a childhood memory," says Everett. "Out in front of School 54 in Buffalo, a policeman was on duty at the beginning and end of the school day. We used to beg him to show us his gun. The world wasn't so violent then, so seeing the gun was a big thrill."

After leaving the bank, Andy drives Barney to Mrs. Kelsey's house. Mrs. Kelsey had to go to Mt. Pilot, and Andy promised to take her laundry off the line. As Barney takes down the clothes, he is joined by Leon, a sandwich-eating boy dressed as a cowboy. Barney confides in Leon that the bank is in such a "sorry state" that he wishes they'd get held up once to see what an easy mark they are. As Barney looks at a dress he has just taken off the line, he has an idea.

"We had the idea that Barney would disguise himself and go back to the bank to attempt a fake robbery," says Everett. "During the actual writing of the script, we had to go back and put in something which would foreshadow this development. That's why we wrote the scene where Barney takes down Mrs. Kelsey's laundry."

"We knew Ronny Howard had a little brother Clint, who had made one previous TAGS appearance. It was his character's peanut-butter-and-jelly sandwiches that initially got us interested. As we thought about the scene, we decided we needed some way to communicate to the audience Barney's thoughts about disguising himself. Having Barney talk to Leon as the idea formed in his mind was the answer."

Barney enters the bank disguised as the cousin of Mrs. McGruder, the regular cleaning lady. Barney explains to Harriet, the bank teller, that Mrs. McGruder is not coming because she has a "fungus of the knee." Barney begins mopping the floor. He works his way over to the open vault and slips a stack of money into his mop bucket.

Harriet is suspicious, so she watches the old woman carefully and discovers it is Barney Fife. Harriet gets the bank president, Mr. Meldrim. Meldrim tells Harriet to "watch this" as he yells, "Stop, thief!" Startled, Barney grabs the vault door and slams it shut behind him. The vault is locked and "won't open again until eight o'clock tomorrow morning." Mr. Meldrim sends Asa over to the filling station to get an acetylene torch.

Gomer returns with Asa and attempts to cut through the vault.

Gomer and Barney in front of the Mayberry bank

TAGSRWC Archives

Meanwhile, Barney has escaped by kicking his way through the vault's back wall into the adjoining beauty shop.

"One of my favorite movies of the time was *The Big Deal on Madonna Street*," says Everett. "It was an Italian picture in which an incompetent group of gangsters dig their way into a kitchen, which they could have reached by walking through a doorway. This inspired the idea to have Barney get locked inside the bank vault and kick his way into the beauty shop. By the way, the beauty-shop customer, Mrs. Rodenbach, who calmly witnesses Barney's escape, was named after Jack Rodenbach, a grammar-school friend of mine."

Barney enters the bank through the front door while Gomer is still working on the vault. Barney explains his escape and complains "that there's not a bank in the whole world that has less security than the Mayberry Security Bank." Barney's remark is overheard by a criminal who is waiting in line to pass a bad check.

After Barney and Andy leave, Mr. Meldrim tells Gomer that he'll pay half of the charge for the torch because the sheriff's department ought to pay the rest. A scream is then heard off-camera. Gomer remarks, "Oh, I forgot to tell you; that door is still hot."

"Audiences love to 'get' a joke from an offstage sound," says Everett. "They have to think to understand the joke, and the laugh is a tribute to their intelligence."

The criminal decides to forgo passing the bad check. Instead, he rejoins his partner, and the two drive off to formulate a plan to rob the bank.

The next day, one of the criminals holds up Mr. Meldrim as he opens the bank. On her way to work, Harriet sees Mr. Meldrim and the criminal through a window. Thinking it is Barney "at it again," she gets Andy. Meanwhile, Asa has entered the bank. The bank robber tells Asa and Mr. Meldrim to get against the wall.

Andy enters the bank with Harriet. Thinking the robber is Barney, Andy casually takes the robber's gun away. The bank robber then crosses the room, grabs Asa, takes his gun, and points it at Andy. He then orders Andy to throw the gun down. Andy complies. Asa breaks away, and the robber pulls the trigger of Asa's gun. The gun, still without screws, falls apart, and the bank robber is apprehended.

Andy rushes outside to check the getaway car and finds Barney writing the bank robber's partner a ticket for overtime parking.

In the epilogue, Andy is shown holding a newspaper with a front-page story about the foiled bank robbery. Barney is on the telephone complaining to the newspaper editor that his name was misspelled. This is somewhat reminiscent of the epilogue for "Convicts at Large." In both episodes, a newspaper headline is featured.

"A newspaper headline had played a prominent role in the 'convicts' epilogue," admits Everett. "But, if we had a story with a beginning, middle, and end, we were so happy that we weren't worried that something similar had been done—especially if it wasn't the week before."

One-Punch Opie

EPISODE #79

FIRST BROADCAST ON DECEMBER 31, 1962

WRITTEN BY HARVEY BULLOCK

DIRECTED BY BOB SWEENEY

> *"The script copy I have of 'One-Punch Opie' is a first draft that was rewritten subsequently either by myself or others. I do have a recollection of writing material not seen in this draft but represented in the finished film."*
>
> Harvey Bullock

"**W**hen I think of this script, I am reminded of a TAGS anecdote," says writer Harvey Bullock. "I once found myself in Aaron Ruben's office with a superb writer, Frank Tarloff. Aaron, Frank, and I were pitching some story ideas, and Aaron finally came up with a story he really liked. I didn't think much of it, but hey, if the producer wanted it, it would be an immediate assignment. But before I could say anything, Frank spoke up, 'That story will never work—never.'

"The meeting broke up soon after. Frank walked out with me, stopped, and asked, 'You really wanted to write that story, didn't you?' I had to admit I truly wanted that assignment. Frank said, 'You'll take that story home, work on it all night and find out what we already know—it won't work. You'd have wasted your time and would have had ulcers by breakfast.'

"The moral of that story is just because a producer is ready to buy doesn't mean the material is right. Take no assignment unless you can sell it to yourself, or else you'll find yourself at three in the morning trying desperately to make a silk purse out of a sow's ear.

"The 'One-Punch' story had a rocky course of many changes, which was to be expected when you juggle 'don't ever fight' and, more importantly, 'never start a fight' with 'there are times when you have to fight for what's right.' Aaron and I labored to get an acceptable approach for Opie to take the challenge and fight the new boy. Using the title 'One-Punch Opie' might have helped by establishing the fight was a one-time-only event. I'm not certain we were able to deliver both messages, but I know we made sizable changes as it went along."

The script introduces a new boy in town, Steve Quincy. The boy is more athletic and muscular in Harvey's script than in the finished film. Steve's father, a college professor who is taking time off to write a book about wildflowers, is featured prominently in the draft's story line.

The original draft of the script provided the basic story line for the filmed episode. The episode begins with Opie asking Andy to allow him "to go fishing with the gang." Andy gives his permission.

Opie's friends have met Steve Quincy. Steve asks the guys what they want to do. One of the boys answers, "Well, we were planning on going fishing." Steve says fishing is "stupid" and suggests the group "go swipe some apples."

Opie arrives and introduces himself to Steve. "What did you say your name was?" Steve asks, "Opie or Dopey?" Opie doesn't like this but backs down when Steve asks him what he's going to do about it. Following Steve's lead, the boys decide "to go get some of those apples."

Meanwhile, Andy has learned that "people from out-of-town have rented a house on Grove Street." When Barney asks who they are, Andy tells Barney that anything they want to know they can learn from

Aunt Bee. Aunt Bee is in the back room of the courthouse picking up some dirty laundry, so Andy gives Barney a made-up description of the new people. When Aunt Bee overhears Andy's description, she tells him that he's got it all wrong. Aunt Bee then describes the newcomers in detail: "The name is Quincy, and they have a child—a boy named Steve, age nine." Mr. Quincy "is a salesman selling farm implements of some sort, and she was married once before to someone in the service, and just before she came here, she had an operation on her foot."

Aunt Bee leaves the courthouse as Opie enters. Opie asks Andy if there is any way he "can stop being sheriff for maybe just ten or fifteen minutes?" It turns out that Opie feels as long as Andy is sheriff, he can't fight. Opie explains that somebody already started a fight and "I just want to get in on it."

Barney decides he should give Opie a "few pointers on how to handle rowdies." Barney believes bracing yourself for the first punch is extremely important. He demonstrates this by "making himself hard all over." He asks Opie to hit him in the stomach "as hard as you can." Opie gives the punch "all he's got," and Barney's eyes bulge out in pain.

The segments in which Aunt Bee shares her knowledge about the Quincys and Barney points out how to handle bullies were included in Harvey's original draft and required only slight revisions.

While Barney is recovering from Opie's punch, Andy asks, "Who is this boy you want to fight, Ope?" Andy learns it is the new boy in town. Andy tells Opie he can't fight just because the boys went off with Steve Quincy. Andy feels Opie should "go out there and see if you can't find something you like about this new boy."

Opie follows Andy's suggestion and finds Steve with his friends. Steve challenges Opie to hit a streetlight with an apple. Opie throws an apple and misses. Steve belittles Opie by saying, "You call that throwing? Try it again, and this time—more like this." Steve throws an apple and shatters the streetlight. Andy drives up, and the boys take off, leaving Opie behind.

Barney is upset when he learns about the broken streetlight. He feels when you see the "first sign of youngsters going wrong, you got to nip it in the bud."

"There's a strange history to 'Nip it in the bud'," says Harvey. "It appeared almost simultaneously in several scripts; each writer evidently thinking of it independently. I was sure 'nipping' was first written in 'One-Punch,' but now I'm not so sure.

"I didn't try to include Barney's trademark phrase whenever possible, even though it was perfect for him and would probably fit into almost every story. Overuse would have left the audience sated, and they were entitled to fresh material. I hated to give the phrase up, but I did. I think I used it only one more time in thirty-one scripts."

All the boys come to the courthouse to have a meeting with the sheriff except Steve Quincy who said "he didn't have to come." Andy gives the boys a warning but adds, "If I catch any of you doing any more of this, I'm going straight to your daddies."

Before the boys leave, Barney offers to add "a word or two" to what Andy said. Barney warns that if you "keep on getting into trouble and breaking the law, it can only lead to one thing—incarceration." Barney steps over to the cells and says, "This is where convicted persons are incarcerated. A man confined to prison is a man who has given up his liberties—no more carefree hours; no more doing what you want, whenever you want; and no more peanut-butter-and-jelly sandwiches." As Barney steps into the cell, he adds, "It definitely is no fun when that iron door clangs shut on you." Barney clangs the door shut to make his point—locking himself inside the cell.

It appears that Barney's speech was added after the first draft of the script. "There is no trace of Barney's 'incarceration' speech in my script," says Harvey.

The next day, Andy decides to take Opie and his friends fishing. While Opie is getting ready, Mr. Foley from the grocery store comes into the courthouse and reports "that them boys came by my store, marked up my window, then grabbed some tomatoes and ran." The new boy started throwing tomatoes at Mr. Foley.

In the filmed version, Andy goes to talk to the boys' daddies. The filmed episode is drastically different from the original script. In the script, Andy meets with Mr. Quincy, Steve's father, who has some interesting insights. He tells Andy that sports have always been an important part of his life. He tells Andy that he won a football scholarship that got him through college. He also boxed professionally to pay his way through graduate school. When he raised his boy, he wanted the boy to be strong. He adds, "I seem to have made a mistake—a bad mistake." Mr. Quincy feels he has taught his son to be strong, but the boy misinterpreted what it means to be tough. Andy suggests that Steve might learn a lesson from another boy.

In the original script, Steve's father follows Andy's suggestion and teaches Opie how to take advantage of his son's one fighting weakness—Steve drops his left and is a sucker for one punch, a right cross.

With his new knowledge, Opie decides to confront Steve. He puts up his fists—ready to fight. At this point, the original script is the same as the filmed version. When Steve dares Opie to "step across this line," Opie does. When Steve places a piece of wood on his shoulder and tells Opie to knock it off, Opie does. Opie continues to accept Steve's dares until Steve finally gives up and "goes home."

"All the dares and rites Steve Quincy goes through with Opie as he builds up to a challenge and fight were as I remembered them from my school days," says Harvey. "The local bully, talking tough, put a piece of wood on his shoulder and challenged, 'Alright, knock it off.' If you accepted the challenge, you knocked the piece of wood off, and the fight was on. There were variations of the challenge such as 'step over this line' or 'step inside this circle.' In the script, I worked the gambit in reverse with Quincy, the bully, not wanting to fight and continuing a list of challenges in hopes of wearing down Opie's resolve."

After Steve leaves, the boys celebrate Opie's heroics and decide to go fishing.

In the epilogue, the boys stop by the courthouse. Barney is cleaning a cell. The cell door is open. Leon, the little, sandwich-eating cowboy, follows the boys inside and remains behind after their departure. The departing boys do not close the courthouse door, so Barney asks Leon to close the door. Leon walks over to the cell and clangs the door shut, locking Barney inside. Then, Leon offers Barney his sandwich. Andy makes the most of the situation by commenting, "He can't have that, Leon. No more carefree hours; no more peanut-butter-and-jelly sandwiches. Right, Barn?"

"The reference to the incarceration speech in the epilogue was obviously another addition to the script," says Harvey. "In my script, Mr. Quincy has donated some used exercise paraphernalia and is moving it into the courthouse. Barney comes in, ready to help. Quincy casually tosses Barney a weighted medicine ball, and the impact projects Barney backward, right out of the room.

"I imagine these additions were the work of Aaron Ruben. Aaron did a masterful job as producer, and he was the supreme homogenizer who tailored the input from dozens of us neurotic writers. He kept the series from farce, deleted obviously intrusive jokes, made knife-edged character delineations, and (with all respect to Nashville) avoided *Hee Haw*. In many, many respects, TAGS is *The Aaron Ruben Show*."

High Noon in Mayberry

EPISODE #80

FIRST BROADCAST ON JANUARY 21, 1963

WRITTEN BY JIM FRITZELL AND
EVERETT GREENBAUM

DIRECTED BY BOB SWEENEY

LEO GORDON GUEST STARS
AS LUKE COMSTOCK

"Yes, this story was inspired by the Gary Cooper picture, High Noon.*"*

Everett Greenbaum

Jim and Everett's "High Noon" script begins with a humorous encounter involving the mailman, Billy Ray. The mailman blows a whistle to announce his presence but will not hand Andy the mail because Andy is not "an authorized receptacle." Responding to the situation, Barney comments, "Put a mail sack on some people, and it goes right to their head."

"Mailmen used to blow a whistle when they delivered the mail," says writer Everett Greenbaum. "I guess Jim and I came up with the mail dialogue because we used to relish writing scenes with Andy and Don together. The mailman provided a non-threatening adversary the two could respond to in a comical manner. As I start to read the script, I realize that we were so young when we wrote it that we refer to Billy Ray Belfast, the mailman, as 'an old codger in his sixties,' and here I am almost seventy-eight."

Billy Ray delivers a letter to Barney that contains a dividend check from Amalgamated Oxidation and Aluminum Corporation of America. The twenty-seven-cent check represents the earnings from one-eighth of a share of stock.

"The name of the company was made up, but it does sound real," admits Everett. "The ideas for the bit and the small amount of the dividend were inspired by the residual checks that writers and actors often get for a few cents."

In the same delivery, Andy receives a letter from Luke Comstock, an ex-convict who was shot in the leg by Andy during a gas station holdup. Comstock writes that he has been wanting to see Andy for a long time "to set things straight between us." Andy is not sure of Comstock's intentions. When Andy shows the letter to Barney, Barney thinks Comstock intends to come to Mayberry to "gun you down for revenge. Everything about that letter says just one thing—r-e-v-e-n-g." Barney suggests that Andy leave town for a week, but Andy refuses. He prefers to see what Luke wants.

"Barney was a wonderful character to write for," says Everett. "The letter from Comstock gave him the opportunity to cleverly analyze its implications and then reveal his lack of knowledge by misspelling revenge. Much of Barney's comedy comes from pretending to have knowledge and then immediately blowing that perception."

Andy takes a telephone call from Mrs. Peterson. After hanging up the phone, Andy tells Barney that "Mrs. Peterson's Fluffy is on the roof again." Barney disgustedly asks, "This is a time for pussycats with a killer on the loose?" Andy answers, "Well, Fluffy's got kittens, and you know how you'd feel seeing your mother on the roof?" As Andy leaves to rescue the cat, Barney offers his gun as protection against Comstock. Andy replies, "I won't need it, Barn. Fluffy and I've been friends for years."

"Mrs. Peterson's call about her cat was inspired by my childhood memory," says Everett. "My cat's name was Fluffy, and she was my pet during the fifteen years I spent growing up."

While Andy is away, Barney deputizes Otis and Gomer to give Andy some protection. Otis is worried "that somebody might get hurt." Gomer wants to know, "Are we going to get guns? Do we get to ride in the patrol car?" When Barney offers the two the opportunity to leave if they feel the "mission" is too dangerous, Otis and Gomer head toward the door. Barney then tells them they are going to be deputies whether they want to be or not.

"This episode is the first time Jim and I wrote Otis Campbell into one of our scripts," says Everett. "He worked well paired up with Gomer in the temporary deputy role and provided a continuous comedic presence throughout the episode. We always liked writing for Otis because we knew that Hal Smith would give it all he had as an actor."

When Barney explains to the deputies that they will be plainclothes operatives, Gomer answers that he has a brown suit "that's pretty plain" and a dark gray one that "might even be better." Barney explains that he doesn't want Andy to know he's being protected, so the deputies should just "happen to be where he is."

That night, Barney plays dominoes with Andy. When he leaves, Otis and Gomer take the second shift and spend the night outside Andy's house.

The next day, Andy tells Barney he doesn't need bodyguards. Andy says he appreciates the protection, but he's not sure Comstock will show up.

At that moment, Luke Comstock steps off the bus. The first shot of Comstock is photographed from the waist down, so his face is not shown.

"Seeing Comstock only from the waist down as he exits the bus was included in our script directions," says Everett. "Bob Sweeney cleverly copied the approach used in the Gary Cooper picture *High Noon* by not showing Comstock's face until near the end of the episode. [The face of the villain in *High Noon* is not revealed until the movie's climactic confrontation.] His decision heightened the audience's feeling of suspense."

That evening, Barney interrupts the Taylors' supper. He tells Andy that Otis saw Comstock carrying a leather shotgun case as he got off the bus. Barney says that he doesn't care what Andy does, but he and the boys are going to "be on our toes." When Andy protests, Barney responds that he won't discuss it further and tells Andy to "tick a lock."

"'Tick a lock' was something my teachers used to say to the class," says Everett. "If teachers wanted kids to be quiet, especially during fire drills or visits to museums, they would make a gesture of locking the lips and say, 'tick a lock.' The phrase seemed right for Barney."

After Barney leaves, the telephone rings. It is Luke Comstock, saying that he wants to come over. After thinking the situation over, Andy suggests that Aunt Bee and Opie go over to Clara's for "a little bit." Before leaving, Opie asks Andy if he is scared. When Andy admits that he is nervous, Opie asks if it is the first time he's ever been nervous. Andy answers that he has been scared many times, to which Opie responds, "Really, Pa? Gosh you sure couldn't tell it." Opie then looks at Andy with an expression of concern before departing.

"Andy and Opie's discussion is somewhat unusual for our writing style," admits Everett. "Jim wrote most of that scene. One of my many failings is a fear of sentiment, or at least of expressing it openly. In all of our scripts, I wrote only one sentimental scene between Andy and Opie."

As the episode continues, Andy takes a gun from the top of the china cabinet. He starts to load the gun but changes his mind and places it back on top of the cabinet.

The suspense of the situation is heightened by camera angles, sound effects, and TAGS musical director Earle Hagen's ominous score. As Comstock's footsteps are heard crossing the Taylors' front porch, two piano chords chime the hour of confrontation. As Comstock is shown pressing the doorbell, the musical score diminishes to one bass note that is sustained for twenty seconds. The note fades to silence as Andy puts his hand on the knob and opens the door.

When Comstock enters the house, the audience gets its first look at his face. Comstock then explains that he reviewed his life while he was recuperating from the "shooting scrape we had." During his reflections, he came to the conclusion that he was wasting his life and decided to change his ways. He began to educate himself and, as a result, he is now leading "the good life."

Comstock announces that he has come to Mayberry to bring Andy a shotgun as a "a little gift of appreciation." Comstock pulls the gun out of its case and holds it in front of Andy.

Meanwhile, Barney, Gomer, and Otis are watching through a front-porch window. Surveying the scene, Gomer says, "It's too late. He's got the drop on him." On the other hand, Barney has an idea. He crosses the porch and throws a breaker in the fuse box, causing the house to go dark.

When Andy and Comstock step out on the porch to check the fuse box, Barney, Gomer, and Otis enter from the back.

As Andy restores power, a commotion is heard inside the house. After the power returns, Andy and Comstock enter the house and find Barney, Gomer, and Otis on the floor bound together with rope. Andy explains to Comstock that this is "our Mayberry knot-tying class. It meets here every Tuesday."

The Loaded Goat

EPISODE #81

FIRST BROADCAST ON JANUARY 28, 1963

WRITTEN BY HARVEY BULLOCK

DIRECTED BY BOB SWEENEY

"I suppose Barney could have said 'kaboom,' but 'blooey' just happened to come to mind first. It seemed right for the character, and there was no reason to replace it. Besides, blooey rolls well on the tongue."

Harvey Bullock

"**P**roducers once had all the power," says writer Harvey Bullock. "They could make you write and rewrite ceaselessly for no extra money. The studios encouraged speculative writing, which paid nothing unless a script was produced, and then the actual money the writer was paid was often less than what was originally agreed upon.

"The Writers Guild finally developed clout and set out a rigid new procedure. First, the writer made an appointment with the producer. At this meeting, you orally pitched new story notions. If the producer didn't find any of your notions to his satisfaction, you left to cook up more ideas, and no money changed hands. However, if the producer indicated there was one of your notions he thought might work, he was then officially committed to buy that notion and at that time paid you 'story money,' which was close to a third of the total contracted $3,500. For this story money, you agreed to deliver a full treatment within a prescribed time. Next you delivered a full written treatment, which the producer could either discard or elect to go forward with. If he decided to proceed with the story, he would then have to pay the writer the remainder of the contracted fee.

"The scripts I wrote for TAGS all varied in one way or another. Some had to endure massive changes, and some sailed right through. 'Mimeograph' was the sweetest word ever heard when you called Aaron Ruben after dropping off the first draft and asked for an appointment with him to discuss changes—to which dear Aaron responded, 'It doesn't need any changes. We're putting the first draft right into mimeograph'."

"The Loaded Goat" episode begins with Andy and the mayor waiting for Floyd to return to the barbershop after lunch. As they await Floyd, dynamite blasts at the construction site of a new underpass are heard in the distance.

Cy "Hudge" Hudgins comes into the barbershop for a haircut. Hudge brings his goat, "Jimmy," into the shop with him. He explains that he has been promising Jimmy that he would "bring him to town."

When he learns Floyd is still at lunch, Hudge decides not to wait. He ties Jimmy to a sidewalk bench while he runs errands. Hudge instructs Jimmy to wait there until he returns.

"Farmer Hudgins talks to Jimmy the goat as if he were a person," says Harvey. "This, of course, is very common with owners of any kind of pet. There is a constant conversation, and it's possible that some little bit of the owner's chatter does really register with the pet. But mainly, it is probably just comforting to the owner. I envisioned Hudge as a loner—someone who would treat his goat as an equal."

As it turns out, Jimmy pays little attention to Hudge's order. He chews on the rope until he is able to free himself. Jimmy then walks to the courthouse, nudges the door open, and enters. Barney is inside

*Andy and Barney find Jimmy the goat after
he has eaten himself full of dynamite.*

TAGSRWC Archives

practicing on his french harp. Startled by Jimmy, Barney shoos the goat outside.

After Jimmy's departure, Andy enters the courthouse. He hears Barney playing his french harp and compliments his performance. At this point, Hudge comes in to report that Jimmy is missing. Barney responds that Jimmy was in the courthouse a few minutes previously. Andy teases Barney that the goat came to the courthouse because he liked Barney's harp-playing. Barney, Andy, and Hudge then go looking for the goat.

Meanwhile, Jimmy has wandered into a shed where dynamite is stored. Jimmy, "who will eat anything he can get his teeth into," stuffs himself with the explosive.

"I'm uncertain about the development of the story line for 'The Loaded Goat'," says Harvey. "But when I was fleshing it out, a goat seemed a natural as something unique to stuff with dynamite.

"Animal handlers are very resourceful, so it never occurred to me that they couldn't come up with a goat to do the scenes as written, or if not, substitute other behaviors the goat had mastered to get the same result."

Andy and Barney learn from Opie that a goat was in the shed behind the hardware store, so they go to investigate. It is dark inside the shed when Barney enters, so he lights a cigarette lighter. When he holds the flame up to a wooden box labeled "Dynamite High Explosives—Dangerous," he realizes the shed is full of dynamite.

Shaken by his discovery, Barney exits and leans against the shed to catch his breath. When Andy goes in the shed to investigate, he finds a piece of Jimmy's rope on the floor. He tells Barney, "Jimmy's been here alright, and what's more he had lunch."

Hudge sees Jimmy entering the courthouse and runs after him, intending to teach Jimmy a lesson by giving him "a good kick." Andy and Barney tell Hudge not to kick the goat because "that goat ate himself full of dynamite. One swift kick and blooey."

Hudge responds, "Ain't that the way it always is. First time he comes to town, he figures he's got to do everything."

"The line about Jimmy coming into town for the first time was developed, just like the rest of the dialogue, by writing and rewriting scenes or just endlessly running them through your mind," says Harvey. "It always helped me to close my eyes, project what the set looked like, and mentally move the characters about, while imagining in my mind what they might say."

As the episode continues, Andy sends Barney to find the engineer with the highway crew. While waiting, Andy decides to place Jimmy in one of the cells. He and Hudge spread straw on the cell's floor and pad the wall with a mattress.

Barney returns with the blasting engineer, Mr. Burton, who advises that it is possible for Jimmy to explode. He explains that he has worked with explosives for twenty years and the one thing he has learned is that "there's nothing you can be sure of."

"I included Mr. Burton, an experienced blasting engineer, in the script to strengthen the possibility that Jimmy could indeed blow up," says Harvey. "Burton responds to the question the audience is asking, 'Is it really possible that Jimmy is a loaded goat?' I knew the audience had been patiently waiting for someone to tell them there was, in fact, a chance that Jimmy could go 'blooey.' Although I felt I couldn't quite quote Burton as firmly believing it, he could say truthfully that you can never be sure what will happen with explosives. His guarded opinion was good enough to maintain the possibility."

After Mr. Burton leaves, Andy and Barney decide to get more hay and pillows to pad the cell.

After they leave, a drunken Otis comes into the courthouse. He opens Jimmy's cell and enters. Otis sees the mattress attached to the wall and attempts to get into bed. He falls to the floor and says, "Wow! This is a new one. First time I ever fell off a bed onto a wall."

"The 'pillows and mattress on the wall' scene evolved when I needed an interesting device for the loaded Otis," says Harvey. "Hal fell off the wall perfectly."

"I hurt my back when I tried to jump on the mattress, and it took me about a week to get over it," says Hal Smith. "The cell floor was hard cement. The abundant amount of straw you see me scrambling under near the end of the scene was added later—after I had fallen off the wall. Originally, they had about an inch of straw spread out. I remember getting my feet up, hitting the mattress, falling back onto the cement floor, and hearing my back pop.

"The TAGS crew was wonderful. If you did something that was unusual or funny, they would wait until the scene ended, and then they would applaud, scream, whistle, and holler. My fall got a big response from the crew, and their approval momentarily made my injury seem less painful."

After his fall, Otis spots Jimmy and asks, "Uncle Nat, what are you doing here?" Otis eventually realizes that the goat is not Uncle Nat and wrestles him out of the cell. When this happens, Jimmy becomes angry.

By the time Andy and Barney return, Jimmy is furious. Andy and Barney are forced to seek refuge on top of Andy's desk. Andy then suggests that Barney play his french harp. This calms Jimmy enough to allow Andy and Barney to ease off the desk and slip a rope around Jimmy's neck.

The scene concludes with a shot of Andy and Barney leading Jimmy down a deserted dirt road. The mournful sound of Barney's harp accompanies the exodus.

"For the end of the second act, I wanted to conclude on a plaintive note," says Harvey. "This would be a distinct change of pace after all the explosions and frantic reaction to the loaded goat. I brought Barney's french harp back to add a soulful background and placed the performers in a desolate setting. The versatility of the performers made writing for them a pleasure, and I know they enjoyed playing this different scene. This was my first try at making an atmospheric no-dialogue ending, and I was extremely pleased with the on-screen result."

Class Reunion

EPISODE #82

FIRST BROADCAST ON FEBRUARY 4, 1963

WRITTEN BY JIM FRITZELL AND
EVERETT GREENBAUM

DIRECTED BY BOB SWEENEY

PEGGY McCAY GUEST STARS AS
SHARON DESPAIN

*"Barney beloved—The tears on my pillow bespeak
the pain that is in my heart."*

Note to Barney from Ramona
Wiley

"The idea for a class-reunion show was stock material in those days
[the early 1960s]," says writer Everett Greenbaum. "Jim and I did it on
almost every series we wrote for."

The opening scene in the "reunion" episode is set in the Taylor garage. Andy and Barney are storing a trunk of Barney's belongings. To
store the trunk, Andy cleans off a shelf positioned against the wall.

Barney tells Andy that his landlady, Mrs. Mendlebright, insisted that
he move the trunk from the cellar because she is planning to grow
mushrooms there. Barney says that she saw a magazine ad that said
"Grow Mushrooms at Home for Fun and Profit."

Barney relates that Mrs. Mendlebright is full of ambition. The previous year she sent away for "a machine that tore car tires into long shreds

Andy and Barney look through **The Cutlass,**
their high-school yearbook.

TAGSRWC Archives

of rubber. She weaved them into floor mats, and purses, and seat covers, and other attractive items."

This scene offers an excellent example of a "cheat shot"—a camera angle that cheats reality. As Andy and Barney talk about Mrs. Mendlebright, the two are seen from a viewpoint on the wall behind the shelf. The actual wall has been removed, giving the viewer the feeling of being part of the scene.

"During the Depression, there were always ads in magazines from outfits selling equipment to grow mushrooms, grow orchids, or shred old tires to earn money," says Everett. "The tire shredders could also get other machines which wove the shredding into sandals, purses, and other useful objects. Sometimes the ads promised to buy all of these products from the makers. Of course, they never bought anything from the poor sucker who is now broke having gone into hock to buy the machine. By the way, one of those shredding-machine people is my next-door neighbor. He served five years and thinks I don't know about it."

As the scene continues, the bottom of the trunk falls out when Andy and Barney lift it to the shelf. As they examine the trunk's contents, they find a tennis racket, an "old" rock Barney used to strike kitchen matches on and hold them to his daddy's pipe when he was "a little fellow," and an old high-school yearbook.

One of the strengths of TAGS was its believability. Mayberry seemed like a real town populated with real residents. A technique used by the writers to create believability was to give the characters a personal history.

The discovery of the yearbook opens the door to a wonderful glimpse into the pasts of Andy and Barney. The minor details surrounding their pasts were inspired in part by the lives of the episode's two writers.

Andy thumbs through the yearbook (*The Cutlass*) and finds their class pictures. As Andy continues thumbing through the book, Barney stops him at a picture of Ramona Wiley. Beneath her picture is the inscription: "Always, Ramona." Barney explains that Ramona was "crazy about me. It was all one-sided. I wasn't interested." Barney, however, will never forget one note Ramona wrote: "Barney beloved—The tears on my pillow bespeak the pain that is in my heart."

Andy's high-school sweetheart was Sharon DeSpain. He and Sharon were voted "Couple of the Year" two years in a row. Barney wonders where Sharon is now. This gives Andy the inspiration to organize a class reunion.

"*The Cutlass* was the name of the yearbook in Jim Fritzell's high school in San Francisco," says Everett. "I think Ramona Wiley came from a list of names my wife made for me of some of the people she knew in Arkansas. Sharon DeSpain went to school with Jim."

"In grade school I was, as yet, quite unformed—really a fetus in sneakers. But the whole school knew I had a crush on a girl named Jane Clark. Another boy, Fred Remington, thought this was hilarious. I once put a little ring on Jane's desk. Fred Remington got hold of a tiny ivory elephant, wrapped it in a gift box, and put it on my desk with the note 'The tears on my pillow bespeak the pain that is in my heart' and signed it 'Jane.' I think we were all in high school when I finally learned that I had been tricked. Small wonder those words should be burned in my mind years later."

Andy's idea is approved and invitations are sent to the members of Mayberry Union High School's Class of 1945.

Sometime afterwards, Mary Lee, a classmate of Andy and Barney, rushes into the courthouse and announces, "We sent out thirty-five invitations, and so far we got twenty acceptances!" When Mary Lee says Sharon DeSpain is not one of the respondents, Andy is clearly disappointed.

In an effort to cheer Andy, Barney says, "Even if she don't come, we're in for the time of our lives. It's going to be great. Yeah, the old orange and blue."

After a moment's reflection, the three former classmates begin singing the Mayberry Union High School song.

"The lyrics for the Mayberry Union High School song were mostly the lyrics from the song of my high school, Bennett High in Buffalo," says Everett. "Orange and blue were Bennett's school colors."

The night of the reunion finally arrives. The auditorium is decorated with balloons and streamers. Carl Benson's Wildcats provide the music.

Andy and Barney struggle to identify names and faces. After the two meet Harry Becktoris, Ramona Wiley's husband, Harry goes to get Ramona. At this point, Barney panics. He doesn't "want to wreck a marriage." Barney decides he will wash the punch glasses. He grabs an armful of glasses, but Ramona walks up before he can make his getaway. Although Ramona remembers Andy, she mistakes Barney for the bartender, which deeply offends Barney.

As the evening progresses, Andy is disappointed that Sharon DeSpain didn't show up. Just then, Mary Lee walks by and says, "Uh, uh, Andy," and points toward the door. Barney turns Andy around so he can see that Sharon has arrived!

The episode takes a dramatic turn after the arrival of Sharon DeSpain. Andy and Sharon dance. Watching the couple, Barney comments, "Look at that. It was one of the great natural romances of all time, and it's still going on."

After dancing, Andy and Sharon step outside and quickly rekindle the passion of their former love. But as the two talk, they quickly remember their differences—Andy likes Mayberry, Sharon prefers the big city. The possibility of reviving "one of the great natural romances of all time" is lost.

In the background, Carl Benson's Wildcats begin playing "Good Night, Sweetheart," and Andy delivers the bittersweet line, "How about a couple of old friends having that last dance?" Sadly, the two former sweethearts realize they will forever be just "old friends."

The episode's epilogue is equally as poignant. Andy and Barney remain after everyone else has left. They sing the school song one last time and reflect upon the departure of their youth. As the epilogue ends the "tears" truly "bespeak the pain that is in their hearts."

Andy and Sharon DeSpain at the class reunion

TAGSRWC Archives

"I was very pleased with the 'Class Reunion' show, although I was always nervous when I saw a show we had written for the first time on the screen," says Everett. "In those days, Jim and I never felt we had the time to thoroughly hash a script over in our minds because we were always late with the next one, and the one after that, and the one after that."

But Everett need not have worried. "Class Reunion" strikes a universal chord. The audience identifies with Andy and Barney as they reminisce about high school, sing the school song, experience the pain of lost love, and acknowledge the passing of time. Andy and Barney's feelings are real to the audience because most members of the audience have felt them firsthand through their own personal experiences. The human feelings projected through their characters enable Andy and Barney to come alive in a powerful way.

Rafe Hollister Sings

EPISODE #83

FIRST BROADCAST ON FEBRUARY 11, 1963

WRITTEN BY HARVEY BULLOCK

DIRECTED BY CHARLES IRVING

JACK PRINCE GUEST STARS
AS RAFE HOLLISTER

"I don't think Harvey wrote this script with a specific actor in mind. The Rafe Hollister role required someone with a fine voice, and Jack Prince fit the bill perfectly."

Aaron Ruben

"Rafe Hollister Sings" begins with Barney loosening up his voice for tryouts for the Ladies League Musicale. Rafe Hollister, a local farmer, stops by the courthouse to drop off "a mess of fresh-picked string beans." When Rafe hears Barney "practicing up on his singing voice," he asks Andy how long Barney has been "ailing."

"When a writer creates a character, he automatically develops a picture of that person in his mind," says writer Harvey Bullock. "However, when the script is shot, the writer will often see an actor who looks entirely different. At first look, Jack Prince didn't seem to be quite the same as my mental image of Rafe Hollister. Not that Jack wasn't right for the role, it was simply that the casting director, Ruth Birch, had her mental picture too. The differences I perceived were all minor things, and when Jack got into the role, the differences disappeared."

"I think TAGS director Bob Sweeney may have suggested me for the Rafe Hollister role," said Jack Prince. "Bob directed a second-season episode I appeared in called 'The County Nurse.' I didn't sing in that episode, but during the week we worked together, he learned that I was a professional singer."

As Barney continues his practice session, he brings Andy's guitar out of the back room and asks Andy to play a "C" chord so he can check his pitch. When Andy asks Barney what he plans to sing at the tryouts, Barney answers, "I thought I'd do something from the light classics—sort of a tossup between 'Tico Tico' and 'The Umbrella Man.' I might even go all the way with 'The Moon of Manicura'."

"All the titles Barney mentions as possibilities for his Ladies League Musicale audition were actual songs," says Harvey. "'Tico Tico' was played endlessly by every accordion player big enough to strap on a keyboard. It supposedly showed off their fast finger work. 'The Umbrella Man' is 'a one-a and a two-a' trite little ballad. 'The Moon of Manicura' was crooned by Bing Crosby to Dorothy Lamour in one of their 'road' pictures and had a slow and syrupy style. These songs were selected because each one had fame for a second, then a complete fadeout. I always enjoyed using quaint, old remembrances in my scripts."

Andy suggests that Barney warm up with "Believe Me If All These Endearing Young Charms." As Barney begins the song, Rafe interrupts by saying, "Barney, that ain't the way it goes." Andy suggests that Rafe "join along and sing with Barn." Rafe does, and his voice is beautiful.

Andy suggests that Barney take Rafe along to the tryouts. Barney feels doing so would be a mistake because they might ask questions that "only a trained musician would understand." To make his point, Barney asks Rafe, "Suppose they was to ask you, can you sing 'a cappella'? Would you know what to do?" Andy asks Barney, "Supposing they was to ask you, can you sing 'a cappella'? What would you do?" Barney answers with a short rendition of a song.

Accompanied by Andy on guitar, Rafe Hollister
sings beautifully during the Ladies League Musicale.

TAGSRWC Archives

"Barney constantly thinks he knows something when he really doesn't," says Harvey. "When Andy asks if he can sing a cappella, he assumes a cappella to be the name of a song. Since the song seems to be Latino, he gives it the music of 'La Cucaracha'."

Despite Barney's apprehensions, Rafe decides to try out. After the tryouts, Barney tells Andy that his audition was "one of those electric moments in the theater."

John Masters, the choral director, enters the courthouse and tells Andy he "has discovered a truly outstanding voice." John then thanks Andy for sending Rafe Hollister.

Barney rationalizes that he was not chosen because he had the "wrong selection. I picked something from the light classics, 'Ciribiribin,' and it was just over their heads."

"'Ciribiribin' was a crazy polka," says Harvey. "It was a song that someone like Barney would enjoy."

When he learns that Rafe Hollister will be the representative at the musicale, Mayor Roy Stoner is upset. Mrs. Jeffries, the head of the Mayberry chapter of the Ladies League, feels Rafe is not "presentable." Since sending Rafe to the tryout was Andy's idea, the two feel Andy should "march himself right out to Rafe's place and tell him he will not be needed."

Andy goes to visit Rafe and realizes that singing at the musicale means "too much" to Rafe and his wife to disappoint them. He says nothing about the mayor and Mrs. Jeffries' opposition.

The mayor is upset when Andy confesses he didn't tell Rafe. The mayor holds Andy "personally responsible for Rafe's appearance."

On the day of the musicale, Rafe shows up dressed in bib overalls, a coat, and a tie. Andy asks Rafe to come back to the courthouse in an hour because he's got some work to do before they go over to the town hall to practice.

When Rafe returns, Andy gives him a suit. Andy explains that he forgot to give Rafe the government clothes when he was "turned loose for moonshine about a year ago."

After Rafe puts on his suit, he and Andy go over to the town hall. When Rafe steps on stage in his new suit, Mrs. Hollister compliments him on his appearance.

"I remember walking on stage in that new suit, and seeing Rafe's wife sitting in the auditorium," said Jack Prince. "I was stunned by the expression of love and pride communicated by Isabel Randolph, the actress cast as the wife. I thought to myself, 'My God, this is an actress.' I never felt her performance was completely captured in the finished film."

Sitting in the back of the hall, Mrs. Hollister overhears Mayor Stoner and Mrs. Jeffries as they agree that Rafe's appearance is all right as long as "he doesn't associate with anyone."

When Andy realizes that Mrs. Hollister has overheard the comment, he takes another tact. On the night of the musicale, Rafe steps on stage dressed in bib overalls. Accompanied by Andy on guitar, Rafe sings beautifully.

"The song Harvey originally scripted for Rafe's musicale performance was 'I'm Coming Back'," said Jack. "Director Charles Irving, Aaron Ruben, and I kicked around a number of songs. 'Lonesome Road' and 'Ridin' That New River Train' were ultimately chosen because they fit the character, and the copyright on both had expired.

"All my vocals in the episode were pre-recorded, and I lip-synced the filmed performances. I remember cringing the first time I saw my performance in the finished film, because I thought my lip movements didn't correspond correctly with the vocals heard on the soundtrack."

"Aaron Ruben would stopwatch a script reading and trim or add as needed," says Harvey. "When a song was included in a script, it was timed as well. Most of my TAGS scripts were thirty-six pages, but this script, which included several musical performances, had only thirty pages.

"I was concerned about holding the audience's attention throughout the musicale performance, so I included directions in the script that numerous camera shots of the audience be shown with Rafe's singing

Rafe's musicale performance

TAGSRWC Archives

over them. This enabled Rafe to get in more of the song without being the focus of the picture endlessly."

At the end of the musicale, Rafe is asked to perform an encore. After the encore, Mrs. Dennis, the president of the Ladies League, says to the mayor and Mrs. Jefferies, "Oh, he's really wonderful, isn't he? And what a perfectly marvelous idea having him appear dressed that way. It made his selection so much more authentic."

In the epilogue, Andy and Opie enter the courthouse and find Barney getting ready for next year's tryouts. Barney tells Andy that this time he's "got the perfect selection—'The Crawdad Song'." Barney hands Andy his guitar and asks for accompaniment.

Harvey's script directions were as follows:

> Andy reluctantly takes guitar and accompanies Barney on 'Crawdad Song.' In the midst of the song, Opie enters, listens a moment, and frowns. They stop. Opie sings last part of song. Barney watches, chagrined. Barney gives Andy a smoldering look and storms out. Andy amused, Opie puzzled as we: FADE OUT.

The epilogue was refined during production and extended a few seconds longer. By repeating the action of the scene in which Rafe is "discovered" by Andy, the audience understands that Barney feels Andy may get the idea to suggest Opie try out at next year's auditions. After Barney storms out, Andy reprises the "Crawdad Song" with a lively guitar accompaniment. Opie joins in, and the joy of song, as well as the harmony of Andy and Opie's relationship, is captured on screen.

Opie and the Spoiled Kid

EPISODE #84

FIRST BROADCAST ON FEBRUARY 18, 1963

WRITTEN BY JIM FRITZELL AND
EVERETT GREENBAUM

DIRECTED BY BOB SWEENEY

"It was always more difficult to write for child actors. Their characters don't have as much history, lore, or aspirations to draw on."

Everett Greenbaum

"Opie and the Spoiled Kid" begins with Andy and Barney walking down Main Street. When they see Mrs. Tarbocks, Barney notes that she is "getting gray for a woman her age." Andy agrees and tells Barney that she's been having trouble with her husband. Barney wants to know what kind of trouble, so Andy explains that her husband wants them to move out of town because people in town gossip too much.

Their discussion is interrupted by a boy riding his bike on the sidewalk. The boy nearly runs over a woman coming out of Foley's Grocery. As Andy and Barney help the woman pick up her scattered groceries, they question her about the boy's identity. The woman has no idea what the boy looked like. She says, "It was just swoosh, and he was gone." Barney tells the woman that a trained professional, like himself, "has a photographic mind." The boy on the bike rides down the sidewalk a second time, nearly running over Barney. Despite the close call, Barney has no idea what the boy looked like. He comments, "It was just swoosh, and he was gone."

As it turns out, the boy on the bike is Arnold Winkler. After his ride through town, Arnold pedals over to visit Opie. Opie is impressed with Arnold's new bike, which is an Intercontinental Flyer.

"Jim Fritzell and I once took two years off from one another to work on separate projects," says writer Everett Greenbaum. "During that time, I moved to California to work on *The George Goble Show* with another writer named Harry Winkler. Harry was a wonderful friend who, unfortunately, died young. Arnold was a name I always thought was kind of ugly. So, when I was thinking of a name for the spoiled kid, the ugly first name and the last name of a former good friend came to mind.

"We wrote that Arnold Winkler should be 'nicely dressed.' The wardrobe department followed our description perfectly. Arnold's button-up shirt, sweater, slacks, and dress shoes gave him the look of worldliness and sophistication we wanted.

"The name we gave Arnold's new bicycle, 'Intercontinental Flyer,' was made up. We thought the name sounded expensive and appropriate for the bike a spoiled kid would have."

Arnold offers to take Opie for a ride. Opie can't because he has to clean the garage or he won't get his "quarter this week." Arnold can't believe Opie works for his allowance. According to Arnold, "allowance is money a kid is allowed to have—and without working for it. It's for being a kid."

Opie decides to talk this over with Andy.

Back at the courthouse, Barney is sorting through a group of wanted posters. The names on the posters are Henry "Shopping Bag" Leonette, Max "the Tongue" Rassmussen, and Benjamin Schuster. Holding the posters, Barney notes that he has "$8,500 American silver cartwheels right in my hands. There's only one small hitch—we don't know where they are."

"We always knew we could get fun out of something like a bunch of wanted posters," says Everett. "So, we used them here to give the scene a humorous beginning. Barney refers to the total reward money on the posters as '$8,500 American silver cartwheels.' I remembered that silver dollars were sometimes called cartwheels, and the phrase, which seemed like something Barney would say, went into the script."

Opie enters and tells Andy he wants to have a talk. Opie then asks Andy if there are rules about how a pa should treat his son. Barney thinks Opie's question "takes the cake." When Andy tells Barney that he and Opie "usually keep these little talks to ourselves," Barney gets the message and steps into the back room.

After Barney leaves, Opie asks Andy whether Barney's feelings are hurt. Barney steps back into the room when he hears Opie say he is "kind of sensitive." Barney explains that he is "spirited, not sensitive."

"I think Barney's feelings had been hurt in some of the previous scripts we had written, but this was the first time his sensitivity was discussed," says Everett.

Andy tells Opie there are no rules for "pas and sons." Each parent raises his child the way he thinks is best. Andy explains that he thinks it's best for Opie to get a quarter and work to get it because "when you give something and get something in return like a quarter, that's the greatest feeling in the world." Opie admits that after working he feels "good and tired." Andy continues to explain that as you get bigger you will do more work for more return and that will make the good feeling even bigger. Opie capsules this philosophy by saying, "The bigger you get, the tireder you get—that makes me kinda sad."

"Andy and Opie's conversation appears in the finished film pretty much like we wrote it," says Everett. "However, Opie's 'The bigger you get, the tireder you get—that makes me kinda sad,' was not in our script. Most likely, it was an addition written by Aaron Ruben."

After Opie leaves, Barney emerges from the back room and tells Andy, "This time you really muffed it." Barney has been reading about childrearing in the magazine section of the Sunday paper. According to the magazine, there is a definite trend toward stronger discipline. Andy asks Barney if his father ever hit him. Barney answers, "Well, he couldn't. I was a lot bigger than he was." Andy replies, "I thought as a child you were sickly." Barney responds, "Well, he was sicklier."

Barney then begins to tell Andy "the way I'd talk to a child of mine," but Andy interrupts. He doesn't want to hear any "imaginary child" theories.

"Barney picked up a lot of information and misinformation, about raising children and other subjects, from the magazine section of the Sunday paper, but in his mind, it was an authoritative source," says Everett. "And the bit about Barney's father never physically disciplining him because Barney was bigger, was a deliberate attempt on our part to get a laugh. We felt we needed one on that page of the script.

"Barney's advice to Andy about raising Opie was inspired by Jim Fritzell's annoying habit of telling Bob Sweeney and me how we should raise our daughters. Jim had no children of his own. In fact, he never even got married, but he was always full of parental advice."

Opie shares with Arnold the result of his man-to-man talk with Andy. After listening to Opie, Arnold explains that "talking is a waste of time. You have to take action—temper tantrums, holding your breath, kicking a table leg, rolling around on the floor, pretending you can't stop crying." Opie is not sure about Arnold's advice. To demonstrate the effectiveness of his technique, Arnold starts crying. When Opie rushes to comfort him, Arnold looks up from his fake crying and says, "It works every time."

The boys' two conversations both take place in front of the Taylors' garage. In the first conversation, Opie stands in front of a barrel. During this conversation, Opie sits on the side of the open barrel.

"Jim and I didn't put it in our script that Opie was to sit on a barrel during his second conversation with Arnold," says Everett. "This type of action, though minor and probably unnoticed by the majority of the audience, was the input of Bob Sweeney and was done in an effort to prevent the two conversation scenes from looking exactly alike."

Later in the day, Barney warns Arnold about riding on the sidewalk. Arnold promises not to do it again. He rides across the street and immediately gets back on the sidewalk. Andy then stops Arnold and impounds his bike.

Barney takes the bike away, and Andy proceeds to the courthouse. Before entering, Andy stops and watches a man who is sitting on the sidewalk bench while he whittles a stick. Andy asks, "How's it coming?" After carefully examining the stick, Andy says, "When you're finished with it, tell me what it is, and I'll give you fifty cents for it."

"The whittler and his nondescript handiwork were our ideas," says Everett. "His presence on the courthouse bench seemed like the sort of thing you'd see in a town where people had a lot of spare time."

Acting on Arnold's advice, Opie stops by the courthouse and tells Andy that he doesn't want to work for his allowance any more. Andy says, "Fine, you don't have to—no work, no allowance." At this point, Opie yells, "That's not fair" and throws a temper tantrum. He holds his breath, cries, and lies on the floor kicking uncontrollably. Andy casually reminds Opie not to "get your clothes all dirty."

"Andy's casual reaction to Opie's temper tantrum is the result of his knowing that the tantrum is fake," explains Everett. "Andy suspects that Opie picked it up from Arnold, so he more or less ignores it."

Arnold and his father enter the courthouse. Mr. Winkler demands that Andy return Arnold's bike. Andy informs Mr. Winkler that if he is not going to take responsibility for his son's actions, perhaps he should be locked up. Upon hearing this, Arnold encourages Andy to put his dad in jail. He then pounds Andy's desk and yells, "I want my bike!" Mr. Winkler now understands his son's priorities. He asks Andy for the bike, saying he plans to sell it.

"The scene with Arnold and his father was shot exactly as it was scripted," says Everett. "Jim and I included Arnold's yelling, crying, and desk-pounding in our script directions."

In the epilogue, Opie wonders if Andy "needs someone to clean the garage and do odd jobs." Opie apologizes to Andy for "the way I acted."

Andy acknowledges the effort it took for Opie to apologize and agrees to raise his allowance to twenty-seven cents a week.

The epilogue's master shot is photographed where the wall behind Andy's desk would usually be. The scene begins with the camera positioned behind the wall's corner file cabinet. Andy, who is filing papers, turns as Opie enters. The camera pans left with Andy as he moves to his desk chair. The camera is thus perfectly positioned to photograph the special encounter between an apologetic son and his forgiving father.

The Great Filling Station Robbery

EPISODE #85

FIRST BROADCAST ON FEBRUARY 25, 1963

WRITTEN BY HARVEY BULLOCK

DIRECTED BY BOB SWEENEY

> "I respected the audience's knowledge of mythology and used the Trojan horse idea without any hesitation."
>
> Harvey Bullock

"The Great Filling Station Robbery" begins in the courthouse where Barney is setting up an intercom system. As Andy and Opie enter, Barney is busy wiring a speaker in one of the cells.

Barney tells how he plans to use the intercom to communicate with the prisoners. Andy interrupts Barney to ask him to take the squad car to get a new carburetor put on. Although Barney agrees to do that task, he still continues to talk about the intercom. He explains that the intercom works both ways, so he will be able to hear what the prisoners are saying. Barney calls the intercom his own "little spy in the sky." To demonstrate its effectiveness, Barney enters the cell and imitates a prisoner by saying, "Alright Lefty, you and me's busting out tonight."

Andy can hear Barney plainly, even though the intercom is turned off. Barney then tells Andy to turn the intercom on so he can show him how it will even pick up whispers. Barney gets Opie to sit on the cell cot and whisper, "Alright Lefty. . ." Andy can't hear Opie because he is too far from the speaker. Barney moves Opie closer two times, but the sound "is still no good." Barney finally holds Opie up to the speaker, and the sound is perfect.

"Writing the opening scene with Opie doing his 'Alright Lefty, you and me's busting out of here tonight' line four times was taking a chance we might make that scene overlong," says writer Harvey Bullock. "But knowing how skillfully Opie and Barney interplayed, I took the chance, hoping the repetition would build the joke. This scene was also important because it helped set up the bit with the surveillance camera used later in the episode."

Since Barney is busy with the intercom, Andy decides to get the carburetor put on himself. Before leaving he signs off, "This is Mercury Control, over, a-OK, and out."

"I always regarded the show as set in the thirties, even though it played in the sixties," says Harvey. "Barney's 'spy in the sky' line had been used in military lingo for decades, but it is also identifiable with NASA rocket missions. And Andy's 'mercury control' reference is definitely a catchword of the early space program. I don't think the audience was too concerned about precisely nailing down the show's era. The main thing in their minds was whether the show's characters delivered the stories."

Gomer greets Andy when he arrives at the filling station. He tells Andy that Wally is away for the week, and he is the one who will need to attach the carburetor. Gomer informs Andy that he doesn't do engine work, "just gas and oil, water and air."

"'The Filling Station' script was the first time I had written for Gomer Pyle," says Harvey. "I enjoyed writing for Gomer. The fact that the character was created by Everett Greenbaum and Jim Fritzell didn't disturb me in the least. A writer constantly had to write for characters created by other writers, and we felt great satisfaction that we could write for any character the story called for.

"One reason I enjoyed working with Jim Nabors is that he's really such a nice guy. Jim had previously been a film-cutter at NBC and performed his big opera tunes nightly at The Horn tavern in Santa Monica. Someone saw him and told Andy. Andy saw Jim's show, called his manager, Richard Linke, and Linke grabbed Jim up. Jim was so grateful and polite, we kept asking him if he had turned into a 'scummy' star yet, and he'd just get more bashful.

"He never did become a monster—just the opposite. Jim was and is a delightful guy who somehow survived the showbiz pressure cooker. And, he's very bright. Jim was an overnight sensation, a true star, yet he still called me 'sir' until I threatened to wreak extreme bodily harm upon him."

As the episode continues, the Hanson brothers, who have been parking their car inside the filling station during Wally's absence, stop by while Andy is talking to Gomer. They promise to "see" Gomer later that day.

Before Andy leaves, a local businessman named Mr. Carter brings Jimmy Morgan, a teenager he has hired to make deliveries, to the station. Carter accuses Jimmy of stealing the battery out of his truck. Jimmy claims he just borrowed the battery to connect it to a starter motor he built. Because the battery was greasy, Jimmy dropped it and broke it.

"My only script description of the Jimmy Morgan character was almost no description at all," says Harvey. "Here it is: 'Teenager Jimmy Morgan.' The role didn't call for any special wardrobe or physical characteristics, so that was all the description needed."

While Andy and Carter are talking, Jimmy inspects the carburetor Andy wants installed. Jimmy tells Gomer that the carburetor will really boost the power. He tells Andy to "put on dual points, advance the timing, switch the manifold—that would really hop her up."

Jimmy's obvious knowledge of cars gives Andy an idea. He asks Jimmy to install the carburetor. Then, Jimmy can buy Mr. Carter a new battery with the money he will earn. Gomer agrees to let Jimmy work at the station while Wally is away.

"I know nothing about cars, so I asked the local garageman a few valid terms to help me with Jimmy's mechanical dialogue," says Harvey. "He found out I was with TAGS, so I was stuck there while he expounded enthusiastically about the TAGS episodes he had seen and the great ideas he had for others.

"I take it as a compliment that TAGS was so deceptively simple and its characters so real and engaging that many fans felt confident that they could come up with a good episode or two themselves.

"It was not at all uncommon to encounter fans who were eager to make suggestions. It even happened to me once in the barbershop. Sal, the barber, knew I wrote for the show and greeted me with 'I'm glad you came in today. I got a great idea for an Andy Griffin [sic] episode. It just came to me out of nowhere, and boy, is it a beauty.' Then Sal turned to the other barber, 'Charley, is it a great story, or isn't it?' Charley says, 'Yeah.' Then Sal continues, 'What a real winner—a knockout! Boy, oh, boy, you will love it. Got everything? You ready, you want to hear it?'

"How could I say no? I nodded. Sal takes a stance, 'You ready? Now get this: THE KID WON'T EAT HIS SUPPER.' That was it in its entirety! Naturally, I told him it had promise, and I'd see what I could do with it. He asked again if I got the idea and repeated it all the way through the haircut."

The next morning, Barney telephones Juanita, a waitress at the Bluebird Diner. Barney calls during the breakfast shift and greets Juanita, "Good morning, cocka-doodle-doo." Andy walks in and overhears the conversation.

"I had Barney sweet-talk Juanita twice in this episode," says Harvey. "Barney, of course, considers himself a knowing Romeo. His 'cocka-doodle-doo' line was a little flourish to remind Juanita how cute and clever a rascal he was.

"I enjoyed writing for Barney immensely. It was intriguing to start writing a Barney scene and to become aware of how many different words and actions could be given him, and Don Knotts would knock your socks off with any of them. It was also fun to come up with a word or moral for Barney to explain."

After Barney hangs up, Gomer rushes into the courthouse to report that the box with all of Wally's brand-new tools is missing. He tells Andy that Jimmy worked late and was the one who locked up.

When Andy and Barney go to the station to investigate, they find that none of the locks have been tampered with. While they are looking around, one of the Hanson brothers stops by to pick up their car.

Because Andy believes that the robber is taking advantage of the fact that Wally is out of town, he is sure the culprit will be back, so he plans an all-night stake-out.

Barney feels there is something additional they can do, so he sets up a surveillance camera in the filling station. He rigs the front door so that anyone who opens it will trigger the camera and get his picture "took." To test the camera, Barney opens the door and waves to the camera. Gomer is amazed by Barney's idea and remarks, "Shazzam, Captain Marvel wouldn't think of that, Barney."

"Gomer's 'Shazzam' appears in this script, but I don't think I originated its use," says Harvey. "I was pleased to see how perfectly it fit the character in the 'surveillance camera' scene. Whoever did introduce the phrase helped all the writers who followed afterwards."

That night, Barney and Gomer stake out the station. Inside the station, one of the Hanson brothers quietly emerges from the trunk of their car. As Barney and Gomer stand in front of the station, a hand can be seen through the window in the background lifting merchandise off the counter.

The next morning, Gomer discovers the missing merchandise. Andy realizes that whoever stole the merchandise "didn't bust in, they got in quiet-like with a key." All the evidence points toward Jimmy, so Andy goes to pick him up.

After Andy leaves, Barney learns from Gomer that Jimmy's key fits the front door. Barney remembers the surveillance camera and says excitedly, "Gomer, we got ourselves a picture!" Barney removes the film from the camera, and Gomer takes it to the drugstore to be developed.

A short time later, Andy brings Jimmy in for questioning. Jimmy says he knows nothing about the missing merchandise. Barney tells Jimmy that he'd better "come clean" because he was under "high-speed surveillance." Gomer arrives soon afterwards with the developed photo. Barney pulls the picture out of its envelope only to discover himself waving hello to the camera!

Jimmy escapes while Andy, Barney, and Gomer look at the picture. Andy goes after him, leaving Barney and Gomer behind. Gomer admires Barney's picture and suggests he have "a whole bunch of wallet-sizes printed up."

"The inspiration for the wallet-sized prints line goes back to when my high-school class picture was being taken and some wise guy called out he'd like a few wallet-sized prints," say Harvey. "The expression tickled us all and stayed in my memory."

Andy is unable to find Jimmy. That night, he and Barney receive a call from Gomer saying that someone is moving around inside the filling station.

Andy and Barney arrive at the station and find Jimmy hot-wiring the cash register. Jimmy has attached one end of a wire to the register and the other to a group of batteries that will send a charge through anyone who touches the register. Andy approaches Jimmy to make an arrest. At that moment, a painful scream comes from inside the station. Andy and Barney rush in to find Prothro Hanson attempting to rob the cash register. He is being shocked by Jimmy's trap. Andy realizes Prothro has been hiding in the trunk and refers to the situation as "a regular Trojan horse."

The crime's solution comes almost too quickly to be credible.

"If you reexamine the story, you will find the solution to the crime didn't really come so easily and quickly as to be incredible," says Harvey. "Prothro Hanson (named after the football coach Tommy Prothro, by the way) is shown coming out of the car trunk way before the second act's conclusion. The audience now knows the perpetrator, but Andy and Barney's gradual solution of the crime continues right to the end of the second act. This keeps the audience's attention, since they are now in the know and able to see both the miscues and the developing solution. The possible guilt of Jimmy is thus a working sub-plot."

In the epilogue, Barney telephones Juanita. Barney tells her that he has finished the poem he has been working on. He asks if she wants to hear it. Barney then reads the poem. As Barney is reading, Andy quietly walks up behind him and begins to read the poem along with Barney. Upon hearing Andy's voice, Barney slams the receiver down and musses up his hair in frustration.

"The love poem was further evidence to Barney of his high-powered 'animal magnetism'," says Harvey. "He was positive Juanita would be swept off her feet by all the special attention (and more than likely she was.)"

The Darlings Are Coming

EPISODE #88

FIRST BROADCAST ON MARCH 18, 1963

WRITTEN BY JIM FRITZELL
AND EVERETT GREENBAUM

DIRECTED BY BOB SWEENEY

DENVER PYLE, MAGGIE PETERSON, AND
THE DILLARDS (DOUG DILLARD,
RODNEY DILLARD, MITCH JAYNE, AND
DEAN WEBB) GUEST STAR AS
THE DARLINGS

"Back in our hometown of Salem, Missouri, all the activities stopped on the night 'The Darlings Are Coming' was shown, and the local National Guard meeting was called off so everyone could watch."
Mitch Jayne

"Andy knew about the Dillards and wanted to use them. We didn't know if they could act and thought it would be funny if they were silent. As it turned out, they were wonderful!"
Everett Greenbaum

"To the best of my knowledge, the Darling family was one of the many brainchildren of Jim Fritzell and Everett Greenbaum and was a concept before they furnished it with characters," says Mitch Jayne. "The Dillard audition for Andy occurred when Andy's manager, Dick Linke, knowing that TAGS producer Aaron Ruben and Andy liked the Darling concept, read about Elektra records signing a bluegrass group from Missouri. Dick then called Elektra, who referred him to our manager Norman Malkin.

"Norman took us over to the Desilu lot, and we carried our instruments onto the first sound stage any of us had ever seen. We were introduced to Andy, Aaron Ruben, Dick Linke, and Bob Sweeney. Andy asked us to do a couple of songs—just whatever suited us. We played several things, and I was comfortable enough to talk about where we were from, just like I did in our stage act. Andy walked off a way to listen and look, exchanging comments with Bob Sweeney and Aaron Ruben.

"Andy always liked to weave music into the show and had previously used the Golden State Boys (a California-based bluegrass group) in two shows. For one reason or another, he and Bob Sweeney had definite types in mind for the Darling boys. It wasn't just musical ability. They wanted to go in a different direction.

"On that first meeting, Andy used us to perpetrate what would be our first of a long line of running jokes on Bob Sweeney who, like Barney in the 'choir' episode, 'couldn't sing a lick.' Bob asked us if we knew 'Big Rock Candy Mountain' and said it was his favorite song. Andy said, 'Of course these boys know that Bob, and they'll probably do it if you'll sing.' I, for one, didn't know the song and was petrified. (I had been playing bass for only four months and only knew our material.) Andy borrowed Rodney's guitar, hit a cord, and insisted that Bob sing the first verse, and then we realized the joke. It was the first and most comforting thing we could have found out about Andy—that his good nature and sense of humor was never far from his professional side."

Jim and Everett developed the "Darling" concept into a well-written comedy script. Their script begins with the Darlings driving into Mayberry. Briscoe Darling stops their truck in front of "The David Mendlebright Memorial" water trough because the truck's radiator is boiling over.

The script instructions introduced the Darlings as follows:

A vintage flatbed truck is coming down the street. The radiator is boiling, and the motor is missing a little. On the

Andy and the Darlings greet Dud Wash
when he returns from the army.

TAGSRWC Archives

flatbed are the Darlings: long, gangly, mountain-type boys. Driving the truck is the father of the clan, Briscoe Darling. Seated alongside Briscoe is the daughter, Charlene Darling. The truck stops at a watering trough alongside the curb.

"A canister of dry ice and water hidden under the hood caused the Darling truck radiator to boil," recalls Mitch. "The truck's standard Model A transmission, used in the episode, was later replaced by an automatic. That wild ride into town, with its stops and starts, damn near flung us out the back of the truck and came close to wrecking our instruments."

Briscoe uses his hat to fill the radiator with water from the trough. Charlene gets out of the truck and joins Briscoe. As Andy walks up, Charlene looks at Andy with approval and calls him "a pretty man."

Briscoe orders Charlene to get back in the truck and tells Andy that "she's promised—Private First-Class Dudley A. Wash, U.S.A. Army, honorably discharged."

The Darlings are in town to meet Dud, a boy from the mountains who is coming in on the next day's bus. It seems that Dud and Charlene have been betrothed since Charlene was five. Briscoe warns Andy not to "go making any fancies for her."

Andy informs Briscoe that he is breaking two city ordinances: parking in front of the trough, which is for horses only, and dipping his hat into the water. Andy gives Briscoe a warning instead of arresting him. Before driving away, Briscoe asks where he and his family "might bed down." Andy suggests the Mayberry Hotel.

Briscoe enters the hotel lobby alone and requests "a room as far back as I can get." The rest of the family sneaks into the room soon after he settles in.

The Darlings decide to play some music while "that clerking fellow" is gone to supper. When John Masters, the hotel clerk, returns, he hears the Darlings "raising the roof in there." He summons Andy. Andy tells John he knows who they are and remarks that he had "warned them earlier today on a 907—Dipping your hat in a horse trough."

"I believe Don Knotts's contract allowed him a week off now and then," says writer Everett Greenbaum. "The city-ordinance number was more characteristic of Barney than Andy, but we needed a joke there. Due to Don's absence, we gave it to Andy."

When Andy knocks on Briscoe's door, the music stops. When Briscoe opens the door, he is the only person in the room. Andy spots a rope tied to the room's radiator and leaves.

Andy then steps outside the hotel and stands beneath the window of Briscoe's room. The music resumes, so Masters knocks on the door again. The four Darling boys and Charlene shimmy down the rope into Andy's arms.

Later that evening, as Andy and Aunt Bee relax on the front porch, Aunt Bee asks Andy if he liked the white beans he had for supper. Andy grunts his approval. Aunt Bee comments that he didn't say anything about them at dinner. Andy responds, "Well, I ate four bowls. If that ain't a tribute to white beans I don't know what is."

As Andy and Aunt Bee sit on the porch, the Darlings can be heard playing their instruments in the distance. Andy goes to see what "they're up to."

The front-porch scene is photographed in one long, sustained sequence (one minute fifteen seconds in length). The sustained shot, which eliminates the editing together of numerous camera angles, gives the scene a relaxing visual presentation and assists in the on-screen creation of a tranquil Mayberry night.

The scene also shows an excellent way to present humor by using everyday conversation. Andy and Aunt Bee's discussion of "white beans" is comically realistic. The humor results from what they say to each other, rather than from a joke followed by a punch line.

When Andy finds the Darlings inside an abandoned store, he informs them they are in violation of "317—Occupancy of private property without permission of the owner." Andy offers to put the Darlings up for the night in the courthouse cells.

After a supper of Aunt Bee's white beans, the Darlings and Andy play two songs, "Tearin' Up Your Old Clothes for Rags" and "Salty Dog."

"'Salty Dog' is a real song," says Everett. "The rest of the stuff, the mountain dialogue and the song titles, we made up. Briscoe's 'More power to you' was a saying of my father-in-law, Tom Ward, who was from Arkansas. Jim suggested the first song title, 'Tearin' Up Your Old Clothes for Rags,' and that got us into the style or rhythm for them."

"Everett and Jim loved those ridiculous gag-song names, and, of course, we did too," says Mitch. "Briscoe delivered the outrageous titles straight-faced, and the excuse for us to play something from our own material was that the gag song made Charlene cry.

"We were always allowed to play our own stuff as long as it fit. I remember Andy was delighted that we had written most of our own material, and he talked to us about that. He wanted original material and a new look at this very old music. Incidentally, knowing that we would make royalty money on our own songs, Andy encouraged us to come up with our own music. That piece of thoughtfulness has paid wonderful dividends over the years, and all of us are grateful. Whereas the actor's screen residuals ran out, in most cases long ago, the Dillards are paid as musicians each time a Darling show is rerun.

"All the musical numbers done on the show were pre-recorded at Glen-Glenn Sound studios and synched to the live performance. All of the music on the series was done that way. Andy wanted the music to be studio quality, which made all of us appreciate the respect he had for our work."

Prominently featured in all of the episode's musical performances is the sound of Briscoe's jugging. The jug sound, however, somewhat dominated the presentation of the music.

"After the first show, Rodney objected to the jug," remembers Mitch. "He was nice about it but very alarmed at the way the overdone sound took away from the music. Andy agreed that, though the jug was a necessary prop for Denver, thereafter it would be only that. The jug notes had been done on a separate track by a studio jug player, if you can believe such a thing. In the following shows, the jug sound was left up to the viewer's imagination."

The next day, the Darlings walk to the bus stop to meet Dud. Five minutes before the bus's arrival, Briscoe realizes that Charlene is missing. The boys are sent to find her.

Charlene is inside the courthouse chasing Andy. She wants to "snuggle up a little." Briscoe enters and accuses Andy of "egging" Charlene on. He tells Andy that he and Dud will have to "fight it out" to see who gets Charlene.

The Darlings and Andy walk to the bus. After Dud steps off, he gives Charlene a gift—"a tiger-eye ring right out of Spokane, Washington." Dud reveals that he carries Charlene's letters, her hair ribbon, and "the remainders of that mountain gladioli you gave me the day I departed to fulfill my country's needs" around his waist in a money belt. This impresses Charlene. She hugs Dud, and the two kiss.

Briscoe consoles Andy, now that he's lost Charlene. Andy responds by saying, "Well, some got it, and some ain't."

In the epilogue, Andy performs Dud and Charlene's wedding ceremony. Instead of the usual $2.00 fee, Andy is paid with a song.

"'The Darlings Are Coming' was an important show for more reasons than we knew at the time," admits Mitch. "It was the Dillards' first appearance on television and gave us national recognition as bluegrass musicians. The immense impact that first show had on bluegrass music itself is hard to guess, coming at a time when only Flatt and Scruggs had ever managed to get prime-time exposure on a top-rated television show. Even with our following appearances, nothing jarred the bluegrass world as much as that first Andy Griffith show, because so much of it was devoted to our music, and the Darling family was such an outrageous concept.

"Of all the shows we did, 'The Darlings Are Coming' is easiest to capture in memory because we met three people who were to change our lives considerably: Andy, Denver, and Maggie. It was also our first exposure to television on what we would later learn was known as a 'happy set,' a set where the star's disposition determined the attitudes of the cast and crew. In later years, after dozens of television shows, we were to understand how fortunate we were to have been initiated into that grueling business by the kindest and most understanding of professionals—Andy Griffith."

Andy's English Valet

EPISODE #89

FIRST BROADCAST ON MARCH 25, 1963

WRITTEN BY HARVEY BULLOCK

DIRECTED BY BOB SWEENEY

BERNARD FOX GUEST STARS
AS MALCOLM MERRIWEATHER

"Bernard Fox brought Malcolm Merriweather to life in his own gifted fashion. I can't imagine another performer in the role."

Harvey Bullock

"In 1957 Ray Saffian Allen was asked to come to London to write a new series, *Dick and the Duchess*, for CBS," says Harvey Bullock. "Ray asked if I would like to be his partner, and I leapt with joy. We went to London and wrote twenty-six episodes. Working with talented British actors was a delight. Thus, we met Bernard Fox.

"After *Dick* was completed, I returned to America, but Ray stayed on to try his hand at producing sitcoms. He worked with Bernie, and I believe he was instrumental in convincing the talented Mr. Fox to come to the states. More pressure came from a pretty American girl, Jackie, whom Bernie later married."

"A fellow by the name of Ray Saffian Allen produced a TV series in

England titled, *Three Live Wires*," says Bernard Fox. "I was one of the stars playing a Malcolm-type of character. When Ray returned to America, he told me that if I came to Hollywood he would write me into something. That turned out to be one episode of *The Danny Thomas Show*."

"Back in California, Ray and I were writing Danny Thomas shows," says Harvey. "We convinced Danny to use Bernie and then wrote an episode for him, 'Danny's English Friend,' in August 1962. Bernie was great playing the part of a totally fouled-up waiter in Danny's night club.

"Bernie did a follow-up episode as the same character in Danny's 'Girl Shy' episode the next year. I recall Danny admiring Bernie's gifts. He once said, 'That man is sprinkled with star dust'."

"I evidently caused something of a sensation because I was asked to do a pilot for a series," says Bernard. "Sadly, to save expense, Danny Thomas and Sheldon Leonard decided to do a spin-off instead. Danny appeared at the beginning and again at the end, which left me about fifteen minutes to develop a character and very little time for a story line.

"At the script reading, I ventured to suggest that it wasn't going to work. Naturally, I was overruled, but it was an abysmal flop and nothing came of the series. Happily for me, *The Andy Griffith Show* was shooting on the same lot, and they were anxious to utilize my talent."

"Andy's English Valet" begins with Aunt Bee making final preparations for a trip. She is worried that Andy and Opie will not be able to care for themselves in her absence and is hesitant to leave. As the two walk down the driveway, Aunt Bee reminds Andy that Mrs. Edwards is leaving her car, and Andy is free to use it. Aunt Bee returns to the house to get a scarf.

As Andy waits, a man on a bicycle rides up and asks Andy if he is the constable. The man, Malcolm Merriweather, is an Englishman from Heckmandyke [script spelling] who is touring America. Malcolm asks for directions to Route 43.

"I thought an elegantly mannered but affable character would make an interesting contrast with the honest and uncontrived Mayberry folk," says Harvey. "Producer Aaron Ruben agreed, so I wrote the story—the 'fish out of water' genre, an English valet bicycling across America."

"In the script reading, when I was asked where Malcolm might have come from I remembered the name of a village in Derbyshire called Heckmonwyke, which was always turning up in the Boy Scout magazines as having a particularly inept troop of scouts," says Bernard.

"I think I devised the name Malcolm Merriweather, but I know Bernie added immensely to the episode," says Harvey. "I remembered such colorful terms as 'Bubble and Squeak' (which I think was corned beef and cabbage) and a few others from my London writing venture. But Bernie came up with almost all the 'Englishisms.' "

While pedaling through Mayberry's business area, Malcolm reads his road map and recklessly rides his bicycle into the path of a truck, causing the driver to run into a pile of packing crates.

Barney sees the accident happen. He untangles Malcolm from the scattered crates and takes him to the courthouse. Andy estimates that Malcolm will have to pay "upwards toward forty dollars" to repair the damage to the wrecked truck.

Malcolm doesn't have the money, so Barney wants to lock him up. Andy, however, sympathizes with Malcolm and suggests he might be able to help around the house to work off the debt. A grateful Malcolm responds, "Aren't you kind?"

Malcolm begins working off the debt by repairing an upstairs window at Andy's house. When Malcolm adjusts the height on the ladder, he catches his head between the rungs.

The script gave the following directions for the scene in which Malcolm gets entangled with the ladder: "Malcolm lies where he fell in the shrubbery, his foot through the bottom of the bushel basket, the ladder almost on top of him. He struggles to his feet and walks with his foot still through the basket."

The filmed version is simplified, but still comically effective.

"Quite a lot of the comedy stuff was suggested by me," says Bernard. "The ladder business was my idea."

"Bernie added all the grace notes that made this episode work," says Harvey. "He has infallible comic instinct honed by his work on music-hall stages. He has the rare ability to do farce, which I think is the most difficult style of comedy."

After Malcolm adjusts the ladder, Opie walks up and introduces himself. As Malcolm continues the repair, he accidentally breaks the window pane when he raises the ladder.

Just then, Andy drives up. He looks at the broken window but doesn't complain. Andy simply says he's going inside to fix lunch. At this point, Malcolm offers to prepare the meal because it is a bit more "in my line." It turns out that Malcolm worked in England as a gentleman's gentleman.

That evening when Andy comes home, he is greeted by Opie, who is "dressed for dinner" in a suit and bow tie. The table is elegantly set.

The next morning, Malcolm, acting in the capacity of a gentleman's gentleman, offers to help Andy put on his pants. Andy refuses.

Malcolm then prepares breakfast. He even draws a face on Opie's boiled egg. Malcolm delivers Andy's morning paper to the table, reports the weather conditions, and brushes Andy's cap.

Another of Bernard's ideas was to have Malcolm draw a face on Opie's egg. The idea resulted in an interesting response from TAGS sponsor, General Foods, the manufacturer of Sanka Coffee and Post cereals.

"I had been reading how American sponsors interfered with shows—you couldn't have a person commit suicide in a gas oven if the sponsor was a gas company," says Bernard. "So I mentioned to the prop man, Reggie Smith, that I was surprised that nobody had complained about having a boiled egg in the show. He said, 'Are you kidding?' He then pulled open his desk drawer that held a stack of letters detailing what had to be in evidence on the table around the egg—all General Food products."

Malcolm's attention makes Andy uncomfortable. When Malcolm steps into the kitchen, Andy quietly sneaks out the front door. He carefully crosses the front porch, turns, and walks into Malcolm, who is waiting for him beside Mrs. Edwards's car.

Flawless editing of a variety of camera angles presents Andy's attempted escape in an effective manner. The fifty-second scene begins with a shot of Andy getting up from the table and walking to the door. A second shot shows Andy crossing the front porch. The action continues with a third shot of Andy and Malcolm standing beside the open car door. The fourth camera angle is a closeup of Andy and Malcolm. The scene concludes with a shot of Andy sitting in the back seat, a shawl pulled over his legs. This scene is filmed with the camera positioned inside the car.

"I didn't really notice how camera angles and musical backgrounds were effective," admits Harvey. "While watching an episode, I was tuned to the words and storytelling. The fact I don't remember all those goodies is the supreme test—they were so good they weren't evident."

Andy tells Barney that Malcolm makes him uncomfortable. Barney suggests that Andy just tell Malcolm how he feels. When Andy comes home, he overhears Malcolm telling Opie how much he enjoys taking care of Andy and Opie. After hearing this, Andy decides he will wait for the right moment to talk to Malcolm.

During the course of the evening, Malcolm overhears Barney telling Andy that "the guy is just making a grade A pest of himself." Malcolm overhears this front-porch conversation through an open window. With this realization, Malcolm leaves a note saying he had to "leave on urgent business."

When Andy finds a glass of milk that Malcolm was taking up to Opie by the open window, he realizes that Malcolm left because he overheard Barney's comments. Andy then goes looking for Malcolm.

"The idea for the telltale milk in the window was worked out by hopscotching back and forth in scripting—planting and then reaping," says Harvey. "The word is 'construction,' not much in vogue today, but to me one of the fun things in writing. I truly enjoyed flipping about, stitching in small unifying bits of dialogue or business."

When he finds Malcolm pedaling out of town, Andy says he doesn't care what Malcolm overheard, but he'd better get back to work. Malcolm replies, "Right away, sir" and pedals back into town.

The theme that musical director Earle Hagen composed for Malcolm is excellent and adds to the overall presentation of the character. The theme is used to highlight the emotions that the character experiences—a slower tempo to express sadness when Malcolm overhears the front-porch conversation, a faster tempo to communicate the joy he feels as he pedals back to Mayberry.

Harvey initially saw the finished version of his script when the episode was broadcast by the network. "There were no special screenings for the writers. Time and economics did not permit them," says Harvey. "We pitched stories, then wrote and polished them, after which the script became the producer and director's sole property—and we were off rushing about to seek other assignments. However, when TAGS came on the air I was right there at home in front of the set with my four kids. We loved it!"

Bernard Fox had a very different experience. "I had just finished watching myself on *The Andy Griffith Show*," says Bernard. "At that time I was very, very new to Hollywood. There was little money in the bank and no signs of immediate work. So, I was sitting there thinking that the future looked fairly bleak when the phone rang. It was Andy, full of praise for my work. He mentioned that it was one of the best shows they had done, and that they were definitely going to do more—my spirits soared."

Barney's First Car

EPISODE #90

FIRST BROADCAST ON APRIL 1, 1963

WRITTEN BY JIM FRITZELL
AND EVERETT GREENBAUM

DIRECTED BY BOB SWEENEY

ELLEN CORBY GUEST STARS AS
MRS. MYRT "HUBCAPS" LESH

*"I was not surprised at all when 'Barney's First Car'
won the Writers Guild of America award. This script
was Jim and Ev at their funny best."*
Aaron Ruben

"**B**arney's First Car' was a good show," says Everett Greenbaum. "The story line grew out of the fact that cars are so important in our lives. I had forgotten that we won the Writers Guild award for this script even though the brass award plaque, with the script's title engraved on it, is hanging in my office."

Jim and Everett's award-winning script begins with Barney happily entering the courthouse. Barney has withdrawn three hundred dollars from his bank account to buy a car. He announces that he will soon be "Mr. Independent Wheels."

Barney reads some of the ads in the newspaper. One describes a "fixer-upper—a 1949 Hudson Terraplane. Was fallen on last Saturday by a thirty-ton semi-trailer. Lots of miles left in the rubber. Cash or swap for twelve good laying hens." He finally finds an ad that "looks right up my street," which describes "a beautifully maintained low-mileage 1954 Ford sedan."

"The wording in the car ads was just basic comedy writing," says Everett. "The reason we selected a 1954 Ford sedan for Barney to purchase was that we wanted the car to be commonplace, and that model fit that description perfectly."

Barney arranges to have the owner drive the car to Mayberry so he can "give her a once-over." While waiting impatiently for the car's arrival, Barney tells Andy about another major purchase he once made—an all-steel, reinforced septic tank given to his parents on their anniversary.

"Many of the gifts Jim and I included in our scripts were very basic—like giving an aunt electrolysis treatments to remove excess facial hair," says Everett.

"The acting in the 'septic tank present' scene had to be very sincere in order for the scene to work. Don and Andy did a great job and felt the scene was so successful that they performed it at parties for years.

Two blasts from the car's horn, followed by swelling harps and trumpets, dramatically announce the arrival of Barney's car.

The car's owner is Mrs. Lesh. A harpsichord soundtrack reinforces Mrs. Lesh's "little old lady" demeanor.

Mrs. Lesh says she never drives "the machine" over twenty-five miles an hour. She also says that her late husband Bernard "loved and cherished the machine," so she wants to be sure it finds a good home.

"My ancestors, including my father, called the family car 'the machine'," says Everett. "I remembered this and gave the line to Mrs. Lesh."

Although Barney is eager to purchase the car, Andy advises him to take it on a test drive. He also advises Barney to take it to the filling station and have Wally look it over, but Barney refuses because he doesn't want to insult Mrs. Lesh.

Barney makes "the deal right here and now." Mrs. Lesh sadly hands over the keys. She then lovingly caresses the machine's door handle,

Mrs. Lesh sells her late husband's
"machine" to Barney.

TAGSRWC Archives

takes a few steps, and hesitates. Barney advises, "Don't look back."

"The line 'Don't look back' was a phrase used in a lot of corny 1930s movies," says Everett. "It seemed like something that sentimental Barney would say to the departing Mrs. Lesh."

As the episode continues, Mrs. Lesh is picked up a few blocks away by her "nephew." After getting into the car, the man inquires, "How did you do, Myrt?" Mrs. Lesh replies, "Unloaded another one, Jake. Three hundred easy clams from the sucker of the world."

Barney then takes Andy, Aunt Bee, Opie, Thelma Lou and Gomer on his new car's maiden voyage. He assigns each person a seat, so the weight will be distributed evenly. Gomer is assigned the middle position in the back seat. After learning that Gomer might get car sick, Barney reassigns him to a seat near a window.

As Barney drives through the countryside, everyone is enjoying the ride—even Gomer, who announces, "I'm sick as a dog but having the time of my life."

"One of the lines of dialogue I always liked was Gomer's line, 'Sick as a dog but having the time of my life'," says Everett. "Jim and I decided to further develop the character, so we emphasized Gomer's pleasant personality to offset his lack of intelligence. Only the sweetest person on earth would say the 'sick as a dog' line."

Barney's face beams with satisfaction as he drives along. His satisfaction, however, is soon shattered when something that looks like a snake starts lifting the steering column. Gomer sums up the situation when he says, "It looks to me like you got too much grease in your steering column."

"The inspiration for the grease coming out of the steering wheel came from something that happened to a very good friend of mine who worked in a gas station while attending medical school," says Everett. "He once had trouble getting the grease to go into the fitting in the steering of a Packard convertible. The boss told him to force it, so he did. When the owner, who was wearing a white suit, drove away, the car hit a bump, and a snake of grease arose, taking the horn button with it. The grease held together for a second and then flopped down on the white suit."

"The scene inside the car was very special because it showed Barney's hilarious reaction to the rising steering column, his mood change, and his bewilderment over the situation," says producer Aaron Ruben. "The car was stationary and photographed inside the studio. The passing scenery, which is seen through the windows, was done with rear-projection shots."

When Barney stops the car, the motor begins "boiling but good," and Andy, Gomer, Opie, and Aunt Bee wind up pushing the vehicle as Thelma Lou steers. Barney is so heartbroken he can neither push nor steer.

The next day, Wally checks the car and finds sawdust in the car's deferential and transmission.

"Sawdust in the transmission used to be a trick of used-car dealers," says Everett. "It made the gears run smoothly for a couple hundred miles and seemed like the kind of scheme Mrs. Lesh would pull on an unsuspecting buyer."

Andy tells Barney that the sawdust "is all the evidence we'll need. Let's take that car right back to the little old lady in Mt. Pilot."

The car breaks down on the way to Mt. Pilot. Andy leaves Barney with the car and walks to a telephone to call Gomer to come give them a tow.

When Andy returns to the car, he and Barney crawl in the back seat to take a nap. The two are awakened sometime later by the car's movement. Andy notices that the tow truck that is pulling them does not belong to Wally. He tells Barney to stay hidden so they can see where the tow truck is taking the car.

"We decided to put Andy and Barney in the car's back seat because there was more room for napping that way, and, of course, it makes them invisible to the tow-truck driver, which helped our story," says Everett.

The car is towed into a garage. After the tow truck stops, Andy and

Barney quietly get out of the car. Barney puts his bullet in his gun. Mrs. Lesh, who is inside the garage, inspects the car and recognizes it "as that clunker I sold that boob in Mayberry."

At that point, Andy and Barney emerge from their hiding place and arrest Mrs. Lesh and her gang. Mrs. Lesh tries to bribe her way out of the arrest by offering them a deal on a "sweet 1958 custom sedan."

Although Barney is interested, Andy doesn't let him make the same mistake twice.

The Rivals

EPISODE #91

FIRST BROADCAST ON APRIL 8, 1963

WRITTEN BY HARVEY BULLOCK

DIRECTED BY BOB SWEENEY

> *"Opie's question, 'Just what can you do with a grown woman?' is one of the best lines—and that's covering a lot of ground."*
>
> Harvey Bullock

"The Rivals" begins with Opie seated on the steps of the Mayberry Hotel. He looks down the sidewalk and sees someone coming. He licks his palms and slicks down his hair just before Karen Burgess, one of his classmates, walks by. Opie begins walking beside her. As they near the courthouse, Opie asks her if she would like to see the inside of a real jail. Karen is interested.

"This script deals with Opie at that wondrous age before sophistication," says writer Harvey Bullock. "Most of us experienced the same sweetness and utter confusion of first love and asked the same disarming questions that Opie asks.

"I opened the episode with Opie seated on the hotel steps, waiting for Karen to pass by. In my script Opie does all that's indicated except for licking his hand and slicking down his hair. This adolescent behavior sounds like a touch the director, Bob Sweeney, added.

"The name of Opie's girlfriend, Karen Burgess, was taken from a girl named 'Karen Birch,' who was best friends with one of my daughters."

Opie introduces Karen to Andy and then shows her "the layout"— the file cabinet, the gun rack, the cells, and "the door I go through when I empty out the trash baskets."

After the tour, Opie offers to carry Karen's books, but Karen turns down the offer.

That night, Opie talks to Andy about "liking someone a whole lot." Opie asks Andy how he can get Karen to like him. Andy suggests that Opie treat her "as nice as you can."

The next day, Barney and Thelma Lou see Opie sitting on the hotel steps. He looks depressed. When Barney sees Andy, he asks Andy, "What's wrong with Opie? He's moping around out there like he doesn't have a friend in the world." Andy explains that Opie has a crush on Karen.

Opie's crush reminds Barney of an experience he had when he "wasn't no bigger than Opie." He met a girl named Vickie Harmes at the ice cream parlor. He describes his reaction, "I stepped outside one day with my raspberry snow cone, and there she was." Barney knew it was love because "icy chills just ran all over me." Vickie was stuckup because "her daddy was in civil service." She also used to do one thing that really irritated Barney. When Barney offered her a bite of his snow cone, Vickie would bite off the end, sip out all the syrup, and leave him with "nothing but the ice." Knowing what he knows now, he would do things differently. If he had a date with Vickie Harmes today, he would ring her doorbell, bite off the end of his snow cone, sip out the syrup, and hand her the ice.

"Vickie Harmes, the name of Barney's former heartthrob, was taken from my niece of that exact name," says Harvey. "Barney's snow-cone problem was inspired by the strict procedures we boys all used to keep an ice cream cone from melting too quickly. Different theories were ardently advocated—lick around the edge, bite with your teeth, or wrap a paper napkin around the cone for insulation. The latter theory was seldom used by boys because the paper napkin smacked of sissyhood. Also ice cream was never ever ordered in a cup, always in a cone. Cups and spoons were for elders who dripped a lot.

"Girls who wanted boys to like them would always order cones. Girls who asked for cups were definitely snooty because boys saw no point in having a non-edible, such as a cardboard cup, between them and the ice cream. A similar protocol existed with snow cones, just as Barney elaborates. Draining the syrup immediately was world-class ignorant behavior."

That afternoon, Opie waits in front of the grocery for Karen to walk by. When she arrives, Opie does a handstand to impress her, but she is unimpressed.

Thelma Lou comes out of the grocery after Karen leaves. She needs someone to carry her packages, so Andy volunteers Opie. Thelma Lou plans to make some fudge brownies when she gets home. She needs a "test pilot" to sample the brownies along with her homemade peach ice cream.

"Fudge brownies were the mainstay goodie at our home, which was the social center for all the kids in the neighborhood," says Harvey. "My daughter Diana had devised a super-satanic recipe for fudge brownies by adding chocolate pudding to the already extra-chocolate mix.

"Earlier in my career, I had written for a daily variety show in New York. In one of our skits we talked about peaches from South Carolina. The South Carolina Peach Growers Association caught it, enjoyed the publicity, and sent me a bushel of their finest. We invited all the neighbors over, got thick whipping cream, processed those glorious peaches, hand cranked the freezer, and produced the most magnificent ice cream devised since the earth began to cool. That was almost fifty years ago— and I remain ruined for any other.

"Fudge brownies and homemade peach ice cream were minor details that seemed right for Mayberry. Sometimes a minor detail wasn't quite satisfying, and I would spend hours tweaking and changing. I actually enjoyed the rewrite process. You have the whole story finished, then if time permits before the script-due deadline, you can go back and make improvements. The trap, of course, is you start deleting a word or two, and soon you are rewriting the whole scene.

"My writing partner on some of the TAGS scripts, the late Ray Allen, was amused, but realistic, about my tendency to rewrite. He would occasionally come to my desk when I was agonizing over a change, pull the paper out of the typewriter, and call out, 'Good enough—next!' Mostly he was right, I was micro-polishing."

Opie agrees to accompany Thelma Lou. Barney walks up while Opie is retrieving Thelma Lou's packages. He invites Thelma Lou to go get a cup of coffee, but Thelma Lou explains she has "made some plans with Opie."

As Thelma Lou and Opie walk away, Karen Burgess is standing around the corner of the courthouse. She silently watches as the two pass by.

When Barney enters the courthouse later that afternoon, Andy is painting a partition. Barney decides to telephone Thelma Lou and "invite her to go for a little ride tonight. There's going to be a moon. Maybe we'll just go up to the duck pond and park."

"Andy did no painting in my script," says Harvey. "I imagine the painting was added just to have something different happening in the scene and to place Andy in the background while Barney calls Thelma Lou."

Thelma Lou's telephone rings. She asks Opie to answer it. When Barney asks to speak to Thelma Lou, she asks Opie to just relay the message because she's busy. Barney tells Opie to ask Thelma Lou if she would like to go for "a little ride tonight to the duck pond." Opie asks why Barney would want to go to the duck pond at night when "you can't see the ducks." Thelma Lou enjoys the situation, so she encourages Opie to ask Barney again why he wants to go to the duck pond. Barney hangs up in frustration.

"In the kitchen scene, Thelma Lou is tickled by Barney's embarrassment when the duck pond is mentioned," says Harvey. "She manipulates him marvelously by using the oblivious Opie. The script's inclusion of the duck pond is as close to my heart as fudge brownies and homemade peach ice cream. In my upstate New York home, there was a duck pond with a scandalous reputation for being where lots of kissing was going on. As soon as you got a driver's license, the first stop you made, with any luck, was the duck pond. Even if you went there very properly and left quickly, it was still considered absolute big-time."

The next day, Opie waits on the hotel steps for his girl. Barney sees Opie and sits down beside him. Barney then gives Opie some "fast tips" that will get his girl back.

When Opie sees his girl coming, he follows Barney's advice. He walks up to Thelma Lou and says, "Well, here I am, you lucky girl. You play your cards right, maybe I'll let you walk with me." Thelma Lou tells Opie that she'll take him "up on that." When Barney realizes that Opie has become his rival, he is upset.

After Opie and Thelma Lou depart, Karen walks by the hotel. She stops, looks around, and realizes Opie is not in his usual place.

On Saturday, Barney eagerly prepares for a date with Thelma Lou. Opie enters the courthouse and announces to Andy that he hardly thinks of Karen anymore, "now that Thelma Lou's my girl." When Opie tells Andy that he plans to spend the whole day with Thelma Lou, Barney storms out.

After Barney leaves, Andy asks Opie what he and Thelma Lou plan to do. Andy suggests that they ride bikes, climb apple trees, or go see a cowboy "shoot-em-up picture." After making these suggestions, Andy observes that none of these activities would appeal to "a grown woman."

Opie then asks, "Pa, just what can you do with a grown woman?"

Andy answers, "Sometimes they take you shopping with them. You set around while the woman tries on dresses and hats. Then you set around her house while the woman gets dressed up. And then you go over to visit the woman's mother—so, it's a fun day."

"As a habitual theatergoer (Suburban Theater on Main Street, Saturday afternoon, ten-cent admission) I always called the cowboy pictures, 'shoot-em-ups'," says Harvey. "The other Saturday activities suggested by Andy—going bike riding and climbing apple trees—were mostly taken from personal childhood memories.

"Andy's description of a day with a woman was the sort of explanation which would occur easily to Andy on his way to wrapping up with, 'So, it's a fun day.' The scene also illustrates what Andy does extremely well. He doesn't voice stern disapproval to Opie. Instead he assumes a seemingly enthusiastic and helpful acceptance of Opie's fun day with Thelma Lou and slides in the negatives very smoothly."

Andy looks out the window. When he sees Karen standing outside, he rushes Opie out the door.

As Opie exits, Karen comes up to him and asks, "Are you going to the movies?" This invitation interests Opie. He steps back inside the courthouse and asks Andy if he will explain things to Thelma Lou. Andy agrees.

Opie and Karen walk off hand-in-hand. Opie starts out on Karen's right but switches over to her left, walking closest to the street.

"In the script, the second-act fadeout does not have the Opie/Karen crossovers," says Harvey. "It seems like a very nice touch—boyhood chivalry at work."

In the epilogue, Andy looks out the window and sees Thelma Lou walking toward the courthouse. He tells Barney. Barney decides he is going to show Thelma Lou that he was not just sitting around waiting for her while she spent time with Opie.

Barney picks up the telephone and holds down the receiver with his thumb. As Thelma Lou enters, Barney says, "I'm sorry, Sally. I really can't say yes or no about going to the movies tonight." As he is supposedly talking on the telephone, it rings. Because Barney is closer, Andy suggests he take the call. After Barney hangs up, Thelma Lou says, "I'm sorry you're going to be busy at the movies, Barney. I was hoping we could drive up to the duck pond."

"Ray Allen and I used the 'holding down the telephone and pretending to be talking to someone' gimmick in a sitcom we wrote in London in 1958 or so," says Harvey. "I have seen it used occasionally on other shows, but it never seemed terribly effective. The gimmick popped into my head while writing for Don Knotts, and I used it in the epilogue of this show. Don cast his magic with the scene, his ruse all smoked out, and it was tastier than anyone else has ever done it.

"'The Rivals' has always been one of my favorite episodes because its structure gave each of the four main characters time enough to get into a role instead of just making short appearances. Barney has a lot of funny dating experiences to talk about, Opie has lots of screen time, Andy is the clever and humorous arbitrator, and Thelma Lou, portrayed by the wonderful Betty Lynn, works throughout. It was a team experience with all four at the top of their game."

Dogs, Dogs, Dogs

EPISODE #93

FIRST BROADCAST ON APRIL 22, 1963

WRITTEN BY JIM FRITZELL
AND EVERETT GREENBAUM

DIRECTED BY BOB SWEENEY

"The script was a real departure for the series and fun to do."

Aaron Ruben

"I believe TAGS director Bob Sweeney suggested a story with dogs overrunning the town," says producer Aaron Ruben. "I liked the idea and gave Jim and Everett the assignment. They wrote a great script, although it was something of a departure for the series. Believability was always a concern, since Mayberry was a real town with real people, flaky as they might be. The story line's need for an ever-increasing number of dogs may have pushed the limits of reality."

Jim and Everett's script begins early in the morning. Aunt Bee has left "a nice big breakfast" at the courthouse for Otis Campbell. After a night of drinking, Otis feels bad, so Andy prepares him a "fixer-upper"—a raw egg, hot sauce, etc. Otis drinks the mixture reluctantly and instantly perks up.

"The opening scene in which Otis wakes up appears on-screen

exactly as it was scripted," says writer Everett Greenbaum. "In those days drunkenness was still considered funny, and we felt having Otis drink a morning-after elixir would be a good comedy gag. Jim and I suggested the ingredients for the mixture, as well as we could remember, from seeing it prepared in movies."

The humor of the gag is enhanced by Earle Hagen's musical sound effects. Music comically traces the mixture's journey from the glass to Otis's stomach and perfectly accompanies Hal Smith's hilarious response.

"I actually drank the mixture that Andy prepared in the episode," said Hal Smith, who portrayed Otis Campbell. "The raw eggs Andy put in the drink were not mixed thoroughly and one of them stuck in my throat on its way down. My reaction to the drink was partly the result of the momentary choking I experienced from the egg."

In the day's mail is a response to an application Andy made for additional funds for the office and jail. The letter announces that a state investigator will be coming to Mayberry to see if the funds are necessary.

Otis asks Barney what they need money for. Barney answers that one of the things they need the money for is to have a charge account at the diner so they can pay for Otis's meals instead of having Aunt Bee fix the meals at Andy's expense. On hearing this, Otis threatens to "take his business somewhere else" because the food at the diner is "too spicy." Otis claims the food is bad for his liver. Barney then yells at Otis, "If you can drink anything, you can eat anything. Otis, you got a pickled liver."

"This was the first script in which we verbally pitted Otis and Barney against one another, and it worked very well," says Everett. "A writer learns little tricks along the way. For instance, it's very easy to drift into the habit of writing dialogue between two actors in a straight question-and-answer format. But, people don't talk that way. There are infinite ways of making a scene more effective by using pauses, answering a question with another question, or changing the subject and turning defensive rather than informative. The dialogue between Otis and Barney reflects their personalities and, thanks to Hal and Don's

Opie wants to feed the stray dog because it looks hungry.

TAGSRWC Archives

great talent, is delivered in a natural way with pauses and agitation."

At this point in the episode, Opie enters with a dog in tow. Opie wants to feed the dog because it looks hungry. Over in his cell, Otis quickly finishes his breakfast so he will not have to share. Andy gets Barney's lunch bag from the desk and gives the dog a sandwich and a Mr. Cookie bar.

After the dog eats, Barney suggests that they get it out of the office because the state investigator is coming. Opie begs to keep the dog, and Andy reluctantly agrees.

Later in the day, Opie tells Andy and Barney that the dog got away. When the three enter the courthouse, they find Opie's dog and three new dogs.

Barney emphasizes the need to get rid of the dogs before the investigator comes. He comes up with the idea that Otis should take them home.

Otis returns a short time later and announces that the dogs are gone again. As he turns to leave, he opens the door and is stampeded by eleven dogs.

Andy, Barney, Otis, and Opie discuss what to do with the dogs. Otis suggests taking them to the dog pound, but his idea is rejected. Andy wants to think about it, so he takes Opie to the filling station to get a bottle of pop.

Meanwhile, Barney tries to think of a place eleven dogs would be happy. He suddenly has an inspiration, so he rounds up the dogs, herds them into the squad car, and drives away.

When Andy and Opie return to the courthouse, the dogs are gone. Just then, Barney walks in. He proudly tells Andy and Opie that he took the dogs to "a nice, big field out in the country." Opie is not convinced the dogs will "be fine."

"Whenever we had an episode dealing with an animal we called a company, and they would send over a trainer with the requested animal," says Aaron Ruben. "All the dogs used in this episode were well trained. We had no problem getting them to follow Otis when he left the courthouse or with their jumping into the squad car after Barney decided to drive them to the country. The trainer would simply give a command, and the dogs eagerly responded."

Andy sends Opie home. As Opie opens the door to leave, thunder crashes in the distance. Since a storm is coming, Andy decides it would be better for Opie to stay at the office awhile.

Opie begins to worry about the dogs' welfare. Barney reassures Opie that a dog can't be struck by lightning because it is too close to the ground. He adds that "if they was giraffes out there in that field—then we'd be in trouble."

Still trying to convince Opie (and himself) that the dogs will be fine, Barney continues to talk. The thunder crashes again. With every flash of lightning, Barney's discourse loses assurance. Barney continues, "Dogs are short. They take care of their own. Giraffes don't. No, giraffes don't at all. Boy, giraffes are selfish."

"My copy of the script must be a shooting script because Barney's 'giraffe' speech is included," says Everett. "I remember that Aaron either created it or made additions to our original speech, and I was very pleased with the final results.

"There were very few monumental script changes on the Griffith show. The stories had been so carefully detailed in outlines and drafts that not many changes were needed. And if changes were made, Aaron, also a superb writer, would only improve the scenes."

"Jim and Ev give me credit for the giraffe speech," says Aaron. "The speech just seemed to fit the character and the story. The line, 'Boy, giraffes are selfish,' was Barney's inflated idea on a subject he knew very little about."

When another crash of thunder booms, Barney asks Andy, "Are you just going to sit there or are you coming with me to get them dogs? Are you coming with me?"

After retrieving the dogs, Barney responds to Andy's comment that he's "all heart" by reciting the lines, "The quality of mercy is not strained. It droppeth as the gentle rain from heaven."

"Jim and I thought it would be a nice surprise to have Barney quote Shakespeare," says Everett. "After all, he isn't a jerk, you know!"

Although Barney is sympathetic to keeping the dogs in the courthouse, he still fears they can "kiss that application for new funds goodbye." The telephone rings. State Investigator Somerset is on his way over.

Opie takes the dogs out back.

When Somerset arrives, he is all business and somewhat negative. He looks around and announces that everything seems to be "adequately supplied."

As Somerset walks into the back room, the dogs rush in and knock him to the floor. His demeanor changes instantly. It turns out that he is a dog lover. The requested funds are cordially approved.

Some viewers think Somerset's dramatic change and the solution to the problem caused by the dogs' presence seem to come too abruptly to be credible and somewhat hurt the story.

Everett concurs, "Yes, the ending of this show is too quick, too easy, and very sitcom-like by Mayberry standards. This may be why I disowned the episode in my memory bank."

In the epilogue, Andy and Barney wearily enter the courthouse. They have just finished finding homes for the eleven dogs. Just then, a man comes to the office looking for his eleven dogs. Andy and Barney exit wearily—to retrieve the dogs.

Mountain Wedding

EPISODE #94

FIRST BROADCAST ON APRIL 29, 1963

WRITTEN BY JIM FRITZELL
AND EVERETT GREENBAUM

DIRECTED BY BOB SWEENEY

HOWARD MORRIS GUEST STARS
AS ERNEST T. BASS

"Ernest T. grew out of interest in the Darlings and their environment."

Everett Greenbaum

"When the William Morris Agency contracted to handle the Dillards after our first appearance on TAGS, one of the first things our assigned representative told us was, 'You guys act like every job you get is the only one you'll get'," says Mitch Jayne, the Dillards' bass player. "He, of course, hit the nail on the head. We were so new to the Hollywood scene that each job was a once-in-a-lifetime chance to us. When you consider that five months prior to our first Griffith show we had been watching Andy Griffith at home in the Ozarks, never dreaming we would even meet these people, much less be part of the show, it isn't hard to imagine our excitement at being asked to come back for a second one."

Jim and Everett's second Darling script begins on the sidewalk in front of Foley's Grocery. Andy and Barney are watching a sign painter. The painter is painting an advertisement on the grocery window, which Barney calls "a delicate piece of artistic work." Barney questions Andy about the painter's spelling of "chicken." Andy reminds Barney that the rule is, "*i* before *e* except after *c*, and *e* before *n* in chicken."

"The chicken sign was not in our script," says writer Everett Greenbaum. "We began with a routine about Barney's fingerprint kit. The routine was either replaced during rewrite or on the stage."

Andy looks down the street and sees Briscoe Darling's truck parked in front of the courthouse. He and Barney walk to the office and find Briscoe inside. Briscoe has come down out of the mountains because there is trouble. Briscoe explains that "there's this fellow up home, Ernest T. Bass, he just don't take to Dud and Charlene being married." It seems that Ernest T. keeps bothering Charlene because he doesn't believe she is really married. Since he doesn't recognize her marriage, Ernest T. wants to court her himself. He comes to the cabin during the night and yells at Charlene and throws rocks through the windows. Briscoe asks Andy if he will come to the mountains and "straighten this thing out." Andy agrees.

Barney decides to sleep at the courthouse so he and Andy can get an early start. The next morning, Andy comes by to pick up Barney but has difficulty waking him. Yelling "wake up," ringing an alarm clock, and blowing a whistle in his ear all have no effect. When Andy finally snaps his fingers, Barney awakes instantly.

Andy and Barney arrive sometime later at the Darlings' mountain cabin.

"The Darling cabin was set in Decker Canyon, the same location I believe for most of the outdoor shots," says Mitch. "The cabin interior was shot, as usual, on the Desilu set. This was interesting to us four boys, learning for the first time how interior shots had to be filmed in entirely different locations, even when conversation had to be spliced as someone went out the door. Like most TAGS watchers, we supposed that the action happened linearly, and we were amazed when things happened totally out of sequence, a fact that the actors, of course, took for granted. Someone would walk out the door on Monday and maybe continue that action, or complete that sentence thirty miles away on Wednesday, when the set moved to location."

The Darlings are playing their instruments when Andy and Barney arrive. The two enter the cabin and are warmly welcomed by Briscoe, Charlene, Dud, and the boys.

Briscoe asks Dud if he told Ernest T. Bass the sheriff was looking for him. Dud was unable to find Ernest T. because he "went off into the woods to kill a mockingbird."

"We thought it was clever to use 'to kill a mockingbird' in the script," says Everett. "It was the title of a hit movie that year."

Dud advises Andy to stay at the cabin. He explains that Ernest T. "is a pestilence, and a pestilence will find you." Briscoe suggests they play some music while they wait for Ernest T. to come along. The Darlings, with Andy playing guitar, break into "Dooley."

"One of the songs we performed early in the episode was 'Dooley'," says Mitch. "We didn't write the song for the show, but it fit in perfectly. I'd known a few moonshiners and made up the lyrics. Rodney Dillard wrote the tune and sang the song in the episode. Rodney's inspiration for the tune came from a song that had the words 'Do Lord' in it that a black group sang at some club we played. That sounded like 'Dooley' to me, and that's what we called the song."

At the conclusion of "Dooley," Andy compliments the boys on their playing. The compliments are interrupted by the breaking of one of the cabin's windows. Andy, Barney, and Briscoe step outside and confront Ernest T. Bass.

"The second show gave us an opportunity to meet and work with Howie Morris," says Mitch. "Watching Howie was a wonderful way for the Dillards to be introduced to this business of being with actors. This educated, camera-wise pro plunged into the Ernest T. role with complete abandon. It made us more comfortable with the oafish roles we were playing. He let us understand that any role you play is as good as you choose to make it, and that acting was its own reward. One example of this impressed me: Howie hates guns and told us so. But he knew that Ernest T. would have a mountaineer's knowledge of handling them. I am still struck when I watch 'Mountain Wedding' by how well and easily he handled that .30-30 in the scenes where he carried it and shot it. He looked as if he had packed the thing through the woods all his life. It was the same way with the voice he invented for Ernest T. It was almost menacing and in anyone less bizarre it might have been feminine—a perfect foil for the wildness of this crazy little man who threw rocks."

Andy explains to Ernest T. that he is a justice of the peace. He goes on to tell Ernest that he performed Dud and Charlene's wedding ceremony and has a copy of the marriage license with him. Ernest T. is unimpressed. He doesn't believe Dud and Charlene "are rightly married" unless the ceremony is performed by a preacher.

Ernest T. refuses to leave Charlene alone, so Andy comes up with a solution that will keep anyone from getting hurt. The circuit preacher will come by on Sunday to marry Dud and Charlene again. Ernest T. is overjoyed because he still has twenty-four hours "to sweet-talk, woo, and charm" Charlene.

If you look closely, you will notice a continuity error in the scene. Andy, Barney, and Briscoe are shown facing the camera with Andy on the left, Briscoe in the middle, and Barney on the right. The scene's concluding shot, following a cut-away of Ernest T. retreating into the woods, has Andy and Barney in reversed positions.

That night, Andy, Barney, and the Darlings all bed down in the cabin. Andy and Barney can't sleep because the Darlings are all snoring loudly.

"I think the snoring scene that opens the second act was the single funniest thing Denver Pyle, who portrayed Briscoe Darling, ever created on that show," says Mitch. "It was intended to be ridiculous, of course, with Andy and Don trying to sleep through this Darling racket, but Denver was the one who invented that incredible maelstrom of noise and directed the Dillards like some sort of insane Leonard

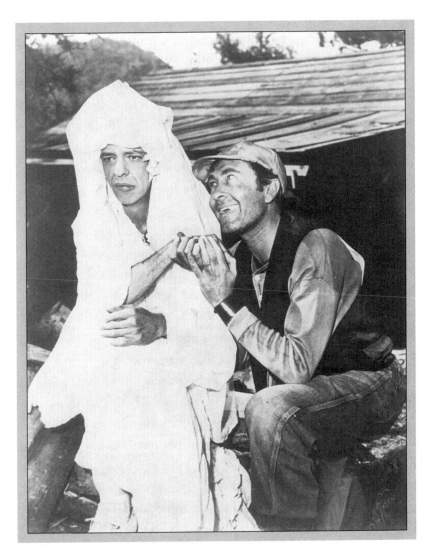

*Ernest T. asks the "lady sheriff," who is still dressed
in a wedding gown, to dance.*

TAGSRWC Archives

Bernstein. It was so unbelievably colorful that it created an ambience more like a hog killing than anything else; a cacophony of all the best snores each of us had heard, piled onto one another car-wreck style, until you couldn't believe it was human. Neither Don nor Andy could handle it. Each time we would try a take, the two of them would slide out of their chairs onto the floor, helpless. Of course, that would free us up to laugh, and I remember Rodney laughed so hard he fell out of bed. Director Bob Sweeney was too weak from laughing to do anything but just wave his hands like flippers, and I personally was so cracked up that I had to lie with my arm over my face and mash on it to get any kind of control.

"To the best of my memory, we shot that scene for half an hour trying to get it right. Don and Andy would do pretty good until they looked at each other. Andy's eyes would start to squinch up, his mouth would get grim. Don would see that and just collapse. Oh Lord, that was fun and still is today when I see the reruns and remember the sound crew, the grips, the lightmen, and the entire cast, just down pounding the floor or hanging over something, wiping their eyes, helpless with the outrageousness of it all, wondering if we were going to make this scene. It's the only time I ever saw Andy Griffith lose it."

The Darlings' snoring is interrupted by the breaking of a window. Ernest T. Bass is paying another visit. In response, Barney yells, "You listen to me out there. I'm armed. If you don't go away, I'm just liable to take a shot out this window." Ernest T. answers with a flurry of rocks.

"The cabin windows Ernest T. breaks in order to wake the family and get Charlene's attention were made of candy glass, which doesn't make much noise, so the breaking-glass sound effects had to be added later," says Mitch. "You'll notice that when the stagehand tosses the rocks through the windows no one is directly in the line of fire. The rocks themselves were furnished by the prop department and were lava rock, which weigh almost nothing."

At this point, Andy suggests that if they let Ernest T. "speak his piece" he might go home. When Charlene steps to the window, Ernest T.

"declares" for her. He serenades her while accompanying himself by tapping on a gas can, chins himself on a tree limb, and asks if he can "come over there and kiss you on the jaw."

At this point, Dud steps in and denies Ernest T.'s request to kiss Charlene. He tells Ernest T. that they are "having a preacher wedding" the next day just to satisfy him. Ernest T. is not so sure.

"Ernest T. serenades Charlene with the poem, 'Aunt Maria'," says Everett. "I got the poem from my wife Deane. It was a jump-rope song she recalled from her childhood days in Arkansas."

The next day, Briscoe and the boys are dressed for the wedding. Charlene steps out from the back room in her wedding gown.

The scene begins with a shot of the Darling boys. Mitch reaches in his pocket for a match, doesn't find one, then stands and walks left toward the kitchen. The camera, following Mitch, stops on Briscoe and Andy as Mitch passes behind them.

"My move was simply to direct the eye across the kitchen set to the principle actors so the viewer can see where everybody is without posing them," explains Mitch. "I didn't feel any special notice doing the shot, I was just the only one moving—a Bob Sweeney trick. I noticed that Bob often used crossing shots like this to get the most coverage with the one camera before resetting it. Since this was the first TV I had ever seen filmed, I took these shots for granted, supposing all TV was done this way. I seem to remember that we were the only sitcom being filmed at that time with only one camera. I also remember hearing that it was Andy's decision. He liked the intimacy of one-camera shots and hated the way two or three cameras interfered with the actor's attention.

"I don't remember any special reaction to Maggie Peterson's first on-screen appearance in the wedding dress, but that's probably because we all told her how nice she looked off set. By the time we had done a half-dozen light settings, rehearsals, walk-throughs and all the standing around inherent in that process, we had all seen the dress and what the effect would be. Denver's line, 'You look just like your Ma,' and his

Barney dresses in Charlene's bridal gown
and stands in for Charlene.

expression says it all. One of Maggie's charms is that she shone like a new penny regardless of what she had on."

Before the ceremony begins, Ernest T. Bass throws a rock through the window with a message attached. The note reads: "Maybe you going to have a preacher, and maybe you going to have an altar, but maybe you not going to have a bride. You ever think about that?"

After considering how to foil Ernest T., Andy has an idea. Barney dresses in Charlene's bridal gown and stands in for Charlene.

The ceremony proceeds through the first hymn without interruption. As the preacher starts the wedding vows, three rifle shots ring out. Ernest T. emerges from the underbrush and kidnaps the bride.

As soon as Ernest T. is out of sight, Charlene comes out of her hiding place. The preacher quickly performs the ceremony.

After the ceremony, Barney emerges from the woods and runs toward Andy. He is hotly pursued by Ernest T. Bass.

A WREATH OF SMOKE

I always smoked a pipe on stage, so it was more of a Dillard prop than a Darling one. I started out smoking a pipe, using it as a storyteller's tool, to make myself comfortable with these strange California audiences. When someone broke a string on stage, which happened all the time, I would use it as an excuse to light my pipe. It was a physical sight thing that helped me start a story that kept the audience's attention away from string repairs and tuning. Finding that it worked wonders with an audience who enjoyed the look and the laid-back nature of the pipe, I used it to audition for the Griffith show. Apparently, Andy thought it was part of the charm too. Bob Sweeney never told me when to light it or how to do anything with it. Because Bob considered every detail, I think he thought the more natural I was with it, the more natural the boys would be. And sure enough, the wreath of smoke that followed me when I moved the bass around worked for us.

Mitch Jayne

"The idea of Barney dressing up as the bride came from the movie, 'Some Like It Hot'," says Everett. "Fleeing from gangsters, Jack Lemmon and Tony Curtis were disguised as women, and Joe E. Brown tries to marry Lemmon."

In the epilogue, Ernest T. reluctantly shakes Dud's hand. The Darlings play a song so Dud and Charlene can dance. Ernest T. enjoys the music, gets an idea, and asks the "lady sheriff," who is still dressed in a wedding gown, to dance.

"Looking back on it, 'Mountain Wedding' was a major show for us," says Mitch. "We met Don Knotts and saw firsthand the magic interaction between him and Andy—two pros who really got off on each other's work. We got to meet Howie, who was always on and full of stories, and we experienced that raw energy he exudes. We were accepted by the cast and crew as good guys who were no trouble to work with and who took direction instantly. Even the pragmatic assistant director, Bob Saunders, who was always pinned to the clock and the budget, seemed to like the way we did things and took time to share some of his Hollywood humor and behind-the-scenes jokes with us.

"With 'Mountain Wedding,' the Dillards became comfortable with the whole idea of representing our music this way. The first show had bothered Rodney, since some people said we looked like a family out of *Deliverance*. In the good-natured and forgiving climate of TAGS, however, we were more like idiot savants, letting Briscoe interpret us as we played our instruments with incredible expertise but acted like blocks of wood. It was fun along the lines of Harpo Marx, and we got into it—the stunned and stuporous look of boys who had only one means of expression, their music.

"The most important part of that show for the Dillards was the friends we made on the set. We were treated as professionals. We were part of the overall plan, important to the development of ideas and direction. Both George Lindsey and Jim Nabors came by to see the filming of that show. TAGS executive producer Sheldon Leonard dropped in too, and we began to be aware that the Andy Griffith set was basically a friendly, successful place where everybody felt at home and wanted to see what was happening. People felt involved in the show, curious and interested in this rural phenomenon that had captured the number-one spot in the TV ratings. Most significant, the Darlings, whatever they represented, had been approved and would be seen again."

The Big House

EPISODE #95

FIRST BROADCAST ON MAY 6, 1963

WRITTEN BY HARVEY BULLOCK

DIRECTED BY BOB SWEENEY

Rule #1: Obey all rules.
Rule #2: Do not write on the walls, as it takes a
lot of work to erase writing on the walls.
"Rules at the Rock"

"The Big House" begins with Barney, Gomer, and Opie listening to a news bulletin on the radio. Four bandits have pulled off "a daring holdup." The bulletin goes on to say that two members of the gang have been captured and will be held temporarily in the Mayberry jail.

After hearing that the two criminals are coming to Mayberry, Barney tells Andy, "Those two hoods are in for a big surprise when they get here. They're going to come in here expecting some small-town, two-bit lockup. Well, they're going to find out different."

Barney suggests hiring an extra deputy and takes it upon himself to find "his assistant."

When Andy returns to the courthouse later in the day, Barney proudly introduces "our number three man." Dressed in a deputy's uniform, Gomer marches from the back room.

"The details for Gomer's appearance in his deputy's uniform were not spelled out in the script," says writer Harvey Bullock. "Gomer was simply described as 'having on an ill-fitting uniform, a peaked hat like Barney's, a gun in a holster, and a badge.' That's all the description I felt was needed. I knew that the director Bob Sweeney would work out the details.

"Generally, a three-character story is more effective than a two-character story. More angles can be covered without the continuous 'talking-head' shots of the same two people. Gomer Pyle was an extremely useful character with his colorful twangy speech and guileless good nature. In 'The Big House,' both Barney and Andy play off him effectively.

"I enjoyed including Gomer in this script because I knew Jim Nabors would bring an engaging and very likable performance to the story. Jim was open, energetic, and a most dependable, talented guy."

Andy is hesitant about having Gomer around the jailhouse. Barney insists that Gomer has "learned a lot from me already" and assures Andy that he is putting Gomer through a crash program. Barney pleads with Andy to give Gomer a chance.

The two prisoners arrive. Minutes after they are jailed, Barney tells them the "Rules at the Rock." The two prisoners listen stonefaced, but Gomer is spellbound.

"Having Barney proclaim the 'Rules at the Rock' is a prime example of his unmatchable comic character," says Harvey. "Barney is so transparent, assuming importance, and emulating the behavior he thinks proper for a big-time lawman. Don Knotts is a true magician. His performance made the rules speech sound better than I imagined it would."

Four different camera angles are used to photograph Barney's speech. The speech begins with a wide-angle shot of Andy, Gomer, and Barney standing in front of the jail cells. As Barney begins to recite the rules, the camera is repositioned inside the cell, so Barney is seen from the prisoner's point of view. Two medium shots of Andy and Gomer bookend a wonderful closeup of the spellbound Gomer. The speech then concludes, as it began, with a wide-angle shot.

"I wrote camera directions only when I felt they were critical to the story and might have escaped the director's attention in the hectic pace of doing the series," says Harvey. "The shooting and cutting to 'singles' [one person in a shot] is fairly routine, and I had great confidence in Bob Sweeney. I knew Bob would be sure to shoot effective coverage as the scene required.

"A typical scene is first shot from a slight distance to contain most of the characters. This is the master shot. Then the scene is shot again with the camera on one character for his lines and reactions. Then, if warranted, a third take is made on another character. Often the single takes are mostly reactions to lines being read off-camera. Lots of film was thus shot, giving the director all kinds of dramatic/comedic ammunition.

"The film cutters (editors) made a tremendously important contribution to the finished film. It is amazing how they can take the most disparate footage and make a final cut that flows seamlessly."

"In one-camera photography, the director shoots the master shot, the closeups, the over-the-shoulder shots, and then the editor puts it together the way he sees it," says Jay Sandrich, assistant to the producer. "On TAGS, Bob Sweeney was directing most of the shows, so he didn't always have time to sit in the editing room and work with the editor. Bob would usually get a rough cut of the editor's work, view it, and then give the editor notes to change this or to use a closeup instead of a wide-angle shot. Then the producer, who has the final authority, would view the corrected cut and say, 'Yeah, that's good,' or 'Let's make some changes.' So editing was a collaborative process.

"An episode's post-production time would sometimes vary, but it usually would take two weeks to edit a show and another week to add the music and the laugh track. After all that was done, the film would have to go to the laboratory to make sure it really looked good. Post production thus averaged about four to six weeks per episode."

At the conclusion of Barney's speech, Andy leaves to look for the two criminals who are still on the loose. He returns sometime later and learns that things at the courthouse have "gone as smooth as clockwork." To demonstrate, Barney announces that "it's time for mealtime formation." When Barney blows a whistle, the prisoners jump to attention and march to the adjoining cell.

Andy inquires about Gomer's whereabouts. Barney says he has Gomer "stationed outside, manning the blockhouse lookout." He and Andy step outside. Andy looks up and sees Gomer's feet hanging over the side of roof of the courthouse.

When Barney yells, "Attention," Gomer drops his gun over the side of the building.

Andy and Barney go up on the roof to return Gomer's gun. The roof is cluttered with decorations left from a past Christmas. Andy reminds Barney that he was supposed to have cleaned this up. Andy then gives the cleanup assignment to Gomer.

"The 'courthouse roof' scene was written after I finally came up with a way for one man, with no regular weapons, to fool four hardened would-be escapees," says Harvey. "The discarded decorations explained the presence of the Christmas lights, which play a prominent role in the episode's conclusion, and the rooftop setting was a nice change."

Meanwhile, the two prisoners agree to let the "hick deputy think he's a big shot. Lead him on far enough and that hick deputy is going to be our free pass out of here."

Andy gets a call that two men, who may be the two other members of the holdup gang, have been spotted around Mayberry. He leaves to investigate.

After Andy departs, the prisoners, in Barney's presence, talk about the similarities between the Mayberry jail and the state pen. They note there is one major difference. The Mayberry jail has not had a "shake down." They say that all prisoners are taken out of their cells while "the screws make a surprise inspection of the mattresses for guns and knives." Barney immediately yells, "Shake down" and flings open the cell door.

"I was looking for a routine the prisoners might devise that would get them out of their cell," says Harvey. "The prisoners had Barney sized up as loving to play warden so much that they could out-think him by saying the Mayberry jail wasn't as highly regarded as other 'big houses,' which had shake downs."

While Barney is busy "shaking down" the cell, the prisoners walk out. When Barney realizes they are gone, he picks up the phone and frantically yells "May Day" to Sarah, the telephone operator.

"Sarah was very helpful," says Harvey. "For one thing, having a phone operator who knew all the numbers in town (instead of a soulless dial) was a constant reminder we were in a small town."

While Barney is still on the telephone, the door to the courthouse opens. The two prisoners walk in, followed by Andy. Andy tells Barney that it was a good thing he was still outside the office.

After Andy leaves, Barney exhibits his anger. He walks over to the cell and tells the prisoners that there will be "no more Mr. Nice Guy." As he routinely does, he hangs the cell keys on the wall peg and goes into the back room to get a cup of coffee.

While Barney is out of the room, one of the prisoners reaches through the cell bars, takes the keys off the wall, and unlocks the cell.

Andy enters the courthouse at this point and thwarts the prisoners again.

Once again Andy leaves. He returns later in the day with two plain-clothes policemen. The two want to use the Mayberry jail as "a trap." The policemen believe the other two gang members will try to free their buddies.

Andy doesn't tell Barney about the two plainclothes policemen or their plan. Instead, he sends Barney up on the roof with Gomer.

Andy rejoins the two policemen and is assigned a position on the other side of the street.

As anticipated, the other two gang members arrive, but they decide to "case the joint" before attempting to spring their buddies. Meanwhile, Gomer is placing Christmas lights in a basket. Barney senses that something is amiss. He looks into the alley and sees the two policemen. Mistaking them for the missing gang members, he disarms them and locks them in the jail.

Meanwhile, the real missing gang members enter from the back room. They then force Barney into the cell with the two policemen, and all four gang members escape through the back room.

Andy sees the escape and yells for Gomer to assist. Gomer drops his gun over the side of the building, knocking Andy's gun out of his hands. As Gomer looks over the side of the building, he knocks over the basket of Christmas lights. The lights fall to the street in rapid succession. With their backs turned, the gang members think the breaking bulbs are machine-gun fire, so they give up.

After locking the four criminals in a cell, Andy unselfishly gives Barney the credit saying, "Great work, Barn. Your scheme worked."

The 'Christmas-light, machine-gun-effect' capture was carefully detailed in the outline before a word of the script was typed," says Harvey. "The outline was broken into actual scenes to be written. This helped me to make sure all the prominent points were in order, and insured that the story came to a logical conclusion."

In the epilogue, Barney and Gomer are taking steps to keep themselves "razor sharp for the next emergency." When Andy enters the courthouse, Barney asks Gomer to show Andy what he's learned. Gomer draws his gun and accidentally throws it through the glass of the bookcase. Barney reprimands him saying, "If you don't know how to handle one of these things, you got no business carrying one." At this point, Barney places his own pistol back in its holster and accidentally fires it into the floor. Andy then extends his hand, and Barney hands over his pistol.

"The scripted epilogue does not have Barney accidentally firing his pistol," says Harvey. "Instead, Gomer gives Barney a bill. Gomer wants to pay to cover the cost of all the light bulbs he broke. Barney generously tears up the bill, throws it away, and Gomer promptly writes Barney a ticket for littering."

1963-64

Briscoe Declares for Aunt Bee

EPISODE #96

FIRST BROADCAST ON OCTOBER 28, 1963

WRITTEN BY JIM FRITZELL AND
EVERETT GREENBAUM

DIRECTED BY EARL BELLAMY

DENVER PYLE GUEST STARS
AS BRISCOE DARLING

"Andy always wondered how a Swede from San Francisco and a Jew from Buffalo were able to write The Andy Griffith Show. *I should have told him that God wanted it that way because I can't explain it otherwise."*

Everett Greenbaum

"We were never told by Aaron Ruben that our two previous Darlings scripts were a success," says writer Everett Greenbaum. "We were just tickled not to be fired, and that was all the praise we needed."

Jim and Everett's third Darlings script begins with Andy responding to a call from Nick's Cafe. As Andy arrives, Briscoe Darling and the boys are exiting the cafe. When Andy questions Briscoe about the trouble, Briscoe explains he was taking "normal safeguards for eating in a strange place." He just wanted to sit in the kitchen to watch while his meal was cooked. As a result, Nick refused to serve Briscoe and the boys.

"Jim Fritzell was a large, raw-boned man, always worried about his company manners," says Everett. "He was somewhat like Briscoe and served as a model for the character. Although Briscoe's language did not really exist in life, it mysteriously poured out of Jim. I often thought it was because he watched every western movie ever made. He would have loved to have been a cowboy (except for his fear of horses)."

Andy invites Briscoe and the boys to have supper at his house. Before supper, Andy and the boys pass the time playing a bluegrass instrumental.

"The first bluegrass instrumental we performed in the episode was 'Mockin' Banjos,' our arrangement of 'Dueling Banjos,' originally written by Arthur Smith," says Mitch Jayne, the Dillards' bass player. "We retitled it because our version featured the mandolin and banjo, but we wanted to keep the tune recognizable. We were allowed to pick our own music for the episode, unless the script called for a tune familiar to Andy. We selected 'Mockin' Banjos' because it was so fast and showy."

Aunt Bee prepares the supper under Briscoe's watchful eye. Impressed by what he sees, he remarks, "That's the cleanest cooking woman I ever did see."

When the meal is served, the bread is passed first. The boys each take a piece. By the time the plate gets to Briscoe, it is empty. Briscoe yells to Aunt Bee in the kitchen, "Bread!"

The potatoes are passed next. The boys each help themselves. By the time the bowl gets to Briscoe, it too is empty. Briscoe yells, "Taters!"

When the meat is passed, Briscoe gets the dish first. By the time the plate gets to Opie, it is empty. Opie yells, "Meat!"

"The gag that begins the first act's dining scene developed gradually," says Everett. "We started with the line, 'Bread,' then with 'Taters' we began to see what we called a routine develop. A routine is like a little plot. In this case, the payoff was Opie following Briscoe's example and yelling, 'Meat'."

Aunt Bee eventually finishes in the kitchen and takes a place beside Briscoe at the table. From the supper conversation, Aunt Bee learns that since Charlene got married, Briscoe and the boys have been cooking for themselves. Briscoe says the boys are "just about the worst cooks they is."

"This story was clearer without Charlene, so we did not include her in the script," says Everett. "Her absence freed us to aim all the female attention toward Aunt Bee.

In response to Briscoe's comments about the poor meals he has eaten since Charlene's marriage, Aunt Bee gives him special attention. She serves Briscoe extra butter, more pot roast, and pearly onions. Briscoe takes note that she "specializes on him" and gives Aunt Bee an appreciative wink.

The supper scene's master shot was photographed with the back wall of the dining area removed and the camera positioned in the place normally occupied by the china cabinet. This shot is supplemented with closeups, especially during the interaction between Briscoe and Aunt Bee.

"To the best of my memory, all extraneous cast members and settings were moved for the closeups," says Mitch. "The single camera dictated the place the Darling boys occupied in the wide-angle shot."

After supper, the Taylors and the Darlings gather for some entertainment. Accompanied by Andy on guitar, the Darlings play "Doug's Tune." Opie and Andy sing "Old Dan Tucker." After some coaxing, Aunt Bee recites the poem, "A Fading Flower of Forgotten Love" by Agnes Ellicott Strong.

"Jim and I usually handed in forty pages per script and let Aaron Ruben figure out what was to be cut out if the episode ran too long," says Everett. "In this case, because of the after-dinner music and poetry recitation, we turned in five pages less.

"Several years ago, a woman wrote to me. She was trying to locate Agnes Ellicott Strong, the author of 'A Fading Flower of Forgotten Love.' This is the poem Aunt Bee recites. I had to tell her I was Agnes Ellicott Strong. By the way, Briscoe calls the poem 'rose poetry' because a rose is mentioned in it."

Briscoe is awestruck by the recitation. He feels Aunt Bee's heart "talking" to his heart. In response, Briscoe says, "I want you to be my bride."

Andy and Aunt Bee are dumbfounded and immediately protest the declaration. Briscoe tells Aunt Bee, "You get your clothes, and your sewing, and your potholders packed, and I'll be by for you the first thing in the morning."

When Briscoe realizes that Aunt Bee is upset by his boldness, he decides her negative reaction is because the courtship is too speedy. He says he'll "put on my square wheels so things won't get to rolling too fast."

Later that night, Aunt Bee is awakened by Briscoe's singing. Following a "lifelong custom" of his people, Briscoe is serenading his beloved.

"Dean Webb, the Dillards' mandolin player, is the one who supplied 'Low and Lonely' for the serenading scene," says Mitch. "Denver had asked us to find him a suitable courting song. Dean came up with 'Low and Lonely' after finding it in an old Roy Acuff songbook and taught it to Denver. I don't remember any particular difficulties with the serenading scene. It was filmed on an interior set. Because the vocals and music were pre-recorded, it was a fairly simple scene."

Aunt Bee is not impressed by Briscoe's caterwauling and slams her bedroom window shut. In response, Briscoe decides "to think this thing out."

The next day, Opie rushes into the courthouse to report that Aunt Bee is missing. When he went home for lunch, Opie found a note that said, "She's with me—Briscoe Darling."

Andy immediately heads to the mountains to get Aunt Bee.

Andy arrives at the Darling cabin and finds Aunt Bee unharmed. Although Aunt Bee and Andy again decline Briscoe's declaration, he refuses to give up.

Andy has an idea. He asks Aunt Bee to step outside, so the two can have "a little talk." When they return, Aunt Bee accepts Briscoe's declaration.

Briscoe is overjoyed. When he hugs Aunt Bee, Andy warns him, "Easy, Mr. Darling. You might break her. You're pretty strong, you know."

Andy's comment leads Briscoe to show off his arm muscle. He lifts the bed so his muscle will "bug." Aunt Bee can't see because the light in the cabin isn't very good, so Briscoe and the boys take the bed outside.

This gives Aunt Bee an opening. She says, "As long as we have the bed out here, why don't we clean that part of the floor?"

The floor cleaning turns into a complete house scrubbing. The scrubbing is followed by baths.

Later that evening, Aunt Bee prepares and serves supper. The potatoes are served first. Briscoe is instructed to take one and pass to the left. Briscoe takes his fork, gets one potato, and passes the potato on the fork to the left. He is immediately corrected by Aunt Bee who tells him to put one on the plate and pass the bowl to the left. Briscoe informs her that they don't do things "that way here." Aunt Bee responds that they "do now," and whacks Briscoe on the back of the hand with a wooden serving spoon.

"Jim and I decided to begin the cabin dinner scene by having Briscoe incorrectly pass a potato around the table," says Everett. "We liked the potato-passing gag so much we used it again with Ernest T. in the episode 'My Fair Ernest T. Bass'."

When Briscoe places his elbows on the table, Aunt Bee hits his elbow with her spoon and says, "No elbows on the table."

When Briscoe places his napkin under his chin, Aunt Bee removes the napkin with one swift wave of her spoon and says, "Napkins go in the lap."

When Briscoe reaches for the salt, Aunt Bee whacks him on the back of the hand.

"The dinner scene with the wooden spoon was a joy to watch," says Mitch. "My favorite part of the scene was Aunt Bee's work with the spoon, and in particular, her expertise at lifting the napkin from Briscoe's bib and putting it in his lap, which was a good trick that she managed three times for the camera, laying it in exactly the same place each time. The spoon had a thick styrofoam pad, cut to spoon shape, and she handled that thing like a baton. It hurt to watch her whack Briscoe with it, and it was always hard not to laugh. But we usually learned to get that out of our systems when we rehearsed the scene, so we could play the filming as solemn as owls."

Aunt Bee's spoon gets the best of Briscoe. He jumps up from the table and calls off the declaration saying, "This has gone just far enough. I can take some manners, and I can take some cleaning up, and I can take a bossy mouth, but I ain't about to be beat to death with no spoon."

In the epilogue, Andy and Aunt Bee are preparing to return to Mayberry. Aunt Bee calls Briscoe over to the car, kisses him on the cheek, and thanks him for "wanting" her. Briscoe appreciates the gesture and replies, "Well, Miss Bee, your kisses are awful nice and highly valuable, but to be perfectly honest with you, it just ain't worth the pain."

"Earl Bellamy directed this episode instead of Bob Sweeney," says Mitch. "As far as I could see, Earl directed with the same level of competence that all directors of TAGS seemed to assume when they did that show. It was almost as if Mayberry was larger than the sum of its parts. The director was merely moving pieces around to get a nice camera angle, while the place itself set the movements and happenings. I know this sounds dumb, and probably is, but I can't imagine a directing talent that wouldn't be able to do a good job of holding the magic of something that Bob Sweeney and Andy Griffith had already captured and frozen in time."

Gomer the House Guest

EPISODE #97

FIRST BROADCAST ON NOVEMBER 4, 1963

WRITTEN BY JIM FRITZELL AND
   EVERETT GREENBAUM

DIRECTED BY EARL BELLAMY

> *ANDY: Do you know anything about cutting meat?*
> *GOMER: Do you think they'll ask me that?*
> Dialogue after Gomer tells
> Andy he is applying for an
> experienced butcher position

"The structure of this script could have resulted in a very ordinary sitcom," says writer Everett Greenbaum. "But we hoped to avoid that flavor by featuring Gomer, who was a fresh new face on the small screen."

"Gomer the House Guest" begins as Andy pulls up to the gas pumps at Wally's Service Station. Gomer, who is waiting on Jake, tells Andy that he will get to him "in a couple of shakes." Since Andy is in no hurry, he gets a bottle of pop and listens as Gomer tells about a recent fishing trip with "Birdy" Blush. Gomer tells how he caught a fish after baiting his hook "with a dab of Limburger cheese and a slice of onion." He goes on to say he dropped his hook at the base of Lover's Leap Rock and relates the legend behind the naming of the rock. Legend has it that "a Confederate colonel plunged to his everlasting calling there after being spurned by a Yankee woman."

"'In a couple of shakes' was a very popular phrase in the time of my childhood, and it seemed right for Gomer," says Everett. "We then had Gomer tell his 'Birdy Blush' story in detail to get the point across that he was in no hurry to wait on the station's customers. The story and its details, such as using Limburger cheese and onion to catch a trout and the legend of Lover's Leap Rock, came about from letting our imaginations roam and using things resting in our subconscious."

Another customer drives up as Gomer tells the story. This customer gets "testy" because of the wait. When Wally, the station owner, arrives, he notices the testy customer and tells Gomer to finish up.

Gomer continues to talk with Jake. He explains that the trouble Jake was having with his car was caused by corrosion on his battery terminals. Gomer took soda pop and "cleared it right up."

"Soda pop will, in fact, clear up corrosion," says Everett. "I was a mechanic in my younger years. I later attended M.I.T. for three years but flunked out. (The Boston theaters and the airport were too tempting for me.) At the age of twenty, I received a patent for an automatic-flush rivet countersink, which I worked out when I was a riveter at Bell Aircraft. The countersink was made by a company in Boston who lost their shirts. By that time I was in naval pilot training. All of this is to explain how I knew about soda on the battery terminals. Not to brag, because I can't do any sports, and I don't understand anything about business."

The testy customer angrily drives away. Wally is furious and warns Gomer that he had "better start snapping to."

Gomer eventually waits on Andy and begins to retell the Birdy Blush story. Another customer drives up to the gas pumps, but Gomer is in no hurry and continues the story.

Later that day, Opie stops by the courthouse to collect his allowance. Andy compliments Opie on not "having to be reminded one time to do

*After supper, the Taylors and Gomer gather around
the radio to listen to the* **Shep and Ralph Show.**

your chores." Opie replies that he didn't have to be reminded because he wrote his chores on his wrist.

"As a naval pilot trainer, I learned that World War II pilots often wrote important time settings, radio frequencies, headings, and altitudes on their wrists," says Everett. "This knowledge inspired the idea to have Opie remember his chores by writing them on his wrist."

As Opie leaves, Gomer enters. He tells Andy that he's been fired. His firing also means that Gomer had to give up the room he had in the back of the station, so he doesn't have anywhere to sleep. Gomer asks Andy if he can sleep in a cell until he "can settle on my feet someplace." At this point, Andy invites Gomer to stay at his house, and Gomer accepts.

That evening after supper, the Taylors and Gomer gather around the radio to listen to the *Shep and Ralph Show.* Gomer, who sits on the floor with his legs extended beneath the coffee table, talks throughout the program.

"Gomer's floor posture fit the character perfectly," says Everett. "The idea to sit on the floor must have come up on the set because it was not included in our script."

After the program, the Taylors go to bed. Gomer, however, "sits up a spell." Before the family retires, Gomer asks if he can do some chores to pay for his board. Although Andy feels it isn't necessary, Gomer insists.

Later that night, Gomer decides to saw some firewood. Awakened by the noise, Andy asks him to stop.

A few hours later, Gomer gets out Andy's vacuum cleaner. He notices the toggle switch is loose, tightens it, and accidentally locks the switch to on. The noise again wakes the Taylors.

Andy encourages Gomer to go to bed. Gomer agrees, even though he is not really tired.

Gomer, however, does not go to bed immediately. He walks loudly across the floor, slams the bathroom door, gargles, and sings "No Account Mule" as he looks at himself in the mirror.

Due to lack of sleep, Andy can't concentrate on his work the next day. When he leans back in his chair to take a short nap, he is interrupted by Gomer. When Andy explains to Gomer that he couldn't sleep last night due to all the racket, Gomer promises to be "quieter tonight."

That night, Andy turns off the house's lights before going upstairs to bed. The scene is interestingly photographed. Director Earl Bellamy positions the camera outside the Taylor house. Andy is shown in silhouette against the closed curtains. The camera then pans left across the front porch and through the closed front door as it follows Andy up the stairs. Positioning the camera outside the house presents the scene in a unique and interesting way.

This night, Gomer also goes to bed. He is quietly reading a comic book when the quiet is interrupted by one of Gomer's former customers. The man parks his car outside Andy's house and revs the engine so Gomer can analyze its problem. Gomer diagnoses the problem immediately and advises the man to pull out his choke.

Gomer goes back to his reading but is interrupted by a second customer who stops by with squeaky shocks.

The next morning, the Taylors are all irritable because no one has had enough sleep. Andy decides to ask Gomer to leave.

Gomer enters the kitchen enthusiastically, unaware that he has caused the Taylors a second night of sleeplessness. Aware of Gomer's good mood and innocence, Andy puts off asking him to leave.

Later in the day Andy stops by Wally's Service Station. Wally tells Andy that he is "the first customer in here all day."

When Andy returns home, he finds his driveway overflowing with "folks needing some repairs." Andy orders everyone into their cars. Accompanied by Gomer, Andy leads everyone to Wally's.

Back at the station, the customers huddle around Gomer as he retells the Birdy Blush story. As Gomer tells the story, Andy says to Wally, "See that fellow there?" Wally answers, "Yeah, that's Gomer." Andy replies, "That's more than Gomer. That's your business." After Wally thinks the situation over, he rehires Gomer "with pleasure."

"Jim and I hoped no one would notice Gomer's varying mechanical ability between 'Man in a Hurry' and this show." says Everett. "In the earlier episode he knows nothing about engines, only how to pump gas. The resolution to losing his job depended upon Gomer's mechanical expertise and his likable personality, so we increased Gomer's mechanical skills to fit the story. We felt we could get by with the change because we thought the audience would have forgotten the earlier show by the time this story aired."

Some viewers think the conclusion of the second act in which Andy leads everyone back to Wally's is not well developed. "The solution was very, very important in comedy writing," says Everett. "Sometimes a perfectly good story had to be discarded because we couldn't think of a credible solution. This was nearly the case with this script. Even after much thought, the solution we came up with arrives too quickly and flaws the story."

The Haunted House

EPISODE #98

FIRST BROADCAST ON OCTOBER 7, 1963

WRITTEN BY HARVEY BULLOCK

DIRECTED BY EARL BELLAMY

"I think the cast enjoyed filming this episode because it had the hint of special effects, a bit of suspense, and a different setting than most other stories."

Harvey Bullock

"The Haunted House" begins with Opie and a friend walking down the road that runs in front of the deserted Rimshaw house. Opie is carrying a baseball bat and his friend has a baseball and glove. The two are discussing Whitey Ford's pitching and Mickey Mantle's hitting. Opie's friend, who imitates Whitey Ford, gets ready to pitch to Opie, who imitates Mickey Mantle. Before the pitch is thrown, Opie uses the bat to knock the dirt off his tennis shoes.

"The scene in which Opie knocks the dirt off his shoes before hitting the ball was scripted," says writer Harvey Bullock. "This action grew out of the fact that young fans adopt the mannerisms of their heroes and emulate anything their favorite players do—even if their shoes have no cleats."

Barney consoles Gomer by saying,
"It's just the lightning, like Andy said."

TAGSRWC Archives

Opie hits the baseball through the window in the front door of the Rimshaw house. The boys are reluctant to retrieve the ball because they fear the house is haunted. Opie assures his friend that there won't be any "spooks" in the daytime. As the boys slowly approach the house, they hear a wail coming from within and run away.

"I decided to write this script because haunted houses are fixtures in small towns, and ghosts and spooks catch an audience's attention," says Harvey. "Stark fear oddly can be comic if the audience feels nothing really fearful will happen.

"When I wrote the script I did not have a Halloween broadcast date in mind and never bothered to suggest it. Haunted-house stories can be aired any time. A few others, like the wonderful Christmas story that features Ben Weaver, are better screened during the holidays. Aaron Ruben did the scheduling, shifting scripts to fit actors' availability and also to evenly distribute shows starring specific cast members."

Meanwhile at the courthouse, Andy is releasing Otis. Barney enters as Otis is unlocking his cell. Barney doesn't think Otis is sober yet, so he suggests they give him a sobriety test. Barney steps into the back room and returns with a rope. He reasons that if Otis is "steady enough to jump rope, he's steady enough to be turned loose."

Otis is reluctant to take Barney's sobriety test. Barney agrees to forgo the test if Otis will tell where he has been getting his moonshine, but Otis refuses.

Barney has Otis and Andy turn the rope as he demonstrates the test. As he jumps the rope, Barney recites, "Call for the doctor. Call for the nurse. Call for the lady with the alligator purse."

After Barney's demonstration, Otis prepares to jump into the turning rope. As he watches the rope carefully, he recites an improvised rhyme, "Slow it down and let me in, or I'll go out and get some gin." This infuriates Barney.

"The idea of Barney giving Otis the rope-jumping sobriety test was the result of going through the script backwards and forwards and re-writing over and over," says Harvey. "The jump-rope idea eventually came to mind. It seemed funny and could be used in the epilogue. I got the notion from my wife's Girl Scout troop, which met in our garage and played with jump ropes after their meetings. The rhyming verses the girls recited while jumping were hilarious. I especially liked 'Call for the doctor.' I could envision Barney doing that chant and felt it was a perfect fit. Having Otis do his own verse seemed like a natural topper."

At this point, Opie and his friend burst into the courthouse. They tell Andy about hitting the baseball into the Rimshaw house and the ghostly sounds they heard. Andy is surprised that "great big boys like you" would be talking about ghosts. He explains that the sound was "probably just the wind blowing." Barney agrees and adds, "There's nothing to fear but fear itself."

Andy tells the boys to stay away from the Rimshaw house because it's not safe. He promises to get the baseball and tells the boys to "run along."

After the boys leave, Barney tells Andy that he should have sent the boys back to the Rimshaw house to get the ball. He says, "That would cure them of the squidgets."

"I don't know where *squidgets* originated," says Harvey. "I suspect it was just a word I made up that sounded right coming from Barney."

When Andy suggests that Barney go to the Rimshaw house and get the ball for the boys, Barney is hesitant. He thinks the situation over and then realizes that he can't leave because he has to finish administering Otis's sobriety test.

When Andy asks Barney if he's "shying away from going to the Rimshaw place," Barney responds angrily that he's going.

Gomer enters to deliver a car battery as Barney walks toward the door, so Barney invites Gomer to "go for a little ride." Gomer agrees.

Gomer is surprised when Barney parks the squad car in front of the Rimshaw house. Barney sends Gomer inside to retrieve the ball. As Gomer starts toward the house, he stops and asks Barney if he's coming. Barney stalls by saying he has to check the timing on the engine.

When Gomer volunteers to check the engine, Barney replies, "I'll check the engine. I said it first."

"Barney's 'I'll check the engine' is a variation of a formula line for spooky stories where the self-styled brave man uses outrageous excuses not to tangle with possible ghosts," says Harvey. "When Gomer contests the order, Barney says, 'I said it first.' Again, a timeless recognizable phrase with children, and hence a good line for Barney."

Gomer continues to balk at going into the Rimshaw house alone, so Barney reluctantly agrees to go with him. The two slowly approach the house. As Barney opens the door, a moan is heard coming from inside the house. Barney and Gomer make a hasty retreat.

Barney, Gomer, and Andy look around the Rimshaw house.

TAGSRWC Archives

Barney bursts into the courthouse and tells Andy, "When Old Man Rimshaw died, he said he didn't want that place disturbed, and I think we ought to respect the wishes of the dear departed." Andy asks Barney about his "nothing to fear but fear itself" speech. Barney answers, "Well, that's exactly what I got—fear itself."

"Reading this script for the first time in thirty-some years, one small line doesn't seem right," says Harvey. "Barney's 'Well, that's exactly what I got—fear itself.' This open admission by Barney that he's afraid after he's gone to great lengths to conceal it doesn't seem consistent. I probably fell in love with Franklin Roosevelt's famous line and didn't realize it went somewhat counter to the character and scene."

Otis is still at the courthouse. He agrees with Barney's suggestion to stay away from the Rimshaw place. Otis says that he has heard that "the walls move, pictures with eyes follow you all around the room, and axes float in the air."

Andy suggests that he, Barney, and Gomer go over to the Rimshaw house to get the baseball.

After they retrieve the ball, Andy suggests they look around a bit. Andy walks to the rear of the house, while Gomer and Barney remain in the front room.

When Andy returns, he notices that the wallpaper beside the fireplace is torn. He examines the tear and discovers that the wall around the tear is warm.

Barney looks above the fireplace and sees a portrait of Old Man Rimshaw. According to local legends, Rimshaw put chains on his hired man and killed him with an ax. Barney then notices that the "eyes in the painting are staring at us."

The script directions for "Old Man Rimshaw's" portrait were as follows: "On the wall adjacent to the fireplace hangs a commanding, forbidding portrait of a man. The features are sinister, the picture weird, the eyes strangely alive."

"I had no concern about any problems with the props when writing the ghost scenes," says Harvey. "I knew that Aaron Ruben could tone down the effects if the props became too complicated or costly."

Barney brings Rimshaw's moving eyes to Andy's attention and suggests they leave. By this time the eyes have changed, so Andy doesn't see anything strange about the portrait. He suggests that it is probably just the way the light strikes the portrait.

Andy feels that perhaps some tramps are staying in the house and decides to look upstairs. Barney and Gomer check the cellar.

As the two proceed toward the cellar, they notice the eyes in the portrait are following them again. Barney consoles Gomer by saying, "It's just the lighting, like Andy said."

They open the cellar door and see an ax attached to the inside of the door. Gomer now consoles Barney by suggesting that the ax is "probably just the lighting."

"The running gag is a part of the writer's comedy kit, but it required careful handling so it wouldn't be just repetitive and dull," says Harvey. "The repetition of 'It's just the lighting, like Andy said' seemed to work because it progressed. The line gave comfort and was used by Barney and Gomer as they clung to the hope that it *was* the light."

Andy returns, notices the ax, and asks if everything is all right. Barney answers, "Just fine, knock on wood." When Barney knocks on the wall, three knocks answer! Andy knocks three times on the fireplace mantel, and three knocks reply! In a loud voice, Andy says, "You're right. This is no place for us. Let's get out of here."

Barney and Gomer retreat out the front door.

After the room is cleared, Otis and Big Jack Anderson, a local moonshiner, emerge from their hiding place. Big Jack is ecstatic. He believes he's found a place to run his still for twenty years.

Big Jack and Otis celebrate with a "snort." After the drink, Otis looks up and sees an ax floating in the air. Then what appear to be footsteps are heard coming down the stairs.

"Andy starts the hint to the audience that he's on to something by saying in an extra-loud voice, 'Let's get outta here!'," says Harvey. "Andy's scheme to uncover the truth continues with the floating ax and the baseball bouncing down the stairs. I realized that some of the audience may not have caught on to Andy's discovery and ruse yet, so I had Big Jack and Otis come out of the paneling to explain everything."

Meanwhile, Barney and Gomer realize that Andy is not with them. Barney believes Andy is still inside and courageously goes to get him.

"The audience knows about Otis and the moonshiner's presence in the house before Barney," says Harvey. "It was absolutely vital that Barney swallow his fear and go in the house to rescue Andy. He had avoided any direct contact with the spooks, but when Andy might need him, Barney, shaky knees and all, will respond. It was important for Barney to overcome his fear because I didn't want him to be a non-dimensional figure who goes through the whole story just being scared."

After seeing the floating ax and hearing the footsteps, Big Jack and Otis make a fearful retreat out the front door. As Barney enters the house from the back, he sees the floating ax and the moving eyes of Old Man Rimshaw's portrait and almost faints. Andy calls out, "Barney, wait. It's OK, it's me."

"Barney does get a bit faint when he sees the floating ax, but I would never have him actually faint," says Harvey. "It's a matter of degree, but if Barney really fainted it would be much too broad and unbelievable. Barney is affected by the happenings but not to the nth degree. Besides, I wanted Barney conscious. I needed his lines and presence to make the remainder of the scene work."

Andy pulls down the ax that he strung to the ceiling and tells Barney they now have to bust up a still. Barney then takes the stance that he thought it was "something along them very lines." The two then head toward the cellar to bust up the Rimshaw "spirits."

Ernest T. Bass Joins the Army

EPISODE #99

FIRST BROADCAST ON OCTOBER 14, 1963

WRITTEN BY JIM FRITZELL AND
EVERETT GREENBAUM

DIRECTED BY RICHARD CRENNA

HOWARD MORRIS RETURNS
AS ERNEST T. BASS

"My late brother worked for a movie-titles producer named Saul Bass. On Mr. Peepers, *Jim and I called the football coach Frank T. Whip, and that's where the T came from. Ernest had the proper rhythm."*

Everett Greenbaum

"Ernest T. Bass Joins the Army" begins with Andy and Barney sitting in the squad car. As the townspeople walk by, Andy and Barney discuss each one. It seems the doctor made Mrs. McKnight lose weight because "her ankles were too skinny to hold up all that heft." Mrs. Devereaux "is just as ugly as homemade soap." Cecil Gurney "has two sets of false teeth." When Barney see Viola Slat walking toward them, he drives away because she "is the biggest gossip in this town. Once she gets started, you never hear the end of it."

"My script does not open with Andy and Barney gossiping about the townsfolk," says writer Everett Greenbaum. "The dialogue about Mrs. McKnight, Viola Slat, and the others must have been written by either Andy or Aaron."

As Barney drives down the street, he and Andy see a group of men scuffling on the sidewalk. The two break up the scuffle and discover Ernest T. Bass at its center. Ernest T. caused the disturbance when he tried to break into the "soldiering" line of potential enlistees waiting outside the army recruitment office.

Ernest T. tells Andy he wants to "soldier." Andy suggests that Ernest T. go on home because the army's "no place for you." An army sergeant who has come outside to see what the ruckus is all about encourages Ernest T. to stay. He announces that they will take all able-bodied men.

Before leaving, Andy and Barney warn the sergeant about Ernest T. Andy believes the sergeant would make a mistake to take him, while Barney simply says, "He's a nut."

"I don't remember how we came about doing this one," says Everett. "We knew that Andy and Aaron Ruben loved Howard Morris as Ernest T., so we knew a funny story line featuring him was likely to be approved.

"Andy informs Ernest T. that he is in the *soldiering* line. Soldiering was a real word used in England. I thought it sounded right for Mayberry."

Ernest T. stays in the soldiering line and eventually gets his physical examination. The doctor begins the exam by probing inside Ernest T.'s mouth with a stick. Ernest T. tells him that the inside of his mouth will be nicer after he gets his gold tooth. Ernest T. explains that he plans to knock out his three front teeth and "put the gold one right in the center—leave a space on each side." He explains that it will stand out better that way, "especially when I'm dancing."

The doctor tests Ernest T.'s hearing by having him repeat numbers. The doctor says a number and slowly walks away as he says the other numbers. The doctor is unaware that Ernest T. is following right behind. The sergeant informs Ernest T. that he is supposed to remain standing where he was. Ernest T. tells the doctor that if he did that, he might not hear him.

"We realized that lots of funny physical-examination scenes had been done previously in movies and on TV, but we decided to write an examination scene because we knew that Ernest T. would bring a wildness to it that had not been seen before," says Everett.

The sergeant has seen enough. He tells Ernest T., "Boy, was that sheriff ever right about you. OK, buddy, out. We're turning you down."

Ernest T. becomes angry when he realizes he's "not going to get my uniform" and swears revenge on everyone—especially Andy.

After lunch, Andy and Barney return from the diner and discuss the eighty-cent meal they have just finished—"three Vienna sausages, heavy on the tomato purée, a slice of bread, and a pat of butter on a paper dish." During the conversation, Andy and Barney discover that they both left Olive, their waitress, a quarter tip. Barney suggests that he go back to the diner and put his hat down on one of the quarters to retrieve it.

"Every morning for thirty years I had to listen to Jim tell me what he had for dinner the night before," says Everett. "The idea to have Barney and Andy discuss their meal was inspired by this. Jim and I also enjoyed describing awful meals and jumped at the chance to work it into the script.

"Barney's concern about the abundant tip grew out of our memories of when having a quarter was like owning a treasure. So, the Depression played its part in the Griffith show."

The sergeant enters and warns Andy about Ernest T.'s sworn revenge. Moments later the front window of the courthouse is shattered.

Andy, Barney, and the sergeant step outside and see Ernest T. retreating down the street. Referring to Ernest T., Barney again comments, "He's a nut."

"Sometimes we would repeat a short sentence throughout a script," says Everett. "It usually had a humorous effect and was called a reprise. Barney's 'He's a nut!' description of Ernest T. is an example of this, and we used it several times for a laugh."

Later that day, Andy gets several telephone calls about broken windows. From the calls he realizes Ernest T. is coming their way. Andy goes to the back and Barney goes to the front to wait for Ernest T.

When Ernest T. meets Barney in front of the office, he says, "If I'd a seen you coming, I'd knowed what to do. I'd a-riz both arms, and I'd a-wove at you." Barney then orders Ernest T. "to stand still." Ernest T. replies, "If a duck stands still, you can catch him by the bill."

"Ernest T.'s rhyme, 'If a duck stands still, you can catch him by the bill,' is in my script, but 'If I'd seen you coming' isn't," says Everett. "Howard Morris made up some of the rhymes, and the second one was his creation."

Andy quietly sneaks up behind Ernest T. while he is taunting Barney. After a struggle, Andy locks Ernest T. in a cell.

The next morning, Barney has breakfast at the diner. The customer sitting beside him at the counter is reading a newspaper. Barney asks the fellow to pass the sugar. As the man lowers the newspaper, Barney discovers that it is Ernest T. Bass. Barney marches Ernest T. back to the courthouse and locks him in the cell.

Barney calls Andy to ask if he let Ernest T. out of the cell to get breakfast. Andy says he did not. Barney then goes to pick up Andy.

While Barney is away, Ernest T. escapes again. Andy and Barney chase Ernest T. all over town but are unable to recapture him. Andy spots the delivery men bringing a new window for the courthouse. Andy and Barney follow the two men delivering the window, well aware that if Ernest T. is still in town he won't be able to pass up the opportunity to break the new window.

As the two men near the courthouse, Ernest T. jumps from behind a storefront with a rock in hand. Barney orders Ernest T. to stand back and says, "Now you drop that rock, and you get over here." Emphasizing the command with a backward gesture of his pistol, Barney shatters the new window.

The gesture is the end result of the serious thought given to how Barney would break the window in a natural and credible way. "Barney's breaking the new window was another addition to our script," says Everett. "It's a very good idea and was either added in a rewrite or worked out on the stage during rehearsals."

As the episode continues, Ernest T. takes off down the street. His route leads Andy and Barney back to the courthouse. The two enter and find Ernest T. relaxing on his cell bunk.

The fact that Ernest T. can get in and out of the locked cell is making Andy and Barney nervous and angry. Ernest T. tells Andy that he will continue to escape until Andy gets the army to give him a uniform. When Andy tells Ernest T. that it won't work if he joins the army, Ernest T. reveals that he had no intention of joining the army. He just wanted a uniform for "girls and love." He had noticed how the girls "flit around Jelsick Sturman when he come back home with his uniform. 'Jelsick, walk with me. Jelsick, dance with me. Jelsick, kiss my mouth'."

"By this time we had learned what Howie Morris could do with certain words, so we tried to find them," says Everett. "The name 'Jelsick Sturman' and the line, 'Kiss my mouth' contained some great sounding words and were perfect for Howie's unique pronunciation."

Pondering Ernest T.'s problem out loud, Andy wonders where they could find a small-size uniform. When he looks at Barney, Barney protest that he had his uniform made in Raleigh and that it's "genuine whiplash cord."

A short time later, Ernest T. exits the courthouse proudly wearing a uniform. He is followed by Andy. As Ernest T. marches away, Barney emerges dressed in a raincoat and white panama hat. He watches Ernest T. depart and says, "There goes a happy nut."

"The idea for Barney's 'genuine whiplash cord' uniform came from Jim's army life," says Everett. "After giving the uniform to Ernest T., we put Barney in a raincoat. The white hat that he wears in the filmed episode was added on the stage during rehearsals."

In the epilogue, Barney is searching Ernest T.'s cell. He finds a fork under the mattress and calls Andy into the cell. Barney slams the cell door shut, sticks the fork into the lock to demonstrate how Ernest T. unlocked the door, and turns the fork—nothing happens. Andy and Barney are now locked inside. The keys are in the filing cabinet. When

Andy asks, "What do you suggest we do now?" Barney answers by yelling, "Help!"

"We always thought the audience loved to see 'here we go again' epilogues, so we concluded this script with the boys locking themselves in the jail cell," says Everett. "Aaron never asked us to repeat a gag, like this one, which had been used successfully in previous episodes. I think he was always hoping we'd write a new one."

Opie the Birdman

EPISODE #101

FIRST BROADCAST ON SEPTEMBER 30, 1963

WRITTEN BY HARVEY BULLOCK

DIRECTED BY RICHARD CRENNA

"This script was a gem from the start."
Aaron Ruben

Wynken, Blynken & Nod one night
Sailed off in a wooden shoe
Sailed on a river of crystal light—
Into a sea of dew.

Eugene Field

"'Opie the Birdman' is one of my favorites," says writer Harvey Bullock. "Despite that, my memories about its origin are unclear. I'm uncertain whether or not the story originated at the Griffith show seminars in which a half-dozen writers would meet two or three days in the off-season with Aaron Ruben, Sheldon Leonard, and, sometimes, Andy to collectively pitch story ideas. Or it may have been an individual story idea I pitched to Aaron. However, I know it was one of Aaron's favorites, and he scheduled it to open one season."

The episode begins with Barney tutoring Opie in the history and shooting technique of slingshots. In his younger days, Barney asserts that he was "a pretty good shot." He could perform numerous tricks—"Over the Mountain, Behind the Barn, Under the Bridge"—but his best shot was "The Tail Gunner." Barney's lecture concludes with a visual demonstration. Against Andy's protests, he performs the "Tail Gunner" and accidentally breaks the glass in the bookcase.

"Someone off-camera threw a stone, or perhaps even used a slingshot, to break the bookcase on cue," explains producer Aaron Ruben.

Andy warns Opie to be careful with the slingshot. In his front yard, Opie shoots into a tree and accidentally kills a bird. The bird falls to the ground. Opie walks over to the bird, gently picks it up, and begs it "to fly away." When there is no response, Opie becomes upset. He drops the bird and runs into the house.

On the way into the house that evening, Andy stops to pick up the newspaper and notices the dead bird. He hears chirping overhead, looks up, and sees a nest containing baby birds.

Opie has no appetite at supper. During the meal, Andy says to Aunt Bee, "Next time you see Mrs. Snyder tell her to keep her cat at home. That thing killed one of our songbirds today." Aunt Bee responds that it couldn't because Mrs Snyder is visiting her sister and took her cat with her. Opie immediately gets up from the table and runs upstairs. Andy now realizes what happened to the bird.

One of the strengths of TAGS was its attention to realistic detail. During the supper scene numerous cooked foods (sweet potatoes, rolls, etc.) are visible.

"The property department with its own kitchen, complete with pantry, stove, and refrigerator, usually prepared the food," says Aaron. "Nothing was ever thrown away. After the scene was over and the food was no longer needed, there were plenty of volunteers to polish off the leftovers."

Andy enters Opie's bedroom and finds Opie on his bed. Opie admits that he killed the bird and gives his slingshot to Andy. When Opie says he's sorry, Andy replies that sorry won't bring the bird back. "Sorry is not the magic word that makes everything right again."

Opie asks if he is going to get a whipping. Instead, Andy walks to the window and raises it. The chirping of baby birds fills the room. Andy says, "That's those young birds chirping for their mama who's never coming back. You just listen to that for a while." Andy then walks out.

One interesting aspect of the background in this scene comes when Andy opens the window. The curtains fluttering in the breeze add a realistic touch. This was an interior studio set and an off-camera wind machine was used to make the curtains move.

"During production I realized that 'Opie the Birdman' was special because it had so many outstanding elements: death, guilt, redemption, humor, and, most importantly, the wise and judicious way Andy handled the situation—sparing the rod but teaching a child how to solve his own problems," says Aaron.

"The fact that Andy does not whip Opie is the most vital treatment of the story," concurs Harvey. "Physical punishment would have reduced the situation to a trite single-dimension, two-party standoff, an unequal confrontation between angry adult and guilty boy. It is far more interesting that Opie has to be his own punisher while Andy is the enlightener."

The next morning, Opie is up early. Andy walks onto the front porch and finds Opies fixing breakfast for the little birds. Opie has decided that he is going to feed them since it is his fault that their mother won't be coming back. Opie names the three birds Winkin, Blinkin, and Nod.

"A writer's mind is like a huge cluttered attic," says Harvey. "If you seek to write, become an eclectic reader to help stuff your attic with word toys. Not necessarily formal knowledge but all sorts of neat nonsense.

"The names for the motherless songbirds, Winkin, Blinkin, and Nod, were inspired by a prowl through the attic. Seeking a fun-named threesome, those names popped into mind. I liked the sound and rhyme, so in they went—by the way, Wynken and Blynken are misspelled in the script. The names come from a lullaby poem by Eugene Field."

Andy looks on as Opie admires his songbirds.

A few days later, Mrs. Snyder returns from visiting her sister. During breakfast, Mrs. Snyder's cat cries out. Andy, Opie, Barney (who has stopped by to pick up Andy), and Aunt Bee realize that the cat may be attacking the birds and rush outdoors.

The birds are put in a cage for safety and placed on the Taylor front porch. After they admire the birds in their new cage, Andy warns Opie that he will soon have to let them go.

A few weeks later, Barney stops by to pick up Andy and give Opie a lift to school. While Opie is upstairs getting his books, Barney mentions how much the birds are growing. Andy tells Barney that "we both know them birds are big enough to be off on their own."

Andy decides to talk with Opie about the birds when he comes down. When Andy mentions that the birds have been flopping around in their cage, Opie answers that "maybe we should get a larger cage. They need a bigger place." Andy agrees, but Opie suddenly realizes Andy is referring to turning the birds loose. Opie feels he "just can't." Andy reminds Opie that he took over for the bird's ma, and she would have let them go "to be free like they was intended to be."

Opie knows what he must do. He removes the cage from its stand and walks to the front yard. One by one he sets his birds free.

The script directions following the release were as follows: "Opie pauses, looks up at the trees. Cut to tree—shooting over Opie and Andy. High lift shot. The chorus of songbirds is heard."

"It seemed dramatically fulfilling to end the scene with a high lift shot," explains Harvey. "I indicated the camera angle because it was ultra-important to the action. In rereading the ending scene I see my script called for Barney and Aunt Bee to appear at the screen door. In the filmed scene they were not used—a wise decision, probably made by the director."

In the epilogue, Andy is talking on the telephone. He tells Otis that Otis forgot his pocket transistor radio. Andy says he will keep it until Otis comes back. Andy places the radio in the top drawer of his desk.

Barney enters with a fish bowl. He has bought Opie some goldfish.

Andy asks Barney if fish talk to one another. Barney answers, "Of course they do. They've made recordings of fish talking to one another down on the bottom of the ocean." Andy secretly opens the desk drawer and turns on Otis's radio.

As Barney leans over the bowl to feed the fish, he hears voices. He asks Andy if he hears talking and proudly nods that his statement is confirmed. At that point, Andy pulls the radio out of the drawer and says he'll turn it off if it "bothers you."

"The epilogue was shot as a continuous scene [two minutes in duration] because there were no dramatic moments that needed highlighting, no need for closeups for reactions," says Aaron. "It was just a closing joke and needed no stops or interruptions."

The epilogue is somewhat flawed by an omission. It was probably shortened because the episode was running too long. After hearing a voice coming from the direction of the fish bowl, Barney was to say, "I gotta get away. I've been under strain." This dialogue implies that Barney questions what he is hearing. The dialogue is omitted, however, from the filmed scene, and it hurts the character. Barney would not unquestioningly believe that fish communicate in human voices.

Overlooking this minor weakness, "Opie the Birdman" is an exceptional TAGS episode. There is a magical quality to it that leaves the viewer with the feeling that the writer, production crew, and actors got everything exactly right.

"From the first, I felt the story was solid and watching it grow was delightful," says Harvey. "And it typed fast, which is usually an indication the script flows well.

"Sometimes words or expressions just spring into existence on their own, totally unbidden. It's one of the most awesome and joyous experiences in writing when the paper suddenly comes to life. It seems to push you aside and, for a brief moment, the story takes over and literally writes itself.

"I have one keen memory of this. I was completing the final scene in which Andy and Opie go out in the front yard to release the young birds Opie has raised. I was typing away. I got them outside, and Opie released the birds. Suddenly, I stopped, unsure of exactly what to say. But the typewriter kept going. I looked in amazement at the words being typed out. I was only a spectator, the story was writing itself."

The following words were typed on the paper:

> Opie looks upward, then he turns and looks at the empty cage, its door open.
> OPIE: (wistfully) Cage sure looks awful empty, don't it, Pa?
> ANDY: Yes, son, it does. But don't the trees seem nice and full.

"I never rewrote even a comma," says Harvey. "It went right into production just like it was. It was without doubt the best ending of any of the shows I did. I'd gladly give proper credit to the real writer—if I only knew who he was!"

Up in Barney's Room

EPISODE #104

FIRST BROADCAST ON DECEMBER 2, 1963

WRITTEN BY JIM FRITZELL
AND EVERETT GREENBAUM

DIRECTED BY JEFFREY HAYDEN

ENID MARKEY GUEST STARS
AS MRS. MENDLEBRIGHT

"I enjoyed directing the Griffith show. The scripts were terrific, and the cast was great. We had a good time, and I think it shows."

Jeffrey Hayden

"I'd been directing the *Donna Reed Show* for three consecutive seasons when I received a call from Aaron Ruben," says Jeffrey Hayden. "Bob Sweeney had left, and Aaron needed someone to direct. I directed eight episodes and left at the end of the season to work on one-hour dramas.

"The atmosphere on the Griffith show was the best. Everyone was very loose and pleasant, which was very conducive to good work. There were a lot of laughs in between the hard work of rehearsing and shooting the script."

"Up in Barney's Room" begins with Barney outside the Mendlebright Park Apartments. He has been grocery shopping, but the sign outside the apartments states: "No Cooking." Barney looks around to be sure the coast is clear. He hides his groceries in his pockets and under his shirt.

Inside the house, Mrs. Mendlebright is talking to Mr. Fields. Mr. Fields has recently moved to Mayberry and is pleading with Mrs. Mendlebright to give him a room. According to Fields, part of the appeal of the Mendlebright apartments is Mrs. Mendlebright herself because she is nice.

Barney enters the house and is stopped by Mrs. Mendlebright. She introduces Barney to Mr. Fields. When Barney shakes Fields's hand, the handshake causes a bottle of milk, which Barney has hidden under his shirt, to slip. As Barney adjusts the bottle, Mrs. Mendlebright asks if something is wrong with his back. Barney answers, "It's just that dampness and humidity kinda work on my disks sometimes." Mrs. Mendlebright is concerned and tells Barney to go lie down awhile.

"Barney's landlady, Mrs. Mendlebright, was based on my landlady in a rooming house in New York," says writer Everett Greenbaum. "Enid Markey was a perfect Mrs. Mendlebright. By the way, in silent movies she was the first Jane in a Tarzan film."

Barney goes to his room, removes his groceries from his clothing, sets a hot plate on Mrs. Mendlebright's dresser, and prepares a pot of chili. When Andy drops by to bring Barney's paycheck, Barney offers Andy a little chili and a glass of sweet cider. Andy declines the offer.

The master shot of Barney's room is photographed with the camera positioned behind Mrs. Mendlebright's dresser. "I would roughly work out the master shot and the other camera angles at home the night before a scene was shot," says Jeffrey Hayden. "These would then be adjusted and readjusted after rehearsing the scene with the actors."

Andy looks around Barney's room and notices that Barney has made a lot of changes since Andy's last visit. Barney proudly points out that he has "picked the room right up" with a "set of bound copies of *True Blue Detective* magazine that go back to 1959." Barney's walls are decorated with his old Mayberry High School pennant and framed copies of newspaper clippings.

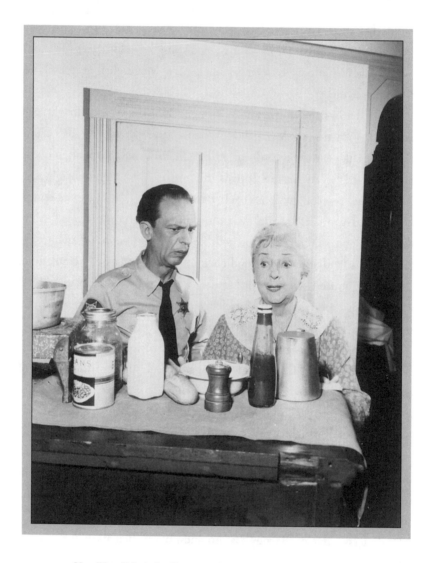

Mrs. Mendlebright discovers Barney cooking in his room.

TAGSRWC Archives

"The appearance of Barney's room was important in bringing the script to life," says Everett. "Several items were added to our description of the room's decor. In my copy of the script, I don't have the magazines. In place of the bound volumes, we had a hunk of driftwood, which Barney considers great art because he thinks it looks like a horse. The Mayberry High School pennant and the framed newspaper clippings were the proud contribution of the set decorator."

The chili begins to burn! Mrs. Mendlebright knocks on the door, and Barney quickly hides the hot plate in the top drawer of the dresser.

Mrs. Mendlebright enters the room, discovers the hot plate, and becomes very upset. She notes that the dresser "came by bus all the way from Fort Lauderdale."

"People always bragged about items of furniture which had come with them from Europe," says Everett. "We gave this a comic twist and placed a dresser in Barney's room that came all the way by bus from Fort Lauderdale."

Mrs. Mendlebright also removes Barney's 75-watt light bulb from its socket. She reminds Barney that "the rule is no bulbs over 40 watts." Mrs. Mendlebright has seen Barney sleeping with the light on and accuses him of being afraid of the dark. This angers Barney, so he calls Mrs. Mendlebright a "snoop and a bulb-snatcher."

"Jim and I both lived in rooming houses during our struggling days," says Everett. "Forty-watt light bulbs and cooking on a hot plate were part of that experience, and we included them in this script."

Mrs. Mendlebright asks Barney "to kindly leave my house. There is someone [Mr. Fields] who is a real gentleman who can use this room."

Barney agrees to do so "with pleasure." He gathers his belongings and leaves.

Barney decides to temporarily live in the back room of the courthouse. He moves his belongings in and decorates the room.

Barney proudly shows the back room to Thelma Lou. He offers Thelma Lou some sweet cider before dinner, but Thelma Lou declines. Barney plugs up the hot plate and begins cooking dinner.

Later that evening, Andy and Opie are walking home after a movie. The movie starred Gregory Peck. As the two walk, Opie comments that Gregory Peck "has an accent." Andy explains that's because "he's a Northern person." Opie mentions that the last time they had seen Gregory Peck in a movie, "he talked like you." Andy explains, "That's the actor of the man."

"The movie Opie is referring to was *To Kill a Mockingbird*," says Everett. "I can't explain how we invented the speech patterns such as Andy's 'actor of the man.' You just picture a character in your mind and let him or her talk."

As Andy and Opie approach the courthouse, they notice the lights flickering off and on. Barney and Thelma Lou are still inside. Barney has Thelma Lou cornered against the wall. Everytime he turns off the lights and sneaks a kiss, Thelma Lou playfully turns the lights back on.

Andy and Opie enter. Barney quickly opens the filing cabinet and hides his lipstick-smeared face. Opie walks over to the filing cabinet and begins telling Barney about the movie. Barney mumbles a reply, but Opie continues to talk. Barney finally becomes aggravated and pulls his face out of the filing cabinet. When Opie sees the lipstick, he thinks Barney's face is bleeding.

Andy returns from the back room and quickly ushers Opie out. Before walking out, Andy sternly whispers to Barney, "You better get yourself a room."

"The scene in which Andy and Opie walk in on Barney and Thelma Lou in the midst of a passionate moment was fun to write," says Everett. "When you come up with a natural comic set-up, like Barney hiding his lipstick-covered face in the filing cabinet, the writing begins to flow."

Barney's efforts to find a room are unsuccessful. He and Andy discuss the situation. Andy suggests that Barney apologize to Mrs. Mendlebright, but Barney feels it won't do any good because she's already rented the room. Andy still thinks it's worth a try.

Andy and Barney drive over to Mrs. Mendlebright's. Although Barney

Andy and Opie walk in on
Barney and Thelma Lou during a passionate moment.

TAGSRWC Archives

agrees to talk with Mrs. Mendlebright, he insists that he'll "bend a little but no crawling."

Barney and Mrs. Mendlebright apologize to each another, and Barney pleads to have his room back. Mrs. Mendlebright then tells Barney that she is giving up the rooming business and selling her house because she's getting married.

In response to the news, Andy proclaims, "No you're not!"

Andy Griffith's timing, tone of voice, and expression are perfect. His response is an example of an actor taking a simple line and making it special.

"We wrote simply 'no'," says Everett. "Andy improved it with a little bit of the way he himself speaks. He is, after all, a man of great talent."

Mrs. Mendlebright says she plans to marry Mr. Fields. Andy wishes the couple well, but Barney later tells Andy he "doesn't like it. I hope it ends in a quickie Mexican divorce."

"Mexican divorces were common in California at the time but wrong for Mayberry," admits Everett. "We decided to use it in the script anyway because the phrase contained good words for Don Knotts to pronounce."

The next day, Barney is standing outside the bank. Mrs. Mendlebright comes out and tells Barney she and Mr. Fields are going to buy a house in Raleigh. Mrs. Mendlebright has just drawn out her savings to help make the down payment.

Barney decides Fields is up to no good and rushes to the courthouse. When he gets to the office, he bumps into Andy, who is standing beside the water cooler. Barney causes Andy to spill a cup of water.

The water cooler is located beside the bookcase near the back room. Earlier in the episode, when Barney is moving his belongings into the courthouse, the cooler is positioned in its normal location between the jail cells. The spilled water helps communicate Barney's urgency. So the cooler, an important prop, was repositioned to simplify Barney's movement.

Barney tells Andy about Mrs. Mendlebright's withdrawal and his suspicion that Mr. Fields is attempting to "pull the old take-her-money-and-run game." Andy decides the best thing to do is to call the state police and get a rundown on Fields. The state police agree to call Andy as soon as the rundown is completed.

Barney drinks a cup of sweet cider while waiting for the telephone call and explains the logic behind his suspicions: "A) A guy moves into town. B) He has no job. C) He wants to marry Mrs. Mendlebright."

The cider brings back pleasant memories of Mrs. Mendlebright and life at the rooming house. Barney tells Andy that he and Mrs. Mendlebright used to have a glass of cider together every evening. "We'd go out on the porch and sit, drink cider, count cars."

Mrs. Mendlebright reminds Barney of his mother. He reflects that "she's a good soul" and "the most faithful member we got at church." Barney recalls the time Mrs. Mendlebright received a white Bible.

"Sitting on the porch and counting cars was a pastime in my hometown of Buffalo," says Everett. "A white Bible was a common award in Sunday schools."

While Andy is listening to Barney, he is seated at his desk. He picks up the gavel and begins marking on it with a pencil.

"Andy's wonderful business with the gavel was not scripted. It was his own input," says Everett.

Barney continues to drink cider. He repeats the logic behind his suspicions: "A) A guy moves into town. 2) He has no job. C) He wants to marry Mrs. Bendlemight."

Hearing the illogical numbering and mispronounced name, Andy looks carefully at Barney and proclaims, "Barney, you're gassed!" Andy takes Barney's cup, smells its contents, and realizes the cider has turned hard.

"I can't explain the creation of Barney's 'A - 2 - C'," says Everett. "It's just comedy writing. And yes, you can get drunk on hard cider."

Meanwhile, Mr. Fields is getting Mrs. Mendlebright gassed on the cider left by her former tenant.

The telephone call from the state police finally comes. Fields is indeed a con artist—"a bunko man all the way."

Andy and Barney hurry to Mrs. Mendlebright's. They arrive in time to catch Fields running off with Mrs. Mendlebright's purse.

Andy explains the situation to Mrs. Mendlebright. Barney comforts her, the two embrace, and have a tearful reconciliation.

A Date for Gomer

EPISODE #105

FIRST BROADCAST ON NOVEMBER 25, 1963

WRITTEN BY EVERETT GREENBAUM
AND JIM FRITZELL

DIRECTED BY RICHARD CRENNA

MARY GRACE CANFIELD GUEST STARS
AS THELMA LOU'S COUSIN,
MARY GRACE GOSSAGE

"I remember the 'guys' really enjoying this episode."

Aaron Ruben

"This was one of our favorites. It was one of the wonderful times in the business when the writing and the casting came together perfectly."

Everett Greenbaum

"**A**s time went by, we realized Gomer Pyle was becoming a big hit," says writer Everett Greenbaum. "This script was written after Aaron Ruben called us wanting a new show featuring Gomer. We met Aaron and suggested a couple of story ideas. Aaron decided which one to use. We then went back to our workplace, made a two-page outline, got it approved the next day, and got to work writing.

"This was the way we worked most of the time. Early on in the show, before the season began, there were daily conferences with Andy, Sheldon Leonard, Aaron Ruben, and the writers in attendance. For a week we came up with story ideas and by week's end it was decided who would write which shows. This practice was later ended by the Writers Guild because the writers were actually working that week for nothing."

The filming of the completed script was overseen by director Richard Crenna. "Dick Crenna was one of the stars on *The Real McCoys* with which Sheldon Leonard was associated," says Aaron Ruben. "Sheldon was also executive producer of the Griffith show. Maybe Dick asked Sheldon for a chance to direct, or maybe Sheldon saw some potential in Dick as a director. Dick was fine as a director. Actors, for the most part, make good directors since they enjoy a kinship and sympathy with the performers they are directing."

"A Date for Gomer" begins as Andy and Opie are exiting the barbershop. Andy has just gotten his hair cut for the Chamber of Commerce dance on Saturday night. Through the shop window, Floyd can be seen readying the barber chair for his next customer. A close viewing of the scene reveals that an extra, rather than Howard McNear, is portraying Floyd Lawson.

"The reason Howard McNear does not appear in the episode could be due to the fact that he might have been too ill," explains Aaron. "Or, since there wasn't anything of substance for Howard in the piece, we just used the barbershop locale. It was a neat way to set up the Saturday night dance."

Opie asks Andy to give him a ride home, but Andy can't. It seems Barney is using the squad car for "a very important mission."

Barney is actually making an ice-cream delivery to Thelma Lou's house. The ice cream, "West Indian Licorice Mocha Delight," was purchased at "Murphy's House of the Nine Flavors."

"Murphy's House of the Nine Flavors was a combination of two local firms—International House of Pancakes and Baskin Robbins Thirty-one Flavors," explains Everett.

The telephone rings while Barney is at Thelma Lou's. It is Thelma Lou's cousin, Mary Grace Gossage. Mary Grace is coming to Mayberry for a visit.

"Jim and I had used Mary Grace Canfield in New York on *Mr. Peepers*," says Everett. "We knew she was going to play Gomer's date, so we named her character Mary Grace Gossage."

Mary Grace's visit causes a problem. Thelma Lou can't go to the dance with Barney and leave Mary Grace all alone. Thelma Lou tells Barney they'll have to get her a date or Thelma Lou won't go.

Barney remembers meeting Mary Grace previously. He recalls that Mary Grace was not very attractive. In fact, he describes her as "a dog." Barney doesn't think he can get her a date, but Thelma Lou insists that he ask Andy to take Mary Grace to the dance.

Andy declines because he's taking Helen Crump. Andy and Barney discuss other possibilities, but the bachelors they think of are either unavailable (Nate Bushy is taking his mother) or not right for Mary Grace (Luke Taft hits the sauce). Barney feels "we've got to get a guy who's not been around too much. Some guy with not too much upstairs, in other words, a real dope." Just as he finishes his statement, Gomer Pyle enters the courthouse.

Andy asks Gomer if he's given any thought to the dance, but Gomer hasn't. Barney then asks if he'd like to "come along with us in the company of a young lady?" Barney tells Gomer he knows a young lady who is dying to go but doesn't know anybody in town because she's a stranger. Gomer asks if she's pretty, to which Barney and Andy respond that "she's so nice."

"'She's so nice' was dialogue used in our time when friends tried to convince you to take a blind date with a girl unknown to you," says Everett.

Gomer agrees to take Mary Grace to the dance.

Thelma Lou is not enthusiastic about Barney's selection. Barney assures her that if she "took the trouble to get under all that oil and gasoline smell, you'd find a heck of a human being." Thelma Lou reluctantly agrees.

After Mary Grace's arrival, Thelma Lou and Helen tell her about the dance and her date. At first, Mary Grace is hesitant, but she eventually agrees to go to the dance with Gomer.

Thelma Lou telephones Barney at the courthouse to tell him that the date is set. Barney is ecstatic. He hangs up and demonstrates his dance steps.

The scene in which Barney demonstrates his dance steps begins with the camera positioned behind the corner file cabinet. The camera pans left and stops at the map that hangs on the wall behind Andy's desk.

"The decision to use this camera angle was made by the director," says Everett. "Ordinarily, cinematographers and directors do not like the writers to suggest camera angles, unless it is necessary to understanding the story."

Gomer comes by to show Andy and Barney the "whole new set of accessories" he has purchased. Gomer proudly shows off a pair of yellow non-porous socks, a brown belt with a horseshoe buckle on it, a purple tie with acorns on it, and a pair of $8.00 shoes.

"Gomer's accessories were typical of Jim Fritzell's stuff," says Everett.

Gomer feels the money he spent on the "matching things" is worth it because "this Mary Grace could be Miss Right." Andy advises Gomer not to "over expect." Barney explains, "What Andy is trying to say, Gomer, is during our lifetime we travel many roads. There are big roads and little roads, rocky roads and smooth roads. . . " Andy interrupts and says, "Gomer, do me a favor. Just don't over expect."

"Barney's 'we travel many roads' monologue arose from his love to preach now and then, especially when he was talking to someone more ignorant than himself," says Everett.

Andy, Barney, and Gomer meet at Andy's house before the dance. Aunt Bee insists on ironing Andy's pants because no nephew of hers is going to a dance with "wrinkled knees." Opie asks Gomer if this is the first time he has been out with a girl. Gomer asks if cousins count, but Opie doesn't think it does. Gomer replies, "Then this is the first time."

"Seeing Aunt Bee help Andy get ready added to the importance and suspense of the big date," says Everett.

"Aunt Bee's and Opie's appearances added some color and a human touch, along with providing us with some pleasant jokes," explains Aaron.

Gomer is nervous and asks Barney what they will talk about. Barney assures Gomer that "a million things will pop into your mind, you'll see." Gomer replies, "It's easy for you Barney, you're so 'swave' and worldly. And you've been out with waitresses and even a registered nurse."

"The importance placed on dating a nurse came from dirty boyhood talk. The hottest women were nurses, preferably registered," says Everett.

Andy, Barney, and Gomer drive to Thelma Lou's to pick up their dates. The couples sit and talk before leaving for the dance. Andy comments on the weather, and everyone agrees the evening is perfect. The conversation lags. Andy recalls an incident from earlier in the day. He says a shaved collie dog walked into the grocery, and Al Becker was standing there. Andy stops and asks if anyone knows Al Becker. No one does. Andy stops his story and says, "It doesn't mean anything if you don't know Al Becker."

"I don't remember the shaved collie dog, but Al Becker lived across the street from me in Buffalo," says Everett. "The device of Andy's unfinished story is a surprise to the audience, and we used this technique a lot."

At this point, Gomer jumps up from the sofa, says, "Would you folks excuse me, there is something I got to do," and walks out the door.

Mary Grace claims she has a headache and insists that the others go on to the dance without her. Thelma Lou and Helen reluctantly agree.

One of the funniest moments in the episode occurs as Andy, Helen, Barney, and Thelma Lou are departing for the dance. Barney escorts the angry Thelma Lou to the back seat of the squad car and proceeds to "have a little fun." The camera immediately cuts to Andy and Helen in the front seat, and a sharp off-screen punch is heard. The camera pans from front seat to back revealing Barney holding a handkerchief to his wounded nose.

"The off-screen event that leads to a laugh is a higher form of humor, which pleases the audience because they've figured out what happened on their own," says Everett.

A short time later, Mary Grace answers a knock on the door. It is Gomer with "your flowers—your cor-sage." Gomer explains that he noticed the other girls had one and she didn't. Gomer left to get the flower because it wouldn't be right for Mary Grace "to go to the dance unadorned." Mary Grace invites Gomer in.

"We wanted Gomer to be loved," says Everett. "And so, he was good." Gomer's goodness is beautifully expressed when he gives a corsage to the "unadorned" Mary Grace.

Thelma Lou refuses to get out of the car at the dance because she has a headache. Helen thinks it's best if she stays in the car with Thelma Lou. Barney doesn't want to go inside and "stand in no stag line with old Mr. Perkins and a bunch of slumped-over teenage boys," so Andy decides to drive everyone back home.

The two couples are surprised when they return to Thelma Lou's and hear loud music coming from inside the house. They open the door and find Gomer and Mary Grace dancing. The couple's concluding dance is a celebration of two "nice" people setting physical appearances aside and enjoying one another's company. Gomer prances over and says to Andy and Barney, "You know something? She's just like you said. She's nice. She's real nice."

"For the closing scene we included the script directions, 'they are doing a wild jazz dance,' hoping Jim Nabors could dance," says Everett. "And he was terrific!"

"Gomer had instant popularity," says Aaron. "It wasn't long before Andy was urging me to come up with something for Jim. Happily for all, that turned out to be *Gomer Pyle, U.S.M.C.*"

Citizen's Arrest

EPISODE #106

FIRST BROADCAST ON DECEMBER 16, 1963

WRITTEN BY JIM FRITZELL
AND EVERETT GREENBAUM

DIRECTED BY RICHARD CRENNA

> *"By this time, we knew how Jim Nabors would say, 'Citizen's arrest!'."*
>
> Everett Greenbaum

"Citizen's Arrest" begins with Andy and Barney sorting through some old files. The two sing as they work.

"The singing that opens this episode was not scripted," says writer Everett Greenbaum. "Andy and Don loved to sing together on the set, and sometimes on camera. I imagine Andy selected the song after it was decided that singing would be a good way to begin the episode."

Barney comes across "some of old Sheriff Pinkley's stuff" and asks Andy if he should keep it or throw it out. Andy sees that the paper is a record of the arrest of Purcell Branch for riding down Main Street in a Reo Flying Cloud with the cut-out open.

"The Reo Flying Cloud was an actual car built, I think, in the thirties," says Everett. "The cut-out was a switch that bypassed the muffler.

When the switch was turned on, the car made more noise and went faster."

Barney asks Andy if he took over after Pinkley. Andy lists the names of all the sheriffs who proceeded him. Barney asks where Frieberger, a name Andy had not mentioned, fit in. Andy answers that Frieberger was a sewer inspector. When Barney says that Frieberger once gave his father a speeding ticket, Andy jokingly remarks, "Maybe your daddy was speeding through a sewer."

"The name of the overzealous Mayberry sewer inspector was borrowed from Freddie Frieberger, a fellow writer and friend at the time," says Everett.

Andy continues sorting through papers and comes across the custody receipt for the first revolver Barney was issued. According to the receipt it has been ten years and one month since Andy swore Barney in. Andy tells Barney, "I owe you a lot, Barn. I really do. We been through a lot together. You been a fine deputy. A true public servant. You can feel right proud of yourself." Barney is overcome with emotion and becomes teary-eyed.

"Jim and I enjoyed exploring facets of the Mayberry characters," says Everett. "After all, we were with them for years. We ended the opening scene with Barney getting emotional over Andy's praise for the fine job he has done as deputy. We enjoyed developing Barney's sentimental side because it made the character multi-dimensional, and Barney's emotional displays were usually comical."

Later that day, Barney is sitting in the squad car observing traffic. He sees Gomer walk out of the post office, get into his truck, and make a U-turn. Barney immediately turns on the car's siren and pursues Gomer. When Gomer stops, Barney demands an explanation for the U-turn. Gomer answers that he's in "an emergency vehicle." Barney makes the point that the vehicle is not on an emergency run by reaching into the truck and examining Gomer's mail— "a postcard and a copy of *Mechanics Monthly*." Barney takes out his ticket book and writes Gomer "a ticket for committing a 911."

"The idea to use a U-turn in the story came about because I had gotten tickets for two illegal turns that year," says Everett. "The 911 code number Barney cites for the violation was made up. We never verified any of the numbers we gave the various violations with an actual code book."

As Gomer protests the ticket, a crowd attracted by the commotion begins to gather.

When Barney hands Gomer the ticket, Gomer mumbles a response. Barney asks, "What was that?" And Gomer answers, "You just go up an alley and holler fish."

"'You just go up an alley and holler fish,' was one of my mother's sayings," says Everett. "It meant 'hush up' and came from the vendors who sold food in the alleys of her Philadelphia childhood."

Barney explains to Gomer that the law must be upheld. He says if he was just "plain John Doe, an ordinary citizen" and saw someone making a U-turn, he'd have to make "a citizen's arrest."

At this point, Barney gets into the squad car, backs up, pulls away from the curb, and makes a U-turn.

Gomer immediately yells, "Barney, stop! Citizen's arrest! Citizen's arrest!"

Barney stops the car and explains to Gomer that "this little black-and-white baby here [the squad car] is a *real* emergency vehicle." Gomer points out that Barney wasn't on an emergency call and orders Barney to write himself a ticket. The crowd gathered around the two cheers.

Attracted by the cheering, Andy comes over to investigate. When the situation is explained, Andy asks Barney to write himself a ticket. Then they can go to the courthouse and settle everything in private.

Andy repeatedly asks Barney to write out the ticket. Barney finally complies but becomes furious while doing so.

In the courthouse, Barney explodes in anger. He refuses to pay his five dollar fine and will not allow Andy to pay it. Barney removes his badge, places it on Andy's desk, and locks himself in a cell. He says he prefers to serve five days in jail rather than pay the fine. Barney tells

Andy that "when word gets out that your deputy, and ex-best friend, has been jailed for a minor offense, you'll be the fool."

That night, Andy returns to the courthouse to check on Barney. Barney has started smoking during Andy's absence. As Andy approaches his cell, Barney marks off a day on his cell calendar and asks, "What did you come back for, bed check?"

"All of Barney's in-jail behavior (his smoking, marking off the days on the calendar, and asking Andy if he would like to make a bed check) was inspired by Edward G. Robinson and James Cagney gangster movies," says Everett.

Andy asks Barney if he is going to stay in the cell all night. Since Barney is determined to remain in the cell, Andy walks toward the door. A drunken Otis enters.

Otis sees Barney behind bars and becomes confused. Otis thinks Barney is out and he's the one locked in the cell. He then looks at Andy, standing beside him, and realizes Andy wouldn't be in a cell. Otis panics and says, "I ain't in, and I ain't out. I'm in the twilight zone."

"Otis's dialogue in response to seeing Barney behind bars was an acknowledgment of the popularity of the series created by Rod Serling," says Everett. "By the way, Rod used to follow Jim and me around New York before he got started."

Andy explains to Otis that Barney is in—he's a prisoner. Andy escorts Otis into his cell and Otis begins to sing, "I'm Sorry I Broke Your Heart, Mother." The singing irritates Barney, so he yells, "Pipe down, Otis!"

Otis can't resist taunting Barney. He taps on his cell bars with a tin cup and chants, "Barney's in jail. Barney's in jail."

"We used Otis as a comic antagonist for Barney in this script," says Everett. "The song Otis sings was specifically requested in our script. The idea to have Otis tap the cell bars with a tin cup (the jailhouse code for 'Barney's in jail') was borrowed from gangster movies. Having Barney and Otis fight was funny, but only in short doses."

The next morning, Barney comes out of his cell and hands Andy a letter of resignation. Andy accepts the resignation calmly and tells Barney he'll take it to the town council the first chance he gets. Andy then walks out.

Surprised by Andy's reaction, Barney walks slowly back into his cell and closes the door behind him. The clang of the door startles him. He looks back at the door and realizes that perhaps he is also closing the door on his work as a deputy.

The renewal of Andy and Barney's personal and professional relationship is set in motion when Opie stops by Wally's Service Station. Opie tells Gomer that Barney quit. He tells Gomer that it all started with the citizen's arrest. Gomer is stunned by the news. Opie continues his story staying, "Barney gave Pa his resignation and then he went to sleep. Pa said to Aunt Bee, 'He made his bed, let him sleep'." As Opie leaves, Gomer says his famous line, "Tell your Aunt Bee Gomer says, 'Hey'."

"Opie's misinterpretation of a statement or a situation was a comic approach we seldom used," says Everett. "A little use of childish misunderstanding was OK, but at the time, Jim and I felt it was overused in radio and TV.

"We concluded the scene with the phrase, 'Gomer says, "Hey".' We somehow thought that 'so and so says hey' was widely used in the South. Maybe we were wrong, but the phrase was right for Gomer."

After talking with Opie, Gomer decides to take action to get Andy and Barney back together. He telephones the courthouse to report a robbery. Because Andy is not in the office, Otis, who is still sleeping in his cell, answers the telephone. Otis tells Barney that there's been a holdup at Wally's. Otis runs out, yelling for Andy, but Barney remains locked in his cell.

Andy learns of the holdup and rushes to the station. Upon seeing Andy, Gomer immediately asks if Barney came with him. Andy tells him to forget Barney and explain what happened. Gomer explains that since he was the one who got the two apart, he thought he'd try to get them back together. He tells Andy he faked the robbery hoping "you and Barney would come together."

Just then, Barney comes running up. He knew Andy would need someone to cover him. Andy tells Barney that Gomer turned in a false alarm. This angers Barney, and he decides to "throw the book at Gomer." Barney writes out several tickets.

After issuing the tickets, Barney walks to the squad car, tells Andy to "come on," and drives away—making a U-turn. Gomer runs after the departing car, yelling at the top of his lungs, "Citizen's arrest! Citizen's arrest!"

"We always enjoyed writing for Gomer and loved watching Jim Nabors perform the role," says Everett. "However, I'm sad to say, we never got to know Jim very well. As soon as *Gomer Pyle, U.S.M.C.* became a hit, Jim became very popular and very social. I recall years later, while being interviewed by Maureen Reagan, President Reagan's daughter, she bragged to me that she was friends with Jim long before President Ford's daughter even met him."

Barney and the Cave Rescue

EPISODE #109

FIRST BROADCAST ON JANUARY 6, 1964

WRITTEN BY HARVEY BULLOCK

DIRECTED BY RICHARD CRENNA

"The differences between this script and the film are sizable. Andy's telling the legend of Lost Lovers' Cave, Barney's dialogue about bats/moths 'flying in your hair,' and Gomer's 'skunk' story were not in the original script. Each was likely the work of Aaron Ruben and was added in the rewrite."

Harvey Bullock

"When Ray Saffian Allen and I were writing *Dick and the Duchess* in London, we were constantly in search of stories," says writer Harvey Bullock. "Somewhere along the line we mulled over a possible rescue story, but it didn't fit the show, so we never developed it. But the idea stuck in my mind and eventually led to the 'Cave Rescue' script."

Harvey's script begins with Andy talking to Helen on the telephone. Helen tells Andy she is taking an apple crumb pie to the town picnic. Andy informs her that Gomer will take care of things at the office while he and Barney attend the picnic.

At this point, Barney and Gomer come out of the back room. Barney is familiarizing Gomer with the layout of the courthouse. Barney points out cell number one and cell number two.

"I began the script with Barney giving Gomer his final instructions: 'Cell #1 is on the right, #2 is on the left,'" says Harvey. "I had no way of knowing whether the cells were numbered one and two in previous episodes by other writers. I was only trying to load Barney with extraneous information to pontificate to Gomer. All of the TAGS writers were free-lance, working alone and remote from the studio. We did not collaborate with one another or even know what stories others were doing."

Gomer is dressed in a deputy's uniform. The uniform's shirt sleeves are too short, the shirt's cuffs and collar are unbuttoned, and the narrow end of Gomer's tie is longer than the wide end.

"Gomer's appearance in his deputy's uniform was not described in the script," says Harvey. "My guess is that the wardrobe people simply duplicated his tie (with the narrow end longer than the wide end) and his ill-fitting uniform from his previous appearance as a deputy."

As Andy leaves the courthouse, he is surprised to see Mr. Meldrim, the bank president, opening the bank on Saturday morning. Meldrim explains that he has a bank examiner coming, so he has been working long hours to prepare for the audit. As a result of the stress, he has a terrible cold and frequently wipes his nose with a handkerchief. Meldrim has trouble unlocking the door because the lock sticks.

The inclusion of Mr. Meldrim in the script has some problems with consistency in his appearance in previous episodes. In the episode, "Up in Barney's Room," originally broadcast two weeks earlier, the name of Meldrim's bank is "Mayberry Bank." In this episode, the name of the bank is "Mayberry Security Bank."

"I don't know if the name 'Meldrim' was purposely written by me," says Harvey. "More likely, Aaron Ruben had done a previous script using the character and changed the name I had scripted for consistency. There is no name of any sort on the bank building in my script. I imagine the name change was just an oversight by the prop department."

The bank examiner arrives, and Andy departs.

Meanwhile, Barney and Gomer are walking down the street. Barney is instructing Gomer to walk through the business district every once in awhile to check what's going on. As Barney looks toward the bank, he sees Mr. Meldrim, but his face is covered by his handkerchief. The man is struggling with the locked front door. The bank examiner is standing with him. Barney deduces that the bank is being robbed.

Barney puts his bullet in his revolver and bravely crosses the street to apprehend the thieves. Barney sneaks up behind the two men only to catch Mr. Meldrim trying to get into his own bank.

Two of the town's loafers see the incident. After Meldrim is identified, they find the situation hilarious. They laugh at and taunt Barney.

Barney returns to the courthouse. He is embarrassed by his mistake. He wants to avoid anyone who might laugh at his error, so he tells Andy that he may not be able to go to the picnic because the paperwork in the office has "been piling up something awful."

Andy asks if his decision has anything to do with "that ruckus over at the bank." Andy tells Barney he did exactly the right thing. "A good lawman can't afford to take chances. Not when he's protecting others."

Barney reconsiders and decides to attend the picnic.

Just then, Opie runs into the courthouse and asks Andy if it's true that Barney pulled a gun on Mr. Meldrim at his own bank. As Opie says that everyone is laughing about it, Andy quickly ushers Opie out the door.

Andy tells the dejected Barney that at the picnic, they will get off by themselves and have their "own private picnic."

At the picnic, Andy, Helen, Barney, and Thelma Lou go off by themselves. The two couples set up their picnic a short distance from "the old mine cave." Andy suggests they explore the cave before eating. Barney doesn't like the idea, so Andy and Helen leave Barney and Thelma Lou at the picnic site and go exploring.

As the two enter the cave, Andy tells Helen that the place was called Lost Lovers' Cave when he was a boy. Andy says the story was that two Indian lovers went into the cave, got separated, and never did come out again. He then adds that even now, if somebody calls out, a voice will answer. Andy yells, "Where are you?" An echo answers.

"The exterior scenes in this episode were shot at Franklin Canyon, where we photographed the opening credits with Andy and Opie walking by the lake," says producer Aaron Ruben. "We only spent one day shooting the exterior scenes, even though a large part of the episode centers around the cave. We reduced the time spent on location by rehearsing many of the exterior scenes on the stage at the studio.

"The cave, made of synthetic material painted with earth colors, was constructed on a stage. The sound engineers easily duplicated Andy's echo."

Thelma Lou eventually talks Barney into exploring the cave. As the two enter the cave, Barney tells Thelma Lou that he never liked caves. He says, "You know what you find in caves? Bats! You know what they do? They fly in your hair and get tangled up in there and lay their eggs, and you go crazy." When Barney hears a noise overhead, he covers his head. Thelma Lou points out that the noise was only a moth. Barney replies, "Well, you don't want a moth in your hair either. They lay these moth eggs. You go crazy from that too."

Further inside the cave, Andy hears a rumble. It turns out to be a rock slide, and Andy and Helen are trapped.

Barney and Thelma Lou also hear the rumble and rush out. Moments later they realize that Andy and Helen are still inside. Barney says, "They're buried alive."

"The roof of the cave was scored in advance and gave way easily to pressure," says Aaron.

Inside the cave, Andy checks the debris left by the slide and realizes the passageway back to the cave's entrance is blocked. He suggests they go a different way, so they head deeper into the cave.

Outside, Barney sends Thelma Lou to the picnic grounds "to round up every able-bodied man." Barney goes back to town to get the emergency equipment.

Andy and Helen find a tunnel that leads to the other side of the cave. When they finally emerge from the cave, they are both covered with dirt. Helen doesn't want anyone to see her, so they decide to hitchhike back to town to clean up. Andy warns Helen that they will have to hurry "before some of them start missing us and worrying." Andy stops a passing motorist, and they ride back to Mayberry.

Back at Helen's house, Andy listens to the radio while he waits for Helen to change. He hears a news bulletin that announces that an earth slide is believed to have trapped two people in a cave. The announcer reports that Deputy Barney Fife has organized the entire town in a "mammoth rescue operation."

Helen picks up the telephone to call the courthouse to report they are not trapped, but Andy stops her. He realizes how embarrassed Barney will feel "if we pop up. That ribbing he took at the bank this morning won't hold a candle to what he's in for now." Andy and Helen agree there has to be somebody in the cave for Barney to rescue.

"I agree with many viewers that the rescue story seems to have questionable timing and validity," says Harvey. "But I feel even stronger that, upon close inspection, elements in the story, although borderline, are in order and plausible.

"Andy and Helen escape from the cave and flag down a truck, but neither thinks anyone else is involved. Even though Andy says, 'We better hurry before some of them start missing us and worrying' this does not imply an overwhelming need for speed. What some viewers forget is that Andy is not in a real rush. He has no idea that, at that moment, Barney is trying to save them."

Meanwhile at the courthouse, Barney is removing the emergency equipment from the back room. While Barney continues to gather the equipment, Gomer tells "about the time my cousin Goober got himself lost in a cave. He was tracking a skunk." When Gomer finishes the story, Barney says to him, "Two people are trapped in a cave, and you stand there yakking about your stupid cousin Goober." Gomer thinks this over and replies, "My cousin Goober ain't stupid. He's ugly, but he ain't stupid."

A short time later, Andy and Helen reenter the cave through the back entrance.

Outside the cave's front entrance, Barney uses a megaphone to orchestrate the rescue. He calls out that "now is the time for all good men to come to the aid of their neighbor."

"As always, Barney takes pride in his pronouncements while instructing the crowd with the megaphone," says Harvey. "If there's a loose cliché around, he'll nab it. Professing authority is his favorite stance. Somewhere he's heard someone say, 'Now is the time for all good men to come to the aid of their party.' It pops into his mind, with the switch of the last word to 'neighbor,' and he's happy with it."

Andy and Helen take their places near the slide just minutes before Barney digs through. Andy and Helen are rescued!

Outside the cave, Andy tells the townsfolk, "It sure was a close call. I don't know what we'd have done if it hadn't been for Barney. It could have been any of us in there. I'd say we're pretty lucky to have a fellow like Barney Fife around." The townsfolk all agree.

As Thelma Lou and Helen stand in the crowd, Thelma Lou says to Helen, "That Barney's really quite a guy." Helen answers, "You're right, he certainly is. As a matter of fact, they both are." These simple lines speak of the close friendship between the two men and acknowledge the audience's awareness that Andy and Helen returned to the cave in order to be rescued by Barney.

"Thelma Lou and Helen's lines were not difficult to write," says Harvey. "As a writer you imagine what has occurred in the story and have the characters react to the situation. The hard part was manufacturing the story in an outline before one word of dialogue was written.

"Primarily, my intent was to tell an interesting story, but when Andy and Helen work to save Barney from humiliation, it teaches an important lesson in friendship. There is another more subtle moral as well—

that lawmen sometimes have to chance appearing ridiculous. A call might be laughable, but it could also be a major crime in progress. The man with the badge can't take the chance of not responding to what may subsequently prove to be a false alarm."

Andy and Opie's Pal

EPISODE #110

FIRST BROADCAST ON JANUARY 13, 1964

WRITTEN BY HARVEY BULLOCK

DIRECTED BY RICHARD CRENNA

DAVID A. BAILEY GUEST STARS
AS TREY BOWDEN

"This script is the simple tale of a boy who feels his father shares too much affection with another boy."

Harvey Bullock

"**A**ndy and Opie's Pal" begins with Opie walking down the street. He is dressed in a football jersey and carries a football. When Opie passes a boy sitting in a front yard, he stops and asks if the boy is "new around here." When the boy answers, "Uh-huh," Opie tells the boy that his football is "a genuine, full-size, regulation football they played with at a state college game." The boy shows little interest. When Opie asks, "You want to be friends," the boy answers, "OK." When Opie says his father is the sheriff, the boy immediately becomes interested.

At the courthouse, Barney is taking a complaint from Gomer by telephone. When Barney hangs up, he tells Andy that Gomer has just come from Pierson's Sweet Shop and is "all riled up again." It seems that the sweet shop is running a giveaway contest. If you purchase a peppermint that has a pink center, you get a free peppermint. If you get a green center, you win a flashlight. On Thursday Gomer bought ten lucky peppermints, all with white centers. Today, he bought twelve more; again all had white centers. Barney says that Gomer is not saying he expects to get a green center right away, but he does think he should have had at least one pink center out of the twenty-two peppermints he bought. Andy responds that he can't believe that Jesse Pierson would ever "run a fixed peppermint box."

"The idea for Pierson's Sweet Shop peppermint contest grew out of my early addiction to gambling," says writer Harvey Bullock. "The neighborhood store kept a box of chocolate mints on the counter for sale at a penny a piece. After you bought one, you immediately bit it in half and checked the color of the filling. Most of the centers were white, but every once in awhile you'd hit it big and bite into a colored center. If it was pink, you won a free mint. But if it was green, hold tight, you won a flashlight!

"I don't recall ever seeing a flashlight awarded, but I did see some pinks—enough to keep me coming back for more. It was exciting, the lure of something for nothing and the admiration of your gang who somehow thought winning a free peppermint was huge proof of masculinity. To have Gomer claim that Pierson runs a fixed peppermint box seemed funny, juxtaposing a gambling term on a most insignificant item."

As the episode continues, Opie enters the courthouse accompanied by his "brand-new friend," Trey Bowden. Opie introduces Trey to Andy and Barney.

Opie explains that Trey is his nickname. His real name is Frederick Bowden the third. Opie says, "Since he's the third, that's why they call him Trey."

"The new boy in Mayberry, Frederick Bowden III, a.k.a. Trey, was named after a neighborhood boy who was a friend of my son Andrew," says writer Harvey Bullock. "The boy's actual first name was Robert, but no one ever called him that. We all called him Trey, because both his father and grandfather were also named Robert Bowden. I liked the sound of Trey for a boy's name and filed it away in my cluttered brain."

When Andy asks Trey about his father, Opie answers that, "he ain't got a pa. He's dead." When Andy asks Trey how he likes "our little town," Opie again answers for Trey.

"Having Opie do all the talking when he introduces Trey to Andy was just a comedy bit to show Opie's initial wild enthusiasm about having a new friend," says Harvey. "It's not that Trey is the quiet type, it's just that he's in a strange room with a real sheriff, and he doesn't get the chance to talk with Opie bubbling over. Opie's enthusiasm contrasts nicely with the later quiet despair he suffers when he feels Trey has supplanted him in Andy's affection."

Before going out to play, Opie asks Andy if Trey can come fishing with them on Saturday and stay at their house that night. Andy says it will be all right with him.

Opie and Trey's new friendship causes Andy and Barney to reminisce about their own relationship. Their discussion reminds Barney of "a little set-to" concerning a visit by the Queen of the State Apricot Festival.

The Queen of the State Apricot Festival visited Mayberry and Barney thought he was going to be her escort. Instead Andy met her "at the city line and took her around." Andy had nearly forgotten "that little mix-up." Barney agrees, "That's all it was—a little mix-up" and continues talking. He recalls the actual date—"June 23, 1952 on a Saturday afternoon." Barney reflects momentarily on what happened and adds, "Patterson's, three ninety-five. Three ninety-five, that's what I paid at Patterson's for a brand-new shirt to meet her while you were off squiring her around." The more he thinks about it, the angrier he becomes. He says, "I stood out on that corner under a blazing sun for two hours waiting, while you two were off gallivanting around. Why should you take the Apricot Queen around? Who eats all the apricots around here anyway? I do, that's who."

"The term *set-to* means a disagreement or fight," says Harvey. "The June 23 date for the visit of the apricot queen was picked at random. The date had no significance except to Barney who will remember that date as the day that Andy took the apricot queen away from him."

After Barney calms down, Andy decides to go on patrol. Before leaving, he reminds Barney that he's invited to the Taylor house for supper that night.

That evening, Opie and Trey quickly finish their supper and rush upstairs to Opie's room. Andy, Barney, and Aunt Bee remain at the table. Aunt Bee picks up the bread basket and says, "One roll left." When she asks Barney if he would like it, he responds, "OK, but I hate to be the old maid."

"I would often include words or phrases in common usage when writing dialogue," says Harvey. "An example of this is when Barney eats dinner with the Taylors and reluctantly takes the last roll. He says in explanation, 'I hate to be the old maid.' That expression was frequently said by anybody who took the last of any dish."

After hearing Trey and Opie bumping around upstairs, Andy recalls how he and Barney used to do the same thing whenever they spent the night together. The two would stay up most of the night, and Barney would "make up for it the next day by sleeping in Sunday school."

"Andy's dialogue about sleeping in Sunday school was inspired by a childhood memory," says Harvey. "As a child, my Sunday school classes were taught by one of the dads. These men were not teachers or public speakers, so often the class was deadly dull and the room overheated. If you had been out late the Saturday before, you were weary, and sleep would overtake you."

When the bumping gets louder, Andy goes upstairs to investigate.

The boys hear Andy coming, quickly jump into bed, and turn off the lights.

Andy tells the boys they have to get some sleep, so one of them will have to come in Andy's room. Opie gets up, but Andy chooses Trey to go to his bed. Andy explains to Opie that he'll bring Trey back as soon as he dozes off.

Opie gets back in bed. Opie overhears Andy asking Trey out in the hallway if he would like a glass of milk and a piece of pie. He lies in bed and thinks the situation over intently before falling to sleep.

The next morning, Trey is up early. When Trey joins Andy and Barney on the front porch, Barney notices that Trey is interested in the "old roscoe." Trey doesn't understand what Barney is talking about, so Barney explains: "Roscoe—revolver. That's what the civilians call it. We refer to it as a roscoe, or a heater, or an old persuader, or a rod."

Barney tells Trey that the important thing with any firearm is safety. Then Barney demonstrates a safe draw and accidentally fires the revolver into the floor.

Andy holds out his hand, and Barney places the revolver in it. Andy tells him to wait in the car.

"Barney's reeling off slang names for his revolver is not in my script, but the accidental firing of his weapon was," says Harvey. "I felt this gag had to be used judiciously, so it wouldn't wear out, but it proved to be hearty stuff, and all the writers got a lot of mileage out of it."

After Barney leaves, Andy checks the revolver to be sure it is empty and allows Trey to hold it. Opie watches the two through the screen door.

Later that day, Opie visits the courthouse and asks Andy if he, Andy, and Barney can go fishing without Trey. Barney enters the office through the back room. He has returned from putting gas in the squad car. As Andy steps into the back room, Opie sees Trey through the front window and goes outside. Trey asks if Andy is inside, but Opie tells him that Andy is busy. Opie tells Trey that he has to go to football practice. Since the team will be practicing secret plays, Trey can't come. Opie waits until Trey walks away and reenters the courthouse.

Trey walks around the corner of the courthouse and finds Andy getting into the squad car. Andy is going on lake patrol and invites Trey to come along. When Andy asks Trey where Opie is, Trey says he's at football practice.

Inside the courthouse, Opie asks Barney where Andy is. Barney says he's about to leave for lake patrol. Opie rushes outside just in time to see Andy and Trey driving away.

The mechanics of Opie missing out on the lake patrol provide an example of the careful attention given to detail. Barney enters the courthouse from the back room and parks the squad car on the side street. This allows a logical setup for Andy and Trey's out-of-sight departure when Opie enters the courthouse from the front door.

"My script does not have Barney entering the courthouse from the back room," says Harvey. "This detail was an important addition, however, because it explained why the car was parked on the side street instead of in its usual place in front of the courthouse."

After returning from lake patrol, Trey walks by the yard where Opie and his friends are practicing football. Opie and Trey argue and begin shoving each another. As Barney drives by, he sees Opie and Trey fighting and stops. He breaks up the "little tiff" and warns Opie that if his father found the two had been fighting, it would be "the end of you and Trey."

Barney returns to the courthouse, and Opie enters a short time later. He is covered with bandages and tells Andy that he and Trey have been fighting. He adds, "Guess I can't play with Trey anymore." When Andy lifts a bandage, he sees that there is no injury.

"I decided to have Opie put on fake bandages to convince Andy that he has had a fight with Trey, even though it could be argued that Opie was smart enough to know that his scheme wouldn't fool Andy," says Harvey. "I felt Opie might wishfully consider the bandages plausible. Also, Opie's not thinking too clearly because the possible alienation of Andy is bedeviling him."

Opie then says, "Well, I guess Trey can't come fishing with us tomorrow, uh?" Andy says he doesn't think so. Opie then responds, "Oh, well he's always horning in anyway. From now on, it'll be just you and me, pa."

Andy agrees and adds, "Just you and me will go fishing. Barney was coming, but just me and you will go off together."

When Barney hears that he won't be going along, his feelings are hurt. He storms off into the back room.

Opie questions Andy about excluding Barney. Andy points out that Trey was probably hurt just like Barney when Opie "pushed him off." Opie walks to the entrance of the back room and invites Barney to come fishing with them. Opie then walks to Andy's desk, looks at his father, and proceeds out the door.

After Opie leaves, Andy apologizes to Barney and explains that "the whole thing was just a pretend job. See, I had to show that youngun that you don't drop your friends just like that. It seemed like the only way I could get it across to him was to give him an example."

"My intention with this script was to tell a good story and give it dimension by centering on a pertinent moral," says Harvey. "This episode does deal with friendship. 'Barney and the Cave Rescue' had a similar moral, but, of course, the story was sufficiently different so as not to seem redundant."

That night, Opie stops Andy in the upstairs hallway. Opie tells Andy that he and Trey are friends again and that they can all go fishing tomorrow. Andy says they can call Trey first thing in the morning, but Opie says they won't have to. He leads Andy into his bedroom where Trey is asleep in Opie's bed. He is clutching the "genuine, full-size, regulation" football that Opie has given him. Andy tells Opie that Trey has "gotten something even better. Now he's got a genuine, full-size, regulation friend to match."

"I was very pleased with Andy's ending lines," says Harvey. "The constant mental shuffling of dialogue and ideas helped arrange their placement and later playoff. Sometimes, somehow, the muses take pity on a writer and whisper things like 'genuine, full-size, regulation' in your ear, and you realize what a gift it is—perfectly describing the football—and the boy."

Barney's Sidecar

EPISODE #112

FIRST BROADCAST ON JANUARY 27, 1964

WRITTEN BY JIM FRITZELL
AND EVERETT GREENBAUM

DIRECTED BY COBY RUSKIN

> *"At the age of fourteen, I bought the remains of a World War I Harley Davidson motorcycle in bushel baskets for $4.00. I actually got it running, and memories of that motorcycle inspired this episode."*
>
> Everett Greenbaum

"Barney's Sidecar" begins with Mrs. Beggs entering the courthouse. She explains that she has "just had the most frightening experience" of her life. While driving on Highway 6, a speeder almost ran her off the road. She says that "a woman was driving that car. She was wearing a green hat trimmed with pink baby roses, and a beige cloth jacket with buttons with furry middles like my sister Tilley has on her jacket." Mrs. Beggs goes on to tell Andy that "Tilley is a tall woman with long teeth. In school Tilley was called 'the Beaver.'"

"The humor in the Mrs. Beggs scene derives from the fact that a woman pays attention to completely different details from a man," says

Barney, seated in his sidecar

writer Everett Greenbaum. "Jim Fritzell was the inspiration for the comment about the sister Tilley. Her long teeth were Jim's teeth."

Andy ushers Mrs. Beggs out of the courthouse as Barney enters. When Andy tells Barney about "the speeder up on Highway 6," Barney offers to take the squad car out to the highway and "take a look-see." Andy declines the offer because he needs to use the squad car.

Then Barney suggests they set up a "checkpoint chickie" to "nip this speeding in the bud." Andy reminds him that they only have one car. Barney complains that police departments are the "lowest budgeted public servants of them all, but it's thank you, Johnnie Shaffto, when the guns begin to shoot."

"Barney's 'checkpoint chickie' came from the World War II phrase 'checkpoint Charlie,'" says Everett. "'Thank you, Johnnie Shaffto' was a line from a Rudyard Kipling poem."

Andy returns later in the day and finds Opie in the office. When Andy asks where Barney is, Opie says he doesn't know. He adds that Barney has not been there since he arrived. During this conversation, Opie is writing his name on a board using a wood-burning set that he got for his birthday. Andy asks him to take his wood-burning work home.

As Opie walks toward the door, he says "Abyssinia," to which Andy replies, "See ya Somoa."

"In the thirties it was considered clever to say 'Abyssinia' for 'I'll be seeing ya,'" says Everett. "The reply was 'See ya Somoa' for 'See ya some more a.' That farewell exchange came to mind as we were writing this scene, and it seemed to me that a young boy might say this to his father instead of goodbye."

As Opie leaves, Barney enters. He puts goggles, gloves, and a helmet on Andy's desk. Barney announces that he has been to the war-surplus auction in Mt. Pilot. Barney then asks Andy to come outside, so he can show Andy something. Andy complies.

Parked in front of the courthouse "is a mechanically perfect RJ 300 motorcycle"—with sidecar. Barney believes the motorcycle will be the answer to their problems. He can cover Highway 6 with the motorcycle while Andy is using the squad car. Andy asks what the sidecar is for. Barney answers, "Are you kidding? That's to carry fire-fighting equipment, guns and ammunition, room for another deputy in case of a raid, going back and forth to the store. Besides, that's the way it came."

"We made up the RJ 300 model number of Barney's motorcycle," says Everett. "The motorcycle, however, was based on the World War I Harley that I built as a teenager.

"I always thought sidecars were amusing. As a child, I was fascinated by one that was in my father's tire store. Jim and I agreed that a sidecar attached to Barney's motorcycle would be a wonderful prop and could be developed into some wonderful gags."

The next day, Barney marches into the office wearing a helmet, goggles, and leather gauntlets. Andy greets him by saying, "How you doing, Baron Von Richthofen?"

"Baron Von Richthofen was the leading German ace of World War I," says Everett. "In the comic strip *Peanuts*, Snoopy the dog fantasizes that he is the Baron—so he lives today."

Barney is upset by Andy's kidding. He takes off his helmet, sets it on the desk, and turns his back to Andy. Andy picks up the helmet, puts it on his head, and asks Barney what he thinks. Barney turns around. His eyes get big, and he says, "Don't wear my hat. I can't stand to wear a hat after it's been on somebody else's head. My mother was the same way."

"Barney's not wanting to wear a hat after it's been on somebody else's head and the comment that his mother was the same way, just bubbled up while Jim and I were writing," says Everett.

Andy apologizes and offers to take Barney to lunch to show there are no hard feelings. Barney wants to drive them to lunch in the new motorcycle. He says, "Big fellow, you're going sidecar express to the diner." Andy reluctantly agrees.

As Andy and Barney walk outside, a group of the "boys" are lounging around the door to the courthouse. Andy gets in the sidecar. Barney mounts the motorcycle and fires up the motor. Barney revs the motor, looks at Andy, and asks if he is ready. Andy answers, "Let her rip." Barney rides away, leaving Andy and the sidecar behind.

"I must confess, the joke about the unattached sidecar was not original," admits Everett. "We stole it from the Marx Brothers."

"We had a laugh machine that would take a laugh and cycle it," says Jay Sandrich, who was the assistant to the producer. "The machine had a small laugh with five or six people, a bigger laugh with ten or twelve people, and a really large group laugh. We never wanted the laughs to get too big since the laugh track's purpose was simply to help the audience sitting at home enjoy the show.

"One of the sound editor's responsibilities was to be sure there weren't too many laughs, that they weren't too big, and that the laughs fit the gag. Don Knotts was so funny that it was easy to insert a laugh at every single thing he did, but then there would be too many laughs. So, we tried to include a laugh only when there was something that was very funny.

"There was never any question about inserting a laugh as Barney rides away without the sidecar. In fact, it was one of the few times the large-group laugh was used on TAGS."

Andy laughs at the incident, but Barney is furious. Andy warns Barney that if he keeps the cycle, he is probably in for a lot more problems. Andy asks why Barney doesn't just make his life easier and get rid of it. Barney responds that "every thinking pioneer and inventor has suffered the same kind of ridicule. It's right there in your history books. Take Alexander Graham Bell. People laughed at him over the telephone. Wilbur and Orville, people practically laughed them right off Wright Air Force Base."

"The dialogue about how people laughed at Alexander Graham Bell because of the telephone and how people practically laughed Orville and Wilbur Wright 'right off Wright Air Force Base' grew out of Barney's tendency to pick up a lot of information and only retain some of it," says Everett.

Andy agrees that Barney can keep the motorcycle if he doesn't spend too much time in town. Andy tells him to patrol "way out on Highway 6."

Barney sets up a "checkpoint chickie" and begins stopping trucks on Highway 6. He stops a truck driven by Edgar J. Masters. Barney tells him, "Well, Eddie, I watched you doing forty miles an hour in a thirty-five-mile zone." Edgar Masters explains, "We've always had an understanding about it. We need that extra five miles an hour to get over Turner's grade." Barney gives him a warning and tells him to "move her [the truck] out."

"The scene in which Barney stops the truck driver, asks his name, and then calls him 'Eddie' was inspired by the fact that we had heard that New York City cops did the same first-name thing," says Everett.

At the end of the afternoon, Barney checks in with Andy. Barney tells Andy that "if you ride into the wind with your mouth open and you put your tongue up on the roof of your mouth, it's impossible to pronounce a word that starts with the letter *s*."

"Barney's dialogue about 'riding into the wind with your mouth open' is not in my script," says Everett. "It sounds to me like Aaron Ruben's writing."

Barney tells Andy that he gave out eleven speeding warnings. When Andy asks who was doing all the speeding, Barney answers, "El truckos."

"The Spanish stuff gave Barney a man-of-the-world pose," says Everett.

That night, the truck drivers protest Barney's warnings by loudly revving their engines and keeping the whole town awake.

During the next few days, Barney patrols the town on motorcycle. He gives out a number of tickets and warns motorists about reckless driving. As Aunt Bee exits the grocery, Barney rides by and frightens her. When she drops her groceries, Barney warns her about jaywalking.

The townsfolk complain to Andy that Barney is making "our lives miserable since he got that darn motorcycle." Even Aunt Bee tells Andy that he has to do something about Barney.

Andy helps Aunt Bee carry the groceries home. At home, Aunt Bee says, "You know, I saw this war picture once. These Nazis were riding around on motorcycles, and these guerrillas strung wire across the road so high, and when these Nazis came roaring through on their motorcycles—phfftt." As she says this, Aunt Bee passes her hand across her throat. Andy responds, "Aunt Bee, we don't want to kill him—maybe hurt him a little, but we don't want to kill him."

"The Nazi suggestion was not in our script, and I don't like it for Aunt Bee," says Everett.

As the episode continues, Andy notices a "familiar smell." Aunt Bee tells him that Opie is burning a new house number with his wood-burning set.

Andy goes to investigate and finds Opie burning the number right into the house.

"Jim and I committed many of Opie's mistakes, such as burning numbers into a house, so that is how we knew about them," says Everett.

Andy stops Opie and takes the wood-burner from him. When Barney roars by on the motorcycle, Andy looks at the wood-burner and gets an idea.

The next day, Andy brings some oilcloth to work. He wants Barney to fix up the torn cushion in the sidecar. He removes the cushion and hands it to Barney. Beneath the cushion, Andy finds a wooden plaque with an inscription. The inscription reads: "First motorcycle to cross the Marne River—Battle of Chateau-Thierry, 6-12-18. Passenger: Black Jack Pershing. Driver: Corporal Nate Jackson, A.E.F."

"The battle of Chateau Thierry, the Marne River, and Black Jack Pershing all existed, but we fictitiously bunched them together for the inscription on the plaque," says Everett.

Andy guesses the plaque was "probably done right in combat with a heated bayonet."

"Jim and I ran into a problem after we came up with the sidecar story line," says Everett. "We didn't know how to finish the story. Then we thought of placing a fake plaque under the sidecar's seat and went back to the beginning and put in Opie and the wood-burning set."

Andy tells Barney, "You don't have an ordinary cycle there, Barn. You got a monument on your hands." Barney responds, "You know, it probably ought to be on display someplace—like there in that Smith Brothers' Institution in Washington, D.C." Andy agrees. Barney realizes that Andy means he should give the motorcycle to them. Andy tells Barney, "Your first loyalty is to your town. We got a lot of World War I veterans right here—Al, Bert Stevens, the Milo Boys. Actually this cycle belongs over at the National Guard Armory between the Civil War cannon and the World War II jeep."

"I don't remember where the names of the Mayberry World War I veterans came from," says Everett. "But, 'Al, Bert Stevens, and the Milo Boys' sounded just right."

Barney understands he must give up the motorcycle. He can't, however, bring himself to drive the motorcycle over to the armory. He asks Andy to do it. As Barney turns away, he starts to look over his shoulder. Andy simply says, "Don't look back."

My Fair Ernest T. Bass

EPISODE #113

FIRST BROADCAST ON FEBRUARY 3, 1964

WRITTEN BY JIM FRITZELL
AND EVERETT GREENBAUM

DIRECTED BY EARL BELLAMY

HOWARD MORRIS GUEST STARS
AS ERNEST T. BASS

"You know, if you wrote this into a play no-body would believe it."

Barney Fife

"It was always fun doing an Ernest T. show. Howie was always 'up' and fun-loving, and there was never a dull moment when Howie was around."

Aaron Ruben

"The origins of the Ernest T. Bass character are somewhat hidden," says producer Aaron Ruben. "Apparently, we had talked about introducing a wild mountain character into the quiet and placid town of Mayberry. When the mountain character was decided on, we then looked for someone who could play this untamed and zany guy. I was familiar with Howie's talents, having worked with him on *Caesar's Hour*. Remembering how outrageous and funny Howie could be, both on and off camera, I thought he'd be an ideal choice."

"Aaron Ruben was one of the writers on *Caesar's Hour*," says Howard

Morris. "*Caesar's Hour* was one of the biggest variety shows, and the cast played all kinds of things—every kind of situation there was. As a member of the cast, I was involved in hundreds and hundreds of sketches.

"Aaron remembered the kind of talent and abilities I had brought to *Caesar's Hour*. I hadn't worked with him in some time, and I had never worked the Griffith show. Out of the blue, he called me and said, 'We have a character in an episode, and we don't know quite what to do with it. Would you look at it?' He sent me a script, and I looked at it. I called him up and said, 'I think I can fool around with this.' And he said, 'OK, we'll hire you then.' I came in, the cast read the script, then we did it, and they loved it so much they eventually wrote four more episodes.

"I don't know exactly where my portrayal of Ernest T. came from. Here I was, a guy born and raised in the Bronx of New York City with little or no connection with the South. I was, however, drafted before World War II and sent down to Wilmington, North Carolina, where I spent seven or eight months. I met people there, and I listened and watched. I apparently have a pretty good ear, and I picked up a lot.

"The character developed as I performed. The Griffith show producer and directors were very good to me. They allowed me to write the kind of poetry that I did—the rhyming thing. There were times when they didn't use it, but pretty much they gave me a great deal of creative freedom."

Howard's input was acknowledged and appreciated by the writers. "Howard Morris played Ernest T. perfectly," says Everett Greenbaum. "He added a lot to it in the way of pronunciation and physical moves.

"In 1963, the Broadway musical *My Fair Lady* was a hot ticket," says Everett. "I've always considered it the best American musical comedy, so Jim Fritzell and I decided to do it. We followed the plot of the show—the coaching and educating of Ernest T. and finally the big event, the ball, or in this case, the party at Mrs. Wiley's. But, it didn't seem right to have Ernest T. make a big success of his new persona, so we had him go nuts, ruin his chances. But, the episode ended on an up-note due to Ramona. By the way, when Mrs. Wiley says, 'He's from Back Bay Boston,' it is the same beat the Hungarian linguist uses in *My Fair Lady* when she says, 'She's royalty'."

The episode begins with a closeup of Ernest T.'s arm lifting a rock to throwing position. The camera pans backward to show the breaking of Mrs. Wiley's window.

"The window panes were made of candy set in a mold," says Howard. "It was called candy glass because it looked like real glass but broke harmlessly."

When Andy and Barney arrive, Mrs. Wiley tells the two that a man burst into the house uninvited and started acting in the "most peculiar manner." The man stuck his hand in the punch bowl, ate every bit of the watermelon rind, soaked the paper napkins in the punch, and threw them at the ceiling. The man also demanded "to meet a woman." Mrs. Wiley gives Andy and Barney the rock that the man threw through the window, thinking they "can study it for fingerprints." From Mrs. Wiley's description, Andy is positive the man is Ernest T. Bass.

Andy and Barney look for Ernest T. "on every street, in every store and restaurant, and even under two houses." They return to the courthouse. Andy parks the squad car, and he and Barney discuss what to do next. Andy tells Barney he wishes there was some way they could straighten Ernest T. out. Barney replies that nobody can. "The man's hostility is ingrained. It's carved in the deepest recesses of his subconscious id. I wouldn't touch his id with a ten-foot pole."

Throughout its production, TAGS was filmed with one camera. The scene in which Andy and Barney discuss Ernest T.'s id provides an excellent example of how this technique worked. Preparations for filming the scene began by positioning the camera alongside the driver's door of the squad car. This camera position provided the "master" print of the scene. The actors' performances were photographed by looking into the car over Andy's left side. After this shot was completed, the camera was repositioned alongside the passenger's door for the required secondary shot. The actors repeated their performances and were photographed by the camera looking into the car over Barney's right side. The on-screen version of the scene is the end result of carefully combining the two separately photographed viewpoints.

When Andy and Barney go inside the courthouse, Barney's old uniform, which was given to Ernest T. Bass the last time he was in town, is on Andy's desk. Ernest T. is sitting in one of the cells.

Ernest T. explains that the uniform did not have the effect on girls that he had anticipated. He says the girls "gazed right on through me" when he wore Barney's uniform. Ernest T. tells Andy and Barney he tried "courtin'" old Hog Winslow's daughter, Hogette. He wrote Hogette a love note, tied it to a rock, and tossed it through her front window. The rock "caught" Hogette on the head. The cut required seven stitches.

Andy suggests Ernest T. "give it another chance with Hogette." Ernest T. explains it's too late because Hogette married the "taxidermist what sewed up her head." Ernest T. feels the best thing to do would be "to find myself a cave and hermitize myself."

"After thirty-two years, all I remember about the Hogette Winslow story is that we had a name, Hog Winslow, and when Jim suggested his daughter be called Hogette, I laughed all day," says Everett.

Andy offers to help Ernest T. get a woman. Andy plans "to clean him up, teach him a few manners—maybe he'll even quit throwing rocks."

Andy begins by inviting Ernest T. over to his house for supper. Ernest T. joins Andy, Aunt Bee, and Opie at the table. Opie asks, "Mr. Bass, will you pass the bread, please?" Ernest T. picks up a piece of break and throws it to Opie. Aunt Bee reprimands him, and Andy explains, "You pass it. You don't throw it."

Andy asks Ernest T., "Would you pass the potatoes, please?" Ernest T. picks up a potato and hands it to Andy. Andy explains, "You don't pass one. You pass the whole thing." Ernest T. picks up every potato in the bowl and hands them to Andy.

After supper, Barney stops by to find out "how the big experiment with Ernest T. is coming." Ernest T. is upstairs cleaning up. Andy tells Barney that Ernest T. is "showing progress." Andy plans to keep working with him and try to pass him off at Mrs. Wiley's upcoming party.

Ernest T. stomps down the upstairs hallway, leaps over the banister, and jumps into a chair. Andy decides it's time to talk with Ernest T. about how to come into a room. Andy asks Barney to show Ernest T. the proper way to come into a room. Andy points out that Barney "is a perfect example of a young man-about-town." Ernest T. compliments Barney by saying, "You can afford to be mighty proud of yourself."

The colorful words and phrases that Ernest T. uses, such as "hermitizing," and "you can afford to be mighty proud of yourself," arose from the freedom the writers felt when creating dialogue for fictional characters.

"No one ever spoke the way our mountain people talked," says Everett. "It was just something that happened when Jim and I got into a room with a pile of yellow paper and a typewriter."

Barney agrees to show Ernest T. "how to come into a room." Before doing so, he quizzes Andy about what type of an affair he is supposed to be attending and the number of people present. Andy asks, "Are you gonna enter, or are you planning on bringing the sandwiches?" Barney angrily replies, "If you're gonna do something, do it right. There are different entrances for different affairs." He walks toward the door to make his entrance and mutters, "Jiminy Christmas."

"In middle America, my generation had many euphemisms for curse words," says Everett. "One was Jiminy Christmas."

Barney enters and silently mouths his amenities. Ernest T. and Andy are both thrown off by Barney's "mouth work."

"We had once written a scene for a show on *Mr. Peepers*, in which Tony Randall taught Wally Cox how to sell encyclopedias door to door," recalls Everett. "It was a case of the naive teaching the naive—only the first naif thinks he is the sharpest living human on earth. It worked well and fit the Barney and Ernest T. characters perfectly."

The night finally arrives when Ernest T. is ready to attend Mrs. Wiley's social. He is dressed immaculately. Barney stops by to drive Andy and Ernest T. to Mrs. Wiley's and doesn't even recognize him. This is one night Barney would "just love to be a wall at Mrs. Wiley's." Andy suggests that Barney join them at the social.

At the party, Andy introduces Ernest T. as Oliver Gossage, his cousin from Raleigh. Mrs. Wiley takes Oliver aside. She wants to get better acquainted. After hearing Ernest T.'s accent, Mrs. Wiley arrives at the conclusion that he must be from "Back Bay Boston."

Barney arrives while Ernest T. and Mrs. Wiley are talking. He is greeted by Andy. As Barney looks around the room, he comments that "Ernest T.'s sure got slim pickin's here. Dogs. Nothing but dogs. If you flew a quail through this room, every woman in it would point."

"The line 'If you flew a quail through this room . . . ' was suggested by a writer friend who had once gone away for a weekend at a popular resort back East," says Aaron. "It was a spot where unmarried young ladies went in search of husbands. On the weekend he was there, he walked into the dining room and looked at the many females at the tables who were, unfortunately, not very attractive. And like Barney he said, 'Dogs, all dogs,' followed by the 'quail' line."

Andy tells Ernest T. that he's "coming off like a million dollars." Andy suggests that Ernest T. "get a girl and dance a little." Andy points out Ramona Ancrum. Ernest T. gets the rhythm by bobbing up and down to the music and walks over to Ramona. She is "delighted" to dance.

Mrs. Wiley stops the music and announces that the next dance will be a tag dance. "When you're tagged you give up your partner." Ernest T. and Ramona begin the dance together. When Ernest T. is tagged and another man takes his place, he doesn't like it. He tags Ramona's new partner and is ignored. Andy tells Ernest T. "to give it [the tag] to him firm." Ernest T. tags the man and is again ignored. He walks to a table, picks up a flower vase, and breaks it over the man's head. At this point, Ernest T.'s cover is blown. Mrs. Wiley yells, "Oh no, it's him. That animal, that creature."

Andy and Barney wrestle Ernest T. out the door. Ernest T. eventually calms down and thanks Andy for trying to help. He decides to "give up his thoughts of femaling."

As Andy and Barney lead Ernest T. away, Ramona comes out on Mrs. Wiley's front porch and yells, "Mr. Gossage, wait. Wait for me." She runs to Ernest T. and asks, "You're not leaving, are you? I was hoping we could spend some more time together."

Ernest T. joyfully lifts Ramona off her feet and carries her across Mrs. Wiley's front yard. After he puts her down, the two leapfrog a stump and scamper away.

"We wrote that Ernest T. and Ramona leapfrog a hydrant," recalls Everett. "I guess there was a stump on the set but not a hydrant."

The stump that the couple leapfrogs was located one house away from the exterior set that served as the front of Andy's home. The familiar set can be identified by its oblong front window and twin-support porch columns that are present in the scene's background.

"Sets were often used a number of times with some minor changes to suit the locale," says Aaron. "It never concerned us that the audience would remember a set. We always felt the story was more meaningful than trivia."

"'My Fair Ernest T. Bass' began production on Thursday, November 21, 1963. The second day's production was interrupted by startling news," Howard recalls. "We were reading around the table and in came the assistant director Robert Saunders. He said, 'I have a very sad announcement to make. President Kennedy has been shot and killed.' Boy, were we upset! It delayed the production schedule for a day, but the show must go on, and it did."

"I remember coming out of my office onto the studio street to walk to the stage, having just heard the news," recalls Aaron. "And there was Howie wandering aimlessly, it seemed, a stricken look on his face. He was repeating loudly, to no one in particular, 'They killed him. They killed the President.' That evening many of the people connected with the show gathered at one of the actors' homes. We tried to console one another and read some meaning into this senseless tragedy. Like the rest of the country, we were in shock."

"I have no other specific memories of working on 'My Fair Ernest T. Bass' or any of the other episodes," says Howard. "They kind of run together as a very happy and joyful experience. It was a remarkable place to be, with these wonderful people, back in a better time for the United States and culture in general."

Prisoner of Love

EPISODE #114

FIRST BROADCAST ON FEBRUARY 10, 1964
(TO COINCIDE WITH VALENTINE'S DAY)

WRITTEN HARVEY BULLOCK

DIRECTED BY EARL BELLAMY

SUSAN OLIVER GUEST STARS
AS THE PRISONER

"Andy Griffith enjoyed this total departure."
Aaron Ruben

"Barney turns to look back toward the angel in the cell to make sure the vision really exists."

Directions from the
"Prisoner of Love" script

"**P**risoner of Love" begins with Andy and Barney talking outside the courthouse. It is early evening. A train whistle is heard in the distance. Barney tells Andy, "Know what I just might do tonight? Go home, change, drop by Thelma Lou's, and watch that George Raft movie on TV." Barney repeats the statement three times. Andy remarks that he might go over to choir meeting "because they're voting on new robes for next year."

"TAGS was the only show on television that could spend three or more minutes with just two men on a porch casually rocking and neither saying much of a thing—pure artistry," says writer Harvey Bullock. "I had previously seen a TAGS episode that had Barney repeating over and over what he planned to do later in the day. I thought the scene was wonderful and patterned the opening dialogue in this script after it.

"George Raft was a popular actor in the thirties and forties who performed in a zillion B movies. Whatever his part, he always played it the same way. He would stride into a room, hair slicked back, camel's hair coat draped over his shoulders, glossy patent leather shoes, and tell the gorgeous blonde, 'Grab your stuff. We're leaving.'

"Andy's remark about the pending crisis at the choir meeting over the color of the robes underscored to me the casual, laid back, affable, small-town atmosphere of Mayberry."

The evening's tranquility is interrupted by the ringing of the telephone. Andy answers the call and learns the state police have captured a criminal. They would like to "park" their prisoner in the Mayberry jail. The unexpected "guest" means that either Andy or Barney will have to stay overnight. Andy eventually agrees to do so because he wouldn't "feel right having Thelma Lou spend a whole evening alone in a dark room with George Raft."

Andy asks Barney to stay just long enough for him "to run over to the drugstore and get a magazine." The state police arrive while Barney is waiting for Andy's return. Much to Barney's surprise, the prisoner is a beautiful woman.

When writing the script, Harvey had a vivid image of the prisoner. He described her in his script as "breathtakingly beautiful. There is nothing of the criminal about her, nothing cheap or brassy. Her beauty is classic, soft, beguiling, feminine. The room, upon her entrance, pulsates with sex appeal."

"I named the prisoner 'Angela Carroll,'" says Harvey. "Oddly, as the writing progressed, I realized there didn't seem any need to mention her name. It wasn't a plot point or an enhancement to her extraordinary femininity.

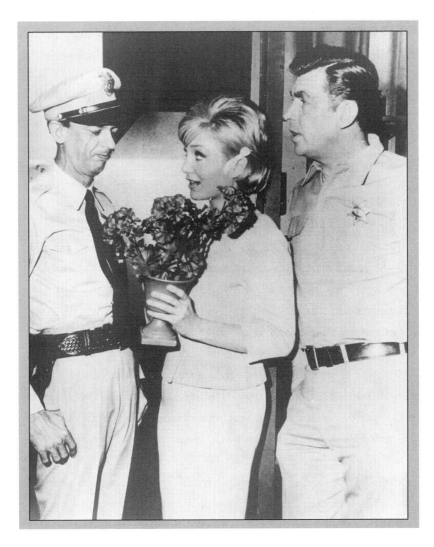

Barney and Andy with Angela, the prisoner

TAGSRWC Archives

"I wanted the prisoner's crime to be elegant, with high stakes but no violence. Grand larceny for stealing jewels seemed to me the type of crime someone like Angela, who was all charm and breathless beauty, would be charged with.

"I didn't know who would be cast in the role while I was writing the script and had no real nominees after the script was finished. But I had infinite faith in TAGS casting director Ruth Burch. The actress she selected for the role, Susan Oliver, was the perfect, absolute perfect Angela Carroll."

"Susan Oliver was indeed a joy to work with," says producer Aaron Ruben. "She was a fine actress and fit everyone's image of the prisoner."

"Whenever Barney was flustered, it was always solid stuff," says Harvey. "When it is in connection with a beautiful woman like Angela, he is rendered helpless. When Angela asks his name, Barney momentarily forgets. This gag was somewhat predictable, but again, Don Knotts made everything seem new."

Barney lights a cigarette for the prisoner. According to the script directions, "she blows smoke toward Barney, which he drinks in like perfume."

"Barney's lighting the cigarette for Angela was a typical romantic gesture of the sixties," says Harvey. "The smoke emanating from that Venus would be delightfully intimate, and Barney revels in it. If I wrote this script today, there wouldn't be a cigarette in sight. It would be a no-smoker script and just as effective."

After Barney's departure, Andy has his first conversation with the prisoner, which is interestingly photographed. A closeup shows Andy saying, "Evening." A second closeup shows Angela with no cell bars visible. She answers, "Evening." Andy then asks, "Are you the prisoner?" Angela replies, "That's what they tell me." As Angela rises from the bed, the camera pans backward. For the first time, the bars around her face become visible.

From the audience's point of view, nothing separates Andy and Angela in the preceding closeups. They are simply a man and a woman meeting each other. When the camera pulls back, revealing the cell bars, the true nature of their relationship is visually established.

Barney eventually returns and tells Andy that he "has checked in the paper about that movie, and it is one I have already seen." Andy and Barney decide they will both "guard" the prisoner. They make final preparations for the night by giving Angela an extra pillow and hanging a sheet in front of her cell. Both the pillow and sheet are taken from the other cell.

When the lights are turned off, the prisoner, silhouetted behind the sheet, prepares for bed under Andy and Barney's watchful eyes. The evening's quiet, however, is abruptly interrupted by the arrival of Otis.

"When the smashed Otis barged into the jail, it added some physical comedy to a conversational script and gave the story a bit more dimension," says Harvey. "Back in the sixties, the drunk was a standard character who could get laughs with his stupor. Writers would bring a staggering Otis into a scene without batting an eye. Over the past thirty years comedic drunks have gotten scarce. Too many families, blighted by alcoholism, don't find the drunk fool amusing."

Upon seeing the pillow and sheet missing from his cell, Otis says, "What happened? Hey, where's everything? There's been a drunk in this cell."

"Otis's speech makes sense only if he suspects crooks, not drunks," says Harvey. "How did this get by? In my script, the line is, 'There's been a crook in this cell.' Possibly this scene was the last shot of the day, or they were running behind time, or perhaps the director automatically associated Otis with a drunk and didn't catch the mistake."

Andy tells Otis they can't take him tonight. He must go home. Otis objects and demands to be locked up. Andy and Barney physically force him outside. Barney loses the flip of a coin to see who drives Otis home.

Andy and Angela have a friendly conversation while Barney is away.

At the end of the conversation, Angela asks Andy if he will help her open a troublesome lock on her case. Andy enters the cell, works on the lock, but becomes distracted by the proximity of Angela. The two look at each other longingly, but the possibilities of the moment are shattered when Barney is heard returning in the squad car.

Somewhat shaken by his attraction to Angela, Andy decides to go home and let Barney take over.

"This episode has become the subject of much argument with some viewers who say the story wasn't right for TAGS. Some say the characters acted differently from their usual roles, the attraction of upright Andy to a female stranger was distasteful, the show seemed dark, etc.," says Harvey.

"I did want this episode to be a little different by showing Andy involved and intrigued (if only slightly) with a Venus such as Mayberry had never produced. I had never before brought him face to face with a mind-numbing angel. And understandably, she did affect him. He found her company appealing—but so would the Pope!

"I guess from the start Angela tried instinctively to size up the rural jail for a means of escape. But more telling, she found herself for once with people who were not judgmental but genuinely friendly. The steady, upright Andy finds an attraction for the beautiful Angela—she's fun, appealing, and vulnerable. Nevertheless, Andy remains in control. He senses her loneliness and talks to her softly but never makes the slightest improper move. Andy shows a glimpse of his personal side. He is not totally cold steel, but he isn't foolish either."

Later that evening, Andy is edgy at home because he senses that Barney is no match for Angela. If Andy goes back to the courthouse, it might crush Barney who would feel he wasn't dependable and had to have every move double-checked.

Andy finally returns to the courthouse. He walks up to the door, reaches for the knob, then pauses, filled with self-doubt. He asks himself one more time if he really should vex Barney by checking on him. He is torn because he also feels the proper conduct of his job is paramount. He decides to chance the vexation and make sure that all is under control. Just as the decision is made, the door opens, and the escaping Angela walks out.

Andy escorts Angela back into the office and finds Barney locked in her cell. His earlier suspicion that Barney is no match for Angela is confirmed, and luckily the prisoner's escape has been prevented.

The train whistle heard in the opening scene foretold the episode's poignant epilogue. On her departure the next day, the prisoner says to Andy and Barney, "You both are kind of 'specially nice guys. I really mean it. And if things were different, well. . ." This is indeed a rare and bittersweet moment in Mayberry—a place where most often things are as they should be.

Hot Rod Otis

EPISODE #115

FIRST BROADCAST ON FEBRUARY 17, 1964

WRITTEN BY HARVEY BULLOCK

DIRECTED BY EARL BELLAMY

"We shall meet, but we shall miss him
There will be one vacant chair . . .
We shall linger to caress him
When we breathe our ev'ning prayer."
"The Vacant Chair"

"I began this script with Andy and Barney playing a game of gin rummy because it was a typical jailhouse pastime," says writer Harvey Bullock. "The game also provided the opportunity to have Otis advise Barney which card to play. Otis's poor advice results in an argument between the two and prevented what could have been a wordy opening scene from becoming terminally bland.

"Otis is somewhat unstable even when sober, so Hal Smith could play the character as broadly as he wished, at times even childlike. When Barney scraps with Otis this childlike attitude rubs off on him, and he ends up arguing on Otis's terms and vernacular.

"I ended this scene with Barney saying to Andy, 'He [Otis] sure does soak up the sauce, doesn't he?' If Andy had responded with an easy reply, he would have answered, 'He sure does.'

"This would have been dialogue standing still. Instead, I wanted to move away from having Andy's reply being nothing more than just a colorless agreement with Barney. I tried a new tack rather than the predictable and had Andy respond with mock reproach, 'Now, Barney, is that any way to talk about your card partner?'

"This is a minor illustration of dialogue construction. Not a big thing, but a very helpful maxim for writing interesting dialogue. And Andy Griffith made the most of it. He was always superb at twisting lines, pulling off repetition with the correct spin, admonishing with the right twinkle, and closing out scenes with finality."

After the card game, Andy leads Otis to his cell. Before going to sleep, Otis asks to be "called at 8:00 in the morning."

The next morning, Barney wakes Otis at 8:00 A.M. Surprisingly, Otis is pleased. He asks Andy for a sip of his coffee as he exits his cell. Otis explains that today is the day he is going to buy something he has always had his heart set on. Andy and Barney question Otis about his purchase, but Otis wants to surprise them and refuses to say any more.

"Otis's request for a sip of Andy's coffee was scripted," says Harvey. "The request and Andy's compliance were intended to show how close Andy, Otis, and Barney were. The bond between the threesome explains why Andy and Barney went to such lengths to help Otis later on.

"Barney speculates that Otis's big purchase may be a vacation to 'the Natural Bridge in Virginia' or to 'an alligator farm in Florida.' Both spots are among the most familiar, and, to be frank, possibly the least exciting destinations to anybody but a Mayberrian."

Later that morning, Andy and Barney's speculation is interrupted by the honking of a car horn. The two step outside and find Otis seated in a newly purchased car.

"The prop department got an old outdated car for Otis's 'hot rod'," says producer Aaron Ruben. "The car stood out and seemed funnier than having a new sleek vehicle."

Barney feels Otis is now a "mechanized drunk," and he can not "just stand by and do nothing while this town gets creamed off the map." Barney decides to call Otis in for a driving test. He gives the test using toy cars.

"Taking a driver's test with toy cars had many advantages," says Harvey. "An outdoor test with a real car would necessitate Otis actually driving and would have required hours of production time, drivers, and stunt drivers, etc. With toy cars, I got a comic effect without all the production woes and had a greater ease of dialogue between Otis and Barney than if they were in an actual car. With a real car, if Otis didn't pass, the story would be over. On the other hand, if he did pass, Barney's spying on Otis later in the episode would be weakened because Otis has already demonstrated his driving ability. All of these problems were avoided with toy cars, which would never convince Barney that Otis could drive."

At first Otis protests the test. After seeing the toy cars, he tells Barney he "ain't never going to get in that thing." Barney warns Otis to not get "facitious." Otis eventually consents and good-naturedly imitates a car motor so the test will be "more authentic."

"Barney's mispronunciations were always funny," says Harvey. "In the written script *facetious* was spelled correctly, and no directions were given how it should be mispronounced. It is a likely word to twist, and Don Knotts or the director may have come up with it.

"The motor sounds Otis made were requested in the script and grew out of the fact that when any red-blooded American picks up a toy car, he will make a motor sound without realizing it. The sound will sometimes be loud, sometimes faint, depending on the person's sophistication. A mute reaction when a toy car is picked up labels the picker-upper indelibly and absolutely as a poseur of questionable birth with not a trace of wonder."

The driving test ends with Barney being totally frustrated by Otis's performance. After Otis leaves, Andy tells Barney "if it will make you feel better, why don't you watch him for awhile?"

"Barney's surveillance of Otis triggered many possibilities, such as

Barney's camouflaged hat," says Harvey. "I also toyed with flashlight codes, Barney holding a glass to the side of Otis's house, the use of a flash camera, and Barney hiding in Otis's car."

Returning from his surveillance, Barney walks down Main Street, stops at a gumball machine, gives it a shake, and takes out a free gumball. Barney's behavior surprises the audience and is comical because it is so unexpected.

"In the script, Barney pauses briefly by the gumball machine to fish for any gum which might be accidentally left in the chute," says Harvey. "Then he continues ambling along. Whoever changed this to Barney actually shaking down the machine and getting a freebie gumball made a distinct improvement."

Barney relates the results of his surveillance. He discloses that Otis was "spotted over at The County Line Cafe buying himself a bottle of the old red-eye." Otis then went over to "Charlie Varney's place to get himself gassed." After Barney shares this information with Andy, the two go over to the Varney residence to check on Otis.

Soon after their arrival, Otis staggers out of the house and passes out beside his car. Barney asks Andy if he can imagine what would have happened if Otis had gotten behind that wheel. After a moment's reflection, Andy comes up with "a way to fix it so Otis will never want to drive again."

Andy and Barney take Otis back to the courthouse, place him in a cell, and douse him with water. When Otis comes to, he finds Andy and Barney reacting to his "driving through the railing, into the river—drowned."

"The fake death story is an ageless standby," says Harvey. "I don't recall any concern from Aaron Ruben even though 'The County Nurse' [Episode #56] had a similar scene. I never saw that show, incidentally, and my approach must have varied enough that it didn't seem repetitive.

"The script stated that the speeches in Andy and Barney's staged 'Otis is dead' performance were to be delivered in 'a wooden, overdone, innocent voice.' Andy and Barney's amateur acting status was important to the scene. If their performance had been too polished it would have reminded the audience that the characters were in reality being portrayed by actors."

"I specifically requested that Andy and Barney sing 'The Vacant Chair.' It was a song I had used when writing hero/villain melodramas for an off-off Broadway dinner/drama house back in the fifties, and it fit perfectly into the scene. 'Chair' is what I asked for and 'Chair' is what I got—sung, by the way, in great harmony."

Otis is so moved by Andy and Barney's performance that he joins them in singing. Eventually, he is overcome with grief and collapses on the bed. Taking advantage of the moment, Andy douses him again with water and tells the startled Otis that he must have been having a nightmare.

Otis promises Andy and Barney he "ain't never going to drive another car again as long as I live—you can get drowned that way." When Barney asks Otis if his "nightmare" was a factor in his decision, Otis explains that he sold his car to Charlie Varney before he took his first drink. Otis continues, "The dream didn't have anything to do with that. Just another of those nutty nightmares. I have them all the time."

"The epilogue for this episode was more serious than most, and the humor arises from Barney's personality," says Harvey. "I had Barney tearful about Otis. Even though the scheme worked, and Otis is hale and hearty, Barney is still carried away. All the theatrics re-echo, and he can't shake it off. He goes in the back room to have a cry over a tragedy which he knows never happened!"

The Songfesters

EPISODE #116

FIRST BROADCAST ON FEBRUARY 24, 1964

WRITTEN BY JIM FRITZELL
AND EVERETT GREENBAUM

DIRECTED BY EARL BELLAMY

"Me they, me they, I-O-U, I-O-U. . ."
Barney's voice-box
calisthenics

"**I** first heard the word *songfester* from TAGS director Alan Rafkin," says writer Everett Greenbaum. "I liked the word and thought it would be a good title for a script that featured music."

Jim and Everett's "Songfesters" script centers on the Mayberry choir's preparation for a concert. Barney, the only tenor, is a featured soloist. During choir practice, however, director John Masters comes to the realization that Barney's "terrible." Mr. Masters calls Andy aside at the end of the practice and tells him that he is going to look for a "decent" tenor. If one is found, he will replace Barney.

Barney has been taking voice lessons to prepare for his solo. After practice, Barney wants to begin his next lesson while his "voice box and muscles are still loose."

"Barney's voice teacher, Eleanora Poultice, was named after Eleanora

Duse, a dramatic actress in the early American theater," says Everett. "Jim and I created the character with Reta Shaw in mind. We felt she always gave a great performance, and both of us were pleased when we learned she had been cast in the role."

Before beginning his lesson, Barney proudly tells Miss Poultice that he did his solo today and "knocked them dead." In response, Miss Poultice predicts that Barney is "going to be another Leonard Blush." We learn that Mr. Blush walked in off the street one day and "two years later he sang the 'Star Spangled Banner' at the opening of the county insecticide convention." His rise to the "big time" was "meteoric." For awhile he had to wear a black mask while singing to cover a skin condition, which was "probably emotional." At this point, Mr. Blush has a radio program, the third Tuesday of every month on station YLRB in Mt. Pilot.

"I began my writing career in New York City," says Everett. "For awhile, my only New York friends were the Schactel family. Irv Schactel was a young lawyer, who at age thirty, became the president of Sonotone Corporation. But he loved show business. At three P.M. every Wednesday afternoon, he would get into a cab, put on a black mask, and go to a radio station where he was 'the masked crooner' for fifteen minutes. Mayberry's 'masked singer,' Leonard Blush, was inspired by this memory."

After returning to the courthouse after his lesson, Barney anounces that he may be another Leonard Blush. Andy isn't familiar with Mr. Blush, so Barney explains that Leonard Blush "used to sing all the vocals on the Ethel Page organ recital shows." Andy doesn't recall ever hearing "any human words on the show—only a canary singing." Barney replies that the "canary hasn't sung with her since she performed on Sunday afternoons at the Pot O' Honey restaurant."

"The dialogue about Ethel Page and the canary was inspired by radio shows I remembered from the thirties where an organ played and canaries sang," says Everett. "This was before radio stations were allowed to broadcast recorded music. Ethel Page was named after Ethyl Shutte, who was a famous organist. The name of the restaurant, Pot O' Honey, came from the Bit O' Honey candy bar."

Andy warns Barney that he's "pumping up his heels too fast." If John Masters can find another tenor, Barney will be replaced.

Andy's warning becomes a reality during the next practice. Gomer is outside the auditorium repairing a flat tire. When he overhears the choir singing, he joins in. Gomer's voice is wonderful! Following an audition, John Masters decides that Gomer Pyle will be the new soloist.

"After Gomer Pyle's appearance in the 'Man in a Hurry' episode, we realized the character had potential," says producer Aaron Ruben. "We decided to develop the character slowly and didn't want to immediately overload him with talents. That is why we waited awhile before introducing Gomer's singing ability."

"Andy Griffith first heard Jim Nabors sing at The Horn, a coffeehouse that was a spawning ground for new talent," says Everett. "Andy told us that the really odd thing about Jim's singing voice was that it was completely different from his speaking voice. So we decided that if Jim Nabors could talk one way and sing another, Gomer could too."

"Andy Griffith's wife, Barbara, was a gifted musician, so we cast her in this episode," says Aaron. "She appears as Sharon, a member of the Mayberry choir. A wordless role would have made her no more than an extra, so we gave Barbara one line of dialogue: 'I'm sorry, Mr. Masters.'

"Ric Riccardi supervised all of the episode's choral music. Ric was a gifted musician and the owner of The Horn, where Jim Nabors was discovered. The song the choir sings, 'Santa Lucia,' was probably Andy Griffith's selection. Andy taught choir for a time before becoming an actor and was very knowledgeable about choral music."

Before breaking the news to Barney, Andy reminds him of advice he once gave Gomer. In the episode "A Date for Gomer," Barney gives his "life is like a road" speech after learning that Gomer had high expectations for his blind date with Mary Grace Gossage.

"Jim and I didn't mind referring to a previous show," says Everett.

"We liked Barney's 'life is like a road' advice and felt that having Andy use it showed how concerned he was about hurting Barney's feelings. Andy also realized he was speaking in a way that Barney, having previously given the advice, would understand."

Barney is devastated by the news and seeks solitude in the back of the darkened auditorium. The sorrow he feels is communicated powerfully in the script:

> In the last row of the hall we see a figure. We TIGHTEN to reveal Barney slumped down in a seat. He gets up slowly—his face very sad— and walks toward the stage. He mounts the stage a forlorn, defeated figure.
>
> He looks around, thinking how it could have been. He runs his hand caressingly over the piano and spots the sheet of music left by Gomer. He picks it up and looks at it sadly. GOMER COMES BACK—UNSEEN.
>
> The lonely figure of Barney stands center stage looking at the sheet music. In a small, weak voice he sings the solo that might have been his. He doesn't get through it. He puts the music down almost in tears and leaves.

The scene's impact is enhanced by Don Knotts's brilliant dramatic performance and Earle Hagen's poignant musical score. Both Gomer, watching from the auditorium's entrance, and the audience are touched by Barney's sense of loss.

Gomer responds to Barney's sorrow by pretending to lose his voice, thus giving Barney his chance to sing. Right before the concert begins, Gomer enthusiastically reveals the truth by shouting, "Sing it good, Barney!" The scene then concludes with the comic dilemma of who will sing the solo—Andy, Barney, Gomer, or all three.

The Shoplifters

EPISODE #117

FIRST BROADCAST ON MARCH 2, 1964

WRITTEN BY BILL IDELSON AND SAM BOBRICK

DIRECTED BY COBY RUSKIN

"We submitted this script to the Writers Guild of America and were totally surprised when it won an award for episodic comedy writing. It was a big thrill."

Sam Bobrick

"Bill Persky and Sam Denoff, producers of *The Dick Van Dyke Show*, suggested Bill Idelson and I team up," says writer Sam Bobrick. "Soon afterwards, Bill suggested an idea for a script. The idea was based on a sketch he had written years earlier about a clerk in a department store who volunteered to catch a shoplifter by posing as a mannequin."

"Bill Idelson pursued us for an assignment," says producer Aaron Ruben. "He and Sam Bobrick came in with a funny idea for an episode. I liked their idea, gave them the assignment, and they wrote an excellent script."

"Aaron Ruben and Sheldon Leonard helped us work out the story," says Sam. "It was my first attempt at writing situation comedy. I had previously written mostly for game shows and *Captain Kangaroo*.

"After the first draft was completed, Aaron read through it and gave us some notes, which we incorporated into the finished script. 'The Shoplifters' was a joy to write, and Aaron was the best producer I ever worked with. He knew exactly what he wanted, which made the writing easier."

"I remember there was a lot of laughter around the table when the actors first read Bill and Sam's script," says Aaron Ruben. "The idea of Barney posing as a mannequin was hilarious, and everyone agreed that the script worked well."

"I was always a big fan of the Griffith show and knew most of the characters," says Sam. "Asa Breeney, the night watchman, and Ben Weaver, the store owner, were written into the script because I remembered them from previous episodes. I also remembered Leon, the

SKY PILOT

Bill Idelson is a curmudgeon. I am very fond of the man, but he takes a bit of understanding.

All through my youth, and his, he played the son Rush on a wonderful radio show from Chicago—*Vic and Sade*. So he has been in show biz longer than any of us and is rather casual about it.

It isn't generally known but Billy was quite a war hero in World War II. He was a night fighter pilot on aircraft carriers. He was highly decorated, having shot down several planes right over Tokyo. Unlike me, who loved flying, he hated it, which makes it even more heroic.

He will never mention this except to me, since we both wore the navy wings of gold. I was mostly an instructor.

But he is an eccentric, which we all allow him to be.

Incidentally, he is a wonderful teacher of comedy writing. Many of his students have found employment in the industry.

Everett Greenbaum

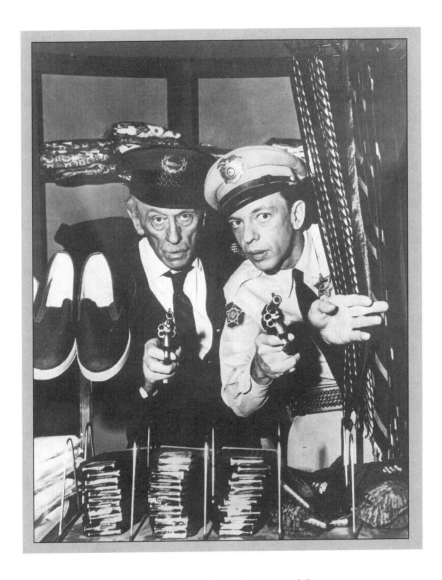

*Asa Breeney, the night watchman, and Barney
stake out Weaver's Department Store.*

little cowboy with the sandwich, and knew he would be perfect interacting with Barney in the mannequin scene.

"Barney was always easy to write for because you instinctively knew what his actions would be in any situation. An example of this is his reaction when he first hears about the robberies at Weaver's Department Store. He immediately pulls out his gun and wants to line the customers up against the wall. I knew instinctively the reaction fit Barney as soon as we wrote it."

After learning about the robberies, Barney decides to "stake out" the store. He telephones Thelma Lou to call off their date. "The movies are out," he says. "Something big has come up." After a brief pause, he adds, "No, it has nothing to do with trash cans!"

Thelma Lou has assumed that a crime involving trash cans, perhaps a vandal turning them over, could be the "something big that has come up." Barney's response requires that the audience figure out what Thelma Lou has said over the telephone. Her assumption reflects the status of crime in Mayberry. Vandalism of trash cans rather than shoplifting is the norm. Her statement also shows her awareness of Barney's tendency to make a minor crime sound important.

"Barney's telephone dialogue was based more on our understanding of the character than on joke construction," says Sam. "Bill and I never tried to write a joke simply for the sake of a joke. Our goal was to have the humor arise from the personalities of the characters and the situations they were involved in."

Barney stakes out Weaver's Department Store later that evening. Ben Weaver also suspects a nighttime robber and is inside the store with Asa Breeney. Barney and Ben, each unaware of the other's identity, scurry through the store's aisles in pursuit of the "robber." The pursuit and the accidental interaction with the store's merchandise (a talking toy clown, a glassware display, etc.) are carefully choreographed. TAGS musical director Earle Hagen's score effectively accompanies the stakeout. The sound effects (a ringing cash register, clanging glass, etc.) bring the scene to life.

Barney, disguised as a mannequin

TAGSRWC Archives

The episode's second act begins with Barney explaining his theory that Ben Weaver is stealing from himself. In Weaver's defense, Andy says, "Weaver is one of our best churchgoing members. He knows every hymn in the book." Barney replies, "Oh, that's just a front. You watch him sometime when we're singing 'Leanin' on the Everlasting Arms.' He don't even know the words. He just moves his lips."

"Individual bits of dialogue, such as Andy and Barney's discussion about Weaver, are born in exactly the same way for all comedy writers," says writer Bill Idelson. "The process goes like this: Two partners sit in a room, create the scene for themselves, and then improvise, sometimes assuming one character, sometimes another. It's kind of a stream-ofconsciousness thing. The writers probe and investigate the working of the minds of their characters. Naturally, a lot of garbage emerges, but when something seems funny, believable and right, they seize it and write it down."

Andy disagrees with Barney's theory and assures him that what they are looking for "is a plain, ordinary shoplifter." Andy sends Barney over to Weaver's store to give Ben "the feeling that we are giving him a little cooperation."

Andy arrives at Weaver's store a short time later to relieve Barney and is unable to find him. Andy causally walks around the store and discovers Barney, disguised as a mannequin. Barney tells Andy "I have my eye on our bird right now." Afraid that Andy will blow his cover, Barney quickly shoos him away.

Barney continues to watch his suspect but is repeatedly interrupted by the store's customers. Aware that his cover is "blown," Barney decides "to make his move." He approaches his suspect—a little old lady. The woman is outraged, and no shoplifted merchandise is found in her possession.

After the suspect appears to be innocent, Andy and Barney step outside. Andy explains to Barney that you never arrest a shoplifter inside a store. Andy then says he has a line on a suspect himself and adds, "There's our man now." The dialogue keeps the audience guessing. The scene immediately cuts to a shot of Barney's "little old lady."

Andy sends Barney into the store for a bathroom scale. After Barney returns, Andy asks the little old lady to step on the scales. Her weight is a surprising 163 pounds! Andy unbuttons her coat. The coat is lined with "a traveling pawnshop" of stolen merchandise.

"TAGS was always a wonderful writing experience," says Sam. "But a show is only as good as those in control of it. Aaron Ruben, Sheldon Leonard, Andy Griffith, and Don Knotts were not only brilliant in what they did but were the nicest people you could ever work for. As a young writer, I was very lucky. Billy Idelson was also a great partner. I owe him a lot."

Andy's Vacation

EPISODE #118

FIRST BROADCAST ON MARCH 9, 1964

WRITTEN BY JIM FRITZELL
AND EVERETT GREENBAUM

DIRECTED BY JEFFREY HAYDEN

"I've had it! I'm sick of sheriffing! I'm sick of this room! I'm sick of this town!"
Andy Taylor

Jim and Everett's "vacation" script begins with Barney bringing in a couple for fighting. Andy has repeatedly warned the couple and angrily fines them "ten dollars or ten days in jail." Barney is shocked by the severity of the fine.

Andy explains that he's just "beat to the socks." Barney encourages Andy to take a vacation and suggests a trip to Miami. Andy agrees to take some time off. He plans to "lay around home, read the *Geographic*, and just take it easy."

"Early in the episode we established Andy's need for a vacation and had Barney advise him to go to Miami Beach and 'take in one of those rabbit girl clubs'," says writer Everett Greenbaum. "Of course, Barney meant the 'Bunny' clubs. The suggestion grew out of the image Barney has of himself as quite a man of the world.

"It seemed that everyone got the *National Geographic* and saved all the copies. However, no one ever read it. Everyone said, 'One day, I'm going to catch up on my *National Geographics*.' This fact inspired Andy's comment about reading the magazine during his vacation."

Barney summons Andy back to the courthouse soon after his vacation begins. He wants Andy to inspect Gomer, who is serving as a temporary deputy.

"Jim and I first used Gomer as a temporary deputy in 'High Noon in Mayberry' and liked the results," says Everett. "Andy's absence set up the perfect opportunity to use Gomer in the position again, so we did. We were well aware that Barney's supervision of Gomer would lead to some good comedy."

Barney and Gomer interrupt Andy's vacation again when they stop by to get a set of handcuff keys. They are standing on the Taylors' front porch, talking to Andy through an open window. While waiting for the keys, Gomer requests an apple. When he reaches through the window to get the apple, Gomer reveals that he and Barney are cuffed together.

"We originally set the handcuff scene outdoors where Andy was pruning an apricot tree," says Everett. "Gomer asks for an apricot and reveals his cuffed wrist. We later changed the setting to the interior of the house and used the window and apple. This decision saved the production a half-day outdoors."

Andy eventually comes to the realization that if he is to have any peace he "has to get away from here." He decides to go to the mountains for a week.

"The mountain exteriors were shot at Coldwater Canyon in Beverly Hills," says director Jeffrey Hayden. "We traveled to the end of the canyon road, and they would unlock a gate for us. We then proceeded to the reservoir above. The area had no homes and was very rustic."

After Andy's departure, the state police bring an escaped convict to the Mayberry jail. The convict is to stay overnight. Gomer feels Andy should be contacted, but Barney disagrees. The two discuss the situation with their backs turned toward the cells. Unnoticed by Barney and Gomer, the convict reaches for the key hanging outside the cell, unlocks the door, and escapes.

The convict heads to the mountains and stumbles on Andy. Tipped off by the convict's prison shoes, Andy apprehends him, ties him to a tree, and goes off for help.

"I was never crazy about this episode," says Everett. "I worried that the audience might feel that the escaped convict coming across Andy in the mountains was too much of a coincidence. But the encounter paid off in fun and moved the story along, so we went with it."

Barney and Gomer arrive a short time afterwards. They have come to find Andy. Gomer suggests they "make animal noises in case they get separated."

"Gomer's suggestion that he and Barney make animal noises to stay in contact was one of Jim Fritzell's ideas," says Everett. "Using an animal noise as a warning was often used in movies—especially westerns, which were Jim's favorites."

Barney begins the search by looking through a set of binoculars. Gomer wants to take a look too and reaches for the binoculars strapped around Barney's neck. He lifts them to his eyes, momentarily strangling Barney, and spots a man tied to a tree.

"The binoculars were included in our script," says Everett. "But Gomer wanting to see and almost strangling Barney with the strap was inserted on the set."

Barney and Gomer come to the aid of the tied-up convict. The convict hides his face and disguises his voice. He explains that an escaped convict jumped him and tied him to a tree. Barney and Gomer free the man and allow him to leave.

Barney and Gomer continue their search. They come up on Andy. Because Andy's back is turned toward them, Barney mistakes him for the convict. Barney courageously sneaks up on the "convict," jumps on his back, and is overtaken by Andy.

"We felt it didn't hurt to see Barney being truly brave once in awhile, so we had him mistake Andy for the escaped prisoner and courageously attack him from behind," says Everett. "We did, however, temper his courage by having him repeatedly ask Gomer, 'Are you ready?' before making his advance."

As the episode continues, Andy, Barney, and Gomer split up to search for the convict. Andy soon finds the convict and apprehends him. Meanwhile, Barney and Gomer stalk each other.

"While Barney and Gomer search for the prisoner, we used the old visual gag of having them circle a tree, each thinking the other is the prisoner," says Everett. "This was a very tired routine and the weakest part of the show."

In the epilogue, Barney is reading a newspaper article that reports the arrest of the convict. Barney discovers that his name is misspelled.

"We repeated the gag of misspelling Barney's name in the epilogue. We first introduced it in 'The Bank Job.' Barney constantly thirsted for publicity. When the paper misspelled his name, F-i-k-e, it always worked."

"We concluded the epilogue with Andy suggesting to Barney that he take a week off and 'get a corner room at the Y in Raleigh.' Staying at the Y enabled young fellows with little money to travel. That's how I got to see New York City in my teens. I never, however, stayed in a corner room—that's a writer's embellishment."

Andy Saves Gomer

EPISODE #119

FIRST BROADCAST ON MARCH 16, 1964

WRITTEN BY HARVEY BULLOCK

DIRECTED BY JEFFREY HAYDEN

"I'm sure the average viewer has no concept of the effort required to put together a thirty-six page script—nor should they. I would rather have them join us in Mayberry and enjoy the doings than have them dissect it. Perhaps the best stories are those where the viewers forget they are watching a written play and are completely caught up with the characters and action."

Harvey Bullock

"**A**ndy Saves Gomer" begins with Opie rushing into the courthouse with a letter from Barney. Barney and his cousin Virgil are vacationing in Raleigh.

"I have no recall why Don Knotts wasn't in this script," says writer Harvey Bullock. "Maybe he had another show to do, or a trip, or an illness. I was told he wasn't available, so I knew ahead of time and fashioned whatever I could without him."

Andy reads the letter to Opie and Floyd.

"This was the first episode Howard McNear appeared in following his stroke," says producer Aaron Ruben. "We wanted to make Howard feel he was still part of the series despite his handicap and invited him back for this scene. His reactions to the contents of Barney's letter were hilarious."

Barney writes:

> Last night was really wild. We went to the arcade and played four games of Skee-Ball. Then we went in a booth where you get four pictures taken for a quarter. I was going to send you one, but it turned all brown later. After that, we had supper at a waffle shop where the waitresses all dress alike in peek-a-boo blouses. Have to close now. Having fun, but money sure doesn't last. Been here only three days and already gone through ten dollars.

"In my script, most of the first three pages are devoted to Andy reading Barney's letter," says Harvey. "Some of the highlights of Barney's vacation were taken from my own recollections, especially the photo booths where you got four prints, which all turned brown later, for a quarter."

Andy decides to show the letter to Gomer. When he arrives at Wally's Service Station, he finds Gomer asleep. The trash can inside the station is smoking. Andy wakes Gomer and puts out the fire, which "was more smoke than anything else."

"The trash can in the filling station contained some inflammable material, like film, that would only smoke and not flame up," says Aaron.

Gomer thanks Andy for saving his life. He is very appreciative and offers Andy free gas and oil, but Andy declines.

The next morning, Andy joins Opie at the breakfast table. Opie's hair is slicked down and neatly combed in preparation for school.

"The slicked-down hair was not included in the script," says Harvey. "If every detail of wardrobe, props, makeup, camera location, and actor's intonations were in the script, it would have been a hundred pages long and too cluttered to follow. So I wrote directions only when they were critically important. All of the production crew knew their jobs, knew the script, and each contributed his particular expertise without being told. The slicked-down hair was probably the suggestion of the director or Andy."

Gomer enters the kitchen with "a mess of fish." He got up "special early" to catch the fish for Andy's breakfast. Gomer feels it "is little enough for the man who saved my life." He dramatically describes the rescue to Aunt Bee and Opie.

Gomer has already washed and polished the squad car. He offers to fix Andy's fence, trim the back hedges, sweep out the garage, and clean out the "ease" troughs.

"Gomer says *ease* troughs for *eaves* troughs," says Harvey. "He occasionally slurs words and phrases to make them phonetic sound-alikes."

That afternoon, Andy returns home and finds Gomer "setting him up with some firewood." Stacked firewood covers the front porch. Inside the house, firewood is stacked up to the ceiling. A stunned Andy observes that "there's enough wood there for seven winters."

"The load of firewood Gomer cuts was acquired by the prop department, who were masters at getting anything a script required," says Aaron.

Andy tells Gomer that he's done enough. Andy says he will see Gomer at the station on the weekend, and "we'll have a bottle of pop." Andy ushers Gomer out the door.

"There is interesting and endless speculation among many of TAGS viewers as to whether bottle of pop is right or whether we should have said coca cola, or dopes, or dranks," says Harvey. "It seems to vary from place to place, so any one name could be justified. When I was a kid in New York state, it was always bottle of pop, so that's what I put down without a second thought."

After Gomer leaves, Aunt Bee comes down the stairs. Gomer insisted on straightening the attic. She has spent the past hour "putting things back where I can find them." Aunt Bee tells Andy that Carter

Finch called. He said "they're having a boiled dinner down at the firehouse and cribbage afterwards."

"Aunt Bee's line about 'a boiled dinner down at the firehouse and cribbage afterwards' was probably a total mystery to most Southerners," admits Harvey. "I can only plead attrition in my Dixie roots which allowed me to think that Yankee phrase was universal. After all, I left North Carolina when I was only three and hadn't absorbed much of a decent vocabulary."

On his way to the boiled dinner, Andy bumps into Gomer. Gomer tells him that he will not forget the good deed Andy has done for him. He says, "If I live to be a hundred, I intend to be by your side to help you out every day of my life. Good-bye, lifesaver man."

"'Lifesaver man' was a madeup phrase that comes from mentally running a scene over and over through your mind, putting yourself inside the character, and then letting your thoughts run amuck until something seems to work," says Harvey.

The next morning at breakfast, Aunt Bee tells Andy she is going to do some baking. She asks him which he would prefer—applesauce cake or angel food cake. "You choose which. You can have your favorite." Andy chooses applesauce cake. Aunt Bee immediately replies, "I think I'll make angel food. I have a lot of egg whites."

"Asking what kind of cake Andy would like for supper and then deciding on another kind was right out of the Bullock household," says Harvey. "As I was leaving for work in the morning, my wife Betty would often ask what I'd like for dinner and then usually give me a choice. I might pick lamb chops. All day I would be salivating all over the typewriter in anticipation—LAMB CHOPS!

"Then I'd come home, zoom into the kitchen, and she'd say offhand, 'ready in ten minutes. We're having meat loaf.' She had found some ground beef in the freezer and decided to make a meat loaf, completely oblivious to the fact that my whole system was crying out for the promised lamb chops."

Gomer comes into the kitchen while Andy is having breakfast. He offers to cut Andy's grass. Andy declines because that's Opie's job. Instead, Gomer trims the hedges. Afterwards, he takes Opie roller skating.

Later that day, Opie comes to the courthouse to complain about Gomer. Andy is working on the gas line to the heater. Opie tells Andy that Gomer puts on his skates for him and picks him up when he falls down. Opie is upset because "all the guys laugh." Opie looks out the window and sees Gomer walking towards the office. He hides under Andy's desk.

Gomer enters, asks about Opie, and decides to wait until Opie comes by. Andy tells him that Opie will probably be heading home because Aunt Bee is baking, and he likes to be "close by when there's any cake baking." Gomer rushes off to help Aunt Bee.

That evening, Andy, Aunt Bee, and Opie hide in one of the cells. They drape a blanket over the cell's bars and have supper. When Aunt Bee leaves, Andy tells her that he may be late because he has to fix a leaky heater.

Opie asks if they are going to have to eat in the courthouse all the time. Andy assures him that things will return to normal once Gomer figures he's done enough. Andy adds, "Course, with him, he may not figure we're even until he saves my life for me." This statement gives Andy an idea, and he tells Opie to run along.

Andy telephones his house and asks Gomer to bring his jacket to the courthouse. Andy explains that the gas heater is broken, and it's chilly in the office. He adds that there is no real problem unless the gas should start to leak. Then it would "asphyxiate whoever was here. But you would smell the gas if that was happening."

After hanging up, Andy opens the valve on the gas line, lies down on the floor, and closes his eyes.

"The idea for the gas leak in the courthouse came from pondering what prop would work best to make Andy a possible victim," says

Harvey. "Drowning and a fake car wreck were considered, but the gas line seemed by far the most acceptable and easiest to understand. It also didn't require a lot of production time."

Before Gomer arrives, Opie enters through the back room. He walks over to Andy and asks, "Pa?" Andy immediately starts doing push-ups.

"I used Opie's walking in on the passed-out Andy to further frustrate Andy while he waits for Gomer's arrival," says Harvey. "It would have been too pat to have Gomer enter the scene immediately. Opie's interruption left Andy concerned that the fakery wouldn't work and created more story tension."

Opie has come to the office because he needs Andy's help. His skate is stuck in the sidewalk grate. Andy agrees to free the skate. As the two walk out, Opie remarks that he smells gas.

Gomer enters moments later. He smells gas too and attempts to turn it off. The gas, however, overcomes Gomer, and he passes out. Andy returns, sees Gomer, shuts off the gas, and wakes Gomer up. Andy says, "It's just lucky I came back," then realizes this will simply mean another debt.

Gomer is still drowsy, so Andy leans back against the cell and tells Gomer, "Thank heavens you come by when you did. Fast thinking, Gomer, to turn the gas off like you did and pull me away. No two ways about it, Gomer, you saved my life. And if I live to be a hundred, I'll never forget it. I'll be by your side every day."

Gomer replies, "Oh, you don't have to do all that." Andy then suggests that they're even for saving each other's lives. They can now go back to "being what we were before."

In the epilogue, Aunt Bee asks Andy if turning on the gas was taking a chance. Andy answers, "Not really. All's well that ends well. . .Happy days are here again." This sounds somewhat strange, since Andy doesn't usually use clichés.

"I suppose some more colorful phrases could have been devised, but it was important that Andy reveal his exact feelings," says Harvey. "These two old standbys are right on target. Also colorful terms sometime divert attention away from the story point the scene needs to make. I felt Andy was needed as a complete straight man in this scene, so I felt the obvious clichés were OK."

At this point, Gomer enters and tells Andy that he's noticed that Andy is accident prone. Gomer says, "There's no question about it. You need somebody around to keep an eye on you." Gomer has decided to be that person.

"This episode is a rare instance in which the problem is not completely solved," says Harvey. "Gomer feels Andy is accident prone and vows to stay by his side, but his attention will soon wane as other problems and puzzles intrigue him. I plead guilty, however, to using the 'here we go again' finish. I tried not to use it. I experimented with alternates and wasn't thrilled by them. Time was short, so I succumbed. I promised to never do another 'here we go again'—unless time got short, and I wasn't thrilled with alternates."

Divorce, Mountain Style

EPISODE #121

FIRST BROADCAST ON MARCH 30, 1964

WRITTEN BY JIM FRITZELL
AND EVERETT GREENBAUM

DIRECTED BY JEFFREY HAYDEN

"You can't explain how the details arise. You just sit down together with the typewriter and usually things just bubble up. On bad days, nothing bubbles."

Everett Greenbaum

"**D**ivorce, Mountain Style" begins with Andy and Barney in the courthouse. Andy asks what Barney and Thelma Lou did after the movie the night before. Barney tells Andy that they dropped by Nelson's Hardware Store. Barney says, "He's got a new window display—bicycle accessories. He's featuring a transparent plastic tool kit. They're really practical, you know that? Say you got a pair of pliers, a screwdriver, a wrench, and half a candy bar. Well, you know at a glance what you got." Andy responds that he prefers the solid black kits because "what I got in my bicycle kit is my business."

Mitch Jayne, the Dillards' bass player, offers some observations on this opening scene: "Denver Pyle, who had sort of taken us under his wing, went to great lengths to explain just what an actor did. He urged us to see what Don and Andy did with a script, not altering the words so much as interpreting them and letting the characters take over. This was particularly impressive in the little intro things they would do, usually on the bench in front of the courthouse. Just the two of them with a few ridiculous lines like this episode's 'bicycle tool kit' bit, which they would transform into a marvelous comedy sketch. I have the feeling Everett and Jim relished these little character vignettes, which played so lovingly with the premise.

"Since the little introductory bits were part of each show, we usually got to see these filmed. I had always loved the short introductory things. Even watching them back home (without an inkling that we would soon be a part of it all), I realized that this was a supremely clever way to center a viewer who had been elsewhere in TV land and needed a chance to adjust to Mayberry. These, I think, were the keys to the time machine that Mayberry was, and of course, still is."

"Before I met Jim Fritzell he had been a writer on a radio show starring TAGS director Bob Sweeney and his partner Hal March—*Sweeney and March*," says writer Everett Greenbaum. "The tool-kit bit was inspired by a joke written for that show by a comedy madman named Jack Douglas."

Andy and Barney are interrupted by the arrival of Charlene Darling Wash. Charlene is alone. The rest of her family is "still up in the mountains." Andy asks how Charlene made the long trip. In response, Charlene sticks up her thumb and whistles.

"Charlene responds to Andy's question by sticking up her thumb and whistling," says Everett. "In the script, we wrote that Charlene replies, 'I can herd a T Model with the best of them.' The thumb and whistle, which fit the character perfectly, came up on the set.

"When we first introduced Charlene in 'The Darlings Are Coming,' we described the character as 'about seventeen, voluptuous, blonde, etc.' The casting of Maggie Peterson was a surprise to Jim and me. We just never pictured Charlene as long, tall, and thin, but Maggie made the part hers and was excellent."

Andy and the Darlings

TAGSRWC Archives

Charlene has come to town to complete "a tiny errand." She asks Andy if he could help her out, and Andy agrees to do so. Charlene wants Andy to drive her somewhere, but she is mysterious about where she wants to be driven. She will only say, "I'll tell you when we get there."

Andy and Barney drive Charlene out of Mayberry. Charlene has Andy stop the car by an oak tree and asks if there is a shovel in the back of the car. Charlene then digs a hole, buries a sack, motions for Andy to stand by her side, recites an incantation, draws a circle in the dirt, and says to Andy, "Now I can be yours." Charlene has just completed "divorce proceedings. From now until the moon comes full is the waiting period."

"While writing this script, I got several books on superstitions from the library," says Everett. "By altering or combining many of them, we were able to catch the flavor and make up our own."

"Even though we were familiar with the culture of the Ozarks, the

Dillards had no input about the script's mountain folklore," says Mitch. "We figured the scripts weren't seeking accuracy, and, for sure, we didn't think they needed our help."

When asked why she is divorcing Dud, Charlene says he went "fox hunting with Hasty Buford and they didn't come home 'til Wednesday week." According to Charlene, the two "sit around drinking hard cider, punch each other on the arm, and holler, 'flinch.'" Andy tries to offer a defense for Dud by saying that he might have been "getting you the makings for a fox pie."

"Andy's line about the fox pie grew out of a comedy routine of a friend of mine, Eddie Lawrence, in which he offers advice to avoid anyone eating a fox pie," says Everett.

Andy, Barney, and Charlene return to the courthouse. Barney decides to go over to the library to get a book on mountain folklore. He tells Andy that he's going to get him "out of this." When Andy and Charlene enter the courthouse, Briscoe Darling and the boys are waiting inside.

Briscoe learns from Charlene that Andy stood at her side for the divorce incantation. Briscoe accuses Andy of leading Charlene on "since day one." Briscoe doesn't go along with the divorce "but the fact is that the ritual's been performed right and proper. The deed's been done. So, come the next full moon, we's going to have ourselves a ceremony."

Later that evening, Barney returns from the library with a book on mountain folklore. Barney has found an antidote in the book for the divorce proceedings: "If the intended should dig up the proceedings before the moon comes full, the divorce proceedings are null and void." Barney suggests they dig up the proceedings. He justifies this action by saying, "If there's a peaceful way, take it." Andy wants no part of this solution. Digging up "that stuff would mean I believe in all this hocus-pocus."

Dud Wash barges into the courthouse and accuses Andy of being a "homewrecker." Dud wants to "fight it out" with Andy. Andy responds by grabbing Dud by the seat of the pants and ushering him out the door.

"We were all appalled when Hoke Howell, who originally played the role of Dud Wash, was replaced by Bob Denver, even though Bob was a great Dillards fan and a good actor," says Mitch. "Bob just wasn't Hoke. In our brief Hollywood experience, Hoke was like family. It was almost as if all of our characters could be replaced if they could replace Maggie's husband so offhandedly. The only explanation we heard was that Hoke was making a picture and was unavailable. I think we patterned our reaction to Maggie's and Denver's—that's show biz. But I remember that basically this just reinforced my belief that every show was probably our last. You have to remember that in the year this show was made no one, including Andy, dreamed that it would last as long or have as lasting an impact as it did."

"The reason I didn't appear in 'Divorce, Mountain Style' was because CBS wanted to give Bob Denver some prime-time exposure," said Hoke Howell. "The network had just decided to go with *Gilligan's Island* for the following season, and they felt it was important to give Bob, who starred in the series, some advance publicity."

As the story continues, Andy reluctantly agrees to dig up the divorce proceedings. When he and Barney return to the oak tree, Andy begins digging. As he throws aside a shovel of dirt, a shovelful of dirt is immediately thrown back. The Darlings walk up with guns drawn. This frightens Barney, and his hands tremble. Briscoe suggests that Andy "just go on home and forget all this nulling and voiding."

The "digging up the divorce" scene is photographed in part from ground level. When the dirt is thrown back into the hole, Andy is shown from the knees down. Then the legs of Briscoe and the boys enter the frame.

"This camera angle was not mentioned in the script," says Everett. "Another addition to this scene was Barney shaking fearfully when he and Andy are confronted by the Darlings. We just wrote Barney was scared, no shaking. I think this works better, since the Darlings were never a real physical threat, even with their guns drawn."

Later that night, Barney takes another look in the book. He reads aloud the following passage: "If a rider dressed in black rides east to west on a white horse in the light of a full moon and passes a bridegroom, the bridegroom is cursed, and the union is cursed." Andy realizes "that's it." Barney agrees, "All we need is somebody willing to dress up in a black outfit and ride a white horse—some patsy." At this point, Andy looks at Barney.

"The rider dressed in black was an enlargement of something I found in one of the library books on superstitions," says Everett.

The next night, Andy and Barney prepare to "curse the union." Dressed in black, Barney meets Andy at a stable. A white horse is saddled and ready. Barney complains that he feels "like a real idiot. Black makes me look so thin." He begins sneezing. It seems Barney is allergic to horse hair. He says to Andy, "Remember when we were kids? We all had our pictures taken on a pony. Well, not me. I had mine taken sitting on the hood of my uncle's Hudson Terraplane."

"Having Barney ride the white horse opened the door to numerous comic possibilities," says Everett. "His line, 'I feel like a real idiot. Black makes me look so thin' grew out of Barney's concern with his appearance, which was always funny. Barney's comment about his childhood picture was inspired by the memory of a photographer coming around to the neighborhood with a pony, which was a staple in Jim and my childhoods. Using the Hudson was a way of turning the memory into comedy."

The Darlings pass the time prior to Andy and Charlene's wedding by playing "Shady Grove." Charlene dances and whistles during the song's instrumental break.

"Maggie's whistling during 'Shady Grove' was her own touch," says Mitch. "She has a nice tomboy feel for these things and can whistle up a coon hound (or a cab) if she has to."

Andy joins the Darlings. He tells Briscoe that he has decided to go along with "this marriage idea." Andy, Charlene, and the Darlings proceed "down to the preacher's house."

Meanwhile, Barney is having difficulties getting the white horse to travel east to west. The horse walks into Floyd's front yard. Floyd is sitting on the porch and greets Barney by saying, "You seem to be on a horse. The reason I was so surprised—I just wasn't expecting it."

"We didn't get to see any of the horse scenes being filmed, much to my dismay," says Mitch. "I didn't get to meet Howard McNear, who played Floyd the barber either, which was a disappointment because everyone loved him and talked about his incredible sense of humor. I still ache over missing that. I have an idea that Andy added the scene with Howard because it's the kind of thing Andy would have done to ease him back into work."

"Floyd was added later," concurs Everett. "We always loved Howard McNear on screen and off. He was a welcomed presence in this script."

Barney eventually gets the horse to move from east to west. He rides past Andy, Charlene, the Darlings, and Dud (who was waiting for Charlene at the preacher's house). Charlene immediately recognizes "the curse of the white horse." The Darlings back away from Andy, and Charlene and Dud are reunited.

"In the epilogue, Barney dances to the Darlings' music (some very fancy footwork by the way)," says Everett. "There was no music, however, in our epilogue. I'm sure that Andy, with the Darling family present, wanted to do some music, so it was added. Barney's wonderful dancing, which grew out of Andy's suggestion, is just another example of Don's comic genius."

A Deal is a Deal

EPISODE #122

FIRST BROADCAST ON APRIL 6, 1964

WRITTEN BY BILL IDELSON
AND SAM BOBRICK

DIRECTED BY JEFFREY HAYDEN

"Cures poison ivy, athlete's foot, prickly rash, complexion, and spring itch."

The label on
Miracle Salve

"If I thought up a story idea for TAGS, I would call Aaron Ruben for an appointment. He would give me a date and time he'd be available," says writer Harvey Bullock. "These appointments were granted mostly to seasoned writers whose work the producers knew. A novice writer occasionally could crack in, but mostly the veteran writers had the edge because the producer knew they would deliver a script on time, it would be shootable, and the characters would be consistent. However, when a new writer who showed talent came on the scene, the word got around very quickly, and he was sought after."

"Our first script, 'The Shoplifters,' was well received, and Aaron Ruben agreed to meet with Bill and me so we could present an idea for another story," says writer Sam Bobrick. "The idea we presented was one I thought up about boys who are Opie's age selling salve on consignment. Aaron liked it and gave us the go-ahead to write the script."

Bill and Sam's completed script begins with Opie and Johnny Paul arriving at a potential customer's residence at the same time. The boys decide who will make the sales pitch by matching "odds or evens." Opie wins. He rings the doorbell. When the door opens, Opie begins the pitch by saying, "Madam, would you like to buy a jar of. . . ." The door slams shut.

"The 'odds or evens' idea was inspired from memories of our childhoods," says Sam. "A lot of our own realities went into each script. I don't remember what inspired the name Miracle Salve and the list of ailments the salve was supposed to cure but the dilemma the boys faced of not being able to sell the stuff was very real to me. For one week in college, I tried to sell Amana freezers door-to-door, so I knew the plight of a salesman firsthand. Thank God I failed, and the experience was soon behind me."

"The prop department had the boxes printed up with Miracle Salve and Mt. Pilot on them," says director Jeffrey Hayden. "I don't recall how many boxes were printed, but the prop department had the time-consuming job of folding and taping each one together. There was nothing inside any of the boxes, so I showed the boys how to hold them so they would appear to be filled with jars of salve."

Opie dejectedly enters the courthouse after a day of poor sales. Opie tells Andy he is thinking about sending the salve back. When Barney enters, Opie tries to sell him a jar of slave. Barney refuses. He has already purchased a jar and is dissatisfied with the product. He tells Opie that it's supposed to be good for crow's feet, but "I put it on my crow's feet a week ago, and they're still there. See that crease in my cheek—nothing."

Barney thinks Opie's problem may be poor salesmanship. Opie shows Barney his technique. Opie repeats the opening line of his sales pitch and stops. He explains, "That's as far as I get. Then they slam the door in my face." Barney suggests that's his problem. "You can't give them a

Opie and his friends try to sell Miracle Salve.

TAGSRWC Archives

chance to cut you off like that. You got to get your foot in the door and start talking and never stop."

Barney demonstrates. He takes a jar of salve and says to Andy, "Hello, little girl, may I see the lady of the house?"

"Barney's demonstration of a proper sales technique was inspired by my freezer-selling spiel," says Sam. "We gave the speech a comic twist by having Barney say to Andy, 'Hello little girl, may I see the lady of the house? Oh, you are the lady of the house, etc.'"

One of the boys, Trey, decides to return his unsold jars of salve. A short time later, he receives a letter from the Miracle Salve Company. Trey tells Opie and his friends that the manufacturer wrote they were "real disappointed in him as a salesman and are putting him on a blacklist."

None of the boys know what a blacklist is. They rush to the courthouse to have Andy explain it to them. Andy, however, is away, so Barney is consulted.

Barney explains that a blacklist means "you can't get a job." Trey shows Barney the letter. Barney thinks the situation over carefully and asks, "How do you fight fire?" One of the boys answers, "With a hose?" Barney replies, "No, with fire! You fight fire with fire. They scared you with a letter. We'll scare them back with a letter—a lawyer letter."

The master shot for the first part of this scene, from its beginning through Barney's question is photographed from behind Barney's desk. The wall, on which the gun rack is mounted, is removed, and the camera is positioned in its place.

"Much of the action in this episode takes place in the courthouse," says Jeffrey Hayden. "It was my responsibility as the director to select camera angles that would present the action in an interesting way. Placing the camera behind Barney's desk was perfect for photographing the beginning of the scene when Barney is napping. The audience also sees the action from a point of view that was rarely used, which made the scene visually interesting."

Barney dictates a letter to Opie. The letter opens with, "From the office of Bernard P. Fife, attorney-at-law." Opie stops writing after the first few words, but Barney continues a long discourse.

After Barney finishes, one of the boys immediately says, "I don't think fighting fire with fire is going to work."

At this point, Andy enters. When he is told that Trey has been blacklisted, he reassures the boys that the salve company is just trying to intimidate them. He says, "It's their way of getting you to sell more salve." Andy tells the boys "to run along and don't worry about it."

After the boys leave, Barney tells Andy they ought to figure out a way of getting back at the salve company. He suggests that they go to Mt. Pilot to visit the company. Andy cuts him off. He doesn't want to hear Barney's idea. His "mind is closed."

After Andy walks out, Barney immediately telephones Wally's Service Station. When Gomer answers, Barney asks if he would like to "take a little drive with me over to Mt. Pilot."

Barney and Gomer visit the Miracle Salve Company in Mt. Pilot. The two are dressed in suits, and Barney wears wire-rim glasses. When they enter the Miracle Salve office, Gomer introduces himself to one of the owners as Opie Taylor, Senior. He says, "My little boy sent away for some of your salve. Well, he got to experimenting with it, you know like kids do sometimes. So he put some on his dog. You see, Junior's dog had the mange. Well, that mange cured up overnight. So I took some of the salve over to Dr. Pendyke here [Barney]. Dr. Pendyke is a veterinarian."

In a high-pitched voice, Barney confirms what Opie, Senior, has said and tells the owner that they decided they would like to buy the salve and sell it to other veterinarians, or even drugstores.

The owner steps into the back room to get his partner. While the man is away, Gomer asks Barney what is wrong with his voice. Barney explains that it is just part of his disguise. Gomer is amazed. He remarks, "That's good. I wish I could do my voice like that."

When the two owners return, Gomer introduces himself, in a deep voice, to the other man. Dr. Pendyke is told the company has "four or five gross" of Miracle Salve on hand. Pendyke replies, "That's good for a starter, but don't you think you could get some more back from those boys in Mayberry?" The owners agree to try.

"We knew immediately that the idea to have Barney and Gomer visit the Miracle Salve company incognito would work beautifully," says Sam. "Jim Nabors and Don Knotts were wonderful in the scene, and each one's reaction to the other's disguised voice made the scene even better than we had imagined."

After leaving the Miracle Salve office, Barney tells Gomer, "They're on the phone right now, calling every veterinarian and drugstore in the county telling them they got a new mange cure."

A few days later, the company collects all the salve Opie and his friends have been unable to sell.

Assuming their scheme was a success, Barney and Gomer enter the courthouse triumphantly. Barney confidently takes a seat on the edge of Andy's desk, crosses his legs, folds his hands smugly in his lap, and starts to explain the scheme to Andy. Gomer shows his admiration for Barney by mirroring Barney's actions in childlike fashion.

"Gomer's copying of Barney's actions was not suggested in our script," says Sam. "It was probably the idea of the director or one of the actors. Gomer's wonderful pronunciation of salve was likewise not in the script. I imagine it was the idea of either Jim Nabors or Aaron Ruben."

The telephone rings just as Barney is about to begin his explanation. It is Aunt Bee, who is "awful upset." Andy tells her to "just take it easy, and I'll come right home." Barney and Gomer accompany him.

When Andy arrives at home, he finds 946 jars of Miracle Salve billed to Opie Taylor, Senior, with payment due in seven days. Gomer turns to Barney and says, "It didn't work the way you said it would, Barney." Andy is now very interested in hearing all about the scheme.

An important element in most TAGS episodes is the resolution of the problem on which the story line is based. "A Deal is a Deal" twists this premise somewhat. The original problem is solved, but a bigger problem takes its place.

The epilogue centers on Barney's efforts to get rid of the boxes of salve. He has Gomer round up Opie and his friends and bring them to the courthouse. Upon their arrival, the boys are seated. Barney begins a speech to persuade the boys to once again sell the salve.

As he talks, the closeups are photographed with the camera positioned so it looks up into Barney's face. This camera angle draws the audience into the action and allows the viewer to see Barney through the eyes of the seated boys.

The boys listen for a short time, then silently walk out. Without saying a word, Andy rises from his desk, picks up several boxes of the salve, and hands them to Barney and Gomer. The two exit the courthouse yelling, "Salve!"

The Return of Malcolm Merriweather

EPISODE #124

FIRST BROADCAST ON APRIL 20, 1964

WRITTEN BY HARVEY BULLOCK

DIRECTED BY COBY RUSKIN

BERNARD FOX GUEST STARS
AS MALCOLM MERRIWEATHER

"Frances Bavier was a vastly underrated actress."

Harvey Bullock

"I met Bernard Fox while I was in London working on some British sitcoms," says writer Harvey Bullock. "I knew his style and strong points, so it was no problem coming up with a second story line for his character, Malcolm Merriweather. In pitching the idea to Aaron Ruben, I mentioned showing how foreigners often know more about our country than we do. Another point I emphasized was that the properly dignified, well-mannered Englishman was an interesting contrast with local Mayberrians. Malcolm's accidental friction with Aunt Bee, who feared she would be replaced, made it all come together."

"I was, of course, very happy to learn that there was to be another episode of TAGS for me," says Bernard Fox. "Working with Andy, Don, and Ronny Howard was indeed a pleasure.

"I found Andy outgoing and charming, and it seemed to me that he kept a very firm hand on the way the show was headed when we sat and read the script round the conference table. Don was nice, friendly to the newcomer, and, of course, brilliant. I remember young Ronny getting quite enthusiastic when he learned that I was keenly interested in fencing, and we had some long conversations on the subject.

"I didn't get to spend much time with Frances Bavier. She tended to keep to herself in her dressing room, and we only met when rehearsing or when actually filming the scene.

"The director, Coby Ruskin, was a darling man. I knew him vaguely from England, where he was directing a TV series. It was some sort of show with guest entertainers. I was in a comedy at the Garrick Theater London, and a segment from the play was to air on this show. The actors all trooped in for rehearsal with Coby, who was directing the segment. He was just marvelous. When he finished, the segment was better than anything else in our play, and we all wished that he had directed the whole thing. I will never forget it. His talent, his understanding and warmth just enveloped you, filled you with confidence, and made you as steady as a rock. Coby, you were great!"

Harvey began the script for "The Return of Malcolm Merriweather" with Barney impatiently waiting for Aunt Bee to bring lunch to the courthouse. Verbalizing his impatience, Barney comments that he has a clock in his stomach that tells him it is past time to eat. Barney adds that his mother was the same way. Andy responds by asking, "Hey, Barn, these clocks you and your mother have in your stomachs. Did the ticking keep your father awake at night?"

"This opening scene was just an extension of an old wheeze—'I bought one of those Venus de Milo statues with a clock in its stomach, but I'm too embarrassed to wind it'," says Harvey. "It's an American icon, and I used it here because I always found it personally amusing."

Aunt Bee arrives with lunch and apologizes for being late. She says she had to get her wash hung out. Andy compliments her on the lunch and gives her the title, "Miss Luncheon Tray." Aunt Bee has no time "to listen to such blarney." She has "a cake in the oven, and ironing to do, and supper to get."

After Aunt Bee leaves, Andy wonders aloud to Barney if Aunt Bee knows how much they appreciate everything she does. Barney's mouth is full. He starts to answer Andy but can't resist another mouthful of sandwich.

"Because Barney has a mouthful of food, he has to just nod for an answer," says Harvey. "This was scripted. In the script Aunt Bee hasn't left the courthouse when this part of the scene takes place. The script repeated the business of Barney's mouth being too full to talk three times."

The lunch is interrupted by the honking of car horns. The two walk outside to investigate and discover that Englishman Malcolm Merriweather, who is somewhat of a traffic hazard, has returned to Mayberry. Malcolm greets the two with his trademark—holding a hand out for a handshake and changing it instantly to the tipping of his hat when the other person reaches for his hand.

"Malcolm's disappearing handshake and hat-tipping were Bernard's contributions," says Harvey. "He also contributed many expressions to flavor the story such as 'Aren't you kind?' and 'proper Bobby Dazzler.'"

"'Aren't you kind?' originated in the north of England somewhere," says Bernard. "I borrowed it from the actress Dame Thora Hird, who used it frequently as a gag."

After learning that Malcolm is traveling through America, doing odd jobs along the way to finance the trip, Andy asks if he would like to work at the Taylor house for awhile. Andy explains that Aunt Bee's got "a way yonder too much to do. You'd be a big help." He also adds that it would be more than a position. Malcolm would be staying with friends. Andy's proposal beautifully expresses the spirit of Mayberry.

"Andy's offer reflected my desire to make Malcolm's hiring more than a completely business relationship," says Harvey. "I wanted Malcolm's employment at the Taylors to be informal, so they could sup together and be relaxed."

That evening, Malcolm prepares supper and cleans up afterwards. While Malcolm is in the kitchen, Aunt Bee tells Andy that she's not sure about "having a man around the house all day." Andy responds with some very humorous dialogue:

> With Malcolm here you'll have more leisure time to watch TV. You know that show you like where everybody is sick and in the hospital. You can watch the whole thing instead of peeping at it through the kitchen door. Sit right there and watch every operation without missing a single stitch.

"Andy's reminder to Aunt Bee that with Malcolm around she can watch all of her soap opera was a powerful enticement," says Harvey.

When Malcolm finishes in the kitchen, he tells Opie that it's past his bedtime. Before going to bed, Opie asks Malcolm to show him a magic trick.

Malcolm pulls a folded sheet of newspaper out of his sleeve. He makes a simple tear in the newspaper, has Opie hold the ends, says the magic words, and lifts the newspaper, revealing a paper ladder!

"The ladder-tree trick was another idea of mine," says Bernard. "I think Harvey asked me if there was anything I could do in the way of magic that would astonish Ronny. I had a whole paper magic act I was taught as an eleven-year-old boy working the *fit-ups* in Ireland (six plays a week, with a matinee Wednesday and Saturday), so I suggested a paper trick for Malcolm."

The next morning, Aunt Bee oversleeps. When she comes downstairs, she asks Malcolm if Andy and Opie have had their breakfast. Malcolm informs her that they have had breakfast and gone. He then seats Aunt Bee at the table, serves her coffee, hands her the morning newspaper, and goes into the kitchen to get her eggs. Holding the newspaper, Aunt Bee looks at the perfectly set table and seems at a loss.

Later that day, Barney waits impatiently for lunch. Andy notices Barney's restlessness and asks, "Clock in your stomach bothering you?

Your tummy going tick-tock?" Barney replies angrily, "Now don't start up with me, Andy." When Andy starts to speak, Barney sings, "ra-bop-bop-bop" to drown out Andy's voice.

"Andy mentions Barney's inner clock again because it really tickles him," says Harvey. "Barney sings to prove he is not listening to Andy. He wants Andy to know that he is wasting his time teasing."

Aunt Bee enters the courthouse. She has just finished attending a club meeting. When she offers to bring Andy and Barney some lunch, Andy declines.

As Aunt Bee is walking toward the door, Malcolm enters with a "little high tea." He has prepared Cornish pasty. After listening to Andy and Barney's enthusiastic remarks about the lunch, Aunt Bee says, "You boys won't be satisfied with tuna-fish sandwiches anymore, will you?"

"Cornish pastry was not my first choice for the main dish Malcolm serves Andy and Barney," says Bernard. "At one script conference, I was asked by Harvey for a typical English dish. I suggested spotted dick, but Harvey didn't think a British dish called spotted dick was appropriate for TAGS, so I disappointedly suggested Cornish pastry. By the way, I must say the prop man did a nice job of it—meat and potatoes in one end, plum pudding in the other."

"The next night's after-supper scene on the Taylor front porch was written to show the serenity of Mayberry after dark," says Harvey. "Andy is idly picking his guitar, Barney is stretched out on the wicker love seat, rubbing his stomach contentedly, and Aunt Bee is playing solitaire."

After finishing in the kitchen, Malcolm joins the three on the front porch. Barney asks Malcolm about his plans to visit Gettysburg and says, "See, that's famous because that's where Lincoln made his famous Gettysburg Address speech. See, Lincoln, he was what we call a Pres-e-dent. And Washington, you see, was our first president and Lincoln, now he didn't come along till later. He was fourteenth or fifteenth— somewhere along in there." Malcolm immediately replies, "Sixteen" and names the fourteenth and fifteenth presidents.▶

"I definitely wanted Malcolm to be knowledgeable about American history," says Harvey. "This illustrated one of the script's selling points—that our foreign visitors often know more about us than we know ourselves. I felt it was important that Malcolm's knowledge be low-key so as not to seem patronizing. The serenity of the Taylor front porch provided the perfect setting to have Malcolm demonstrate his knowledge.

"Barney's pronunciation of president was scripted, as was the follow-up where Barney isn't sure of Lincoln's number, and Malcolm helpfully spews names of all the early presidents—finally getting to Lincoln at number sixteen."

Before going back into the house, Malcolm makes a play in Aunt Bee's game of solitaire. The play takes her "out." He then places her sweater upon her shoulders, which she pushes off moments after his departure.

"Malcolm is really trying to help Aunt Bee with her cards, but she resents it—especially after all the attention Malcolm has been getting," says Harvey. "Naturally, Aunt Bee is far too well-mannered to lay out any of her personal problems or to betray her anguish over being replaced.

"This script required an extraordinary attention to detail in its progression. It was important that the audience understood that Aunt Bee has a cherished fatigue from doing housework, which in fact gives a center to her life. She is also fearful that Andy and Opie might benefit from having Malcolm around. But she must not seem to be whiny or petulant. Her feelings of apprehension about being replaced have to grow at the right pace. Her feelings are communicated in part from the placement of her closeups, which convey much, even when she has no lines."

Opie joins Malcolm in the kitchen for a glass of milk before going to bed. Malcolm sings as he cleans a pot. Opie asks him if he always sings when he does the dishes. Malcolm answers affirmatively and explains that "you're happiest when you're working because it makes you feel useful." Opie agrees and says, "When Aunt Bee was working, she'd sing all the time." Malcolm thinks about what Opie has said and replies, "I don't think I've heard your Aunt Bee sing."

"I needed a device for Malcolm to realize Aunt Bee's distress and understand that she actually enjoyed keeping up the house and depended on it for her worthiness," says Harvey. "I achieved this by having Opie and Malcolm discuss how Aunt Bee used to sing when she worked. When Malcolm explains that 'you're happiest when you're working because it makes you feel useful,' he arrives at the realization that this likewise applies to Aunt Bee. So he does a bit of self-destruction to bring things back as before."

Malcolm sets up the circumstances for his dismissal by serving Sunday lunch drunk. He pulls the drawer of the china cabinet out and spills the silverware on the floor. He then serves the soup cold right out of the can.

"Malcolm's drunk scene was constructed from waiter's goofs," says Harvey. "In fact, Ray and I had given Bernard a similar but longer scene as an errant waiter in an episode of *Make Room for Daddy*. In that episode, Bernard was truly a goof, not pretending as in this script."

"In order to give myself a slight feel for the drunk scene, I asked the prop man if he had any ideas. He produced a shot of scotch," says Bernard. "He did give me a very old-fashioned look when I asked for a second! As a matter of interest, the assistant prop man was a lad from Liverpool."

Andy, Barney, and Aunt Bee hear a crash in the kitchen. The three go to investigate and find Malcolm sitting on the floor. Barney notices an empty bottle of cooking sherry on the counter and brings it to Andy's attention. He tells Andy that he has no choice but to fire Malcolm. Barney says, "The guy's a wino. Get rid of him." Malcolm overhears and agrees to "pack up my things and leave."

After Malcolm leaves the kitchen, Andy examines the bottle, which Malcolm supposedly emptied. He smells the kitchen sink and realizes the bottle's contents were poured down the drain.

Before leaving, Malcolm tells Opie to try being "a little more help around here, young man." Andy opens the kitchen door to enter and stops. He then overhears Malcolm telling Opie that "when your Aunt Bee starts singing around the house, and she will soon, you just join in and have a regular singalong."

Opie leaves and Andy enters. He acknowledges what Malcolm has done by observing that he "sobered up mighty quick." Malcolm looks around the kitchen and apologizes for the mess. Andy tells him not to worry, that Aunt Bee will take care of it.

Malcolm then tells Andy good-bye, and Andy responds by saying, "Thanks, Malcolm, for everything."

"I made the decision to have Andy realize Malcolm's sacrifice and to thank him obliquely without forcing an admission, which might be uncomfortable for them both," says Harvey. "Having Andy tactfully talk around the subject was very effective and provided a satisfying ending."

The Rumor

EPISODE #125

FIRST BROADCAST ON APRIL 27, 1964

WRITTEN BY JIM FRITZELL
AND EVERETT GREENBAUM

DIRECTED BY COBY RUSKIN

"What a dumb trick. Don't ever call me dumb again."
Gomer talking
to Barney

The situation in this episode is somewhat different from Fritzell and Greenbaum's usual story lines. Instead of a motorcycle or the purchase of a first car causing the problem, the problem in "The Rumor" results from Barney's misinterpretation of Andy and Helen's intentions.

"This is one of the few times that Jim and I stole from ourselves," says writer Everett Greenbaum. "We had done this story with almost the same complications on *Mr. Peepers*. We enjoyed including Aneta Corsaut, who portrayed Helen Crump, in the script. Jim Fritzell was dating Aneta at the time and had encouraged her hiring on the Griffith show. Aneta was a wonderful person and a close friend."

"The Rumor" begins with Andy walking through Mayberry's business district. He looks into the window of Sterling's Jewelry Store and sees

Helen. Andy enters and asks Helen about a bracelet she is holding. Helen tells him it's a charm bracelet for her niece's graduation.

The jeweler steps into the store's back room. While he is away, Andy and Helen kiss.

Barney, who is patrolling the street, walks by the jewelry store and notices Andy and Helen inside. Barney sees the kiss and immediately jumps to the wrong conclusion.

A short time later, Barney tells Thelma Lou that Andy and Helen are "up to something." When Thelma Lou asks why they couldn't just happen to be in the jewelry store together, Barney replies, "Put two and two together. Read the handwriting on the wall. Blow away the smoke and look at the fire." In response to his clichés, Thelma Lou says, "Barney, you're always throwing your education in my face."

Barney responds, "I can't help myself. I'm just a student of the humanity. I guess that's the difference between a sharply honed lawman and just an ordinary jerk wearing a badge."

"It was always fun to write Barney's bull," says Everett. "Barney's dialogue flowed out of us—since the two of us were naturals at doing the same thing."

Barney eventually tells Thelma Lou that he thinks Helen and Andy are getting engaged. He points out that Andy wouldn't kiss anybody "out in public unless he had been hit by a transport of emotion."

"The 'transport of emotion' line was taken from old novels," says Everett.

When Barney tells Thelma Lou to keep the engagement a secret, he says, "I know it's tough on you being a woman, but for heaven's sake don't tell anybody."

Barney's statement is immediately followed by a closeup of Aunt Bee crying over news of the engagement. The camera pulls back, and Barney is revealed as the one who has told the secret.

"This visual joke was included in the script," says Everett. "We set it up with Barney's request for silence from Thelma Lou. The director's decision to begin the next scene with a closeup of Aunt Bee, before showing Barney sitting beside her, made the joke even more effective."

Still emotional over Barney's news, Aunt Bee cries while serving supper later in the evening. When she steps into the kitchen, Opie tells Andy that he thinks "she's got one of those allergics." When Andy asks what he means, Opie explains, "You see, at a certain time of the year bumblebees stand on the flowers, and they get a lot of this flower dust on their legs." Opie points out that the bees spread the dust, and people with "allergics" breathe the dust. He goes on to say, "I guess 'cause they just don't know any better. Well anyways, they get all puffy and their eyes run water."

When Aunt Bee comes back into the room, she starts to take her place at the table but is overcome with emotion and returns to the kitchen.

In response to Aunt Bee's crying, Opie observes that he doesn't think "that's allergic." Aunt Bee's sobs get louder. Opie responds, "I just don't understand it. I washed my hands and face. I emptied all the dirt out of my pants cuffs. My lizard is outside in the lizard house."

Andy explains that things sometimes "set women off." He alludes to certain sounds, smells, music—"a song on the radio reminds them of a rowboat ride or a dance." After listening to Andy, Opie says he doesn't understand. Andy replies, "Well, when you grow up, you won't understand it either, so don't worry about it."

"Opie's bumblebee and flower-dust theory is his way of explaining things—just as Barney has his way," says Everett. "I can't remember how the lizard house came up, but I clearly recall the inspiration for the dirt in the pant's cuffs. In Buffalo I had a radio show called *Greenbaum's Gallery*. A man named Ray Wander wrote it with me. We wrote at Ray's house. As I typed, he brushed out the cuffs of all his pants.

"A lot of Andy's talk about women sprang from Jim Fritzell. To him, women were a race apart—very hard to understand. On the other hand, I was a bit better with them.

"We wrote a brief scene in the first act in which Helen is walking one of her students home. Helen tells the student to remember to have her mother put something on her sty. We included this scene because we wanted to show that Helen was not only a good teacher but deeply concerned with the well-being of her students."

Thelma Lou sees Helen on the sidewalk in front of the student's house. She hugs Helen and tells her how happy she is. Thelma Lou invites Helen to walk downtown with her and do some shopping. Helen replies that she does need some stockings but she can pick them up when she goes to the jeweler's on Friday. She excuses herself from the shopping spree by saying she has papers to grade.

As the plot continues, Barney decides to surprise Andy and Helen with a party. At the planning session for the party, the food is discussed. Aunt Bee asks if Lillian should be asked to bring her meatballs. Barney answers, "They're always terrible—one percent meat and ninety-nine percent bread crumbs. She puts them in the oven, and they vulcanize."

"Vulcanization was the baking of crude rubber, sulphur, and other chemicals to make commercial rubber," explains Everett. "Barney thought it was a clever way to comment on the toughness of the meatballs."

Aunt Bee suggests that the perfect gift for Andy and Helen would be to fix up Andy's bedroom, which "is like an elephant's nest." The room needs fresh paint and wallpaper, new curtains, and a canopy bed "like in the Errol Flynn movie *The Dashing Prince*."

"Aunt Bee's description of Andy's bedroom was inspired by my brother-in-law's father," says Everett. "He said when his sons were boys their room looked like an elephant's nest. The name of the movie with the canopy bed in it was made up."

After the party plans are made, Barney goes around town collecting money to pay for the new decorations in Andy's room. Barney has each person write in a little book their name and the amount given.

The painter and wallpaper hangers are hired. When Barney stops by to see the room, he tells Aunt Bee that everybody will arrive for the surprise party "at eight bells" that night. "Thelma Lou and I will make like we're taking Andy and Helen out to dinner, see. Then we're going to stall them until it's time to get here."

By eight o'clock Andy's room is ready. Aunt Bee proudly shows it to one of the party guests and says that it is her "dream room."

Meanwhile at the courthouse, Barney can't decide where to go for supper. No place suits him. Andy eventually tells Barney to drive him to the market, and he'll get a loaf of bread and some baloney. Barney finally agrees to drive over to Andy's and "get something out of the icebox."

The party guests decide that everybody will go into the kitchen. When Aunt Bee gives the signal, they will come out and yell, "Surprise!" Gomer volunteers to go outside to "do my hoot owl" when he sees them coming.

Andy, Helen, Barney, and Thelma Lou arrive at the Taylors'. Gomer is eating a piece of cake when the squad car drives up. His mouth is full, so he is unable to hoot.

Andy and Helen enter the house. Gomer enters behind them and does his hoot owl. At this point everyone yells, "Surprise!" When Andy wants to know what the surprise is for, Barney says, "Oh, come on, buddy. It's not a secret anymore. We all know." When Helen asks what they know, Thelma Lou answers, "That you're engaged, and you picked up the ring today."

Aunt Bee ushers the speechless Andy and Helen upstairs to see Andy's room. Everyone follows. Aunt Bee announces, "This is your present."

Andy gets everyone's attention and tells them that there has been a mistake. He tells the group that they aren't engaged and have not even discussed the topic. When Barney asks about seeing the kiss, Helen says they were just buying a bracelet for her niece.

At this point, everyone begins to yell at Barney. Andy speaks up and says, "Folks, hold it! A party's a party anyway. And you're all here. There's plenty of food and pop here and everything, so why don't we all go downstairs and have a good time." Everyone leaves the room except Andy and Helen.

The two discuss the possibility of "getting together" in the future.

"The scene between Andy and Helen was difficult to write," says Everett. "The dialogue had to express their immediate feelings of not wanting to get married and the possibility that some day they might. We ended the scene with the couple kissing, which I'm sure Andy Griffith enjoyed—he was always ready to do some kissing."

When Andy and Helen join the party, Andy announces that everyone will get their money back, and Aunt Bee will get the room she's "always dreamed of."

"In the epilogue, Barney loses the book in which he wrote down the amount each person contributed to fix up the bedroom," says Everett. "The scene would have been nothing without the conflict the lost book caused. The discussion about who owes whom and how much each gave is not only conflict but a way to work some of the other characters into the end of the show."

Barney and Thelma Lou, Phffft

EPISODE #126

FIRST BROADCAST ON MAY 4, 1964

WRITTEN BY BILL IDELSON
AND SAM BOBRICK

DIRECTED BY COBY RUSKIN

"Believe me, I'm not worried. I got that little girl right in my hip pocket."

Barney Fife

This was the first episode written by Bill Idelson and Sam Bobrick in which the story line's problem results from difficulties that arise in a relationship. In their two previous TAGS scripts, the problems resulted from a shoplifter and jars of salve.

"An episode, which dealt with relationships, was actually easier to write," says writer Sam Bobrick. "The characters gave better guidelines for developing the story than in our first two scripts where the narrative centered on a comical situation."

The episode begins with a wonderful scene in which Barney and Thelma Lou are window shopping. The two stop in front of a furniture store and fantasize about decorating their future home. Momentarily carried away in their dreaming, the couple speak as if their marriage is a certainty. Barney, however, makes it clear that marriage is at best a distant possibility.

"By the time we started actually filming a scene, Don Knotts was ready, and you really believed whatever he said or did when he looked at you," says Betty Lynn, who portrayed Thelma Lou. "Don's performance always came from the bottom of his heart. Whenever I was in a scene, I played it for real, too.

"I felt that Barney was the love of Thelma Lou's life. She adored Barney. I think Thelma Lou was kind of hurt at times that Barney didn't say, 'Well, let's get married.' She kept hoping, and it never quite happened. It was like 'you're my girl, and somewhere off in the future we might get married, but we don't have to talk about that now.' In a way, there was a longing for Barney in Thelma Lou's heart that was never really satisfied."

The following day, Andy and Barney are busy with monthly reports. Thelma Lou telephones Barney and asks if he can drive her to Mt. Pilot for a dental appointment. Gomer drops by while Barney is on the telephone. He tells Andy that the squad car, which is in the garage getting fixed, won't be ready until that afternoon. Gomer offers Barney the use of his pickup. Barney, however, can't drive the pickup. Nobody can except Gomer, so Gomer volunteers to drive Thelma Lou to Mt. Pilot.

After Barney hangs up, Andy begins to tease him about going along to chaperon. Andy says, "You mean you're sending your girl on a long trip all alone with a handsome fellow like Gomer here? You're liable to lose your girl."

In response, Barney tells Andy and Gomer, "There are a lot of things in this world I might be worried about, but losing Thelma Lou is not one of them. I got that little girl right in my hip pocket."

"The message in this show," says Sam, "was 'let's look at relationships. Are they fair and the same for all parties?' Obviously, most of the time, they aren't.

"One way we demonstrated the difference in Barney and Thelma Lou's feelings about their relationship was to have Barney tell Andy that he had Thelma Lou in his hip pocket. We repeated the line several times in the episode, but when we first wrote it, that was not our intention. The line just worked well as a connector, which is a word or phrase that can be comically repeated. We liked to have connectors, but only when it was natural—like Barney's line was in the context of this story."

After Gomer leaves, Barney refers to Gomer and says, "Sheik."

"This was an example of Barney's tendency to mispronounce words," says Sam. "The word Barney had in mind was *chic*, which is French for sharp, current, or stylish."

During their drive to Mt. Pilot, Gomer asks Thelma Lou when she and Barney are getting married. He tells Thelma Lou that people say "you hardly ever hear one name without the other one." Thelma Lou is pleased. Gomer continues, "If he don't hurry up somebody's going to come along and steal you away." He goes on to add that Barney said "he had you in his hip pocket." Thelma Lou is no longer pleased.

"Gomer and Thelma Lou's conversation during their trip to Mt. Pilot was photographed inside the studio," says producer Aaron Ruben. "The camera was placed in front of the stationary truck. A cloth was placed behind the truck's back windshield to eliminate the need for a rear projection shot of the passing scenery. The shadows that were cast on the truck's hood were done with lights and a cut-out that simulated the shadows that would be cast on the vehicle."

After returning from Mt. Pilot, Gomer shares with Andy and Barney the details of his outing with Thelma Lou. He says, "She bought me lunch—sausages and three eggs, six flapjacks. It must have set her back over seventy cents."

After Gomer leaves, Barney tells Andy that in all the years he's known Thelma Lou, she's never bought him lunch. They've always gone "dutch treat."

"Barney's response to Thelma Lou's buying Gomer's lunch showed an endearing sort of pettiness and insensitivity on his part," says Sam.

Thelma Lou decides to teach Barney a lesson. She breaks their standing Tuesday night date. Barney goes to the courthouse and dejectedly explains to Andy that he was "all dressed up—tie, coat, the works." He called Thelma Lou to tell her he was on his way over, but she acted surprised, "like it completely slipped her mind that it was Tuesday night." Thelma Lou told Barney that she was busy. Barney is amazed because every Tuesday night for as long as he can remember "we're sitting on that couch, a pan of cashew fudge between us, watching that doctor show on TV. Now all of a sudden, it slipped her mind."

"We painted a situation in which the viewer would know instantly that a great date for Barney was not what anyone would consider to be a great date—for Thelma Lou or any other person," explains Sam.

Barney accompanies Andy on his nightly check of Main Street. As the two walk down the street, they see Thelma Lou and Gomer going to the movie.

The next day, Barney tells Andy that it's all his fault that Thelma Lou went with Gomer to the movie. Andy responds by telling Barney he is "acting like a kid. There's nothing serious going on between Thelma Lou and Gomer. So they went to the movie. As far as that goes, you've stepped out a few times yourself." Andy then asks Barney about Juanita who works at the diner. Barney says that's different. When Andy pushes him for an explanation of the difference, Barney says, "Well, if you don't know how it's different, I ain't going to tell you."

"Barney's response to Andy showed the narrow concept of fairness he had," says Sam. "Barney was a very chauvinistic fellow."

Andy advises Barney to go see Thelma Lou. He tells him to take her some flowers and see what's wrong. Barney insists that "she ought to come to me with flowers. I'm the stood-up party."

When Gomer enters, Barney walks out. Andy asks Gomer how he came to take Thelma Lou to the movie. When Gomer replies that Thelma Lou asked him, Andy asks what the two talked about on their way to Mt. Pilot. Gomer answers, "We talked some about Barney. . .and how he thought he had her in his hip pocket."

Andy begins "to get the picture. Thelma Lou is playing a little game with Barney trying to make him jealous." Gomer is upset when he learns that Barney's feelings are hurt. Andy tells him not to worry. The two of them will get over it, but it was a good thing Thelma Lou picked Gomer because sometimes a "thing like that could backfire, you know." When Gomer doesn't understand, Andy explains, "Suppose she had this date with another fellow. This fellow got to liking it, got to liking her, and wanted her to be his steady. I expect she'd drop her game pretty fast and go running back to Barney."

After hearing this, Gomer decides to "scare Thelma Lou back into Barney's arms." He visits Thelma Lou. Soon after his arrival, he asks for a cup of coffee. While Thelma Lou is out of the room, Gomer telephones Andy. He tells Andy he is fixing to "backfire on her." But Thelma Lou overhears Gomer.

Meanwhile, Barney is outside Thelma Lou's house. He has decided to follow Andy's advice and bring Thelma Lou some flowers. When he starts to ring the doorbell, he hears Gomer's voice and stops. Barney walks over to the window and looks in.

Inside, Gomer asks Thelma Lou to "be his steady." Thelma Lou answers, "Gomer, I'd love to," and kisses him on the cheek.

After seeing the kiss, Barney goes to Andy's house. He tells Andy that they were "kissing—hugging and kissing. You couldn't have gotten a piece of tissue paper between them. They were that close."

The doorbell rings, and it is Gomer. Barney immediately raises his fists and tells Gomer to "put 'em up." Andy has to separate the two.

"What we were going for in this scene," says Sam, "was to have Andy come across as an adult trying to separate two children."

Gomer tells Andy that something went wrong with his plan. "She kissed me right flush on the jaw. And you know what that means, don't you? There's only one thing I can do now, only one honorable thing. After she kissed me like that, I got to marry her."

Andy decides "this thing has gone far enough" and takes them all over to Thelma Lou's house.

Barney remains in the squad car while Andy and Gomer talk with

Thelma Lou. Andy explains to Thelma Lou that Gomer comes from a family with a very strict code of conduct. When a girl kisses a fellow "it's marrying time." Thelma Lou tells Andy it was all a joke. Andy asks Gomer if it is a joke when a "girl kisses you like that." Gomer says, "It ain't no joke to me. When a fellow and a girl kiss, it means they got to marry. Shoot, my mama and daddy just shook hands on their deal."

"This dialogue grew out of the character," says Sam. "It communicated Gomer's innocence and the fact that absolutely nothing happened between him and Thelma Lou. This also helped explain Barney's warped look at relationships—in his mind, one kiss implied there was something going on between Thelma Lou and Gomer."

Andy asks Thelma Lou if she would "take the kiss back." Thelma Lou kisses Gomer, taking the first kiss back.

After Andy brings Barney inside, Thelma Lou apologizes to Barney and asks him to "please don't ever say you've got me in your hip pocket." The two are reconciled.

In the epilogue, however, the original cause of the misunderstanding is not resolved—Barney once again confidently tells Andy, "I've got that little girl right in my hip pocket."

"Comedy writing is delivering a message in a clear and easy-to-take way," says Sam. "More than being concerned with solving any problem, we were always more concerned with dealing with the message."

Back to Nature

EPISODE #127

FIRST BROADCAST ON MAY 11, 1964

WRITTEN BY HARVEY BULLOCK

DIRECTED BY COBY RUSKIN

"I just patched some bird words together and came up with web-footed, red-crested lake loon."

Harvey Bullock

"**B**ack to Nature" begins with a conversation between Andy, Barney, and Floyd about modern gadgets. Barney is upset because the new automatic cutoff on the filling-station gas pump has caused a scratch on the squad car. After listening to Barney's complaint, Floyd goes off on a tangent and says he dislikes the new, electric lather makers. He prefers the sound the shaving brush makes in the mug when it goes "klep."

"The script copy I have begins with the scene in the courthouse in which Andy tells the boys about the impending overnight camping trip," says writer Harvey Bullock. "Perhaps producer Aaron Ruben wrote the scene with Howard McNear, who portrayed Floyd Lawson, to add length or variety.

"All writers have a proprietary interest in what they write. I would occasionally feel twinges when I saw changes to my script. Most of the script changes on TAGS, however, enriched the story, and I always felt comfortable with writer-friendly Aaron Ruben at the helm."

The next day, the boys who are going on the camping trip meet with Andy at the courthouse. Andy gives the boys instructions about the trip.

One of the boys is Opie's friend, Trey Bowden. Trey first appeared in the episode "Andy and Opie's Pal" and was named after a friend of Harvey's son, Andy, who lived up the street from the Bullocks.

"The real Trey Bowden was one of the boy campers in this show," says Harvey. "For some reason I can't recall, my son Andy was not used. I was seldom on the set, but I think it was a rare occurrence when friends were used as extras."

After the boys leave, Gomer enters and tells Andy he has decided not to go along on the camping trip. He says, "There's this movie on the TV tomorrow night with Preston Foster I wanna see."

"Preston Foster was a prominent movie star in the 1930s," says Harvey. "He was a leading-man type who played rugged outdoorsy roles— Mounties, Rangers, woodsmen, etc. Gomer felt watching a Foster movie would make up for his not going on the camping trip."

The next morning, Andy, Barney, Gomer (who was finally persuaded to come along), and the boys arrive in the woods and set up camp.

Later that night around the campfire, Barney leads the boys in their request for a ghost story. Andy agrees to tell one. He asks the boys to "be real quiet." A owl hoots in the distance. Andy says the hoot owl reminds him of a story and starts with " a long time ago, right in these very woods, there lived an old hermit."

"As a child, I spent three summers at YMCA Camp Arrowhead in Binghamton, New York," says Harvey. "The experience definitely left memories. What we kids loved best were the ghost stories—either when the whole camp was around a fire or when they were told by individual leaders at bedtime in the cabins. Later I worked at the same camp, in charge of entertainment, and told ghost stories, using moans, groans, and staring eyes. The campers would buy it all, huddle closer, and walk back to their cabins in tight groups with sweeping flashlights.

"As I remember, I told a story like Andy's 'The Hermit with the Golden Arm' early in the summer. Then one of the camp counselors would dress up as the hermit and allow the campers to get a fleeting glance of him. This put the kids in a tizzy, which they loved. We kept up the deception for weeks, even sending search parties after the apparition. Then, finally, we had the hermit walk nonchalantly into the mess hall. I can still hear the kids screaming. The hermit story naturally came to mind when I needed a ghost story to include in the script."

After the story, Barney tells the boys that it was just a story, and that there is "nothing to be frightened about."

Later that night, Andy wakes up. He looks from side to side and sees Barney and Gomer. The two have placed their sleeping bags next to Andy and are wide awake.

"Barney and Gomer's fearful reaction to the story is somewhat ingenious and possibly stretched credibility a little," says Harvey. "But they were out in a strange foreboding place and had just gulped down a horror story told effectively by Andy. And the two were somewhat unsophisticated and impressionable."

The next morning, Trey tells Andy, Barney, and Gomer that Opie's gone. His sleeping bag is still there, but he isn't anywhere around.

Andy goes out searching for Opie. After he leaves, Barney decides he and Gomer will "comb the north slope."

A short time later, Andy returns to camp with Opie. Opie left camp without telling anyone because he wanted to surprise Andy with some berries he picked.

Meanwhile somewhere on the north slope, Barney tells Gomer, "Opie isn't anywhere around here or these old baby blues would have spotted him." He suggests they work their way back to camp. Barney starts back, but Gomer thinks camp is in the opposite direction. Barney insists he knows the way back. As they start walking, a handkerchief in Barney's back pocket gets snagged on a branch and is left behind.

Fletch, a friend of Andy's, arrives in camp. Fletch has brought up a "little archery equipment." Fletch also brought along two roasted chickens, which Aunt Bee sent in case they got "tired of hot dogs." Andy asks Fletch if he has seen Barney and Gomer, but he has not.

Fletch takes the boys "to have some fun with the bows and arrows." While the boys are occupied, Andy decides to go look for Barney and Gomer. He takes Aunt Bee's roasted chickens and leaves camp.

Barney and Gomer continue wandering in the woods. When they stop "to take a breather," Gomer tells Barney that he's starved. He says, "We didn't have no breakfast, and it's already past noon." Barney responds that normally he would make a snare and catch a pheasant or wild bird, but "you can't make a decent snare without a piece of string. If I had a piece of string, I'd catch you a bird dinner you'd never forget." At this point, Gomer pulls a pair of extra shoelaces from his shirt pocket.

"The extra shoelaces are a stretch that I missed," admits Harvey. "It would have been infinitely better if Gomer volunteered the shoestring from his high-top sneakers. Then he could have flopped around with one open sneaker to add to the comedy."

Barney builds a snare and sets it up. He and Gomer then leave, so they won't scare the pheasants away.

Gomer suggests they will need a fire. Barney agrees and asks for a match. While Gomer is searching his pockets, Barney bends over, picks up two sticks and says, "Course, we could start one just as quick by rubbing two sticks together. You know fire by constriction."

"I reveled in giving Barney word miscues—*constriction* for *combustion*, for example," says Harvey. "I tried not to overdo it, but the occasional miscue was tasty."

When Gomer can't find a match, he looks at Barney and says, "I guess you better use those pioneer sticks."

When Barney sits down beside a fallen tree, Gomer observes that the place looks like the same place where they started. When he suggests they are lost and walking in circles, Barney replies, "This is not the same tree, and we are not lost."

Barney sends Gomer "to keep an eye on the snare while I get a fire started." Barney places one of the sticks on the fallen tree and twirls it back and forth between his hands.

Andy finds Gomer while he is checking on the snare. Gomer asks Andy what he's doing there. Andy explains that when they didn't come back to camp, he thought he'd come out to look for them. Gomer tells Andy that he thought they were lost, but Barney had said they weren't. He adds, "Are the boys back at camp going to have fun with this! The laugh is really going to be on him."

Andy explains to Gomer that he's afraid that kind of laugh will "hurt him pretty bad." After a moment's reflection, Gomer observes that Barney was only trying to help. He wishes there were something they could do.

"When Andy explains to Gomer that Barney will be ridiculed for getting lost, he is telling the audience as well to back up their understanding and emphasize the importance of all which follows," says Harvey.

Andy decides there is something they can do. He gives Gomer some matches and tells him to break them off and put the heads in Barney's "firemaker." Andy promises "to watch the snare and get you a pheasant." Gomer then rejoins Barney.

While Barney is away gathering twigs, Gomer puts the match heads in Barney's firemaker.

When Barney walks a short distance away, he finds his handkerchief hanging from a branch and realizes he has been walking in circles. He accepts the realization that he is lost.

Barney walks dejectedly back to Gomer. He is about to admit he is lost when Gomer interrupts and insists that Barney "show me your twirling again." Barney twirls the stick, and a flame shoots up. Barney gets excited and runs off to "get some firewood."

While Barney is away, Andy hands Gomer one of Aunt Bee's roasted chickens and tells him to hold it over the fire. Andy tells Gomer that when he and Barney finish eating, Gomer should listen for a loon call that Andy will make. If Gomer and Barney follow the call, Andy will lead the two back to camp.

Barney returns and is surprised to find Gomer roasting a bird over the fire. He asks incredulously, "You mean that snare worked? And it's [the pheasant] done and everything?" Barney reasons that the "pheasant" cooked so fast because "any fire started pioneer-style is bound to be hotter than fire started with just ordinary matches."

"I spent some mental time seeing how Barney could accept a cooked bird without being suspicious," says Harvey. "A fire seemed a good idea since Barney had claimed expertise in building one and the match heads Gomer put in the firemaker gave Barney all the credit without much suspicion. Barney's question about how the pheasant cooked so fast was an intelligent question which he would ask almost without thinking. Then Barney answers his own question—'pioneer fire is hotter.'

"The viewer has to put themselves in Barney's place. He's lost, apprehensive, and a bit confused. He wants desperately to have caught and cooked that bird and is willing to come up with almost any explanation—especially if it backs up his pioneer moxie. Remember, Barney doesn't question that they caught the bird. He is not aware of any other person or thing involved. The actual bird proves he's on the right track, and no other explanation of the cooking comes to mind—so he accepts it."

Barney and Gomer enjoy the meal. Barney observes that "there's a taste you can't match with anything you'll ever find in the city. Even Aunt Bee couldn't have cooked up anything that good."

Just then, a bird cries out. Gomer asks, "Hear that? That's a lake loon, and it come from that direction." When Barney ignores him, Gomer continues to drop hints that the loon is probably headed toward the lake. Barney still ignores what Gomer is saying until he begins to think out loud, "Probably a web-footed, red-crested lake loon. Where would a web-footed, red-crested lake loon be headed? Toward the lake. We just follow that sound, and it's a shortcut home."

Barney and Gomer follow Andy's bird calls back to camp and triumphantly share their story of survival. As the story is told, Gomer shows the boys the snare Barney made. Interestingly, as the two walked through the woods, neither Gomer nor Barney was carrying the snare. Nevertheless, Gomer has it with him when he emerges into camp.

"Details of continuity were watched by the script supervisor and the director," says producer Aaron Ruben. "The missing snare was simply an oversight that no one caught."

"A lot of pencil plotting went into the structuring and sequencing of this story," says Harvey. "If you have a movie screen in your head, that helps. Close both eyes. Be there in the scene on the screen. Watch where everyone else is, and how it progresses. Then stop and do it another way. Sometimes any approach to the scene seems inadequate. In that case, toss the whole scene away, study the story again, and reset the scene and characters somewhere else. This sounds glib, but consciously or unconsciously that is what most writers do. And here's where a writing partner is so very helpful. Two people bouncing ideas off each other is far more fruitful than one person bouncing ideas off the wallpaper alone."

"'Back to Nature' was Jim Nabors' final TAGS episode," says Aaron. "The *Gomer Pyle, U.S.M.C.* episode, which was broadcast the following week, was actually filmed much earlier in the season. I recall Jim being elated when 'Nature' was completed. He was about to star in a series of his own and was already eagerly anticipating the future."

1964-65

Barney's Bloodhound

EPISODE #128

FIRST BROADCAST ON OCTOBER 26, 1964

WRITTEN BY BILL IDELSON
AND SAM BOBRICK

DIRECTED BY HOWARD MORRIS

"This episode and 'The Case of the Punch in the Nose' were my two favorite scripts."
Sam Bobrick

"Our first two TAGS scripts were well received," says writer Sam Bobrick. "As a result, Bill and I became part of the group of writers who met with executive producer Sheldon Leonard at the beginning of the year to work out story lines for the new season.

"Every morning for about two weeks, the writers met in Sheldon's office and pitched stories until late in the afternoon. During the two weeks, we would come up with ten to twelve stories. 'Barney's Bloodhound' was one of the stories that came out of the seminar."

By the fall of 1964, Howard Morris had directed *The Dick Van Dyke Show, The Bill Dana Show*, and dozens of other shows on different networks. "I was getting known as a director," says Howard, "and TAGS producer Aaron Ruben asked me if I wanted to direct the Griffith show.

I said, 'Sure,' and I did. It fell together quite well."

"Barney's Bloodhound" begins with Barney rushing down the sidewalk to get to the courthouse in time to hear *The Leonard Blush Show* on the radio. The show is interrupted during Leonard Blush's first song by a special news bulletin. The news bulletin reports that a convict, Ralph Neal, has escaped from the state penitentiary.

"The script called for a radio announcer to introduce *The Leonard Blush Show* and then interrupt the program to make the announcement about the escaped convict," says Howard. "I was there on the set, they needed a voice for Leonard Blush and the announcer, so I did them both."

Barney turns off the radio as soon as the news bulletin is completed. He gets excited over the possibility that Neal may be heading for Mayberry and feels he and Andy should be prepared to assist in the capture of the convict. Andy is unconcerned because the state prison is "a long ways from here." Barney is frustrated by Andy's nonchalance and storms out.

That afternoon, Barney asks Andy if there have been any more reports on Neal. Andy answers that a motorist thought he saw him near Mt. Pilot, but "he's probably just imagining." Something pulls Barney away from the doorway where he is standing. When he returns to the doorway, he is pulled away a second time. At this point, Barney announces that he wants to show Andy something.

Barney struggles to enter the courthouse. He is holding a rope. On the other end of the rope is a dog. According to Barney, the dog, who is named Blue, is part bloodhound. Barney says Blue is going to "lead us right straight toward that criminal." Barney then demonstrates Blue's responsiveness to a dog whistle. When Barney blows the whistle, Blue snarls. This causes Andy to comment, "I don't think he likes that."

"The dog cast as Blue fit my image for the animal perfectly," says Sam. "The name Blue was a cliché. We chose that name because we felt it was one that Barney would come up with."

Andy doesn't believe "that dog could find his own food dish." Barney then threatens to make Andy "eat those words. I'm going to give you a little demonstration." On the way to the courthouse, Barney had stopped at the barbershop and picked up one of Floyd's handkerchiefs. Barney has Blue sniff the handkerchief and encourages him to track Floyd. Barney pushes Blue out the door, nudges him down the sidewalk, and guides him into the barbershop.

Floyd watches the dog's work with great interest. Blue eventually walks to Floyd. Floyd responds that "he's probably looking for some more of that candy." When Barney had brought Blue into the barbershop earlier, Floyd gave the dog a lollipop.

"This was the first time Bill and I wrote for Howard McNear, who portrayed Floyd Lawson," says Sam. "Floyd was a very easy character to write for, and we always enjoyed Howard McNear's performance."

"The dog was just wonderful," say Howard Morris. "The trainer would say, 'Show the left side,' and the dog would turn around and show his left side. Or the trainer would say, 'Now do a take. When Barney does a take, you do a take,' and he would. The dog's long gone now but working with him is a memory that I cherish.

"Howard McNear was a lovely man. I'd say, 'Show your left side,' and he would. Howard had had a stroke by this time and was unable to walk around, so he remains seated throughout the scene in the barbershop. In another episode I directed, Howard had to pretend to cut Andy's hair. We built a kind of seat for Howard behind the barber chair, which couldn't be seen. It made Howard appear to be standing. Howard was a lovely, lovely man and a wonderful actor."

Andy tells Barney that the dog will probably lead them straight to the criminal, "providing he's traveling around with a pocketful of lollipops." Barney is not amused. He calls Blue to leave, but Blue does not respond. Barney takes the dog whistle out of his pocket and blows it. Blue snarls angrily and chases Barney out of the barbershop.

Later in the day, the state police visit the courthouse and confirm Barney's suspicion that Neal is in the vicinity. They ask Andy to check out the area north of Mayberry.

After the state police leave, Andy calls Barney into the office. He has

*Barney has Blue sniff Floyd's handkerchief
and encourages him to track Floyd.*

TAGSRWC Archives

been outside, working with Blue. Barney tells Andy that the manhunt couldn't have come at a better time. He is convinced that the dog is going to be "such a help to us."

When Andy protests the use of Blue in the manhunt, Barney offers to show how much the dog has learned. Barney calls Blue, but the dog is asleep on the cot in the back room. Looking at Blue, Andy tells Barney that he'd better leave the dog at the office. "He looks like he needs the rest."

An angry Barney says, "You want to see that dog move?" He then pulls out his gun and says, "All right Blue, there's a man out here with a gun. Get him." Blue continues to sleep. When Barney blows the dog whistle, Blue bounds out of the back room and knocks Barney to the floor.

Andy, Barney, and Blue travel north of Mayberry to assist in the manhunt. Before beginning the search, Barney shows Blue a picture of Neal and talks to the dog as if he were a person. Barney gives Blue his instructions: "That's your man. Now you go get him."

"The idea to have Barney show Blue the wanted poster and then talk to the dog as if it were a person was inspired by the fact that most people talk to their pets," says Sam. "Barney, of course, always pushes a normal situation a little bit farther."

After looking at Neal's picture, Blue takes off. When Andy and Barney decide to split up, Barney follows Blue.

Blue leads Barney to a man who is fishing. The man is dressed in jeans and a dark shirt. As Barney approaches, the man takes off his hat and hides a gun beneath it. Barney warns the man that there's a convict on the loose. As Barney describes Neal physically and shows Neal's picture, he realizes he's talking to Neal.

The first act, which concludes with Barney's capture by the convict, is unusually long (fifteen minutes and twenty-nine seconds).

"We were never concerned with the first act's length or the spacing of the commercial breaks," "says Sam. "That was not a writer's problem."

Neal takes Barney to a cabin where he is held hostage. Neal plans to keep Barney at the cabin until dark. He is going to take Barney along for "a little insurance. Cops don't shoot so quick when you got a hostage."

Meanwhile, Andy has discovered Barney's hat and the picture of Neal at the site where Barney was captured. He walks to the cabin, sees smoke coming from the chimney, and carefully works his way closer to look inside.

Inside the cabin, Neal is asleep. Barney quietly rises from his chair and slowly walks toward the door. Barney is almost at the door when Blue barks. Neal wakes up and orders Barney back to the chair. Neal leaves Blue in charge and goes back to sleep.

By this time, Andy has worked his way to the cabin. He motions to Barney through a window, and the two silently mouth a plan of escape. Barney runs toward the door. As he reaches the door, it opens. Barney runs out, and Andy steps in. Now Andy is the hostage.

Andy warns Neal that he'd better give himself up. He says, "This place will be surrounded by police in a matter of minutes. My deputy is getting a posse right now."

Upon hearing this, Neal decides to leave. He orders Andy to open the door. When the door opens, Barney is standing outside and is recaptured.

Neal puts on Barney's uniform and leads Andy and Barney, who is now dressed in Neal's clothes, to the squad car. Before getting in, Neal asks, "Where's the mutt. Hey, Blue."

Andy explains that the dog's a "little hard of hearing, but you got a whistle in your pocket there. If you blow that, he'll come right to you." Neal blows the whistle. Angered by the annoying whistle, Blue rushes up and jumps on Neal, enabling Andy and Barney to capture him.

The epilogue is extremely well written and uses a TAGS trademark— Andy and Barney locking themselves in a cell—in a clever way. Excited by Blue's capture of Neal, Barney continues to work with the dog. He attempts to have Blue pick the cell-door keys off the floor on command. Andy, who is straightening up a cell, asks Barney for help. Barney enters the cell and shuts the door, locking it behind him. Blue, holding the keys in his mouth, now becomes the center of attention as Andy, Barney, and the locked-up Neal all call his name. Remembering the dog whistle and its effect on Blue, Andy instructs Barney to blow it. The keys are quickly delivered to the cell.

"'Barney's Bloodhound' was an easy script to write," says Sam. "It worked extremely well, and Don Knotts, as always, was a comic genius."

Family Visit

EPISODE #129

FIRST BROADCAST ON OCTOBER 5, 1964

WRITTEN BY JIM FRITZELL
AND EVERETT GREENBAUM

DIRECTED BY HOWARD MORRIS

"I remember that Andy's house was crowded."
Howard Morris, director

"I don't think Don Knotts's contract obligated him to be in every show," says writer Everett Greenbaum. "Producer Aaron Ruben would tell us who was going to be in each script. We wrote 'Family Visit' knowing Don wasn't available."

The opening scene of Jim and Everett's completed script begins with Andy, Aunt Bee, and Opie sitting on the front porch on a Sunday morning. The three have already been to church and are greeting folks who are passing by on their way to the second service. Johnny Paul Jason, one of Opie's friends, walks by, and Opie tells him, "Good sermon today—about Cain and Abel. You see it's about these two brothers, and they had all this trouble." Andy interrupts and tells Opie to hush, but Opie continues, "That's all I can tell you, Johnny Paul, but don't be surprised if somebody gets killed." After Johnny Paul walks off, Andy tells Opie that "Bible knowledge is a fine thing but don't flaunt it."

"The episode's opening scene was inspired by a childhood memory," says Everett. "When I was growing up in Buffalo my family lived next to Saint Mark's Catholic Church. In summer, we could sit on our front veranda and watch the congregation get out of their cars and walk to Saint Mark's. There was an early service and a later service. We didn't know any of the people personally so there was no conversation, but that didn't matter. It still was a peaceful way to spend a Sunday morning.

"Opie's line, 'Don't be surprised if someone gets killed,' was the Greenbaum way of spoiling the ending of a movie or a novel for another family member."

Andy, Aunt Bee, and Opie see the Beamon family on their way to church. Four generations of Beamons—Claude, Sr., Claude, Jr., Plain Claude, and Claudette—are walking together. Opie asks why they call Mr. Beaman "Plain Claude Beamon." Andy answers, "Because he's not a Senior, and he's not a Junior, so they call him Plain Claude Beamon." Aunt Bee says she thought they called him Plain Claude because he was so homely. Andy replies, "He's not homely. He's just got the Beamon overbite, but that's more of a characteristic."

"I remember very little about this one," admits Everett. "I don't even remember seeing it in reruns. I can't recall how the Beamon dialogue originated. But if it hadn't bubbled out, we never would have been paid."

Seeing the Beamon family stirs up Aunt Bee's desire to see her baby sister Nora and her family. After a brief discussion, Andy and Aunt Bee decide to invite Nora, her husband Ollie, and their two sons for a visit.

Ollie, Nora, and the boys arrive the next weekend. Andy helps Ollie unload the car. Ollie tells Andy about how many miles-per-gallon he got on the trip to Mayberry while he hands Andy the luggage. Andy carries four suitcases into the house, while Ollie carries a sack, a pair of shoes, and a small valise.

"Andy's Uncle Ollie was based roughly on Jim Fritzell's cousin Ivor," says Everett. "Ollie's annoying habits of talking about his gas mileage and driving victories were inspired by a routine that had worked well for us on *Mr. Peepers*. One of the characters on that show, Aunt Lil, always enjoyed telling her adventures about driving in her Reo. The idea to have Ollie load Andy down with all the heavy luggage came from my memories of my Uncle Arthur. He somehow always avoided carrying in the luggage whenever my family visited him in Philadelphia."

During supper Aunt Nora mentions a friend of hers, Racine Tyler, who she feels would be a good match for Andy. Nora tells Andy that Racine's deceased husband owned Tyler Bakery. Nora adds that Racine recently collected four thousand dollars on his life-insurance policy. Echoing his wife, Uncle Ollie sums up the situation concisely. "Pretty good deal, Andy. Skinny widow, four thousand dollars, three-year-old bakery truck with the original paint."

"Jim and I felt that Nora had been trying to make a match between Andy and this Racine for some time," says Everett. "Nora felt that the insurance payout was an important selling point for Racine. Ollie's summation of the situation demonstrated what a shallow materialist he was—another of his many annoying attributes."

Following supper, Andy takes his guests for "a little spin around town to see the sights." He stops the car at the Mayberry Gas Works and points out the new, blacktopped parking lot.

"My dad's idea of showing visitors a good time was to drive around Buffalo, pointing out new stores, or better yet, stores having tire sales," says Everett. "My father owned a tire store and was always interested in tire prices. We wanted Andy to show off something even more boring—blacktop."

Due to limited space, Opie must share his bed with Ollie's two sons, Roger and Bruce. Before going to sleep Opie complains to Aunt Bee "that Roger has his foot in the pit of my back." Aunt Bee tells Opie she will "rub it down with witch hazel in the morning." Opie continues to complain that "witch hazel makes my eyes water." Aunt Bee responds, "Well, you won't see as well, but you'll feel better."

"I've always been fond of witch hazel," says Everett. "I love the way it smells and still use it constantly for fleabites, since we have pets. Sleeping in a crowded bed was a memory from childhood, and as the gag developed witch hazel fit in perfectly."

Andy and Ollie share a bed. Before going to sleep, Ollie and Nora get into an argument. According to Ollie, Nora forgot to bring his goose-down pillow. Nora replies that she thought he had it. "After all, you're the one who uses it." When Ollie admits he forgot the pillow, Nora says, "You forget everything. You forgot my birthday. You forgot our anniversary." Ollie explains that he forgot their anniversary because "the foreman sent me around looking for a spindle wrench just at quitting time."

"After I flunked out of M.I.T., I was obliged to go to work at Bell Aircraft as a riveter," says Everett. "It seemed to me that parts chasers always had the best job. The job seemed to fit Ollie."

Ollie is upset by the argument. He tells Andy that he won't sleep "a wink. She's got me all on edge." Andy suggests that Ollie read a little bit. He says, "I always find that when I can't sleep, if I read a little piece out of a magazine, I just doze right off." Andy reaches for a magazine from the nightstand. He hands the magazine to Ollie, but Ollie is already asleep.

The next morning, Andy and Aunt Bee are in the kitchen before Nora and Ollie wake up. Andy tells Aunt Bee that "half the night Ollie had his arm in my mouth. The other half, he was dreaming he was riding a bicycle. All in all, I'd say it was one of the most active nights I ever spent." Aunt Bee assures Andy that everything will work out because they are only visiting for the weekend. Andy replies, "I guess we can stand our loved ones that long."

When Ollie and Nora join Andy and Aunt Bee, Nora talks about how wonderful the visit has been. Aunt Bee and Andy agree. Andy says, "We were just saying what a fine visit it's been, and what a shame it has to be so short." In response, Nora and Ollie decide to stay for a whole week.

During the breakfast scene, Aunt Bee is seated with her back to the stove. The closeups of Aunt Bee show the wall behind her. This wall is rarely seen in the series, since the kitchen is normally photographed with the camera positioned behind the stove with the wall removed.

Later that morning, Ollie visits Andy at the courthouse. Ollie takes a rifle from the gun rack, cocks it, aims toward the door, and pulls the unloaded rifle's trigger. Andy takes the gun away from Ollie and returns it to the gun rack.

When a man stops by to pay a traffic ticket, Ollie reprimands the man.

Wanting to get rid of Ollie, Andy suggests that he go fishing. Ollie follows Andy's suggestion and drives off in the squad car. Andy runs out onto the sidewalk and tries to stop him but is too late.

Floyd is sitting outside his shop. Hoping to catch Ollie, Andy asks if he can borrow Floyd's car. Floyd tells Andy that his car is at Wally's. In reference to his car, Floyd adds, "Oh, the poor dear's in terrible shape. Her transmission, her second gear had a whine like a crying child. Wally opened up her gear box and took one look and closed her right up."

"Using Floyd's comments about his sick car was our way of satirizing the older generation's medical gossip," says Everett. "We took a comment such as 'Dr. Phelps took one look inside her abdomen, found it incurable, and closed her right up' and applied it to Floyd's car. Floyd was always fun to write for and here, as always, Howard McNear delivered Floyd's lines as only he could."

Andy rushes back to the office to use the telephone. Nora is on the telephone talking to Racine Tyler. She insists that Andy talk with Racine. Andy reluctantly complies. After a short conversation, Andy hangs up the telephone and calls Harry's Pond. Andy tells Harry to send "his uncle right back with the squad car."

Later that evening, Andy and Ollie hear a news bulletin over the radio that three convicts have escaped from a South Carolina prison. Ollie tells Andy, "Good thing they [the escapees] are not headed this way. We'd take care of them in two winks."

Andy leaves to "make his rounds." Sometime later, he receives a call at the courthouse that the escapees have been caught. After hanging up the telephone, Andy gets an idea. He telephones his house and tells Ollie that he has great news. "You know those two convicts we heard about on the radio? They've been seen in this area. I'm going after them, but I'm going to need some help. I'll throw an extra rifle in the squad car and come by for you. I'll be there in a few minutes."

This scene has a continuity error. This passage of the script mentions two convicts, while the earlier news bulletin reported three.

Ollie suddenly remembers that he left the gas on at home and makes a hasty departure.

"The resolution of the problem in this episode was typical sitcom and kind of ordinary," says Everett. "I was not very satisfied with it, but we needed an ending. Time was a factor, so we decided it would do."

The episode's epilogue is set on the Taylor front porch. It is evening, and Andy and Aunt Bee are enjoying the peacefulness of life without company. The two-minute scene, photographed in one sustained shot, opens with a closeup of Andy playing his guitar. The camera then pans back, revealing Andy and Aunt Bee. The two comment on Nora and Ollie's visit. When the telephone rings, Aunt Bee rises. The camera pans left and follows her as she enters the house. The camera then pans right and stops on Andy, who listens to Aunt Bee talking on the phone.

The decision to photograph the scene in one sustained shot adds to its peaceful atmosphere. The sustained shot enables the camera to float around the porch and is more visually relaxing than having various camera angles edited together.

"The epilogue in my script is different," says Everett. "It is set in the dining room, and Andy is not playing his guitar."

The change in setting gives the story a sense of symmetry. The episode opens on the front porch. After the relatives leave and peace is restored, it ends there.

Aunt Bee's Romance

EPISODE #130

FIRST BROADCAST ON OCTOBER 19, 1964

WRITTEN BY HARVEY BULLOCK

DIRECTED BY HOWARD MORRIS

WALLACE FORD GUEST STARS
AS ROGER HANOVER

"'Everybody complains about the weather, but nobody does anything about it.' Know who said that? Calvin Coolidge."

Floyd Lawson

"I have a mental blank about this classic 'Floyd' scene. I really can't recall whether it was my contribution or not."

Harvey Bullock

"**A**unt Bee's Romance" begins around the breakfast table. Andy compliments Aunt Bee on "a fine breakfast" and whispers to Opie, "That girl's going to make somebody a fine bride one of these days." Opie asks Andy if he will write "a permission for school, so I can go on a field trip. The whole class is going on a bus to a bakery in Mt. Pilot to see how donuts are made."

"I recall the opening scene of this episode vividly," says writer Harvey Bullock. "The reason I do is because I went on a similar field trip when I was a Boy Scout. Our scoutmaster announced that we would be going to the big Spaulding Bakery. Their huge donut-making machine made a lasting impression on me. Dough was extruded in donut shapes, which dropped onto a pan of gas-heated oil. Then as they drifted along, a paddle turned them over to fry the other side, after which they were deposited into wire baskets moving several times to the ceiling and back on an endless chain to cool them off before they were packaged.

"Then, the highlight—the bakery manager said we could stand at the end of the cooling line and eat as many donuts as we wanted—heaven! We cleaned out basket after basket hurriedly, fearing the miracle would be recalled. The bakery man just smiled, but soon our scoutmaster, seeing we were all desperately and deliciously on a life-threatening donut binge, dragged us away. That's why I selected that field trip for Opie."

While Andy is writing the permission note, the mail is delivered. Several of the letters are addressed to "Occupant," and Opie questions Andy about this.

"Opie and Andy's 'occupant' discussion was of minor importance to the story line," says Harvey. "I actually guided scripts onto little plateaus of idle conversation such as this. The idle conversation emphasized the relaxed relationships that existed among the people of Mayberry."

One of the letters is for Aunt Bee. Aunt Bee is curious about the identity of her letter's sender, but she doesn't open the envelope immediately. Instead she looks at the Raleigh postmark and holds the letter in front of a light. She makes several guesses (Mrs. Deacon, Donna Forbes, or Rita Aiken) before opening the letter and learning it was sent by Roger Hanover, "a boy I used to keep company with."

"I've known folks who try everything to guess who has sent them a letter, including holding a totally opaque envelope up to the light," says Harvey. "Postmarks, blurred mostly, suggest other possible corespondents. It can be maddening, but it's funny to see someone try everything but opening the envelope. Writing the gag for Aunt Bee gave Frances Bavier, who portrayed the character, an acting moment and a chance to do some comedy.

"The names of the ladies Aunt Bee mentions as possible correspondents came from many sources. I needed several names quickly and just wrote down whichever names came to mind. Mrs. Deacon was a friend of my parents and the mother of comic actor Richard Deacon who played Mel Cooley on *The Dick Van Dyke Show*. Veeda Aiken, whose first name was later changed to Rita, was a neighborhood friend whose husband was a sheriff. Gertrude Turner, the name of a lovely woman my widower father tried to marry, was changed to Donna Forbes. The legal department would often change a name, or Aaron Ruben would have one that was better, so I tried not to waste time naming characters."

Aunt Bee answers Roger's letter and invites him to come to Friday night supper.

Friday arrives. Aunt Bee dresses up in preparation for Roger's visit. Andy, returning home with some ice cream, responds to her appearance with some wonderful dialogue. He tells Aunt Bee: "You must be the teenage baby sitter. Aunt Bee, you look good enough to take to Chinatown. New hair-do, red lining in your jacket, peach ice cream." Andy whistles and turns his head.

"Andy's whistle and head turn were not scripted," says Harvey. "He once told me this was something his father did, and he got it from him."

Aunt Bee tells Andy that "Roger phoned and what's more he said he might be able to stay for a few days." Andy asks if he needs to "get out my old shoes and rice." Aunt Bee ignores the remark and reminisces aloud, "Oh, it's so good to hear his voice again." Andy responds, "Try to control your passion, Aunt Bee. You're melting the ice cream."

"The idea of an enticing female melting ice cream has been used in many forms for many moons," says Harvey. "I was always quite comfortable finding old clichéd descriptions and dressing them up a bit to fit a scene or a character."

When Roger arrives, he looks at Aunt Bee and says, "Just as pretty as ever."

Aunt Bee introduces Andy and Opie to Roger. Roger holds out his hand to shake, pulls it back at the last second, sticks his thumb up, and says, "Hang it on the wall." Aunt Bee comments, "I told you he's full of the devil."

Aunt Bee offers to show Roger to his room. Roger moans, steps over his suitcase, and says, "I'm just a little weak. I just got over the grip." Roger then points out the suitcase he stepped over.

"Roger Hanover, who is really annoying, was modeled after an insurance salesman of equal likability," says Harvey. "The salesman was also named Roger. I would give his last name, but he'd probably read this and show up here again. The guy knew all the ancient gags and practical jokes, was overbearingly authoritative, and a real nuisance.

"Roger's jokes are old creaky routines that someone like him would persistently use. His attempts at comedy were inspired by my father, who also spewed old jokes and groaners. But my father was affable about it and, happily, didn't know too many.

"Wallace Ford's portrayal of Roger was wonderful. In fact, I still have viewers tell me how much they disliked the character—which proves that Wallace was an able and convincing actor."

The next morning at breakfast, Roger continues his joking. He emerges from behind the newspaper he is reading wearing a mask and says to Andy, "Take me to your leader." Roger asks Opie if he knows why people have thumbs and answers, "Because if they didn't have thumbs, and you shook hands with somebody, the other fellow's hand would go right up your sleeve and hit you right in the nose." Roger shoves Opie in the nose.

Andy invites Opie to join him for breakfast at the diner. As the two leave the kitchen, Opie asks if Roger is really going to be "our new uncle?" Andy thinks over Opie's question and its implications carefully.

Later in the day, Andy joins Floyd outside the barbershop. It is hot. The temperature is ninety-two degrees. Andy comments, "Well, like Mark Twain said, 'Everybody complains about the weather, but nobody does anything about it'." Floyd remarks that he thought Calvin Coolidge had said that.

Aunt Bee and Roger walk up. After a brief conversation, the two depart. After their departure, Andy confesses to Floyd that he can't stand Roger.

That evening after supper, Andy decides "to fix the cord on that lamp." Roger takes the cord away from Andy and says, "Don't mind me showing you how to do this, do you, boy?" Roger twists the ends too tightly and ruins the cord.

When Aunt Bee asks Andy if he has the plug fixed, Roger responds that he "tried to help the boy." Referring to Andy, he adds, "Funny thing, these electrical gadgets. You have the knack for them, or you haven't."

"I found it was easier to write for a loud brash character like Roger Hanover than for a mild-mannered, polite person," says Harvey. "A brash character produces more friction and energy as he interacts with others, which is good for the story. I simply wrote dialogue that I felt fit Roger's personality."

Roger takes Aunt Bee "on a little stroll." After the two depart, Opie asks Andy, "You don't much like Mr. Hanover, do you?" Andy refuses to give a direct answer and instead tells Opie, "I've tried to bring you up teaching you there's some good in everybody. Now the same goes for Mr. Hanover."

"Andy's statement seemed like an apt moral," says Harvey. "Also, in stating it to Opie, it helped explain to the audience why Andy has been so patient with Roger, instead of ushering him on his way."

The next morning, Andy is potting petunias before he goes to work. Roger comes outside. He is "down to half-a-cigar" and is "going to the store to get a few more." Roger offers to show Andy how to pot petunias, but Andy refuses his help. Andy says, "Roger, I know we don't see eye-to-eye on electricity, but when it comes to potting petunias, I'm a giant." Roger replies, "Just wanted to be helpful, boy."

Roger starts to the store but returns a short time later. He says he left his money in his other pants and asks Andy for a half-dollar. Andy asks Roger what his future plans are. Roger answers, "My original plan was Florida, but things are running along so nicely here I sort of hated to think of leaving."

Roger eventually tells Andy that he needs four hundred dollars to fund a trip to Florida. If he doesn't get the money, he plans to marry Aunt Bee and move in permanently. Roger tells Andy, "Four hundred dollars and I'd be right there on that noon train. Otherwise, I'd say you got yourself a new uncle." Andy tells Roger he can find Aunt Bee in the kitchen. Roger sarcastically responds, "I never expected to have such a grownup nephew. I might have a hand in those petunias yet, Andy."

A short time later, Roger and Aunt Bee join Andy on the porch. Roger says "Andy, I just had a little talk with Bee." Aunt Bee tells Andy that Roger is leaving on the noon train to Florida. She then goes back inside to make Roger some sandwiches. Roger remains behind.

Roger asks, "Sheriff, you ever play poker?" Andy answers, "Yeah, Roger, I used to play. I used to be pretty good at it."

As this scene develops, Roger addresses Andy in a progression—boy, Andy, sheriff. "Boy" places Roger in a superior position. When the showdown comes, and it's man-to-man "Andy" is used. After Roger's bluff is called, it's the respectful "sheriff."

"Roger's request for the needed funds is a shakedown," says Harvey. "Roger will keep moving if Andy gives him four hundred dollars, but Andy never offers to go along. Both men have hidden cards. Andy seemingly takes a chance when he sends Roger into the kitchen to propose to Aunt Bee. Andy is hoping she has gotten over her crush by now. Roger, however, is confident the starry-eyed Bee will grab at his proposal. It's poker, pure and simple. Labeling it so helps the audience be aware of the drama and tension as the two men match wits."

In the episode's epilogue, Aunt Bee comes back into the house after seeing Roger off. She confesses to Andy that "a little of Roger goes a long way. All those tricks and jokes—they're fun for awhile, but you wouldn't want to live with them for the rest of your life, would you?"

Andy answers that he "certainly wouldn't." Aunt Bee then adds, "Fun is fun, but there's a limit to everything." Andy replies that he'll go along with that. "In fact, I'll just shake on it. Hang it on the wall."

"The epilogue serves to restore Aunt Bee to her previous non-gullible status," says Harvey. "She has come to recognize Roger and his annoying habits—and has had more than enough of his jokes. Andy sensed this when he took the big chance of telling Roger to go ahead and make his play for Aunt Bee. The reuse of Roger's trademark, 'Hang it on the wall,' was just a light comic flip to button up the epilogue."

The Education of Ernest T. Bass

EPISODE #133

FIRST BROADCAST ON OCTOBER 12, 1964

WRITTEN BY JIM FRITZELL
AND EVERETT GREENBAUM

DIRECTED BY ALAN RAFKIN

HOWARD MORRIS GUEST STARS
AS ERNEST T. BASS

"I had fun doing this episode. It was great comedy to fool around with. Jim and Everett wrote some wonderful stuff. They were the best."
Howard Morris

"**I**t was always difficult to sit down and produce an outline for a new script," says writer Everett Greenbaum. "In the case of Ernest T., it wasn't as painful because we knew we would have fun with it eventually."

Jim and Everett begin their script with Andy and Barney discussing where they will eat lunch. Andy suggests the diner. Barney has checked the diner's special on the way in—"Chicken wings, rice, and mixed vegetables." He observes that the cook "gives you two wings and usually from a chicken who's done a lot of flying." The discussion is interrupted when Ernest T. Bass throws a rock through the window of the courthouse.

"We did a lot of scenes about eating in everything we wrote," says

Everett. "Eating is a very basic life activity and having Barney and Andy discuss lunch seemed like a good way to begin this episode."

Ernest T. enters the office, drops his bag of rocks on Barney's hand, and explains that he has returned to Mayberry to get an education to please his girlfriend "Romeena." (We were introduced to Ramona Ancrum in "My Fair Ernest T. Bass." Ernest T. calls her Romeena.) Ernest T. tells Andy and Barney he has tried to attract Romeena in other ways, including getting a gold tooth. He tells them he didn't go to a dentist to get his gold tooth. Instead he "had it did at the sign company. Gold leaf, they call it." All of his efforts have been unsuccessful.

"Having Ernest T. drop his bag of rocks on Barney's hand was not scripted," says Everett. "It came up on the set. Ernest T.'s gold tooth was inspired from observing unsophisticated people who considered it fashionable to have a gold tooth flashing at the world."

Ernest T. wants Andy to help him "get some schooling." If Ernest T. can't get an education, he intends to "bust every window in town."

Andy decides to help Ernest T. and enrolls him in Helen Crump's fifth-grade class. Ernest T. joins the class and immediately causes a disruption with his comments about a sentence written on the blackboard. The sentence reads, "The possum hid under the rock."

When Helen asks the class who can point out the preposition, the object, the subject, and the verb, Ernest T. jumps to his feet and asks, "Why don't we break down that rock and find out what that possum's doing under there?" The class laughs.

When Helen calls on Sharon, Ernest T. comments, "Ain't no little girl going to tell you nothing about a possum under a rock. If you want to really find out about a possum under a rock, you find a boy with dirt under his fingernails." Helen responds with, "Mr. Bass, that's quite enough!"

"I've forgotten most of this script," says Everett. "As I read through it, it seems as if it were written by a strange hand. I can't recall how the possum sentence entered our heads, but it is funny."

Ernest T. is upset after his first day in Helen's class and shares his feelings with Andy. He complains that Helen "ain't teaching me nothing." Andy comforts Ernest T. and agrees to help him study.

Andy begins by having Ernest T. read from Opie's first-grade reader. When Andy opens the book, Ernest T. points at the page and says, "I know that word. *Cat*." Andy asks Ernest T. if he figured out the word from the picture on the page. Opie tells Andy to "turn to a page without any pictures." Ernest T. tells Opie to "have more respect for your elders." Andy explains to Ernest T. that Opie was just trying to help. Ernest T. then says apologetically, "Well, I take off my humble hat to you, boy." Opie then goes upstairs and says, "Good night, Ernest T. Bass." Ernest T. replies, "Good night, Opie Taylor."

"Ernest T.'s 'humble hat' line grew out of an expression I once heard, 'He's the button on the cap of kindness,'" explains Everett. "We used the expression in many variations. Ernest T. says, 'Good night, Opie Taylor' because he is trying to fit in and do as the Romans, or, in this case, as Opie does. Opie used Ernest T.'s complete name when he bid him good night, and Ernest T. does likewise."

While working with Ernest T., Andy discovers that he can already read several words. Ernest T. puts the words into a sentence, "No hunt, beware, open, and close, no credit."

The next day at school, Ernest T. wants to write his sentence on the blackboard, but Helen tells him to wait until after arithmetic. Ernest T. refuses, and Helen punishes him by slapping his hand with a ruler. This disciplinary action stirs up strong feelings in Ernest T., and he immediately declares his love for Miss Crump.

That evening, Ernest T. throws a rock through Helen's window with a note attached to it. The note says, "I love you." Andy arrests Ernest T.

The next day, Barney explains to Andy that Ernest T.'s reaction to Helen is psychological, that she has become his "mother figure." Barney tells Andy, "Sigmon Frued wrote a lot about that. Old Sig had this thing pegged years ago."

"I can't remember how the 'mother figure' thing came up," says

Everett. "But 'Sigmon Frued' was an example of Barney's tendency to mispronounce words. We always enjoyed writing these and worked them in whenever we could."

Later that evening, Andy comes home from work and finds Ernest T. sitting in an easy chair. Ernest T. has escaped from jail. Andy questions Ernest T. and learns that his mother used to hit him. Andy explains to him that all of his feelings for his mother came back when Helen hit him with a ruler. Andy goes on to say that Ernest T. is just putting Helen in his mother's place, and Helen has become his mother figure. Ernest T. thanks Andy "for clearing up the whole thing" and invites him to be his "brother figure."

Ernest T. feels "a good son is supposed to help his mother." The following day, he sees Helen coming of the grocery store and offers to carry her groceries. Helen declines the offer and hurries down the sidewalk to Andy. Andy is sitting with Mr. Schwump on the bench outside the courthouse.

"Mr. Schwump was not scripted," says Everett. "The guy probably could have used a day's pay, so they put him in."

Andy ushers Helen inside the office. Andy, Helen, and Barney discuss how to deal with Ernest T. and eventually decide the best thing to do is to get him an education as soon as possible. Andy quickly prepares Ernest T. for a final exam in geography, arithmetic, reading, and writing.

Ernest T. demonstrates his knowledge of geography by reciting "boundaries—Mexico, Canada, Atlantic Ocean, Pacific Ocean, Kelsey's woods, Kelsey's creek, Kelsey's ocean."

"We tried to imagine what the world looked like to Ernest T.," says Everett. "These boundaries reflected his world view."

One of the best visual jokes in the entire series occurs as Ernest T. demonstrates his mathematical skills. Ernest T. counts out two and two by stamping his foot on the floor like a trained horse. The joke would have been great if it had ended there, but it is brilliantly taken one step further by having Ernest T. do a harder problem—twenty-five and twenty-five. The humor comes when he stands and frantically stamps out the answer.

"In the script, Ernest T. pounds on the wall to answer the math problem," says Everett. "Of course, stomping the floor like a horse is much better and must have been added on the set. Whoever thought it up should be commended.

"Another addition to the script was Ernest T. timidly shaking hands with Andy and Barney after receiving his diploma. His humility was a nice counter to his normally wild behavior."

The epilogue repeats the episode's opening. Andy and Barney are discussing where they will eat lunch. Andy suggests the drugstore, and Barney replies, "I don't like to eat at the drugstore—everything tastes like medicine." The two decide to go to the diner instead. Barney thinks aloud, "I wonder how old Ernest T. Bass made out over at Ramona's. I guess everything turned out all right, or we would have heard from him." A rock breaks the front window of the office, and the problem with Ernest T. starts over.

"The epilogue in my script is completely different," says Everett. "More than likely either Aaron Ruben or Andy rewrote it. The rewrite follows the 'here we go again' format and is much better than the original."

EPISODE #135

FIRST BROADCAST ON NOVEMBER 9, 1964

WRITTEN BY BILL IDELSON
AND SAM BOBRICK

DIRECTED BY COBY RUSKIN

ALLAN MELVIN GUEST STARS AS
FRED PLUMMER

Barney's Uniform

"It's perfect for dancing, hangs just right for the dip."

Barney Fife, talking about his
"salt-and-pepper" suit

"This episode had a different type of story than our previous TAGS scripts," says writer Sam Bobrick. "It was more serious and taught an important lesson about respect for the law. Even though it was different, Bill and I didn't find it any more difficult to write. We never had trouble with any story that Don and Andy were in together. Their relationship was so good it made writing for them a pleasure."

The episode opens with Andy taping a poster on the window of the courthouse. The poster announces an upcoming charity dance. Barney approaches and is so mad he can hardly see straight because Fred Goss, the dry cleaner, has misplaced his "salt-and-pepper" suit. Then, Barney notices Fred Plummer, an employee at Foley's Grocery Store, sweeping trash into the street. Barney has warned Plummer previously about littering and decides to "go over there and cut him down to size."

Barney confronts Plummer about "sweeping trash right into the street" and writes him a ticket for littering. Barney makes note of the time, place, weather, and traffic conditions on the ticket.

"We were always looking for ways to insert humor into a script," says Sam. "I enjoyed writing little details, such as Barney's 'weather clear, traffic light' observations as he is writing the ticket. Barney always went a step or two farther than the norm. In this case, he felt his observations should be included on the ticket."

Fred Plummer is angered by the ticket and tells Barney that he is "gonna take this ticket, see, but you and me are gonna meet sometime when you're not wearing that uniform, and I'm going to beat you to a pulp."

In response to Plummer's threat, Barney not only wears his uniform while on duty, but also to church and on his day off.

Unaware of Plummer's threat, Andy questions Barney about wearing his uniform. During their discussion, the two are sitting on the bench outside the courthouse. Fred Plummer steps onto the sidewalk in front of the grocery and glares at Barney. When the telephone rings, Andy goes inside to answer it. He is followed closely by Barney.

The telephone call is from Fred Goss. Barney's suit has been found and is waiting for him at the cleaners. In response to the news, Barney tells Andy, "I figured on wearing something else." When pressed by Andy, Barney starts coming up with excuses for why he can't wear his favorite suit. He doesn't think the suit will fit him anymore. He has been "gaining weight like crazy lately."

When Fred Plummer comes into the courthouse to pay his ticket, Barney leaves.

The master shot for the scene inside the office is photographed from the wall behind Andy's desk and the adjacent wall where the gun rack is usually mounted. Both walls have been removed. The camera is positioned in the corner usually occupied by the filing cabinet. The camera pans right to photograph the conversation between Plummer and Andy.

Fred Plummer warns Barney that he will beat Barney to a pulp
whenever he meets Barney when he's not wearing his uniform.

TAGSRWC Archives

During the conversation, Andy learns that Plummer threatened Barney.

Andy later questions Barney about the situation, and Barney explains that he has resumed his judo class in Mt. Pilot and is wearing his uniform to protect Fred Plummer. Barney feels his knowledge of judo would be an unfair advantage if the two were to fight.

Andy decides to visit Barney's judo school. As Andy exits his car, Earle Hagen's musical score switches to an oriental theme that audibly identifies the school.

Andy learns from Mr. Izamoto, Barney's teacher, that Barney is an excellent student. Mr Izamoto says, "He try very hard." Andy asks for Mr. Izamoto's professional opinion about how Barney would fare if he were to get into a fight. Mr. Izamoto asks how much the other fighter would weigh. When Andy answers two hundred pounds, Mr. Izamoto replies, "You a friend of Barney's? Then you stop that fight. That man kill Barney. Around here we call Barney the 'chicken.' He got bones like chicken, weak bones, they snap. You stop that fight. I like Barney very much. Not want him to get hurt."

As Andy walks toward the door, he gets an idea. He asks Mr. Izamoto what size suit he wears.

Andy puts his plan in motion. After warning Plummer that Barney knows judo and is dangerous, Andy tells him that Barney will be out of uniform when he attends the charity dance that night. Andy also mentions that Barney's suit is in the courthouse. He tells Plummer that Barney plans to change into his civvies for the dance around a quarter to eight.

As he speaks with Plummer, Andy helps himself to some fruit from a stand outside the grocery. Taking the fruit is mildly devious and helps to communicate visually the fact that Andy is sharing some "inside" information while conspiring with Fred Plummer.

Acting on Andy's tip, Plummer confronts the person he thinks is Barney at the designated time on the dimly lit street. Plummer is actually fighting Mr. Izamoto dressed in Barney's suit, and he is no match for the judo instructor.

After Plummer's defeat, Andy decides to teach Barney an important lesson. A good visual joke occurs when Andy knocks on the door to Barney's room. Rushing to get into his uniform, Barney puts his shirt on backwards.

"We were allowed to write whatever we felt was good," says Sam. "Aaron Ruben was a great producer and gave the writers a lot of freedom. Aaron encouraged us to trust our instincts about what would work in a scene. So whenever we felt a visual gag, such as Barney putting his shirt on backwards, would work, we didn't hesitant to include it."

Andy has brought over Barney's suit. Barney, however, hasn't changed his mind about wearing it to the dance. He intends to wear his uniform. Andy tells Barney that he is going to have to face Fred Plummer sooner or later because of "what you are." Andy reminds Barney that they are "symbols of the law. When people look at us they just don't see Barney Fife and Andy Taylor, they see the law. And more than that they have respect for the law. We've worked a long time to get that respect, and I don't think we should give it up. . .We're lawmen no matter what we're wearing."

Barney comes to the realization that he must confront Fred Plummer. Barney's courage to do so is admirable, even though his behavior during the confrontation expresses the fear he still feels.

Barney walks past Foley's grocery and finds Plummer sitting in an alley. In a weak voice, Barney tells Plummer, "Whether I'm wearing my uniform or not, it doesn't make any difference because I'm a symbol of the law, and you got to have respect for the law." A beaten and bruised Plummer says, "You know that judo is something awful. You could kill a person with that."

After realizing that Plummer is afraid, Barney's demeanor suddenly changes. He becomes confident and cocky. (So much so that it somewhat ruins the humanity displayed by his bravery and willingness to learn from Andy's advice.)

"A good rule for this show is that the human spirit must triumph," says Sam. "I think we showed Barney's courage and vulnerability as he confronts Plummer. Perhaps Barney's drastic change in demeanor, after he sees he has the upper hand, was a mistake. Sometimes we were wrong."

In the epilogue Andy helps Barney practice his judo. This scene highlights the wonderful rapport that existed between Don Knotts and Andy Griffith. Barney gives Andy a ruler to use like a knife and instructs him "to try to run me through." As Andy attacks, Barney stops him. He needs another look at his judo manual. Barney studies the manual and goes through the motions of blocking the attack. Once again, he is ready. Andy attacks Barney and overpowers him. After being "let loose," Barney tells Andy, "You didn't do it right." Barney tells Andy that he was holding the ruler wrong. Barney suggests they practice in slow motion. Andy attacks. This time, Barney successfully defends himself. Now Barney is ready. Andy attacks at full speed. He overpowers Barney and gently lowers him to the floor.

Don Knotts and Andy Griffith genuinely seem to be enjoying themselves. Their acting is excellent. Although they remain in character, it is evident they love working together.

The Pageant

EPISODE #138

FIRST BROADCAST ON NOVEMBER 30, 1964

WRITTEN BY HARVEY BULLOCK

DIRECTED BY GENE NELSON

Eventide

The gentle rustling of the leaves
The birds seeking their nests
O, my Happy Valley.

Lady Mayberry's soliloquy

"In my ceiling-staring sessions, when I was seeking a story to write, it crossed my mind that many towns celebrate their lineage, however modest, with a pageant," says writer Harvey Bullock. "My hometown (Binghamton, New York) once had a centennial pageant showing the fine work of Mr. Bingham, who brought the settlers and Indians to a peaceful co-existence. And I was in the cast!

"Staged at the high school, the pageant ran for three nights and was a sellout—a full-blown costumed fantasy with early settlers, Indians, and pioneers. I had a very minor ten-second part as a settler's son who runs across the stage in near panic and announces, 'The Indians are coming.' That was it. Despite it being such a quickie, I experienced the heady elixir of audience approval. The memory of the experience stayed with me and inspired 'The Pageant' script."

Harvey's script begins with Andy, Barney, and Opie discussing the celebration of Mayberry's centennial. The centennial pageant is mentioned, and Barney, who plans to attend the tryouts, demonstrates his elocution by reciting several tongue twisters.

"For some reason, my mother decided my sister should have elocution lessons," says Harvey. "When my sister graduated from high school, it fell to me to continue the lessons. Once a week, I went to Mrs. Merchant's and sat in an overstuffed parlor, spieling off tongue twisters. My mother was determined I should become a better speaker even though the full-hour, single-student rate cost a not inconsiderable fee—fifty cents.

"The tongue twisters 'Peter Piper Picked' and 'How Much Wood Would a Woodchuck Chuck' were too ordinary for Mrs. Merchant's taste. She preferred 'She Sells Sea Shells' and 'With Sturdy Threats and Loudest Boasts.' She is totally responsible for searing them into my limp brain. I jumped at the chance to have Barney recite them and was very pleased to have found a place to use them after all these years. The 'Rubber Baby Buggy Bumpers' twister that stumps Barney was an audience warmup routine that the emcee used with contestants on a quiz show that I once wrote for."

When Aunt Bee enters the courthouse, Andy reminds her not to forget the tryouts that night. Aunt Bee answers that she won't be attending the tryouts because she sews the costumes. Andy points out that there's "a real good woman's part, Lady Mayberry, founding mother of the town." Aunt Bee is sure Mr. Masters has decided to use Clara Edwards for that part.

At home, Aunt Bee tells Opie she is certain she could play the part of Lady Mayberry. She tells him that she was in a church play years ago, and her mother and father both said she was "the best one in it." She shows Opie a review of the play, which was called *The Little Princess*, that appeared in a church publication.

"I had always taken part in school plays and essay readings," says Harvey. "One of the plays I performed in was *The Princess Marries the Page*. It was a two-part play and inspired the name of the play Aunt Bee appeared in."

That night, Andy and Barney try out for the pageant. Andy reads for the James Merriweather role, and Barney reads for Chief Noogatuck.

"The name of Andy's character was James Meredith in my script," says Harvey. "The name of Barney's character, 'Chief Noogatuck,' was conjured up as a correct-sounding but goofy sort of Indian name."

Barney's performance during the tryouts is a classic. He loses his place in the script and delivers his first line, "How," too fast. As he and Andy step down from the stage, Andy says, "Hey, Barn, I know how you can learn your part real good." Barney asks, "How?"

"I was not troubled by using this venerable wheeze," says Harvey. "I thought viewers familiar with it would enjoy hearing its resurrection.

"The scene of the tryouts worked very well. Of course, the material had an edge. The performers were so skilled and comfortable in their roles that they could make any reasonable situation come to life. And a pageant for a friendly town like Mayberry seemed totally believable."

The script directions were artistically interpreted by the director and photographed in one sustained shot. The shot begins with Andy and Barney stepping off the stage. The camera follows the two toward the back of the auditorium. Aunt Bee is seen in the background, seated on the far side of the auditorium. Andy and Barney exit from the frame, and the camera moves with Aunt Bee as she rises from her chair and walks to the stage to speak with John Masters about trying out for the role of Lady Mayberry.

John Masters doesn't give Aunt Bee an opportunity to express her interest in the role. When Aunt Bee mentions Lady Mayberry, Mr. Masters tells her that the costume she makes for Lady Mayberry will be almost as important as the words Lady Mayberry speaks. He then says Clara Edwards will play the role.

"In the filmed episode, Clara is called to tend to her sick sister in

Saberton," says Harvey. "In the script I wrote 'sick sister in Mebane,' which is a real North Carolina town. I selected it because a freshman friend of mine at Duke University came from Mebane, and I always liked the sound of it."

In Aunt Bee's presence, Andy, Barney, and Mr. Masters discuss finding someone else to play Lady Mayberry. Throughout their discussion, Aunt Bee drops hints about her theatrical experience and interest in the role. Andy eventually notices and asks her why she doesn't play the part. Mr. Masters thinks it over and gives Aunt Bee the role.

That night at play practice, Andy, wearing a coonskin hat, and Barney, dressed in an Indian headdress, smoke a peace pipe while rehearsing a scene. Barney coughs after he takes a puff and delivers his lines in a high-pitched voice.

"Barney's high-pitched voice was not scripted," says Harvey. "Don Knotts was masterful with high voices and probably felt it worked well in the scene.

"When Barney and Andy are reading lines, Barney stops to ask the director if they can change his last line, 'Paleface is not a man of his word.' He says that the line is 'just not Noogatuck.' This is an echo of a supposedly true story of an actor who, when playing a role of a Martian in a sci-fi story, asked the director in all seriousness to change his lines because 'a Martian wouldn't talk like that.' Here Barney is stating that he knew how the mind of an Indian worked—even though a hundred years has passed."

After Andy and Barney finish their scene, Mr. Masters calls on Aunt Bee to practice "the opening of the second act, your soliloquy." While Aunt Bee is getting into place, Mr. Masters tells Andy to have the "faintest smile" when Noogatuck calls him "laughing face."

"Having the director ask for a faint smile, which Andy summons up, grew out of my memories of directors who have to make their contribution to everything," says Harvey. "Andy smiles because he, like most cast members, actually wants to be given directions—it's cool."

Aunt Bee walks past the wings and runs back and forth behind the backdrop before eventually making her entrance. Her performance is terrible.

"Frances Bavier actually isn't called upon to do much physical activity," says Harvey. "The stage is small, and it's not very demanding to ask her to change directions to get to the proper side. The running behind the curtain was probably done by a crew member.

"Writing a script calls for absolutely no obligatory interaction between the writer and the performers. In the process of doing thirty-some scripts, however, it was inevitable that I might occasionally run into the actors in the studio commissary. So I met Andy, Don, Ronny Howard, Jim Nabors, etc., and we knew each other. Frances Bavier was never in sight. I heard she was a very private person and quite a disciplinarian on the set. At times she even had Andy tiptoeing about if she was annoyed. Andy was aware of Frances's minor personality quirks and was very deferential, diplomatic, and supportive. Above all, she was a superb actress and totally Mayberry."

After working with Aunt Bee for three hours the previous night, Mr. Masters insists that Andy tell her she is not right for the Lady Mayberry role.

That evening, Aunt Bee complains to Andy that she doesn't think Mr. Masters understands the Lady Mayberry role. Andy replies, "If you don't see eye to eye with him, why don't you just forget it?" Aunt Bee says she won't give up the part for "anything in the world."

As Aunt Bee rushes off to practice, she remembers supper. Andy tells her that they'll pick up something at the diner. Aunt Bee feels she is neglecting Andy and Opie, but she can't "seem to find the time."

After Aunt Bee leaves, the telephone rings. Mr. Masters is calling to say the problem with Lady Mayberry is solved because Clara is back in town. Mr. Masters insists that Andy tell Aunt Bee.

Andy asks Mr. Masters not to say anything to Clara yet. While Andy ponders what to do, Opie mentions that he'll be glad when the pageant is over because he's "getting tired of eating at the diner." Opie's comment gives Andy an idea.

The next day, Aunt Bee is busy planning her day around play prac-tice. Clara comes over because Andy asked her to help out while Aunt Bee is "busy with the pageant." Clara is delighted to help and says she's looking forward "to having someone to cook for."

As Andy and Clara talk, Andy reminds Aunt Bee that she'd "better run along if you expect to get that stuff done." Aunt Bee agrees and mentions that she "still has to work on that opening speech." Clara fondly recalls the opening speech and recites it beautifully.

Aunt Bee leaves reluctantly. As Clara goes into the kitchen, it ap-pears that the plan didn't work.

However, Aunt Bee goes out the front door, walks around the side of the house, and enters the kitchen through the back door. She insists that Clara "take back the part." Clara joyfully accepts, and Aunt Bee willingly prepares Andy and Opie's supper.

In the epilogue, Andy and Barney watch Clara practice the opening speech. She is wonderful. Barney tells Andy, "Well, Aunt Bee tried, but it's just one of them things. Either you got it, or you don't." Barney looks up on stage and sees someone dressed in Chief Noogatuck's head-dress. He yells at the man, jumps up from his chair, and rushes the stage. Mr. Masters stops Barney and takes him aside "to speak privately."

"The epilogue might have been more effective in mime," says Harvey. "Just a slight change is needed. After Barney states that 'either you got it or you don't,' it might have been better to have an actor walk by in Indian headdress. But, perhaps it's too late to change the script."

The Darling Baby

EPISODE #139

FIRST BROADCAST ON DECEMBER 7, 1964

WRITTEN BY JIM FRITZELL AND EVERETT GREENBAUM

DIRECTED BY HOWARD MORRIS

"In my more positive moments I like to think of The Andy Griffith Show *as a sort of modern Charles Dickens oeuvre. After all, most of his work was first published as serials in newspapers."*

Everett Greenbaum

"I don't remember how this story first originated," says writer Everett Greenbaum. "As far as I can remember, Jim Fritzell and I were the only ones to write Ernest T., the Darlings, and, at first, Gomer stories. Then the other writers began writing for Gomer. It wasn't any more difficult to think up a new reason to have the Darlings return to Mayberry than to come up with new ideas for other stories."

Jim and Everett begin their "Darling Baby" script with Andy and Opie in the courthouse. Andy is inspecting a glass jar with an egg inside. Opie shows Andy a rubber wishbone he made by "soaking it in vinegar." Opie learned how to do the tricks, which he calls "facts of science," from the book, *Twenty Scientific Tricks a Boy Can Do at Home* by

Seymour Shreck. Opie's interest in magic and one of his tricks, the use of disappearing ink, will later play a prominent role in solving the episode's problem.

"Opie's interest in magic and the title of his book were inspired by my own childhood interest in magic," says Everett. "As a kid I got a lot of magic tricks from library books with titles like *Twenty Tricks a Boy Can Do at Home.*

"The construction of this story was the same as 'Barney's Sidecar.' In the 'Sidecar' episode, we resolved the problem caused by Barney's motorcycle by having Andy place a fake plaque, which he had inscribed with Opie's wood-burning set, under the sidecar's seat. We then had to go back and insert the wood-burning set into the beginning of that script. This script came later, so this one starts right off with Opie's magic trick, which we reprise for an ending. We remembered the sidecar episode, followed its structure, and had the disappearing ink in mind before we ever began writing this script."

Andy steps outside with Opie and finds Barney sitting on the bench. Although Barney is asleep, when Andy wakes him, he claims he "was watching traffic." He says his eyes were "squinched up so they couldn't see me looking."

At this point, the Darlings' truck comes down Main Street. The Darlings are welcomed warmly by Andy and Barney. Charlene proudly shows off her three-month-old daughter Andelina. Charlene acknowledges that they named her after Andy, since he "done so much to help us."

"Jim and I made up the name Andelina," says Everett. "It was our version of the feminine form of Andy."

While admiring the baby, Barney tries to get Andelina to take his finger, but the baby refuses. Later in the episode's epilogue, Jim and Everett cleverly reprise this gag with a twist—after taking Barney's finger, the baby won't let go.

Andy, Barney and the Darlings go inside the courthouse to "get that baby in here where it's cool." Briscoe tells Andy, "This ain't a to-show trip. It's got purpose. It's a betrothal."

It seems the Darlings have come to Mayberry "to find a young boy to pledge his hand and heart to Andelina." Briscoe informs Andy that "the young fellar that gets Andelina comes in to a pretty good dowry—an eight-by-ten cottage on the back twenty. All it needs is a roof, some fresh mud on the floor. It'd be a real paradise. And a cow comes with it, and two acres of side hill with good strong boulders." Andy and Barney both agree that it sounds like a good deal.

"Andelina's dowry and Briscoe's dialogue were pure Jim Fritzell and are examples of the rapport he had for characters like the Darlings," says Everett.

The Darlings spend their first day in Mayberry looking for a husband for Andelina. Their search is unsuccessful. They came "across one young 'un, but he had a big wart on the end of his nose."

That evening the Darlings drop by the Taylor house to "pick with Andy a little bit." After Charlene sings a love song, Opie comes downstairs to tell Andy good night. Opie takes Andy aside and asks if it would be OK if he doesn't kiss Andy in front of company. Andy understands, and the two shake hands.

"Opie's concern about giving Andy a good-night kiss in front of company grew out of my own experience with my father," says Everett. "My father considered it an insult if you didn't kiss his cheek on arriving, leaving, or going to bed. The older I got, the more embarrassing it became. As an adult, it didn't bother me."

After seeing Opie, the Darlings decide that he would be a perfect match for Andelina. Andy protests, but Briscoe pays no attention. He takes out the betrothal papers for Andy to sign. When Andy refuses, Briscoe thinks that Andy is all "choked up," so he decides "to leave the signing until tomorrow."

The next day Andy tells Barney about the Darlings' intentions for Opie. The situation reminds Barney of an experience he had with a girl named Halcyon Loretta Winslow. Barney describes in detail the experience, which he says was like *A Tale Out of Two Cities*. It all began when Halcyon's father, who owned a prune-pitting factory, saw Barney's picture in the newspaper after he had won four free haircuts in the church raffle. The father wanted Barney to meet Halcyon, so he set up a date for the three at Klein's Coffee House for lunch. Barney tells Andy, "You know me. When opportunity knocks, Old Barn's got to a least take a peep and see if there is anybody on the stoop." During the lunch, Halcyon's father offered Barney one-third interest in the family business, full use of the company car, and a beautiful hillside plot in the Mt. Pilot cemetery.

Halcyon, however, was "Beasto Maristo," and Barney turned down the offer. Barney ends the story by telling Andy that Halcyon later went off to finishing school but is still "ugly, single, and pitting prunes."

During the conversation, Andy gets up from his desk without saying a word and goes into the back room. He returns a short time later with coffee for Barney and himself. This action seems exactly like something someone would do while enjoying a good story. Intent on hearing the story, but also wanting a cup of coffee, Andy quietly gets up without disturbing the storyteller and returns quickly.

"I knew a girl in Buffalo named 'Halcyon'," says Everett. "As for the rest of the stuff about her—it was what happened with Fritzell and Greenbaum and a typewriter on a good day. It was not scripted for Andy to get coffee. This was probably worked out on stage.

"Andy and Don were perfect in the scene. I think they gave the most relaxed performances of their careers, and I often think the best—except for Andy's performance in the movie *A Face in the Crowd*."

After Barney finishes his story, Opie enters the courthouse dressed in a new suit. Opie tells Andy he was walking down the street when Briscoe and Charlene took him into Weaver's Department Store. The next thing he knew he was in a suit that they said was his to keep. With this new development, Andy decides to stop the Darlings.

Andy, Barney, and Opie find the Darlings at Andy's house, where they are having an engagement party. Mr. Darling admires Opie's egg in a bottle. He observes that he "ain't never seen it fixed like that before. I think I'll pass it up for the time being." Briscoe hands the bottle to Andy.

When Barney becomes wrapped up in the celebration and helps himself to the sandwiches, Andy tells him to sit down. Barney sits down in a chair that has a jug of "mulberry squeezings" beside it.

When Charlene hands Andelina to Opie, Opie tell Andy he doesn't want to marry Andelina. When Andy tries to object, Briscoe interrupts by saying, "Don't they make a nice-looking couple. They's matched together like a racy team of buggy mules." As Andy starts to put the egg in a bottle down, he gets an idea. He hands the bottle to Opie, whispers to him, and sends him upstairs.

After Opie leaves, Andy sees Barney sipping from the jug of squeezings. He points out that Barney is still on duty, but Barney replies, "The boys said this was just mulberry squeezings." He takes a sip, coughs, and says in a strained voice, "That's all it is—mulberry squeezings."

At this point, Andy seems to have accepted the betrothal and "joins the boys in a number." After the song, Opie returns with a pen and the bottle of disappearing ink. Andy and Opie seem eager to sign the betrothal papers. Somewhat inebriated by the squeezings, Barney attempts to stop the proceedings. When Briscoe gives Barney a threatening look, Barney returns to his chair.

Andy and Opie prepare to sign but are interrupted by Barney again. This time, Andy sends him into the kitchen.

"We thought it would be a good idea for Barney to get a little drunk," says Everett. "Otherwise, he may never have allowed the signing of the agreement."

Before signing the papers, Andy recites, "Ebum, Shoobem, Shoobem, Shoobem" and explains to Briscoe, "That's just something we say." Andy and Opie sign the papers. Moments later their signatures disappear. The Darlings see the signatures vanish before their eyes. Suspecting "witchery" in Andy's family, they call off the betrothal and depart quickly.

"The idea for the 'witchery' came from Jim, but 'Ebum, Shoobem' was not scripted," says Everett.

In the epilogue, Andy and the Darlings reunite and play a song. Afterwards, Briscoe explains that he and the boys got to talking and decided "since there's some witches that lives up around our place that we visit with and talk to and everything—even go to church with—there ain't no reason we can't associate with you." Andy and the Darlings "seal" their friendship with another song.

"If memory serves me, we felt a little written out on the Griffith show during the time we were writing 'The Darling Baby'," says Everett. "We had also been offered a high-budget movie, *Good Neighbor Sam*. The offer ultimately proved to be too much to resist, and our Mayberry days came to an end."

Andy and Helen Have Their Day

EPISODE #140

FIRST BROADCAST ON DECEMBER 14, 1964

WRITTEN BY BILL IDELSON AND SAM BOBRICK

DIRECTED BY HOWARD MORRIS

"Howard Morris was a fine director. Most actors are. They have empathy for the artist."
George Lindsey

"Goober was invented in 'Man in a Hurry,' but we didn't see him. Gomer mentioned him. I named him after a teacher my wife had in Arkansas—Old Goober Mouth."
Everett Greenbaum

Bill and Sam begin their script with Barney explaining to Andy why he looks tired. Barney explains that he was out late the night before. He says, "I don't think my head hit the pillow before a quarter to eleven." Barney had taken Juanita from the diner to Morelli's and "then over to her house for a little 'quote' TV."

"Bill and I enjoyed writing the details of Barney's date with Juanita," says writer Sam Bobrick. "Barney's expectations of a good time are always hilariously low, so he's very seldom disappointed. A meal at Morelli's and an evening of TV is his idea of an exciting time."

Barney asks Andy if he had a date with Helen the night before. Andy says he plans to take Helen to the movies tonight.

During this conversation, Helen enters the courthouse and tells Andy she will have to break their date because she has papers to grade. As they attempt to reschedule the date, they both have conflicts. Andy promises Helen that "one of these times, I'll take you off somewhere, and we'll spend the whole day."

Overhearing their conversation, Barney agrees to make Andy and Helen "a present of Saturday." He will take care of all their responsibilities, so the two can spend the whole day together at Myers Lake. Barney will not take no for an answer. He tells Andy, "Saturday, you, Helen, picnic, the whole day alone together, the birds and the bees."

"The story line for this script centered on the relationships of the characters more than upon a situation," says Sam. "I always felt it was easier to write character than contrivance-centered stories."

Barney has Goober drive Andy and Helen to the lake. After their arrival, Goober interrupts Andy and Helen's day by hanging around to eat. This begins a pattern that will continue throughout the episode.

"I read the part for 'The Man in a Hurry' script and was told I was going to be Gomer," says George Lindsey, who portrayed Goober Pyle. "At the last minute a change was made, and Jim Nabors got the part. I was later offered the role of Dud Wash in the first Darlings episode but turned it down. I just knew I was going to be on that show, and I figured if I took the minor role of Dud I would never become a regular. It was a decision made in heaven. Jim Nabors eventually left to start his own series, and I was called in to play Goober."

"It was not much different to write for Goober instead of Gomer," says Sam. "The characters were very similar. With both, there was a thin line between dumbness and innocence."

While Goober is eating with Andy and Helen, Barney arrives at the lake to get the key to Helen's house. The television repairman is coming over to work on her TV, and Barney has volunteered to oversee his work. Helen tells Barney that she had left the key under the mat. As Barney leaves, he orders Goober to return to town.

After lunch, Andy and Helen relax by the lake. Andy has his head in Helen's lap, and Helen strokes his hair affectionately. The two start to kiss but are interrupted when Barney yells, "Andy!" and walks up with Opie. Barney wants Andy's permission to take Opie to the movies. When Andy gives his consent, Barney responds, "Let's go, Ope. Let's get out of here, and let them get back to whatever they were doing." Barney then adds, "What were you doing?"

After Barney leaves, Andy suggests that they take a walk. The two find a boat and row to the middle of the lake. Andy tells Helen, "Well, at least nobody can walk right in on us." Andy puts his arm around Helen, and the two start to kiss. The kiss is interrupted by Barney yelling, "Andy!" He is standing on the lake shore with George, the television repairman. It seems Helen's set will have to go into the shop, and Barney wants to be sure she will approve the repair.

"We had no difficulty thinking up reasons to have Barney return to the lake repeatedly," says Sam. "Almost any reason was legitimate from Barney's viewpoint, and this gave us a lot of freedom."

"We were sitting around the table reading the script and came to the part for George the repairman," says director Howard Morris. "They had not yet cast an actor in the role, so I read the part. As I read, I used a nasal voice. They liked what I did and asked me to play the role."

After Barney leaves, Andy and Helen finally have some time alone and decide to go fishing. Andy catches several fish and is stopped by the game warden, who asks to see Andy's fishing license. Andy has left the license in his wallet, which is in the pocket of his uniform back in Mayberry. The unsympathetic game warden escorts the couple to the justice of the peace to set Andy's fine.

"Colin Male was cast as the game warden," says Howard. "Colin was a tall, handsome guy. He had a great voice and was the announcer who introduced the show in the opening credits. I was not privy to the casting people, but I imagine his wonderful voice and appearance are what got him the role."

After arriving at the justice of the peace's office, Andy calls the

Mayberry courthouse. Goober answers the telephone, and Andy asks him to tell Barney that "Helen and I are over at the justice of the peace in Siler City. I was fishing, and I didn't have a license. Tell Barney to get over here as fast as he can with twenty-five dollars." When Goober relates the message to Barney, it becomes, "They are at the justice of the peace in Siler City, and he said something about a license, and he wants you to bring twenty-five dollars as fast as you can."

Barney jumps to the conclusion that Andy and Helen have decided to get married. Barney goes by the Taylor house to pick up Aunt Bee and Opie. The three, plus Goober, head to the "wedding" dressed in their Sunday best.

Barney's conclusion that Andy and Helen are getting married is very similar to the story line of the fourth-season episode, "The Rumor." In that episode, Barney thinks Andy and Helen are getting married after he sees the two kiss in the jewelry store.

"Sometimes we would put a character in a similar situation and see where it would lead us," says Sam. "Apparently, producer Aaron Ruben felt this episode was far enough away from the previous script. He never expressed any concern about repeating a story line."

A SET OF THREADS

The suit Goober wears to the wedding was originally owned by Howard McNear, who portrayed Floyd the barber. The story I was told was that Howard had sent the suit to a funeral home so a friend of his could be buried in it. The suit wouldn't fit, so the funeral home returned it to the studio. Jim Nabors was then given the suit to wear. After Jim left, it was handed on to me. Eventually moths got into the suit, and it had to be thrown away. By then, however, it had become a Goober trademark, so wardrobe made a replica of the suit before discarding the original.

George Lindsey

The four arrive at the justice of the peace. Goober "gets busy" tying shoes and cans to the bumper of the squad car. Barney, Aunt Bee, and Opie rush inside. Aunt Bee embraces Helen, and Opie asks, "Pa, are you really getting married?" Barney gives Andy the twenty-five dollars and says, "You don't have to worry about paying me back. Just take your time." Andy looks at the money and says, "This is for a fishing fine. We're not getting married. You beat anything." Goober enters and begins throwing rice.

In the epilogue, Andy and Helen are relaxing at Helen's house. Andy has sent Barney and Thelma Lou "out into the woods." As Andy hugs Helen, the moment is interrupted when Barney bursts in. He has dropped his fishing pole in the lake and wants to borrow Andy's. Barney apologizes for "barging in," and then asks Andy, "What were you doing?"

Barney Fife, Realtor

EPISODE #143

FIRST BROADCAST ON JANUARY 4, 1965

WRITTEN BY BILL IDELSON
AND SAM BOBRICK

DIRECTED BY PETER BALDWIN

DABBS GREER AND AMZIE STRICKLAND
GUEST STAR AS HARRY AND LILA SIMS

*"If you're selling something, you should tell
the people the truth about it, or else it ain't
honest."*

Opie, repeating Andy's rule
of fair dealing

"**I** don't really remember what inspired the story line for this episode," says writer Sam Bobrick, "but when I first came to Los Angeles everyone was in the real-estate business. We may have gotten the idea from that. I do recall that I enjoyed writing this script."

Bill and Sam begin their script in the courthouse. Andy enters and finds Barney on the telephone. Barney is talking with Mr. Clark about moving the iron bed out of his garage. Barney hangs up the telephone and begins figuring on a piece of paper. Andy says, "Boy, you sure are doing a lot of figuring. What you doing, buying a house?" Barney answers, "Not me personally. I'm in the business."

Barney explains that he recently talked to Mr. Slummer, the real-estate man. According to Barney, all Mr. Slummer does is "sit around in his office all day long, smoking a big, fat cigar, and never stirs unless somebody wants to buy something. Then he takes them out in that old rattle-trap car of his, and if they buy he collects five percent." Barney thinks "a younger guy with some drive" could make some money.

Barney tells Andy he has been in the real-estate business "less than twenty-four hours" and has already learned that "everybody wants to sell their house."

During the conversation, Andy goes into the back room to get a cup of coffee. The coffee pot is covered with a plate instead of a lid. The plate lid is a realistic detail that captures the feel of everyday life.

Andy remarks that he is completely satisfied with the house he's living in. Barney asks, "What if I told you the Williams house was available?" Barney reminds Andy that he always points out the house every time he and Barney drive by it. Barney tells Andy he could put him in "that little unit," if Andy would sell his place and get a mortgage for the difference. Andy eventually asks, "Well, what are we doing? Is this a real-estate office or a sheriff's office?"

Barney replies that the real-estate business is strictly a sideline. The words are just out of his mouth when the phone rings. Without hesitation, Barney answers, "Fife Realty."

"Jokes like this were easy to write," says Sam. "You just had to be sure they fit the character and didn't come off as a joke just for the sake of a laugh."

Later that day Andy returns home and finds Opie and a friend, Howie Williams, examining Opie's bicycle. Opie has decided to sell the bicycle to Howie. Andy asks Opie if he has told Howie that the bicycle's coaster brake slips, the chain comes apart, and the inner tubes are covered with patches. Opie asks Andy if he should have told Howie about the defects. Andy answers, "I think so, Op. If you're selling something, the buyer's got a right to know everything that's wrong with it, otherwise it's not quite honest."

"I don't remember that Bill and I intentionally set out to teach a lesson," says Sam. "The importance of fair dealing to the story line and the interaction between Andy and Opie just developed as we wrote the script."

During supper, Opie tells Andy that he ruined the deal on the bike by being honest. Andy responds, "Ope, let me give you a little talk on fair dealing." Opie asks if he can get a glass of water first. When Opie goes into the kitchen and turns on the water, the plumbing begins to rumble. Andy tells Opie to turn the faucet all the way open.

The rumbling sets Aunt Bee's "teeth on edge." Andy asks her if she would like to move and explains that the Williamses might want to sell their house. Andy says Barney has told him they could afford the Williams place.

After supper, Barney surprises the Taylors by dropping by and asking if he can bring in perspective buyers, the Simses, to look at the house. The Taylors reluctantly agree and quickly "straighten up the place" while Barney goes to the car to get the Simses.

While showing the house, Barney whispers to Mr. Sims, "There is a little work to be done, but with your imagination, you folks could really do something with this place." Andy overhears this and responds with a grimace.

"Andy's grimace grew out of the fact that most people think they live in a perfectly decorated house," says Sam. "People quickly become incensed if someone should think differently."

During the visit, Opie points out that the kitchen ceiling is cracked, that there is a "noise" in the faucet, and that the roof leaks. After hearing about these problems, the Simses quickly lose interest in the house.

"The Griffith show always was a friendly set," says Amzie Strickland, who portrayed Lila Sims. "During breaks, Andy liked to go into his dressing room and play his guitar. Quite often I would go in and sit down and talk. My husband and I knew Andy from his early days in New York. After we moved to California, Andy was kind enough to recommend us for jobs.

"TAGS casting director Ruth Burch would call my agent if they wanted me for an episode and ask if I was free. I was never told what kind of a role it was or anything about it because in those days I was one of a group of actors who played different parts every week. We were very versatile, so the type of role was not important."

"If I was available, they would send over a script a couple of days ahead of time," says Amzie. "In those days, the writing was so good that very few rewrites were required. The scripts were ready in advance, and there were few changes when you got on the set. Once you had a script, you knew that maybe you'd have one line changed but never anything else because the writers knew what they were doing.

"If you were good the first time you were on, they would give you other opportunities to work. If you didn't work in with the show, then they kind of eased you out. The next time a role came up, they wouldn't call you."

After the Simses leave, Andy asks Opie if he pointed out the house's defects just to get even. Opie answers that he was just thinking about what Andy had said about the rule of fair dealing. Andy responds with, "Well, bikes are bikes, and houses are houses." Andy says when he bought the house, the crack was already in the ceiling, and the previous owner had just painted the kitchen so the crack wouldn't show. Andy tells Opie that one owner passes the things wrong with a house on to the next owner.

Opie then asks, "You mean, kids should be honest but the grown-ups don't have to be?" This observation leaves Andy at a loss for words, and he sends Opie to bed.

The next day, Barney is angry because Opie prevented him from making a sale. When the telephone rings, Barney answers it curtly. When Barney realizes it is Mr. Sims, his demeanor changes instantly. He pleads frantically with Mr. Sims for one more chance to show Andy's house. After Sims agrees, Barney says, "Thank you, thank you, and bless you, bless you."

"'Bless you' grew out of Barney's relief that Mr. Sims will give him another chance," says Sam. "A desperate Barney is also relieved that God has not forsaken him."

At the second showing, Barney tells the Simses that there is nothing really wrong with the place. "It's just the boy said those things last night, and we know how kids exaggerate." Andy admits to the Simses that kids do tend to exaggerate, but in this case everything Opie said is true. Opie responds to Andy's honesty with a look of deep admiration.

"Opie's admiration of Andy was called for in the script," says Sam. "The decision to show Opie's face in closeup, however, was the call of the director."

Thinking Andy has got another buyer, Mr. Sims immediately offers to buy the house. Before Andy can sell, however, he must decide if he wants to purchase the Williams house. Barney quickly calls the Williamses, and Andy and Aunt Bee go to look at the house.

Andy and Aunt Bee are greeted by Howie at the Williamses. Howie's feet are wet. He explains that he has "been down in the basement sailing the boat. There's about a foot of water down there. It's great. Sometimes after a heavy rain there is a lot more." Howie turns to his father and says, "The crack in the furnace is getting a lot bigger, and you can see the flame real clear."

"It never concerned us that the audience might wonder where Opie was while Andy and Aunt Bee were at the Williams house," says Sam. "But, it could have given the viewer something to think about. Maybe it was late, and Opie had to study or go to bed. After all, Barney stayed with the Simses at Andy's house. Or perhaps Opie stayed out of sight, down in the flooded basement, sailing a boat."

After thinking over the situation, Andy decides that the best thing would be for everyone to stay where they are. He uses the telephone to "warn Barney." Barney is irate when he learns Andy has decided not to buy the Williams house. Andy lays the telephone down and walks out. Thinking Andy is still listening, Barney continues to protest his decision.

The next day, Barney is busy figuring. Andy asks if he has another real-estate deal. Barney tells Andy he is completely out of that business. When Andy asks what the figures are all about, Barney replies, "Ange, you been wanting a car, haven't you?"

Goober Takes a Car Apart

EPISODE #144

FIRST BROADCAST ON JANUARY 11, 1965

WRITTEN BY BILL IDELSON
AND SAM BOBRICK

DIRECTED BY PETER BALDWIN

"I won't set foot outside that courthouse, Andy, I promise."

Goober Pyle

"This was another script that was fun to write."
Sam Bobrick

The opening scene of "Goober Takes a Car Apart" finds Andy seated on the bench in front of the courthouse. He is reading a letter when Goober drives up in the squad car. Andy asks how the squad car is going. Goober responds, "Running like a scalded dog." When Goober asks Andy what he's reading, Andy tells him that it's a letter from Barney. "He's up in Raleigh. Took his vacation up there." Goober sits down on the bench, and Andy reads Barney's letter out loud.

"Bill Idelson was always great with phrases," says writer Sam Bobrick. "Goober's 'scalded dog' description of the squad car came from him. I don't remember anything in our script about a letter from Barney.

Floyd considered buying the car, but he couldn't
make his mind up with the body off.
Goober "put it together, so Floyd could try it out."

TAGSRWC Archives

I imagine it was added later and written by either producer Aaron Ruben, Andy Griffith, or Don Knotts."

The office telephone rings as Andy finishes reading. A man named Shorty tells Andy he will not be able to answer the sheriff's phone while Andy is attending the Sheriffs' Safety Conference in Mt. Pilot. Goober eagerly offers to take Shorty's place. He tells Andy, "I really would enjoy it. You know how I love to hang around the courthouse." Andy reluctantly accepts Goober's offer. Goober gives Andy his word that he'll be at the office early on Wednesday morning.

"This was the first script that featured Goober," says George Lindsey. "I remember that the script seemed to have miles and miles of dialogue to memorize. I wasn't overly excited when I saw that I had a major role in the script. I was just very pleased that I was getting a job—a good job."

On the day of the conference, Goober fails to show up. Andy goes to Wally's Service Station in search of Goober and finds him working on Gilly Walker's carburetor. Goober imitates different carburetor noises as he explains to Andy the trouble Gilly is having with his engine.

"Goober was a natural mechanic and knew cars so well he could talk their language," says Sam. "In my mind, he was the kind of mechanic who never read a book or went to automotive school. He simply had a feel for working on cars."

Goober tells Andy he will "go right down" to the courthouse, and Andy returns home to finish packing for his trip. While Andy is packing, the telephone rings. Andy learns that there is still no one at the courthouse. Andy goes to investigate and finds Goober outside the courthouse working on Gilly Walker's car.

Frustrated, Andy tells Goober to go back to the filling station. Andy returns home and decides to ask Aunt Bee to take Goober's place. Goober shows up soon afterwards and tells Andy he has fixed Gilly's car and is now free. Goober promises to stay in the office, but Andy refuses the offer. Aunt Bee points out that it might be better if there were a man at the courthouse, so Andy reluctantly agrees. He tells

Goober, "When you get down there, you stay inside the courthouse. Don't you go outside the courthouse."

Gilly drives by and sees Goober walking to the courthouse. He stops to complain about a new problem with his engine. Gilly drives Goober down to the courthouse so he can listen to the engine on the way.

Remembering his promise to Andy, Goober takes Gilly's engine apart and brings it inside "to get it right." Goober begins with the engine but continues until the entire car is disassembled. Gilly and Floyd watch Goober while he works.

"We had three different cars in various stages of being torn apart," says George. "I also know that they actually ran because I would start the engines up."

Andy returns from the conference and is stunned when he enters the office and finds Gilly's car. The telephone rings. Goober starts the engine while Andy is on the telephone. When Andy hangs up the telephone, he tells Goober that he has to go to Mrs. Corey's house. Andy warns Goober that he'd "better have a good start getting this car out of here" by the time he returns.

When Andy returns, he is angered by Goober's slow progress. Andy announces, "Now, Goober, I'm going to get out of here because if I don't I'm liable to start hollering. When I get done hollering, I'm liable to take one of these guns out of this rack here and shoot you. Now, I'm going home, and when I come back here in the morning I want all traces of that car to be gone."

"It never concerned us that Andy was coming across angrier than usual," says Sam. "We thought Andy's anger was justified. After all, most people would get upset if they found a car in their workplace or living room."

When Andy arrives home, Aunt Bee tells him that Sheriff Jackson, the president of the Sheriff's Association called, and Aunt Bee told him Andy was at the courthouse. Sheriff Jackson is planning to pay Andy a visit.

Andy fears that he will become the "laughingstock of the whole state" if Sheriff Jackson sees the car inside the courthouse. He rushes to the office and finds the "car back together." Gilly has decided to sell the car, and Floyd is considering buying it. Floyd, however, couldn't make up his mind with the body off, so Goober "put it together for a few minutes, so Floyd could try it out." Andy frantically tries removing a car door.

Sheriff Jackson and his assistant enter the office. When the sheriff inquires about the car's presence, Goober explains, "I took the car apart piece by piece and got it right in here. It belongs to Gilly Walker. You wouldn't believe how he abuses that car. Speed, speed, speed, that's all he ever thinks about." After thinking the situation over, Sheriff Jackson decides the car is part of a safety display. Andy's reputation is saved.

"Bill and I had decided on this solution to Andy's problem before writing the script," says Sam. "The fact that the visiting officer thinks the car is part of a safety display may be too much of a coincidence to be entirely believable. But sometimes you have to make drastic cuts for time, and sometimes they're not always the right cuts."

In the epilogue, Andy and Goober bid Sheriff Jackson and his assistant good-bye. After their departure, Andy invites Goober inside the office. He walks straight to the gun rack, removes a gun, points it at Goober and says, "Get it out. I said, get it out, right now." Goober immediately goes to work.

The Case of the Punch in the Nose

EPISODE #152

FIRST BROADCAST ON MARCH 15, 1965

WRITTEN BY BILL IDELSON
AND SAM BOBRICK

DIRECTED BY COBY RUSKIN

"The case was never properly disposed of."
Barney Fife

"I once had an uncle who punched several people in the nose for stupid reasons," says writer Sam Bobrick. "I thought an episode inspired by my uncle's behavior would work well on TAGS. We presented the idea to producer Aaron Ruben. He liked it, and we began working on the script."

The opening scene in Bill and Sam's script finds Andy and Barney sorting through some old files. Barney comes across an assault case dated August 9, 1946, that involved Floyd Lawson and Charlie Foley. The case file doesn't say who assaulted whom. Barney reads the file and discovers that the case never came to trial, "nothing resolved, no verdict, no nothing."

"The date of the assault case was picked randomly," says Sam. "We wanted a date far enough in the past to emphasis the fact that Barney had to go a long way to stir up trouble."

Barney feels they ought to do something because "an assault was committed, an arrest was made, and nothing ever happened." Barney decides to reopen the case and begins his investigation by talking to Floyd. Floyd is reading a newspaper when Andy and Barney enter the barbershop. He has just read about the engagement of Bobby Gribble and Emma Larch and shares this news. Andy is interested, but Barney is focused solely on the investigation. He asks Floyd about the assault but gets nowhere.

"Howard McNear was the funniest man in acting I ever worked with," says George Lindsey. "He did something with his role of Floyd Lawson that couldn't be duplicated. He put his own stamp on it. I loved watching him act. I would often go down to the studio and watch him when I wasn't even working."

After leaving the barbershop, Barney goes next door to talk to Charlie Foley. Mr. Foley remembers the case and tells Barney he fell asleep in the barber chair. While he was sleeping, Floyd cut his hair and gave him a shave. He hadn't asked for the shave. When he refused to pay for it, an argument followed, and Floyd punched him in the nose. Foley had an eyewitness to back up his statement. He identifies the witness as "Goober in the garage. He was a little boy then. He saw the whole thing."

While Barney is talking to Mr. Foley, Andy and Floyd are back in the barbershop discussing Barney's interest in the case. Floyd observes that he thinks Barney's trouble is that he's not married. He says, "Now if he was married, these little things wouldn't bother him."

"Bill and I felt that Mayberry's slow pace left Barney with too much time on his hands," says Sam. "We expressed this through Floyd's comment about Barney not being married. Floyd felt Barney needed something like marriage to occupy his time. If he were married he would have been busy trying to make the marriage work and would not have been concerned with petty stuff."

Barney returns to the barbershop and tells Foley's version of what happened. He has asked Mr. Foley and Goober to come by so the assault can be reenacted. While waiting, Floyd gives his version. According to Floyd, Foley "asked for that shave." Floyd denies punching Foley.

When Foley and Goober arrive, Foley and Floyd start arguing about what actually happened. Barney insists that the case be reenacted. Andy takes Barney aside and asks him to stop his investigation. While the two are talking, Floyd and Mr. Foley resume arguing, and Floyd hits Foley in the nose.

Mr. Foley follows Andy into the courthouse and demands that Floyd be arrested. Foley says, "I have three witnesses. You all saw the whole thing." Andy replies that he didn't see anything because he was talking to Barney. Foley insists that Barney and Goober must have seen it. When they enter the office, Foley says to Barney, "All right tell the truth. You saw him haul off and hit me in cold blood."

"Mr. Foley's dialogue was inspired by the title of Truman Capote's book, *In Cold Blood*," says Sam. "The book was very popular at the time, and we thought the phrase would be a comical way to describe a punch in the nose."

Barney tells Foley he didn't see the assault because he was talking to Andy. Goober didn't see anything either because he was reading a comic book. Foley insists Goober saw Floyd "hit me on the nose" and calls Goober a "liar." The two argue, and Foley punches Goober in the nose.

The animosity Barney rekindles between Floyd and Mr. Foley stirs up the whole town, and numerous nose punches follow. Otis, "a distant kin of Foley's," punches Floyd in the nose. Goober punches Gilly Walker in the nose. Opie gets into a fight with his best friend, Johnny Paul. Lamar Tuttle, "a cousin of Floyd's," punches Otis in the nose.

The rash of assaults angers Andy. He tells Barney that things have gone far enough, and he wants them stopped. When Barney responds that the assaults are not their fault, Andy yells, "No, it's not *our* fault. It's *your* fault! You started the whole blame thing!" When Barney attempts to justify his actions, Andy tells him to "shut up."

"We felt that Andy's angry outburst was justified," says Sam. "Andy begged Barney to back off earlier, and Barney refused. Andy knew Barney was the troublemaker, so he had reason to be mad."

Eventually, Andy decides to have Floyd and Mr. Foley sit down and talk about the situation. He sends Barney to get Floyd and Foley and bring them to the courthouse. After the two principals are gathered, Andy begins "a hearing so we can settle this thing between you two fellows once and for all." Barney insists that Goober "really ought to be here," so Andy sends Barney to get him.

After Barney leaves, Andy attempts to have Floyd and Foley "settle this thing like friends." He reminds the two that they are old friends and tells them that being ready to forgive is the first law of friendship. Andy believes that what happened can be made right with "a warm, forgiving handshake." The two realize that Andy is right, shake hands, and forgive each other.

"This is another incidence of an important lesson developing as the script was written," says Sam. "We resolved the problem by having Andy tell the two principles to 'let sleeping dogs lie'."

Barney and Goober enter the courthouse soon after the case is resolved. Dissatisfied with how Andy has handled the situation, Barney wants to continue his investigation. As he rushes out of the office, Goober says, "You know, Andy, Barney's a wonderful fellow, but sometimes I just don't understand him, do you?" Andy answers, "Yeah, he's a nut."

"Barney's actions were justified by the fact that 'justice is blind'," explains Sam. "Barney is leaving no stone unturned to clear up a best-forgotten episode, no matter what the outcome."

When Goober asks where Barney has gone, Andy suddenly realizes that he's gone to the barbershop. Andy and Goober hurry outside and see Barney walking toward them, holding his nose. He has been punched.

In the epilogue, Barney has gotten a haircut. He refuses to pay Floyd an extra twenty-five cents for tonic he says he did not request. This repeats the situation between Floyd and Mr. Foley that led to the first punch in the nose. Hoping to prevent a possible punch in the nose, Andy insists that Barney pay the twenty-five cents.

"Sometimes repetition is important in comedy writing, sometimes it isn't," says Sam. "On the other hand, sometimes it isn't, and sometimes it is. On the other hand. . . ."

Opie's Newspaper

EPISODE #153

FIRST BROADCAST ON MARCH 22, 1965

WRITTEN BY HARVEY BULLOCK

DIRECTED BY COBY RUSKIN

"This is a non-police story. Such episodes lent diversity to story areas."

Harvey Bullock

"**W**hen I was a ten-year-old kid, my pal and I built a lean-to on the side of our garage. Inside was the office of *The Keyhole Journal*," says writer Harvey Bullock. "We 'printed' (we actually duplicated pages by using carbon paper and a gummy roller) about twenty copies of the one-page first edition. All items in the paper were gossip tidbits—whose girl was seen riding in whose car, who really craves whom although she pretends she doesn't. These tidbits would be followed by reports about mysterious doings, such as reports of garments missing from clotheslines, followed by more romantic revelations.

"The other kids didn't react much. Some of the girls named in the paper got oafish. The grown-ups giggled, if they bothered to read it at all. But we did attract one advertiser. A neighbor gave us fifteen cents to run a notice that he was selling Airway vacuum cleaners. We shut down after three issues. Boredom set in, and there were other fields to conquer. But the memory of the experience stayed with me and inspired 'Opie's Newspaper'."

The episode begins with Opie selling Andy a copy of his newspaper, *The Mayberry Sun*. Opie and his friend, Howie, "put the paper out on the print machine Howie got for his birthday." After discussing the paper's poor sales, Opie leaves the courthouse, and Barney enters.

Barney has just come from the barbershop and shares with Andy his distaste for gossip. Barney says his haircut took a long time because Floyd was gossiping with another customer about the widow Saunders. Barney claims he was reading an article in the "Geographic" and "turned a deaf ear to the whole thing." He then proceeds to repeat in great detail the story about the widow Saunders and a dish-towel salesman from Raleigh.

"For some mysterious reason there is comedy in ultra-specifics, notably in small-town gossip where every minute happenstance is fodder for conversation," says Harvey. "The opening scene is heightened by Barney's transparent, disdainful dismissal of gossip, which in reality he avidly cherishes—like everyone else."

After Barney repeats the gossip, Andy reads aloud from Opie's newspaper. In response, Barney comments that the paper is "darn cute."

"The items Andy reads to Barney were about kids and resembled news in *The Keyhole Journal*," says Harvey. "Barney's initial appraisal of the newspaper was all momentary approval to set up the contrast with his upcoming apoplexy when he later realizes how he's been misquoted in the second edition."

Opie returns while Andy and Barney are discussing his paper and tells them the paper's sales have not increased. Barney tells Opie, "If the papers aren't moving, there must be a reason why. Maybe you're not getting the right kind of copy. Copy, that's newspaper talk for stories." Barney goes on to tell how he had his own sports column in high school called "Pick-ups and Splashes From Floor and Pool." He acknowledges that the column only appeared once, because it was "too controversial and ahead of its time." Barney says, "I always had printer's ink in my veins. Guess I always had a nose for news." Barney advises Opie to increase the paper's scope and illustrates the point by pointing out that although Karen Folker, who is mentioned in Opie's paper, may be "hot copy for the fifth grade, uptown she don't mean a thing."

"Barney's exposition on 'hot copy' is another of his great and cherished assumptions as an authority," says Harvey. "He uses newspaper slang to mark himself as a veteran.

"In junior high school, I wrote a sports column with that exact awful name 'Pick-ups and Splashes From Floor and Pool.' I remembered it while writing the script and knew such a cornball title would fit Barney nicely."

Opie shares Barney's advice with Howie and the two decide to model their paper after *The Mayberry Gazette*'s "Mayberry After Midnight" column. The boys begin gathering material.

The two make note of Aunt Bee's comment that "Mrs. Foster's chicken à la king tasted like wallpaper paste," Andy's remark that "sometimes the preacher can be as dry as dust," and Barney's observation that Harold Grigsby's wife is "a blonde right out of a bottle." All three items are reported in *The Mayberry Sun*'s second edition.

"Most of the items in the second edition were tailored to Mayberry folk, with a hidden bomb in each," says Harvey. "I custom-fabricated the gossip items by figuring in advance which ones would lead to Andy, Barney, and Aunt Bee paying penance."

Opie hands papers to Andy, Barney, and Aunt Bee while the three are sitting in the Taylor kitchen. The hot weather is of more importance than the paper, and Barney comments, "Well, the weather's been changed so much lately, it must be the bomb."

"Barney's line about 'it must be the bomb' was an oft-stated casual throw-away line in the aftermath of World War II," says Harvey. "When I see it now in the script, I wince. It was ill-advised because I labored to keep topical items out of Mayberry. The writers were able to present

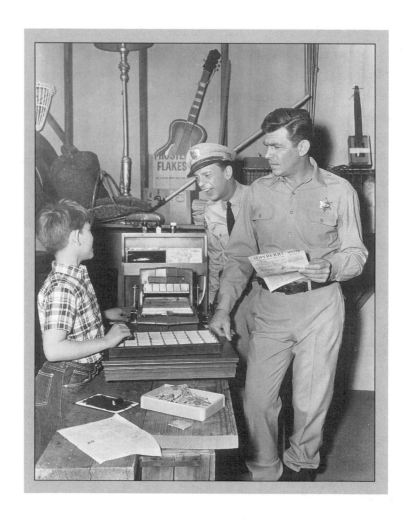

*Andy and Barney watch as
Opie prints* **The Mayberry Sun** *in Howie's garage.*

TAGSRWC Archives

Mayberry as a small Eden, which time had passed. I tried not to make references that would date stories. Also, any reference to the bomb was negative and unnecessary."

Barney casually glances at Opie's paper and sees its contents. Andy, Barney, and Aunt Bee all realize that "this town will be too hot to live in" if the paper is read.

The three find Opie in Howie's garage. Andy asks where he delivered all the papers. When Opie answers, "Just on Willow Avenue, Elm and Maple," the adults rush out in hopes of collecting the papers before they are noticed.

Andy, Aunt Bee, and Barney learn the consequences of gossip while they collect the papers. Mrs. Foster sees her moments after Aunt Bee hs removed Opie's paper from her mailbox. Aunt Bee explains she was just passing by and wanted Mrs. Foster's recipe for chicken à la king. Mrs. Foster invites Aunt Bee and Andy over for a leftover chicken à la king supper. Barney almost gets "a load of buckshot" from Harold Grigsby. Unaware that Barney is retrieving a paper, Grigsby thinks Barney came by to see his wife. After reading Andy's remark in Opie's paper, the preacher has Andy "hog-tied into teaching Sunday School for a full month of Sundays."

"Obviously the gossip was designed so that our characters who swap stories have to eventually pay the price," says Harvey. "It was also fun to write a story where the most upright of citizens are found to have human foibles."

Andy, Barney, and Aunt Bee successfully collect the papers before any great harm is done. Three hours later there have been no telephone calls complaining about the paper. Andy says, "I guess we got away with it. At least it's over. Maybe the boys learned a lesson out of this." Aunt Bee responds, "Maybe all of us could learn something from this. We're responsible for all this loose talk going around town. If we want the boys to behave better, we better set them a better example."

Opie comes in to say good night and apologizes for the trouble the paper caused. He says, "I guess it was kind of dumb of us to print up two whole pages of that stuff." When Andy, Aunt Bee, and Barney begin to panic about another page, Opie explains that they "bundled it up and threw it in the trash. I even saw the truck come pick it up. So nobody will ever get to read it."

Curiosity gets the best of the three adults. Later in the evening, Andy, Barney, and Aunt Bee meet unexpectedly at the city dump. Each supposedly has come to make sure the other page "was burned proper." When the bundled pages are found, Andy says, "We can go ahead and get rid of these. Yes sir, and the quicker the better." Andy removes three pages from the bundle, hands copies to Aunt Bee and Barney, keeps one for himself, and throws the rest into a smoking barrel. The three begin reading.

"The earlier admittance of blame and the steely determination by Aunt Bee (which they all accept) that none of them will ever again indulge in mindless gossip set up the concluding laugh," says Harvey. "All of this noble intent, however, is quickly put aside when they find out more 'hot stuff' is available.

"As I re-read the script, I noticed one major flaw. How did Aunt Bee get to the city dump that night? I keep hoping I will remember some correction or addition I made to cover up this gaping hole, but I can not."

In the epilogue, Opie delivers "a new, revised edition" of *The Mayberry Sun* to the courthouse. Opie assures Andy and Barney that "there's nothing about grown-ups at all" in the paper. After Opie leaves, Andy and Barney read the paper's schoolyard gossip. Barney comments, "Opie told the truth. He's not writing about grown-ups." Andy replies, "No, but they sure caught our style good though, didn't they?"

CLIFFORD IS A RAINDROP

Item in *The Mayberry Sun*: "Myra Lambert got a part in the school play, and she will be a raindrop."

In the Navy, right after World War II, I was assigned as a welfare/recreation officer in Hawaii to work with Joe Delaney, a Red Cross representative. Sailors would often come begging for news of their family back in the states. They had received no mail for some time and were worried and distraught. Kindly Joe would immediately send requests back to the Red Cross field worker in the sailor's hometown. The field worker would then visit the family and report back to Joe.

One concerned sailor pleaded for help in finding out about his family. So Joe sent off a request to the stateside field worker. The worker visited the family and found out all was going well. In fact, Clifford, a younger brother, had been given the role of a raindrop in the school play. In an effort to make her report more colorful, the field worker began with "Clifford is a raindrop."

Joe Delaney got word the report was received, hastily called the sailor into our office, grabbed the report, and read aloud, "Clifford is a raindrop."

Both men were stunned speechless. The poor sailor, staring beseechingly, asked, "What's going on?"

They finally sorted out things, but the ridiculous incident always stuck in my mind. Even now, fifty years later, if someone asks me, "What's new," I almost automatically reply, "Well, Clifford is a raindrop."

Harvey Bullock

The Luck of Newton Monroe

EPISODE #156

FIRST BROADCAST ON APRIL 12, 1965

WRITTEN BY BILL IDELSON AND SAM BOBRICK

DIRECTED BY COBY RUSKIN

DON RICKLES GUEST STARS AS NEWTON MONROE

"I think the 'fly' gag is one of the great pieces of television history."

George Lindsey

"I knew Don Rickles very well," says Andy Griffith's manager Richard O. Linke. "I suggested to Andy that Don would be great in the part of Newton Monroe. I made the suggestion only because Andy allowed me to. Andy said, 'Yeah, you're right. He'd be good in the part.' Andy then passed the suggestion on to producer Aaron Ruben, and Don was hired."

In the opening scene of "The Luck of Newton Monroe," Andy and Barney are relaxing on the Taylor front porch on a Sunday afternoon. A fly catches their attention. The fly lands on Barney's knee. Barney quickly swipes at the fly, catches it, holds his hand up to Andy's ear so he can confirm the catch, and then lets the fly go. "Well, it's Sunday," Barney says in explanation.

After releasing the fly, Barney tells Andy that the next day is Thelma

Lou's birthday, and he needs to buy her a present. He then shares his plans for the rest of the afternoon. He plans to "go down to the filling station, get me a bottle of pop, go home, take a nap, then go over to Thelma Lou's and watch a little TV." Barney repeats the plan three times.

"I don't remember writing the 'fly' gag," says writer Sam Bobrick. "Most likely it was an addition written by either Aaron Ruben, Andy Griffith or Don Knotts. Barney's recitation of his plan for Sunday afternoon was scripted. The afternoon's dull activities were the result of Barney's minimal expectations, especially in his social life."

After leaving Andy, Barney walks to Wally's filling station. Barney is greeted by Goober, who is excited about a transistor radio he has just purchased from a traveling salesman named Newton Monroe. Floyd Lawson is also at Wally's and has purchased a wrist watch.

Newton compliments Floyd on his purchase and tells him the watch goes well with his "green pants and black-and-white sports shoes." Floyd concurs and replies, "Sort of a symphony, isn't it?"

"Floyd was a wonderful character to write for," says Sam. "His lines were shaped primarily by his personality, and they often seemed to write themselves. Floyd's 'symphony' comment just seemed right for the character."

Barney asks Newton if he has anything in the trunk of his car for a girl. Newton suggests a ring, but Barney says he prefers something "a little less personal." When Newton suggests a pencil sharpener, Barney likes the idea. Newton, however, remembers "just the thing"—a fur piece. Barney examines the fur and hands it back to Newton, saying he doesn't want to spend that much because "she has a birthday every year." Newton informs Barney the fur piece sells for "thirteen-and-a-quarter" because he got it at "a fantastic buy at a warehouse." Barney makes the purchase.

The next day, Barney tells Andy how pleased Thelma Lou was with her birthday present. Andy asks Barney how much he paid for the fur. After learning how inexpensive the fur was, Andy voices his suspicion that Newton is "selling stolen goods."

Floyd and Goober are inside the courthouse when Andy and Barney arrive. The two feel they have been "gypped by that fellow selling stuff over at the filling station." Goober's radio "don't play no more," and the second hand on Floyd's watch is "spinning around like a pinwheel."

The telephone rings. It is Thelma Lou, who is upset because the fur on her fur piece is starting to fall out "in bunches."

Andy and Barney learn that Newton is "just up the block" and decide to confront him about the defective merchandise.

The master shot for the confrontation shows Andy, Barney, and Newton standing in front of Dave's Coffee Shop. Apparently, there was an oversight in the editing process, because the medium shots and closeups place the three in front of a jewelry store.

This error was the result of filming the scene with one camera. After the master shot was completed, the camera was moved, perhaps for better lighting, to a different location where the additional shots were photographed.

Newton shows Andy the bill of sale for his merchandise. Although Newton is not selling stolen goods, Andy discovers that he doesn't have a peddler's license to operate in Mayberry. Andy asks Newton to leave town. Newton, however, cannot resist the inquiries of an eager customer and makes another sale after Andy's warning. Barney sees the infraction and "nails" him.

Andy tells Newton, "I'm not going to stand still while you sell that junk on the streets. Now, you were peddling without a license. You're still peddling without a license. I don't know what else to tell you. I'm going to have to book you."

Seeking revenge, Barney doesn't allow Newton to "do much sitting" in jail. He puts Newton to work planting a tree. In the process, Newton breaks a water pipe.

Later in the afternoon, Barney telephones Thelma Lou. He has purchased another birthday present. Barney tells Thelma Lou that it's a surprise, but he promises her that she's "never had anything like it." Andy overhears the conversation. After Barney hangs up, he asks Barney what he got Thelma Lou. Barney answers, "A pineapple skinner from Newton. I looked all over, and I couldn't find anything. It was only two bucks."

"There was no romance in Barney's soul," says Sam. "This is reflected in his idea of an appropriate birthday gift and his satisfaction with his purchase of a pineapple skinner. We selected a pineapple skinner because it seemed funny and very Barney Fife-ish."

Barney has Newton "down in the basement cleaning the furnace." Andy suggests that Barney "let up on" Newton. When Barney responds that he is teaching Newton a lesson, Andy suggests that he's really "getting a little revenge."

"Through Barney's behavior, Bill and I were trying to show that good people can get angry, and it's OK," says Sam. "I always hated shows that were devoid of all human emotions. People get mad, and it's better for them—and Barney—to let it out on occasion."

Andy calls to Newton through the heating vent and asks how's he doing. Newton replies that he's just starting the fire. Andy reminds him to open the flue, but minutes later black smoke pours out of the vent.

After the fire is out, Barney has Newton mop the office floor. Newton "spills the bucket" and breaks the bookcase glass while mopping. Barney yells, "Can't you do anything in this world right? He's inept," and storms out. In response to Barney's reprimand, Newton feels he is "a born loser."

Andy sympathizes with Newton and decides to help him restore his self-confidence. He gives Newton the job of painting the Taylor front porch. Andy tells Newton he can paint the porch when nobody's watching. After Newton finishes, Andy and Barney check his work. The front porch is a mess, so Andy and Barney repaint it.

The next morning, Andy takes Newton to look at the porch. Andy gives Newton the credit for the beautiful paint job. Newton comments that the porch does look great. Andy tells him, "It just shows you what a little confidence will do. And I got a surprise for you. I'm going to suspend your sentence."

Later in the day, Andy and Barney return to the office. Newton is at the front door, paintbrush in hand. With his confidence restored, he joyfully says, "I'm not inept. I'm ept. I don't have to be a salesman, if I don't want to be. I'm a painter. Sheriff, I'm going to paint the courthouse for free."

In the epilogue, Barney questions Andy about the wisdom of getting Newton a sales job at a Mt. Pilot hardware store. Andy responds, "If Newton doesn't do well, they'll get rid of him. Besides he's out of our hair. Let's just forget about it." Andy and Barney find two packages. The packages are "tokens of Newton's gratitude." Barney gets "that pencil sharpener" and Andy gets a "battery-operated razor." When Barney tries out the razor, it grabs the skin on his face and will not let go.

1965-66

Malcolm at the Crossroads

EPISODE #164

FIRST BROADCAST ON SEPTEMBER 27, 1965

WRITTEN BY HARVEY BULLOCK

DIRECTED BY GARY NELSON

BERNARD FOX AND HOWARD MORRIS
GUEST STAR AS MALCOLM
MERRIWEATHER AND ERNEST T. BASS

"This is a bit of a mystery script because of massive changes, including the substitution of Ernest T., which made it more interesting."
Harvey Bullock

"I can't recall the events that led to the massive revisions this script underwent," says writer Harvey Bullock. "It must have been producer Bob Ross's idea. The bully character was originally named Spike Jenson. He never appeared and was replaced (quite wisely) by Ernest T. Bass.

"Bob Ross replaced Aaron Ruben as producer at the beginning of TAGS's sixth season. Aaron Ruben left to produce *Gomer Pyle, U.S.M.C.* Bob was a good friend and very talented. He had written on the old *Amos and Andy* shows, and when I first met him, we shared offices while he was the editor/producer of *I'm Dickens, He's Fenster.*"

The revised script begins with Andy walking down a Mayberry street. He stops and watches Ernest T. Bass., who is working as a school-crossing guard to earn money so he and his girlfriend Romeena can get married. Ernest T. needs twelve dollars for the honeymoon. "Tents cost money," according to Ernest T. He also plans to "get a lantern, too."

At this point, Ernest T. throws a rock at a passing car. Andy warns him that if he throws any more rocks he will be fired. Ernest T. promises he "won't throw one more rock." After Andy walks away, Ernest T. pulls a brick out of his sack and says, "Didn't say nothing about no brick."

On his way back to the courthouse, Andy hears a commotion down the street. Malcolm Merriweather has returned and has recklessly ridden his bicycle into a car. Luckily, Malcolm is unhurt. Andy welcomes him back to Mayberry. Malcolm tells Andy he would like to "stay a bit this time and try my hand at being an American." Malcolm plans to make his "own way" while in Mayberry and is looking for "a solid position." Andy suggests he check out the barbershop bulletin board.

Andy and Malcolm walk to the barbershop where Floyd helps them check the bulletin board. Malcolm says he has experience as a valet and a falcon keeper. Floyd carefully scans the job listings but finds openings for neither. He promises Malcolm, "The first thing that comes in for falcon keeping, I won't give it to no one else."

"I really enjoyed working with Howard McNear, who portrayed Floyd Lawson," says Bernard Fox. "We didn't get to talk much, but the wonderful way he came out with 'falcon keeper, falcon keeper' as he scanned the bulletin board rings in my ears to this day."

Later in the day, Andy returns to the school crossing and sees Ernest T. throwing a brick at a car. He fires Ernest T. and offers the position to Malcolm. Malcolm accepts and performs his new duties in a militaristic style influenced from his experience as a Coldstream Guard. The militaristic style impresses the boys who use the school crossing.

"Bernard Fox was of great help suggesting English phrases," says Harvey. "Although, I think the Coldstream Guard, which was an actual and very historic regiment, was my idea."

"I suggested many of Malcolm's English phrases," says Bernard. "The

Andy, Goober, Floyd, and Ernest T. Bass outside the courthouse

TAGSRWC Archives

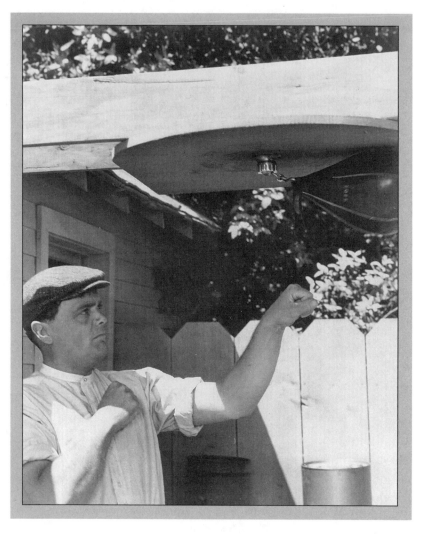

Malcolm Merriweather trains for his fight against Ernest T. Bass.

collarless shirt Malcolm wears was also my idea. Most working-class men in England wore collarless shirts. The idea was that you bought a shirt with two collars so that you could put a fresh collar on without having to wash the whole shirt. Presumably, because of the general coolness of the weather in England, the shirt itself didn't become too offensive."

Ernest T. becomes angry when he discovers that Malcolm has taken his job. To make matters worse, Malcolm is an "Englishter." Ernest T.'s parents were Irish, and, according to Ernest T.'s mother, "Englishters" and the Irish are enemies. Ernest T. thus challenges Malcolm to a fight.

"I also enjoyed working with Howie Morris," says Bernard. "I thought Howie was a very funny man. It was a pleasure to appear with him and act as his straight man."

Malcolm decides to leave town quietly. On his way out of Mayberry, he sees a group of boys imitating his military style at the school crossing and changes his mind. Malcolm seeks out Goober, who used to be a bully when he was younger, and requests fighting lessons. Goober agrees, and Malcolm begins training.

"There was some difference between writing for Goober and writing for Gomer," says Harvey. "Gomer was soft, gullible, and affable. Goober was more slangy, energized, but self-effacing. Their voices also affected the kind of lines that could be written for each. Gomer had a smooth, if sometimes high-pitched voice. Goober's speech was raspy and punchy. But, all in all, there were more similarities between the two than differences."

Malcolm's training reveals his inadequacies as a fighter. He is "decked" by Goober, gets tangled up as he is jumping rope, and hits himself in the face with a punching bag.

"I do believe the punching bag hitting me in the face was my own little bit of masochism," says Bernard. "It took about three takes to get it right. The continued bopping of the nose caused some concern, but it was worth it to get it right."

On the day of the fight, Andy, who is aware that Malcolm will likely "get killed," tells Ernest T. that if he goes through with the fight he is going to jail. Ernest T. doesn't care.

Andy decides to try a different approach. As the fighters are making their final preparations, Andy tells Ernest T. that it will be fun to watch two Irishmen fight. Andy explains that Malcolm's mother is from County Cork. Ernest T. immediately has a change of heart, "Well, never let it be said that Ernest. T. Bass ever spilt a drop of Irish blood." Ernest T. runs toward Malcolm, jumps in his arms, and kisses him on the forehead.

"I recall most clearly the incident of Howie jumping into my arms," says Bernard. "We were rehearsing on the patio of Howie's home. I suggested that Howie leap up and wrap his legs around my neck. The producer and director felt that it couldn't be done. I said I thought it could. I put my fists up, and as Howie took a flying leap, I bent my knees, caught Howie on my arms, and slid him up to my shoulders!

"Incidentally, I had often wondered why we were rehearsing at Howie's home. Only recently, he explained that his wife had just arrived home after giving birth. The producer, director, and Andy had agreed that we would rehearse at his house so that he would be immediately available if needed."

In the epilogue, Andy, Malcolm, and Ernest T. are in the courthouse. Ernest T. invites Malcolm "up to his cave to eat." Ernest T. asks Malcolm what part of County Cork his "mommy" is from. Malcolm answers that she's not from County Cork. He adds that she was born in the heart of London. Ernest T. realizes that Malcolm is a "full-blooded Englishter" after all. Andy jumps up from his desk and positions himself between Ernest T. and Malcolm as Ernest T. lunges for Malcolm. Ernest T. jumps into Andy's arms, and Malcolm crawls through Andy's legs to escape.

"I remember that prior to this episode there was some talk about fitting me in as a series regular," says Bernard. "Ray Saffian Allen, who was a good friend, called me to tell me that the agent who was negotiating for me at the time was screwing things up by telling them that I was practically signed to several other series, none of which was true.

Ray said the agent was going to blow the deal. Ray suggested that I get my tail over there and attempt to patch things up with Aaron Ruben.

"Instead of meeting with Aaron, I was ushered into the presence of Bob Ross, whom I didn't know from Adam. Mr. Ross chomped on a mouthful of food as I explained that the agent was exaggerating, I had no intention of signing with another series, and that I was, in fact, looking forward to joining TAGS. It wasn't easy to make out his speech through a mouthful of mush, but I do believe I heard him say, 'In other words, we have first refusal?' I agreed and left without so much as a 'Bon appetit,' and that was that. Ray Allen did tell me that several scripts were written, but the recurring role never occurred. Inasmuch as the series didn't last that much longer, it really didn't matter very much. But who knows what adventures Malcolm might have cycled into and around Mayberry?"

Off to Hollywood

EPISODE #166

FIRST BROADCAST ON OCTOBER 25, 1965

WRITTEN BY BILL IDELSON
AND SAM BOBRICK

DIRECTED BY ALAN RAFKIN

"Buy something absolutely unnecessary and then it's a blast."

Aunt Bee

"**A**fter five seasons with the Griffith show, Aaron Ruben created *Gomer Pyle, U.S.M.C.*, which was a spinoff from TAGS," says Andy Griffith's manager Richard O. Linke. "Aaron had to leave because he was the producer of the new series. Luckily, fate showed its strong hand. I knew Bob Ross, and so did Andy. He was a writer and took over as producer of TAGS. I want to tell you, it was unreal. It was like we never dropped a beat, and that was unusual. Normally, you might find another producer/writer who is talented but doesn't fit in or who doesn't come up with the goods. But that wasn't the case with Bob. And Bob was such a genteel man, such a nice and talented fellow, that it just flowed."

"Off to Hollywood" begins with Goober and new Mayberry deputy, Warren Ferguson, discussing an unopened letter addressed to Andy from

Belmont Studios, Hollywood, California. The two are curious about the letter's contents. Warren rhetorically asks Goober, "Do you know what your sharpies do when they want to see what's inside a letter?" Warren then follows with his trademark, "huh, huh, huh?" and holds the envelope up to the light.

"Warren's 'huh, huh, huh?' was not scripted," says writer Sam Bobrick. "That was one of Jack Burns's own devices. Writing for Jack was quite different from writing for Don Knotts. No one was ever easier for us to write for than Barney Fife. He was every writer's dream."

Andy enters the office as Warren and Goober are examining the envelope. Andy opens the letter and finds it contains a check for one thousand dollars. Belmont Studios has purchased the rights to make a movie about Andy. The movie is based on the magazine article, "Sheriff Without a Gun." Andy decides to go home and tell the family.

"The idea to have the Taylors travel to Hollywood was Bob Ross's idea," says Sam. "Bob also pointed out to us that a magazine article about Andy had been mentioned in a previous episode ["TV or Not TV," Episode #150] and suggested the story idea that a studio buy the rights to make a movie based on Andy's life."

Aunt Bee and Opie excitedly inspect the check. Aunt Bee wants to call Clara Edwards, but Andy would like to "kind of keep it to ourselves." Opie questions Andy about how he plans to spend the money. Andy "figured we'd put this right in the bank." This disappoints Aunt Bee and Opie. Aunt Bee suggests Andy "spend some of it" on something unnecessary. Andy does feel they "ought to celebrate." He suggests they invite Helen over for supper. Aunt Bee suggests starting the meal "with a crabmeat cocktail. At least, let's do something crazy."

Andy returns to the courthouse and finds it overflowing with people who want to see the check. Goober has spread the word. He takes the check from Andy and proudly shows it off.

Floyd remains behind after everyone else leaves. He says to Andy, "You know those two acres that I've got over on the north side. Well, it's a beautiful spot. Fill in that swamp, and it would be a paradise."

Floyd is willing to sell the land "at two hundred an acre. Of course, if it happened to be a personal friend of mine I'd shave it to one fifty." Although Andy isn't interested, Floyd tells him he doesn't have to make up his mind right away. "Just one of these days, put your wading boots on and go over and have a look at it."

"After learning about Andy's money, Floyd offers to sell him some swampland," says Sam. "By this time Bill and I understood the characters very well and knew the swampland sales pitch was perfect for Floyd. We always enjoyed writing for Floyd and imagining how Howard McNear would perform the material."

That evening at supper, Helen suggests Andy use the money "to live it up a little." She asks, "When was the last time you people took a trip?" Andy mentions the possibility of taking a trip to Asheville, North Carolina, to see cousin Evin Moore.

"The name of Andy Griffith's cousin was not in our script," says Sam. "I imagine Andy used the name to recognize his own cousin. Minor changes like this were usually made during the script read-through and approved by the producer."

Aunt Bee suggests visiting Hollywood, California. Andy protests, "Well, that's three thousand miles away— and the money! We'll have to think about this a lot."

Eventually, Andy is persuaded to spend the money on a trip to Hollywood. After the decision is made, Andy and Aunt Bee concern themselves with preparations for their departure. The two discuss taking Opie out of school, and Andy shares with Aunt Bee his concern about leaving an inexperienced man like Warren in charge of the office. The discussion takes place in the kitchen. Aunt Bee is seated at the table, snapping green beans as she talks.

"I don't think the bean snapping was included in our script," says Sam. "It was a nice realistic Southern touch that was likely the input of either Bob Ross or Andy Griffith."

When Andy arrives at the courthouse, he finds a large number of "the boys." The men have gathered to look at Andy's Hollywood travel folders. The group has picked out a motel for Andy to stay in while in Hollywood. Floyd is excited about a folder from "Senior Citizen's Lodge on Route 66."

Aunt Bee purchases a new outfit for Opie to wear on the trip. The red shorts and a shirt with a white-flower print, along with a pair of sandals are "just what little boys wear in Hollywood." Opie doesn't like the outfit. Hoping to encourage Opie, Andy compliments his appearance. Aunt Bee tells Opie, "I told you your father would like it, and I'm so happy because that comes in men's sizes too. Father-and-son sets, and I got you the same outfit. Andy, why don't you go up and try on your outfit?" Andy protests, "It's so late and everything." Opie asks, "If Pa doesn't have to wear his, do I have to wear mine?" Aunt Bee responds, "Andy!"

This sets up a wonderful visual gag. Andy is shown in closeup, reacting to the news that he has to put on his "Hollywood" outfit. The closeup immediately cuts to another shot of Andy in the same pose. The camera pans backward and reveals Andy and Opie dressed identically.

"The matching father-and-son outfits were what we thought Aunt Bee's image of Hollywood would be," says Sam. "It was the first of several visual gags we used in the script."

Much of the humor in the episode comes from the small town's reaction to the Taylors' trip. Andy receives numerous requests to get an autograph or take a "Hollywood" picture for someone. He is asked to call someone's west-coast relative, and even gets a request to "stand on the corner of Hollywood and Vine and say 'hello' from Floyd."

On the day of their departure, a large group, dressed in their Sunday best, gathers at the bus stop to bid the Taylors farewell. The town band plays.

At the bus stop, Warren volunteers to load Andy's luggage. He throws the bags over the top of the bus. When Andy lifts a suitcase, the handle comes off in his hand.

"Bill and I were somewhat reluctant to use visual gags on the Griffith show because Andy preferred that the humor come from the personalities of the characters," says Sam. "We did, however, occasionally use visual humor if we felt it worked well in a scene."

In the epilogue, the Taylors are shown aboard the airplane on their way to Hollywood. Andy is finally able to relax after the frantic activity of preparing for the trip. Aunt Bee says, "Suddenly Mayberry seems far away, doesn't it? Main Street, and the people, and our house." She looks perplexed and asks, "Andy, did you turn off the gas?" Andy shouts, "Stewardess, stewardess, when's the first stop?"

"There was never any reluctance in ending the episode with the old 'did I turn off the gas' routine," says Sam. "I still have those doubts when I leave the house. The routine is tried but true."

Taylors in Hollywood

EPISODE #167

FIRST BROADCAST ON NOVEMBER 1, 1965

WRITTEN BY BILL IDELSON AND
SAM BOBRICK

DIRECTED BY ALAN RAFKIN

"This is Andy Taylor. I'm the Taylor they're making that movie about, Sheriff Without a Gun.*"*

Andy, on the phone
with Belmont Studios

"The Hollywood-trip idea was conceived as a multi-episode series," says writer Sam Bobrick. "Bill and I got the assignment to write the first two Hollywood episodes. As I recall, this episode seemed tougher than usual to write because much of what happened was an over-exaggeration of reality. Exaggerated situations always seemed to work better in Mayberry than in the outside world."

Bill and Sam begin their script with the Taylors' plane landing in Hollywood. The family is taken by bus to the Piedmont Hotel, where they will be staying during their two-week vacation.

On the way to the hotel, Andy discovers that the man sitting behind him is a relief bus driver originally from Ruby Creek, North Carolina. Andy strikes up a conversation with the man. The fellow points out several famous sites as the bus travels down Sunset Boulevard.

The Taylors' hotel is the last stop on the route. After all the other passengers have gotten off, the relief driver arranges to have the bus go up Beverly Drive so the Taylors can see a movie star's home. The bus stops in front of Caesar Romero's house.

"The famous sites (Dino's restaurant, Schwab's Drugstore, Whiskey a Go Go, and the Blair House) were a combination of places we suggested in the script and those selected by the film crew," says Sam. "I don't know if the house the bus stopped in front of was actually the home of Caesar Romero. We included the stop at a movie star's home because we thought it would be typical small-town behavior to have the Taylors greatly admire anyone connected with film whether they were hot or not. Caesar Romero, by the way, was not."

After the Taylors arrive at their hotel, they are escorted to their room by a bellboy. The bellboy tells Andy that the suite overlooks the pool. When Andy walks to the window, the bellboy says, "If you look over there, you can see the diving board." Andy stands on his tiptoes. After the bellboy gives further instructions about exactly where to look, Andy finally sees the diving board. The bellboy explains how to adjust the air conditioner, holds out his hand for a tip, and says, "If there's anything else, just call room service." Andy doesn't get the hint. The bellboy points to the air-conditioner thermostat and holds out his hand again. Andy finally gets the message and tips him.

"Bellboys have traditionally been comic targets," says Sam. "The view of the pool and the bellboy's desire for a tip were inspired by actual experiences that happened to us. We exaggerated them, of course, for the script."

Once the Taylors are settled in, Aunt Bee insists that Andy call "those movie people" and tell them he is in town. Before making the call, Andy adjusts his tie. Andy identifies himself to the Belmont Pictures's operator, "This is Andy Taylor," and is transferred to the tailor shop. The call is then transferred back to the operator, to the tailor shop again, and back to the operator.

"The adjustment of the tie before placing the phone call was not scripted," says Sam. "It was a nice touch and likely resulted from Andy Griffith's acting instincts. Being transferred to the tailor shop was a routine play on words and a lot of fun to write."

The director of *Sheriff Without a Gun* returns Andy's call and invites the family to come over to the studio to watch the shooting of a scene. The Taylors rush over to the studio and meet the director, A. J. Considine. Mr. Considine introduces the Taylors to the actor who will be portraying Andy in the movie, Bryan Bender. When Andy notices that Bender is bald, he is speechless.

The Taylors watch the shooting of a scene that depicts a cigar-smoking Andy beating up and capturing the Calhoun boys single-handedly. Andy and Opie are thrilled, but Aunt Bee doesn't like the scene "one little bit."

Later that evening after the Taylors have returned to their hotel, Aunt Bee is still quite upset. She tells Andy, "I never saw anything so outlandish in my whole life. It's an exaggeration. It's nothing but a lot of humbug." Aunt Bee feels they are making a "roughneck" out of Andy's character. She insists that Andy "march right up to Mr. Considine and tell him to make things more the way they really are." Andy promises to do so when they return to the studio the following day.

The next day, Andy approaches the director but is asked to wait until the next scene has been shot. The scene is set in the Taylor home. A young and thin Aunt Bee gets a rifle and bravely defends Andy when the Calhoun boys attack the house.

"I was a little uncomfortable with the movie scenes," says Sam. "They were melodramatic, which was acceptable, but we may have exaggerated them a little too much. Even a B film wouldn't have been that bad."

At the scene's conclusion, Andy is going to tell Considine that the scene was "stupid." Aunt Bee stops Andy and says, "Just a minute. I'm not absolutely sure I've been quite right about this." Andy reminds her, "Yesterday you were crying about it." Aunt Bee replies,

"I know, but somehow today it seems a little better. It's a movie, Andy. They have to take liberties in order to make it interesting."

When A.J. Considine comes over and asks Andy what he wanted to talk about, Aunt Bee responds, "We were just going to say how happy we are about the way you're making the picture. And that actress who plays me—she's marvelous."

In the epilogue, the Taylors have returned to their hotel room and are discussing what they are going to do that night. Andy suggests they go down to Grauman's Chinese Theater and take a walk down to Hollywood and Vine. Opie says, "If we were back in Mayberry, do you know what I would be doing right now? Watching the *Jerome Sanger Show* on TV." Aunt Bee responds, "And I would be watching it with you. You know, I'm very fond of that program myself." Andy says, "Yeah, that's a good show, but we're in Hollywood now. What's it going to be?" When Opie and Aunt Bee do not answer, Andy telephones room service and asks them to "send up a television set."

"I was relieved when this script was finished. In the next script, we returned to Mayberry, which was a more familiar and comfortable setting," says Sam.

Aunt Bee Takes a Job

EPISODE #171

FIRST BROADCAST ON DECEMBER 6, 1965

WRITTEN BY BILL IDELSON AND
SAM BOBRICK

DIRECTED BY ALAN RAFKIN

*"With that little lady, Miss Taylor, out front,
this whole thing will take on a complete air
of respectability."*

Ralph Kingsley,
counterfeiter

"I don't remember where the idea for this story came from," says writer Sam Bobrick. "I do, however, remember Frances Bavier, who portrayed Aunt Bee. She was a sweet and talented lady. I enjoyed writing for Aunt Bee. She was an easy character to work with."

Bill and Sam's script begins in the Taylor home. Andy is looking at the evening paper when Aunt Bee asks him to turn to the want ads. She points out a job listing for a receptionist's job, which reads: "Wanted: Female. Easy part-time work, afternoons. Apply in person, 177 Main Street." Aunt Bee shares her intention to apply for the position.

The next day, Aunt Bee goes to the address listed in the paper and finds the job is with a print shop. Aunt Bee enters and waits in the outer office with another applicant, Violet Rose Shumaker. Violet Rose is a shapely young woman, who is surprised when she learns Aunt Bee is also answering the ad.

"Violet Rose Shumaker was inspired by a personal memory," says Sam. "The prettiest girl in my high school was a girl named Violet Rose Daisy. We felt Aunt Bee's competition for the job should be a younger woman, so we made note of that in the script. I don't remember what the actress cast in the role looked like, but I hope she did Violet Rose justice."

Aunt Bee is interviewed by the print shop's owners, Ralph Kingsley and Arnold Finch. She tells the two that she hasn't worked for several years, that she doesn't type or take dictation, and that she isn't very good with figures. She says, "The only reason I'm here is I have too much time on my hands."

Despite these revelations, Aunt Bee is hired. She stops by the courthouse to share the news with Andy. Aunt Bee tells Andy and Warren Ferguson that Mr. Kingsley had said she was just the person they were looking for. Aunt Bee hurries home to get ready for her new job.

After Aunt Bee's departure, Andy tells Warren he wishes the new owners luck because the previous owners did not do well financially. Warren replies, "Oh, that was probably mismanagement, Andy. You know there's nothing wrong with the printing business. A good printing shop can be a moneymaking thing."

In the next scene, a printing press is shown in closeup. As the camera pulls back, Mr. Kingsley and Mr. Finch are revealed. The two are printing ten-dollar bills.

When Andy stops by the print shop, Mr. Kingsley comes out of the back room to greet him. Andy welcomes Mr. Kingsley to town and thanks him for hiring his aunt. Kingsley is pleased to know "the nice lady that works for us is the aunt of a sheriff." He calls Mr. Finch out of the back room and introduces him to Andy.

After Andy leaves, Mr. Finch says, "Ralph, I think we should have hired Violet Rose Shumaker." Mr. Kingsley replies, "No, we couldn't be in better hands."

Aunt Bee begins her first day at work "right on time." A short time after her arrival, she knocks on the door of the back room to give Mr. Kingsley an order from a friend of hers. Mr. Kingsley opens the door and says, "Miss Taylor, about coming in the back. Mr. Finch is something of an artist, you see, and he gets very nervous when he's disturbed." Aunt Bee agrees not to disturb Mr. Finch. She gives Mr. Finch her friend's order and another order for "one hundred business cards for my nephew."

A customer named Mr. Clark enters the print shop. He has come by to pick up a package of wedding announcements, which are actually counterfeit bills. Aunt Bee notifies Mr. Kingsley. While Mr. Kingsley is getting the announcements, Aunt Bee asks Mr. Clark if the announcements are for himself. Mr. Clark is caught off guard and tells her the wedding will be on Thursday.

Later that afternoon, Andy receives a telegram stating that counterfeit bills have turned up in Raleigh. Andy believes the bills might start showing up in Mayberry soon. He decides to warn Mayberry's merchants.

Warren has the responsibility of notifying the owners of the print shop. He enters the shop and walks into the back room unannounced. Warren tells Kingsley and Finch to be on the lookout for counterfeit bills. He then says, "If you do see a bill that looks the least bit phoney, bring it right to me. You see, my eyes are 'specially trained for that type of thing." Warren picks up a newly printed counterfeit bill and points out the differences between it and a phoney.

In this scene, Warren is presented as a one-dimensional, know-it-all character. Bill and Sam use his self-professed "expertise" to set up the humor that results from his total ignorance. This was an approach that was previously used with Barney Fife. Barney, however, was a more fully developed and likeable character. His know-it-all behavior was countered by qualities of caring and, at times, humility.

A few days later, Mr. Clark returns to pick up some birth announcements, again actually counterfeit bills. This surprises Aunt Bee. When she inquires about the matter, Mr. Clark explains, "We're adopting a kid."

"Having the customer pick up wedding and birth announcements within a few days of each other seemed like a funny idea," says Sam. "It worked well, and Frances Bavier's reactions to the situation were wonderful."

Because the bank is closed after Aunt Bee gets off work, she asks Mr. Clark to cash her paycheck for her. Mr. Clark cashes the check with three ten-dollar bills.

Aunt Bee celebrates her first paycheck by purchasing a dress, a football for Opie, groceries, and Andy's business cards. The cards are printed in green ink.

Soon after, Andy gets a telephone call. It is Weaver's Department Store. A counterfeit bill has shown up in Mayberry!

Aunt Bee rushes to the print shop to warn Mr. Kingsley about the counterfeit bills. Mr. Kingsley and Mr. Finch decide "to get out of here." The two tell Aunt Bee they are closing up because they've "hit a slump."

Mr. Kingsley and Mr. Finch carry the printing press outside, load it in their car, and prepare to drive away. Warren, who is "out spreading the word," rushes up in the squad car, accidentally rams the back of the counterfeiters' car, and locks bumpers.

Meanwhile, Andy is at the courthouse considering the facts. He discovers the identity of the counterfeiters by putting together a series of clues. The owners of the grocery, sporting-goods store, and department store have reported counterfeit bills. Aunt Bee made purchases in all three places. Andy's business cards are printed in green ink.

"Bill and I had worked out the details that identify the counterfeiters while constructing the story outline," says Sam. "We knew where we were going before we began writing the script."

Andy rushes to the print shop. Moments before his arrival, Warren and the two counterfeiters unlock the car bumpers. Mr. Kingsley and Mr. Finch jump in their car and make a hasty departure.

Andy runs up, pulls Warren's revolver out of its holster, aims, and shoots out the rear tire of the counterfeiters' car. Aunt Bee says, "I can't believe it. Just because they're going out of business is no reason to shoot at them." Andy runs to the car and arrests the counterfeiters.

In the epilogue, Warren gives the jailed counterfeiters a sandwich. He says to them, "I still get a kick out of you fellows thinking you could pull that counterfeiting deal here in Mayberry. You must think we're real idiots. You think we wear these uniforms for our looks? That's sixty cents for the sandwiches." Mr. Kingsley gives Warren a counterfeit bill and says, "Keep the change." Warren is overjoyed until Andy points out the bill is counterfeit.

"We concluded the script by repeating the comic idea presented earlier," says Sam. "Repetition is an important comic tool. Sometimes it works, sometimes it doesn't. As a writer, you get a sense of these things."

EPISODE #173

FIRST BROADCAST ON DECEMBER 20, 1965

Girl-Shy

WRITTEN BY BILL IDELSON AND
    SAM BOBRICK

DIRECTED BY LEE PHILIPS

*"I never chased a woman in my life. I'm a
gentleman! I'm from Boston!"*
                    Warren Ferguson

"When Don Knotts announced that he didn't want to go on with
the show after the fifth year, we were really disappointed because he
and Andy were a great team," says Andy Griffith's manager Richard O.
Linke. "It worried Andy and me. We could see going into the sixth year
and having the ratings plummet. As soon as that happened, your fate
was determined. You knew the show would be canceled.

"After Don left, the producers were scurrying around, saying, 'we're
going to try this person, we're going to try that person.' There was a
comedy team that was starting to do well, Burns and Schreiber. Somebody told us about the two guys, especially Jack Burns.

"Burns and Schreiber were appearing in a nightclub in San Diego.
Andy flew down with producer Bob Ross and executive producer

Sheldon Leonard with the idea of trying Jack Burns out on TAGS. The three liked what they saw, and Jack was hired."

"I don't remember what inspired the idea to center a story on sleep-walking," says writer Sam Bobrick. "Sometimes ideas came easy, sometimes they didn't. It would take us anywhere from three hours to three days to develop a story idea."

"Girl-Shy" begins with Warren Ferguson bringing his television into the courthouse. Warren explains to Andy that his landlady's brother is visiting, the hotel is full, and he is going to spend the night in the back room so the out-of-town visitor can have his room. The television leads Andy to inquire, "Hey, Warren, how's your social life? You been going out much?" Warren answers, "No, not too much. Actually, I've been pretty busy." Andy tells Warren that he and Helen are "thinking about going to a Chinese restaurant up in Mt. Pilot tonight, and we were wondering if you would like to come along." Warren agrees to come. Andy adds that Helen's "got a little girl she can get for you." Warren is stunned and says, "Girl? You mean a date? I just remembered something, Andy. My blue suit is in the cleaners. If I'm not dressed properly, I just wouldn't enjoy the evening."

Later that evening, Andy stops by the courthouse on his way to Mt. Pilot to pick up a tie clip.

"The courthouse desk may seem an odd place for Andy to keep a tie clip since he normally doesn't wear a tie with his uniform, but we didn't concern ourselves much with it," says Sam.

The telephone rings. There has been a wreck out on the highway, and Andy is needed to help clear the traffic. Helen, who is out in the car, at first decides to wait in the courthouse. She asks Warren if he would like to join her for something to eat, but he declines the invitation. Helen decides to go ahead and get something to eat. She wonders out loud whether she should "come back here and brush up on my typing or go to a movie." Warren replies, "Our typewriter's in pretty bad shape. The s keeps sticking." After hearing this, Helen decides to go to a movie.

After Helen leaves, Goober comes by the courthouse to watch an episode of *International Secret Agent F45* with Warren. Agent F45 is "suave," and the episode includes a "steamy" love scene.

"The *International Secret Agent F45* title was inspired by the popularity of the James Bond movies at the time," says Sam.

After the program, Warren falls asleep in the back room. Helen returns to the courthouse. Influenced by the television love scene, Warren sleepwalks out of the back room. He talks to Helen romantically, just like Secret Agent F45, and chases her into a cell.

Andy eventually returns, and Helen angrily tells him that his "shy, little deputy, Warren, chased me." Andy wakes Warren, but Warren remembers nothing and is shocked by Helen's accusation. Warren claims he was asleep until Andy woke him. He says, "I never chased a woman in my life, I swear. I'm a gentleman! I'm from Boston!"

"Warren's comment that 'he's never chased a woman . . . he's from Boston' seemed to fit," says Sam. "After all, Warren was a bit of a know-it-all, and I'm sure he thought coming from Boston gave him an edge up on Mayberry residents."

The next day Warren tells Goober that he is a sleepwalker, and last night in his sleep he chased Helen Crump all around the courthouse. Something usually triggers Warren's sleepwalking. He thinks the fact that Andy tried to fix him up with a date and he then saw Secret Agent F45 set things in motion. Goober advises Warren to explain this to Andy, but Warren refuses. He feels Andy would not want a sleepwalking deputy. Instead he decides to "stay awake, so it can't happen again."

Meanwhile, Andy visits Helen at school and promises to "straighten this thing out." Andy asks Helen to stop by the office on her way home to see if he has found out anything.

Andy summons Warren to the courthouse. The telephone rings soon after Warren arrives. It is Mrs. Purvis. Andy says, "Oh, yes, Mrs. Purvis. Up in the tree again, is he? Did you try poking him? Look, Mrs. Purvis, I can't come over there every time you and Mr. Purvis have a fight and get him down out of a tree."

"The joke about Mr. Purvis was the result of great comic ingenuity and a touch of immaturity," says Sam. "We presented the joke through a telephone conversation, so the audience would initially think Andy and Mrs. Purvis were talking about a cat up a tree."

Warren falls asleep while Andy is on the telephone. After Andy leaves to get Mr. Purvis out of the tree, Helen stops by on her way home from school. Warren sleepwalks and the "romantic" chase is repeated.

Andy returns, learns about the incident, and fires Warren. Warren goes home and begins packing his belongings. He has decided to leave town.

Goober stops by Warren's room, and Warren asks him if he would like to buy his television set. Warren turns on the television to demonstrate that the set works fine just as a Fred Astaire movie begins.

Goober advises Warren to confess to Andy. He points out that Warren has nothing to lose, so Warren agrees.

Warren goes over to the Taylor home. Andy telephones Helen and asks her to come over. Helen arrives, sees Warren, and becomes angry. While she and Andy argue in the kitchen, Warren falls asleep on the couch. Hoping to drown out Andy and Helen's loud voices, Aunt Bee turns on the radio. Moments later, Andy and Helen are summoned from the kitchen. Warren is dancing in his sleep with Aunt Bee, just like Fred Astaire.

After his sleepwalking is revealed, Andy and Helen take Warren home. Referring to his sleepwalking, Warren says, "I got a feeling it may never happen again. These things, once they're out, that's it—thing of the past." As Andy and Helen leave, the episode concludes with Warren handcuffing himself to his bed before falling asleep.

"We never concerned ourselves with why Warren didn't confess the sleepwalking when it first happened," says Sam. "Perhaps he wasn't aware until later that revealing it would make it disappear. We were simply looking for a quick solution and hoping the audience wouldn't question its logic."

"Jack Burns was a very funny guy," says Richard O. Linke. "Unfortunately, he didn't work out. The ironic thing was, with Don Knotts leaving and Jack not working out, the ratings kept getting better and better. I remember saying to Andy at the time, 'In my mind, you are the star. You set the tempo of the show. You're the focal point, everything revolves around you. The flow of the show depends on the star, not the second or third banana.'"

The Return of Barney Fife

EPISODE #176

FIRST BROADCAST ON JANUARY 10, 1966

WRITTEN BY BILL IDELSON AND SAM BOBRICK

DIRECTED BY ALAN RAFKIN

> *"She was the only girl I ever loved. She's the only girl I ever will love."*
>
> Barney, mourning the
> loss of Thelma Lou

"The class-reunion story line was the idea of producer Bob Ross," says writer Sam Bobrick. "It seemed like a good idea since most people have been to class reunions. We knew Don Knotts was available, and a reunion provided an excuse to bring Barney back to Mayberry."

Bill and Sam begin their reunion script with Andy, Helen, Aunt Bee, and Floss, a former classmate of Andy's, preparing for the 1948 Mayberry Union High School class reunion. Andy hangs a "Welcome Back" banner, while the "girls" work on the name badges. Andy and Aunt Bee look through the letters of the people that are coming. Aunt Bee looks at a letter from Sharon DeSpain, one of Andy's former girlfriends. Andy then opens another letter and says, "Guess who's coming back? Barney!"

The incomparable Barney Fife

TAGSRWC Archives

Many of the details about Andy's graduating class are consistent with the "Class Reunion" episode written by Jim Fritzell and Everett Greenbaum. However, the year Andy graduated is different. In the first "reunion" episode, it is 1945.

"Bill and I tried to be consistent with the first reunion episode, but obviously we slipped up on the year," says Sam. "I don't know why it wasn't corrected. I imagine it was simply overlooked."

Barney returns to Mayberry and is welcomed back by Andy. The two talk about Barney's life in Raleigh. The high-school reunion is also discussed, and Barney asks if Thelma Lou is coming. Andy replies, "Gee, we haven't heard from her yet. She moved out of town about a month after you left. She might show up, though."

It is agreed that Barney will stay at the Taylors' house while in Mayberry. Barney "brought along a few little things." He gives Opie "an official ink pad we use at the print department." Aunt Bee receives a box of imported handkerchiefs from Tijuana. Barney gives Andy a tie clip and says, "A lot of people clip them right on the front of their shirt, even when they don't wear a tie. It's smart."

That evening after supper, Andy and Barney relax on the front porch. Barney asks, "Thelma Lou's not coming, huh?" Andy answers, "I don't guess so." Barney replies, "That's too bad. She'd get a kick out of seeing how I've come up in the world." Andy asks if Barney is still sweet on her. Barney answers, "No, no, once it's gone, it's gone, Ange. You can't go back. Course, sometimes a man wonders."

Andy and Barney reminisce about their high-school days and sing the Mayberry Union High School song. Helen steps onto the porch soon after the singing is finished and tells them that she's just heard that Thelma Lou is coming to the reunion after all. Barney is overjoyed.

On the night of the reunion, Andy impatiently waits for Barney to get ready. Andy says to Aunt Bee, "He hasn't changed much. He's still the slowest man in the world." This remark seems out of place. There was no previous reference in the series to Barney being slow.

"We weren't concerned that Barney had not previously been referred to as slow," says Sam. "Andy's comment fit the scene, so we used it."

Barney eventually comes downstairs. He proudly shows off his shirt "with initials on it." As Andy and Barney depart, Aunt Bee says, "Now, you boys drive carefully and have a good time. Don't stay out too late." Andy replies, "We won't, 'Mama.'"

"Having Aunt Bee remind Andy and Barney to drive carefully, as if they were two teenage boys, and Andy's 'mama' reply were ways of showing that time stands still for some people," says Sam.

At the reunion, Andy and Helen enjoy the music of Carl Benson's Wildcats, and Barney talks with two of his former teachers. When Thelma Lou arrives, Barney walks over and asks her to dance. As the two dance, Barney apologizes "for not writing to you for all that time" and says "a lot of things have been happening to me careerwise. The future looks pretty rosy." Barney shows off the initials on his shirt.

"When Barney points out the initials on his shirt pocket, it is his way of showing growth and sophistication," says Sam.

Floss interrupts Barney and Thelma Lou and asks Thelma Lou to come with her "so she can be registered and get her name badge." While Thelma Lou is away, Barney tells Andy, "She looks just great." Andy asks if "it" is still there, and Barney answers, "Well, I'm not saying it is, and I'm not saying it ain't. I'm not going to rush in to anything. I'll tell you one thing though—she's still crazy about me."

Thelma Lou returns with a male companion and introduces her new husband to Andy and Barney. The two have been married six weeks.

"Barney, of course, was shattered by the news that Thelma Lou was married," says Sam. "The fact that she married just six weeks earlier made it even sadder."

"In my mind, and no one else agreed with me, I decided that Thelma Lou didn't actually get married," says Betty Lynn, who portrayed Thelma Lou. "She knew this fellow at work and when they had the reunion and everyone would be coming back, she said to this fellow, 'Listen, I don't want to go back to Mayberry like I was. I'm going to tell them I got married. Would you do me a favor and come with me?' This was all in my head, and that's what I believed because I knew in my heart that Thelma Lou would never marry anybody but Barney Fife. They all said, 'No, no, you really got married.' But I knew better. Barney was the love of Thelma Lou's life."

Barney consoles himself by attempting to get drunk on the fruit punch. Andy says, "I'm sorry, Barn. I know it must have been a shock." Barney responds in a slurred voice, "Sure, it was a shock. So what? It wasn't the first one in my life. It won't be the last. That's life. Don't worry about it, Ange. I'll get over it. If I can't do it one way, I'll do it another." Barney takes another drink of punch. Andy replies, "Well, if you're trying to get drunk, you won't do it that way. There's nothing in the punch but fruit juice." Barney immediately sobers up.

"Having Barney get drunk on nonalcoholic fruit punch seemed funny, and Don Knotts was wonderful in the scene," says Sam.

Floss joins Andy and Barney. She introduces the two to a former class-mate, Nettie Albright. Nettie ignores Andy and tells Barney, "You know, I've been wanting to talk to you. I hear that wonderful things have been happening to you." Nettie is not surprised by Barney's success. She always knew he would do well. Nettie admits that in school Barney was always her "idol." Barney takes an immediate interest in Nettie and invites her to dance.

"Barney's sudden interest in Nettie was his attempt to bounce back from the devastating news of Thelma Lou's marriage," says Sam.

Thelma Lou's marriage comes close to shattering the series' premise that all problems have a solution. In previous episodes, Andy could solve Barney's problems with a wise word or a face-saving action. But Thelma Lou's marriage is different. There is nothing Andy can say or do that will undo the marriage and make things right. The substitution of Nettie Albright's attention for the loss of Thelma Lou is not believable. This is not the solution to "losing the only girl I'll ever love."

The epilogue captures Barney's sadness over losing Thelma Lou. The school song is played very slowly in the background as Andy and Barney drive home from the reunion. Barney turns off the engine, and the two classmates remain seated in the car. Andy says, "That was something about Thelma Lou being married, wasn't it?" Barney answers, "Yeah," and begins talking enthusiastically about Nettie. Barney falls silent. Andy eventually asks, "You want to go in?" Barney answers, "Yeah."

"It was our intention to end on a melancholy note," says Sam. "The reunion has had an impact on Andy and Barney. In that brief moment of silence in the car, they both realized you can't really 'go home again.'"

The Legend of Barney Fife

EPISODE #177

FIRST BROADCAST ON JANUARY 17, 1966

WRITTEN BY HARVEY BULLOCK

DIRECTED BY ALAN RAFKIN

"A true living legend, that Barney Fife. I mean he's something, isn't he?"

Warren Ferguson

"Don Knotts's picture will always be on every TAGS writer's piano."

Harvey Bullock

"The TAGS writers' seminars had stopped by this time," says writer Harvey Bullock. "There were some writers who found they didn't like the seminar pooling. They would rather cherish and develop their own ideas to fruition. Perhaps some of them thought they were giving away more good ideas than they received. Whatever, I enjoyed the seminars. After the seminars stopped, the producer's door remained open to the writers whose work he knew.

"The big mystery to me is that I don't recall working with producer

Bob Ross. I knew him, of course. He was a very affable, talented friend and neighbor at the studio, but I can't bring up any remembrance of working a Griffith show with him.

"To the best of my recollection, the 'legend' story was devised by Aaron Ruben and myself. Aaron must have known that Don Knotts was available and mentioned it in one of our meetings. I jumped at the chance to write the episode."

Harvey's script begins in the Taylor kitchen. It is the morning after the class reunion, and Barney is still in bed. Andy says he'd better get down to the courthouse. Aunt Bee asks if Andy is going to wait for Barney. Andy answers, "The way he was carrying on at the reunion last night, he's liable to sleep the clock around."

"I had heard the phrase, 'sleep the clock around,' from my parents," says Harvey. "It popped into my head as I was writing the opening scene, and I gave it to Andy."

Barney comes down a short time later. Andy invites Barney to accompany him to the courthouse. Andy wants to introduce Barney to the new deputy, Warren Ferguson. Aunt Bee says that Warren is doing "a wonderful job." Barney is somewhat hesitant to meet his replacement and tells Andy he plans to return to Raleigh as soon as Goober finishes repairing the fuel pump on his car.

While Andy goes to get the keys to the squad car, Barney and Aunt Bee remain in the kitchen. Barney remarks that he is glad the new deputy is working out so well. Aunt Bee responds, "Oh yes, he's a graduate of the sheriff's academy. Finished fourth in his class. Andy was even able to take off two weeks last fall—something he was never able to do before." Barney is hurt by the implication.

Uncomfortable with the praise given to Warren, Barney decides he'd "better head on back to Raleigh." He calls to check on the car and learns it will be an hour before the repairs will be finished. Reluctantly, Barney goes with Andy to the courthouse and is introduced to Warren.

"Jack Burns had just started the show when this script was written," says Harvey. "He had done successful comedy with Avery Schreiber, but anybody who replaced Don Knotts was sticking his head into a guillotine. Viewers were attuned to the incomparable Don Knotts, and they like familiarity. No one else could be the deputy. It was also more difficult for the writers to make Jack's character function. Don had spoiled us. Moreover, I'm sure this was apparent—and depressing to Jack. He couldn't win."

Barney is surprised to learn that Warren admires his work as a former deputy and sees him as "a living legend." Enjoying the adulation, Barney decides there is no real rush to get back to Raleigh.

Warren steps into the back room to fix Barney a cup of coffee. While he

A QUICK ANSWER

I had no idea that "The Legend of Barney Fife" would be my final TAGS script, but that's the way it turned out. At the time, my partner Ray Allen and I were venturing into the beguiling world of feature pictures, which took most of our time and energy. I wrote most of TAGS by myself, and I wanted to get back to a full-time partnership with Ray. We continued the occasional TV script but concentrated primarily on films. In addition, TAGS without Barney wasn't as appealing.

I cherish having written for TAGS and am enormously grateful to the many fans who keep the show alive. TAGS was the central achievement of my writing career, and my relationship to it is my most important and pleasing identity.

When new friends hear I was a TV/film writer, inevitably they ask, "What shows did you write?" Well, after forty years and hundreds of scripts, I have quite a choice. But I never even skip a beat. I simply answer, *The Andy Griffith Show*.

Harvey Bullock

is out of the room, Barney tells Andy that Warren's admiration is understandable. He says, "Lots of persons have an idol." Barney's childhood idol was "Skeets Gallagher, sidekick to Tailspin Tommy."

"I always liked the name 'Skeets Gallagher'," says Harvey. "It was borrowed from a 1930s comic-book series. The name was sort of wacky and sounded funny."

Later in the day, the newspaper sends over a reporter to ask some questions for a story about the high-school reunion. Andy and Warren convince the reporter to include a story on Barney's return to Mayberry. Barney just happens to have packed his deputy's uniform, so Warren drives him over to Andy's house so he can put it on for a picture to accompany the newspaper's story.

Barney and Warren return to the courthouse. The photographer wants to take the picture outside. When Andy, Warren, and the photographer step outside, they are joined by Floyd.

"Floyd has no comedic lines in the street scene," says Harvey. "This can happen when a script is hurriedly trimmed for length. The vital-to-the-story lines are sometimes kept at the expense of cutting optional comedy lines. There's no telling what comic gems Floyd would have spoken if he had been given the time."

Barney remains inside the courthouse to adjust his tie. The telephone rings. When Barney answers, he is told a convict, Avery Noonan, has escaped and may be heading toward Mayberry. Barney was responsible for Noonan's initial arrest and is warned that Noonan may be seeking revenge.

Barney immediately decides to "pass up the newspaper story" and get out of town. Goober telephones to tell Barney he'll be getting a new fuel pump from Mt. Pilot in the morning. Barney instructs Goober to put the old fuel pump back on his car.

Barney decides to go to Andy's house and pack. He exits the courthouse, dressed in Andy's raincoat with his hat pulled down over his eyes. While waiting in the Taylor home for Goober to return his car,

Barney places a dresser in front of his bedroom door.

"I might have been pushing Barney's reaction a little," admits Harvey. "Farce is the most difficult of all comedy to make work, but Don gave the writers such latitude. Putting the dresser up against the door was such a cliché, I hoped it wouldn't be too wild. For a touch of normalcy, I had Andy notice it, and then had Barney offer the almost credible reason that he was looking for a collar button."

Goober returns Barney's car and follows Andy inside the house.

"Goober's main story function is to compound Barney's problem of getting out of town," says Harvey. "He has mostly straight lines that progress the story but are not comedic in themselves."

As Barney is preparing to depart, the warden from the county work farm telephones Andy's house with the news that Noonan "was seen hopping a southbound train" and may be headed toward Mayberry. The warden is surprised that Barney didn't tell Andy about Noonan. Aware that Noonan is out to get Barney, Andy now understands why Barney is in such a hurry to leave Mayberry.

Moments later Warren arrives and tells Andy that he just got a call from the station master. It seems "some fellow by the name of Avery Noonan is sneaking around down at the depot." Warren has brought Barney's old gun and tells him, "I knew you'd want to get in on this one."

Barney rushes outside, and quickly gets into his car, but the old fuel pump falls off when he starts the engine. Barney is thus temporarily stranded in Mayberry and has no reason not to accompany Warren and Andy to the depot.

At the depot, Andy and Warren stalk Noonan while Barney waits by the squad car. In the script, Harvey describes Barney, waiting by the car, as "nervous and unhappy with himself. A battle is going on within him. He finally comes to a decision, swallows, braces himself, and opens the depot door quietly."

Andy has already spotted Noonan inside the depot and is preparing to apprehend him. He changes his plans, however, when he sees Barney enter. Andy gives Noonan time to confront Barney, before he drops a heavy sack on the convict. Andy then unselfishly gives all the credit for the capture to Barney.

As the epilogue begins, Barney is shown closing the cell door on Noonan, signifying that the arrest was his. The newspaper is sending a reporter over, and Barney asks Andy to "swing" the credit for the capture to Warren. Barney says, "Sometimes it don't hurt to shade things a little when you want to help someone. After all, Ange, I've had my place in the sun here for a lot of years. Now a nice fellow like that comes along, a little pat on the back will make him feel good. It's his town out there now, Ange. It's not mine."

"Barney's suggestion that Andy give the credit to Warren is a very satisfying twist," say Harvey. "It shows a touch of maturity coming to Barney. Barney is taking Andy's usual role when he gives up credit to Warren."

Barney exits to look for the newspaper reporter. Warren enters the courthouse and says, "A true living legend that Barney Fife. I mean he's something, isn't he, Andy?" Andy answers, "Yes, he is. He really is."

A Baby in the House

EPISODE #184

FIRST BROADCAST ON MARCH 7, 1966

WRITTEN BY BILL IDELSON AND
SAM BOBRICK

DIRECTED BY ALAN RAFKIN

> *"The baby hates me. She just hates me. Every
> time I pick her up she cries."*
>
> Aunt Bee

> *"I don't remember this one."*
>
> Sam Bobrick

"**I** have no idea where the idea for this story came from," says writer
Sam Bobrick. "I enjoyed writing all our TAGS scripts. Other than that
general recollection, I have no memories of this episode."

Bill and Sam's "forgotten" script begins in the Taylor home. Andy,
Helen, Aunt Bee, and Opie are working on a crossword puzzle. The
pastime is interrupted by a telephone call from Aunt Bee's niece Martha.
Martha would like to leave her six-month-old baby, Evie Joy, with the
Taylors for a few days, while she and her husband attend a wedding in
New Jersey. Aunt Bee is excited about the opportunity, but Andy is

reluctant to have a baby in the house. He eventually consents, but he tells Aunt Bee that she's going to have to "handle the whole thing."

Goober brings some of his old toys for Evie Joy before her arrival. Goober selects the toys he thinks a baby might like—checkers and a checkerboard, an old cigar box, and Goober's favorite toy, a teddy bear named Buster. Goober points out that a baby would get a "big kick" out of knocking the checkerboard over. He also points out he spent hours opening and closing the cigar box.

"Jack Burns, who portrayed deputy Warren Ferguson, was a good actor and a pleasure to work with," says George Lindsey, who portrayed Goober Pyle. "Unfortunately, who's going to take Don Knotts's place? After Jack left the show, I filled in as the comic relief."

When the baby arrives, Martha tells Aunt Bee that the baby "almost never cries."

"Whenever a script required a baby, we would notify casting director Ruth Burch, and she would make the necessary arrangements," says former TAGS producer Aaron Ruben. "There were strict regulations that had to be followed whenever a baby was used. Because you could only use a baby for a limited time, it was standard practice to replace the baby with a doll if the baby's face was not required in a scene."

Martha asks Opie if he would like to hold the baby. Evie Joy is content in Opie's arms. When Aunt Bee takes the baby from Opie, Evie Joy begins to cry. When Andy suggests that she might be hungry, Aunt Bee hands Evie Joy to Andy while she warms a bottle. Evie Joy stops crying as soon as Andy takes her.

Soon after the parents leave, Aunt Bee discovers that Evie Joy cries whenever she holds her. This upsets Aunt Bee. Helen comes by to see how everything is going and notices that Aunt Bee has been crying. Aunt Bee confesses to Helen that "the baby hates me. She just hates me. Every time I pick her up she cries. What am I going to do for the next six days?"

That night Andy is called out to break up a fight between Jed and Carl Darling. The fight began when Jed told Carl there was no Santa

Claus. The next morning Andy is "too tired to eat" breakfast. He decides to go upstairs and "get a little sleep." Andy asks Aunt Bee not to "let the baby start crying."

After Andy leaves the table, Aunt Bee asks Opie if he has to go to school right away. She asks if he would like to give Evie Joy her bottle. When Opie says he'll be late for school, she offers to write him a note. Opie, however, doesn't want to miss first-period gym. At this point, the baby starts whining.

Aunt Bee telephones Goober at the filling station to order a quart of oil and asks if he can bring it over right away. When Goober makes the delivery, Aunt Bee gets him to feed the baby.

Around noon, Evie Joy gets hungry and starts crying again. Andy wakes up and tells Aunt Bee to feed the baby, so he can get some sleep.

A kitchenware salesman rings the doorbell soon after Andy goes back to bed. Aunt Bee invites him in and looks at his merchandise while the salesman feeds Evie Joy.

Later in afternoon, the baby starts crying again. When Andy gets up, Aunt Bee asks him to give the baby her four o'clock feeding. Andy agrees but says he doesn't understand. Aunt Bee begins to cry and tells Andy she doesn't know what to do. She says, "Evie Joy hates me. Every time I pick her up, she cries."

That evening Aunt Bee goes shopping and leaves the baby with Opie and one of his friends. The boys feed Evie Joy filling from a blueberry pie. Some of the filling gets on the baby's face.

Aunt Bee goes to check on the baby when she returns. While she is upstairs, Opie tells Andy he gave the baby some blueberry pie filling. Aunt Bee sees the blue filling around Evie Joy's mouth and thinks the baby is sick. She picks the baby up, rushes downstairs, and tells Andy to call the doctor. Andy explains to Aunt Bee that the boys gave Evie Joy some pie filling.

Once the "crisis" is past, Andy realizes that Aunt Bee is "holding the baby and she isn't crying. She's happy as a lark." He guesses that Evie Joy cried before because she sensed that Aunt Bee was nervous. She is no longer crying because she senses that Aunt Bee picked her up to protect her. The baby now feels safe in Aunt Bee's arms.

In the epilogue, Andy, Helen, Aunt Bee, and Evie Joy (resting in her crib) relax on the front porch. Helen asks if Aunt Bee would like for her to take the baby upstairs. Aunt Bee answers, "Oh, I'll take her. She's so used to me, if anyone else picked her up it might disturb her."

"Frances Bavier was a wonderful actress," says George Lindsey. "When you can work with an actress of her caliber, you're living in the lap of luxury as far as acting is concerned, because she was so good that you didn't have to worry about her. She allowed you the freedom to focus all your attention on what you were doing.

"We had the best cast on television. Every one of them was great! The years with the Griffith show were my 'golden years' of television because those people were so good."

"The Griffith show had a brilliant cast," says Richard O. Linke, Andy Griffith's manager. "When you put a show together and it jells, things work right. You add, subtract, and it grows into something wonderful. With TAGS we had something extra, not only a brilliant cast, but a happy set—and Andy Griffith set that up."

The County Clerk

EPISODE #185

FIRST BROADCAST ON MARCH 14, 1966

WRITTEN BY BILL IDELSON AND
SAM BOBRICK

DIRECTED BY ALAN RAFKIN

JACK DODSON GUEST STARS
AS HOWARD SPRAGUE;
MABEL ALBERTSON PORTRAYS
HOWARD'S MOTHER

*"That Mr. Sprague is kind of a funny fellow,
isn't he, Pa? All the kids think so. You know, he
can't throw a baseball."*

Opie Taylor

"**P**roducer Bob Ross was a masterful writer," said Jack Dodson. "He was largely responsible for Howard Sprague's basic character, yet he gave me the freedom to develop and enlarge the character. Bob was a fine writer and overseer and certainly ranks high among those who have influenced me. I cannot remember specifically his special suggestions for this episode, but I know he had them. They were, as usual, followed closely. To have known and worked with Bob was a great privilege."

"Jack Dodson was a consummate professional," says George Lindsey, who portrayed Goober Pyle. "He came to the Griffith show from Broadway and was a very talented actor. Jack was perfect for the Howard Sprague role."

"Bob Ross wanted to use Jack Dodson and gave us suggestions about the character he had in mind for Jack to portray," says writer Sam Bobrick. "The character, Howard Sprague, was a grown man still tied to his mother's apron strings. Bill and I took this general description and wrote 'The County Clerk'."

Bill and Sam's script begins in the courthouse. Opie is sweeping up. As Andy searches for an accident report, he says, "That beats me." When Opie asks what's wrong, Andy says he can't find the 1953 accident reports. He says the county clerk, Howard Sprague, wants the reports for the last twenty years.

Andy decides to take over the files he has. He walks into Howard's office and meets the new county health officer, Irene Fairchild. Miss Fairchild has taken over Howard's office. Howard has moved next door into a larger office.

Andy steps next door. He delivers the accident reports and discusses "facts and figures" with Howard. While the two are talking, Miss Fairchild returns an undershirt she has found while "cleaning out her files." Howard explains that he took it off one day "when it was rather warm."

After Miss Fairchild leaves, Andy suggests that an "old bachelor" like Howard "might like to try and make a little time there." Howard responds, "Andy, with all the work I've got to do, who's got the time?"

At this point, Howard's mother stops by and greets Andy formally by saying, "Hello, Andrew."

"Mrs. Sprague was a snob," says Sam. "We had her call Andy 'Andrew' to give the audience an idea of the stuffy climate her son was raised in. Mabel Albertson, who portrayed Mrs. Sprague, was wonderful in the role."

Mrs. Sprague reminds Howard "not to be too late coming home tonight. We're playing bridge with the Albrights at seven-thirty." Mrs. Sprague asks Howard whether he had a hot meal for lunch and if he is wearing his undershirt.

That evening Andy tells Helen he was at Howard Sprague's office and noticed that "he's quite a character." Andy goes on to say he went

Jack Dodson portrayed Howard Sprague.

TAGSRWC Archives

through high school with Howard, and "he always was strange." When Helen asks in what way, Andy answers, "He kind of always kept to himself. He never went out much. Most of the time he just went straight home." When Helen wonders why, Andy says, "His mother. I was in the office today, and she came in. Boy, she's got him tied to her apron strings, and there's very little slack."

Andy tells Helen that there's a pretty girl in the office next to Howard, and he doesn't pay much attention to her. After hearing this, Helen decides it would be good for Howard to get out more often. She suggests Andy invite Howard and Irene Fairchild to join them on a dinner date to Morelli's. At first Andy refuses, but when Helen doesn't want to "go to the show" or "take a walk," he is "persuaded" to go along with her idea.

Howard is interested in Andy's invitation, but before he can accept he has to "call mother and make sure there are no plans for tonight."

That evening Andy drops by the Spragues' house to pick up Howard. As the two are leaving, Mrs. Sprague says, "Now, don't you worry. I'm know I'm going to feel much better. It's nothing. Just a little headache." Howard is concerned that his mother may be having "one of her spells" and promises to "check with her later."

Howard and Irene have a wonderful time on their date until Howard calls home and gets no answer. He is concerned that his mother is sick and ends the evening early.

The next day, Andy tells Helen that it's "no good getting involved in other people's lives." Helen replies, "They were having a perfectly wonderful time. It's that mother." Helen asks Andy to talk to Mrs. Sprague about giving Howard some freedom. Andy refuses, but when Helen doesn't want to "go get a cup of coffee" or "go to the show," he is "persuaded" again to do as Helen asks.

Andy decides to handle the situation by flattering Mrs. Sprague. He tells her he's always admired the way she's devoted her life to Howard. He says, "I wouldn't recommend this to everybody, but a charming, attractive woman like yourself—you ought to go out. Go to parties. Go to dances. Have a real life for yourself." Mrs. Sprague replies, "Andrew, you've certainly given me something to think about."

The problem seems to be resolved as the episode comes to an end. Helen, Howard, and Irene are shown seated at a table at Morelli's. The three discuss the possibility of going out the next night, and Howard comments that he hasn't been out this late in years. He notes that it is almost two o'clock. The camera then cuts to the dance floor where Andy and Mrs. Sprague are dancing together.

In the epilogue, Andy expresses his anger at Helen for playing matchmaker. Helen apologizes for asking him to talk to Mrs. Sprague. Helen thinks Mrs. Sprague just needs someone her own age and immediately returns to her matchmaking ways by suggesting that she and Andy introduce Mrs. Sprague to an elderly gentleman named Mr. Judson.

1966-67

Big Fish in a Small Town

EPISODE #198

FIRST BROADCAST ON NOVEMBER 28, 1966

WRITTEN BY BILL IDELSON AND SAM BOBRICK

DIRECTED BY LEE PHILIPS

> *"I like to approach fishing like everything else—from a scientific standpoint."*
> Howard Sprague

> *"I don't have any particular memories of writing this script, except it was hard, back-breaking work, as all of them were."*
> Bill Idelson

"The story idea for 'Big Fish in a Small Town' must have been mine," says writer Bill Idelson. "I was always a rabid fisherman, while Sam Bobrick probably never fished a day in his life, so the notion probably originated with me. I was always struck by the fact that in many places I fished there was a monster, legendary fish. Everyone knew about it, many had claimed to have seen it, a few claimed to have hooked it, but no one had landed it."

Bill and Sam's script begins in the barbershop. Fishing season starts the next day. Floyd and Goober are getting ready and "have a million things to do." Howard drops by for a haircut, learns about the opening of the new season, and hints that he would like to join Floyd and Goober the next day. The two attempt to discourage Howard because he is a "beginner" fisherman. They don't invite him to join them. Howard decides to get his haircut "later in the week."

After leaving the barbershop, Howard steps next door to the courthouse and finds Andy and Opie also getting ready for the new fishing season. Howard asks if he could "tag along" the following day. Andy reluctantly agrees.

The next morning, Howard arrives at the Taylors' house loaded down with fishing gear. Howard has an umbrella, a portable radio, a flashlight, a thermometer, and a depth-finder. Howard has packed "two roast chickens, a quart of potato salad, and a lemon pie."

After arriving at Tucker's Lake, Andy, Opie, and Howard begin a day of fishing. Andy and Opie bait their hooks and discuss the possibility of catching "Old Sam," a legendary silver carp.

"The selection of 'Old Sam' for the fish's name was in part a little inside joke," says Bill. "He was named after Sam Bobrick, but mostly, I think the name was chosen because Old Sam was a homey, sort of appropriate name for the fish.

"We never consulted a fishing manual about anything in the script. There was a lot of bull in these scripts at times. The decision to make Old Sam a silver carp draws a blank. I never fished for such a fish and don't recall hearing about them. I wouldn't be surprised if it wasn't a suggestion from Andy."

"My personal memories of this episode are fairly clear, mostly because it was such an interesting show to shoot and because we had such comradeship on it," said Jack Dodson, who portrayed Howard Sprague. "We normally rehearsed for one day and shot for three days. Rehearsal laid out the scenes for the crew as well as the cast. Changes were made as we shot, but they were rarely major. For this episode, which was almost all on location, we had little blocking rehearsal at the studio. This episode required more location shooting than

Andy assists Howard as he catches "Old Sam."

normal and working on water posed more than the usual problems for the crew, but nothing major.

"The series' regular cast members traveled to the location in their own cars. The crew was transported by bus from the studio. All the fishing sequences and most of the exteriors were shot at the lake in Franklin Canyon, which was about a ten-mile trip from the studio. All the interiors were shot at the Desilu Studios in the heart of Hollywood. Mayberry's street scenes were filmed at Forty Acres near MGM in Culver City, about a half-hour from Desilu."

Determined to catch fish, Howard wanders down to the lake shore. He repeatedly interrupts the other fishermen with his amateur casting. Howard calls on Andy to help him untangle his line from a tree branch. After Andy untangles the line, he says, "If you just wouldn't try casting, Howard. Why don't you bottom-fish like Opie and me?" Influenced by a book he has read, Howard insists on casting. Howard calls Andy a second time to remove his hook from the seat of his pants. Howard requests Andy's assistance a third time, but this time he is not in trouble. Howard has caught a fish, and to everyone's surprise, it is Old Sam!

After catching the fish, Howard returns to town and displays Old Sam in a tank on Main Street. A newspaper reporter interviews Howard for a "front-page" story. Howard tells the reporter, "I had been using a variety of complicated lures, but after lunch I had some potato salad left, and that's what got him."

"The fish was provided by a wildlife facility," said Jack. "The scenes with the fish in the lake were easily set up because the fish was rather passive. The street scene back in Mayberry was shot inside the studio instead of at Forty Acres because of tight schedule demands."

After the interview Howard runs home to change clothes. While Howard is away Goober, Floyd, and Opie wonder aloud what Howard plans to do with the fish and ask Andy to find out.

Andy learns that Howard has decided to donate Old Sam to an aquarium in Raleigh. Goober and Floyd are disappointed with Howard's decision. Floyd says, "That fish doesn't belong in an aquarium. Old Sam was born and bred right in Tucker's Lake and that is where he ought to be." Reflecting on the thought of Old Sam no longer being in Tucker's Lake, Goober says, "It's like the end of something, ain't it?"

Howard invites Opie to join him on a trip to Raleigh to visit the aquarium. Opie agrees but is unenthusiastic when he sees Old Sam. Howard notices Opie's disappointment and points out that he put Old Sam in the aquarium because he thought it would be nice for "a lot of other people to see Old Sam. He's kind of unusual. That's what an aquarium is for." Opie admits that the aquarium is good, but he points out that Old Sam had been in Tucker's Lake so long, "and everybody talked about him so much—tried to catch him all the time."

"Howard was intrinsic to the story, as a villain in a way, since he had recently come to town. For him to land Old Sam was an ironic, even bitter pill to swallow," says Bill. "Another ironic twist was that Howard used potato salad as bait to catch the fish. It was ironic for Old Sam, who had every kind of exotic lure thrown his way, to succumb to an outrageous offering by an alien. If Old Sam were to be landed, it should have been by one of the old residents, who probably would have released him into the lake."

After talking with Opie, Howard realizes Old Sam belongs in Tucker's Lake. Howard and Opie return to Mayberry.

Andy, Goober, and Floyd are fishing at Tucker's Lake when Floyd says, "Hey, did you see that? There was a big one went by. He went right past my line. He was as big as Old Sam. Every bit as big." Andy and Goober think Floyd is "imagining things."

Howard and Opie walk up soon afterwards and are told about the big fish. Howard tells the three that what they saw might have been Old Sam. He goes on to say that a "couple of minutes ago, Opie and I let Old Sam go about fifty yards down there." Floyd asks why he decided to put the fish back in the lake. Howard answers, "You know, Opie and I went up to the aquarium in Raleigh. Well, we were standing by the tank there, and Old Sam came right over to the glass of the tank. . .and started moving his mouth. Well, we stood there and watched him for awhile, and we finally figured out what he was trying to say. He was trying to tell us, 'Gosh, would I like to see Goober, and Floyd, and Andy, and everybody again.' Well, after that, I just had to put him back."

"I think the script also served to further develop Howard as a character, and that was why it was necessary to find a decent, sympathetic resolution to what was going to happen to Old Sam," says Bill. "I remember this came in for a lot of discussion. Putting the fish back in the lake immediately after it was caught was discussed but rejected for some reason, and the final conclusion came about by committee, as many of these things did."

The decision to return Old Sam to the lake was necessary. The town of Mayberry is a small, familiar, and secure place. Traditions and legends are tightly protected. The premise of Mayberry required that Old Sam would swim in Tucker's Lake forever, thus keeping the possibility of catching the legendary fish just one cast away.

"HEY, THAT'S SHELDON'S CHAIR."

At the weekly script read-through, I usually sat across the table from Sheldon Leonard, beside Andy. Bob Ross always sat at the head of the table, the director at the opposite end, and Andy in the middle, to Bob's right.

We actors did not always have the same seat at the table, but there was no competition for the seats. No particular emphasis was placed on where you sat—just that the seats for Sheldon, Bob, Andy, and the director were always reserved.

Jack Dodson

A Visit to Barney Fife

EPISODE #211

FIRST BROADCAST ON JANUARY 16, 1967

WRITTEN BY BILL IDELSON AND SAM BOBRICK

DIRECTED BY LEE PHILIPS

"I'm best on the undercover work; a little slow, but sure."

Barney Fife

"**B**ill and I were told by producer Bob Ross that Don Knotts was available for a TAGS guest appearance," says writer Sam Bobrick. "We were eager to write for Don again and came up with the idea to have Andy visit Barney in Raleigh. Bob liked the idea, and we were given the assignment."

"A Visit to Barney Fife" begins with Andy stopping by the Raleigh Police Department. Andy arrives earlier than expected and finds Barney painting the captain's office. After the two exchange greetings, Andy learns that Barney has been transferred from "fingerprints to the detective bureau." Barney has invited Andy to come by because he "heard that there's going to be an opening in our department, and I immediately thought of you."

Barney introduces Andy to his co-workers, and it quickly becomes evident to Andy that Barney is not respected by the other detectives.

Barney shows Andy his small corner desk and shares with him a newspaper story about a series of supermarket robberies. The master shot for this scene shows Andy in the foreground and Barney seated at his desk with his back against the wall. After the master shot was photographed, the actors performed the scene a second time with the wall behind Barney removed and the camera positioned in its place. The master shot and the secondary shot were then edited together for the finished film.

Barney leaves the office early and takes Andy, who plans to stay a few days, to the boarding house where he has recently moved. Andy meets the Parker family, who owns the house. The family consists of Ma, Ma's boys Leroy and Henny, and daughter Agnes Jean who "is a real charmer." Afterwards, Andy and Barney go up to Barney's room to get settled in.

Barney proudly points out his accommodations and the decorative touches he has made. The room has a private sink with a faucet that "says cold, but it's hot," a double bed, a real leather chair, and a view "between two telephone poles" of city hall. Barney has decorated the room with his Mayberry High School pennant and prints of *The Laughing Cavalier* and *Blue Boy*.

"Bill and I included some suggestions for decorating Barney's room in the script," says Sam. "The prop department added to this, and the end result fit Barney perfectly."

Later at dinner, the Parkers question Barney about the rash of supermarket robberies. Andy reminds Barney that the investigation is confidential. Barney, however, ignores Andy's warning. Flattered by the Parkers' interest in what he has to say, Barney explains in great detail the bureau's "zone detection system."

The next day, Andy meets with Captain Dewhurst about the job opening in the department. Andy is not interested in the job but meets with the captain in order to please Barney. During the meeting, Andy learns that the opening is for Barney's job.

That evening, Andy asks Barney if he's ever thought about coming back to Mayberry and tells him his job is still open. Barney answers, "Well, that's awful nice of you, Ange, but I got everything going for me here—a big job. I got a terrific future."

WHY THEY WATCH

When *The Andy Griffith Show* first came out, Andy was really discouraged because the reviews in New York and Los Angeles were not too good. One columnist called the show 'corn-pone humor.' The critics thought it was a cartoon kind of show with cartoon characters—Andy being the exception.

Andy was really upset. I said to him, 'Forget those guys. Give me Ohio, Kansas. Give me the whole South. Give me Texas, Oklahoma, Indiana, Illinois.

The show found an audience in Middle America and became popular because people identified with it. They had the same problems the people of Mayberry had. Most towns have a goofball like Gomer or Goober Pyle. The audience would see Gomer and Goober, or one of the other wonderful characters we had, and think, 'They remind me of someone I know.'

In the mind of the audience *The Andy Griffith Show* was about real people who lived in a real town—a town where people cared about one another.

Richard O. Linke

I guess *The Andy Griffith Show* will go down as the best show that's ever been on and ever will be on television.

George Lindsey

The Parkers return from shopping and interrupt the conversation. Barney tells Andy that none of the family members go shopping without the others. After the Parkers go into the house, Andy notes that they didn't purchase much. He adds, "I mean, for a whole big family, they just came back with two little sacks."

At this point, a news flash is broadcast over the radio. Another supermarket robbery has occurred, this time on the city's south side. Barney tells Andy that there has to be a leak some place. He notes, "That's the eighth time in a row we've staked out two zones, and they've hit the third."

Andy and Barney rush over to the scene of the robbery. Captain Dewhurst and two detectives have been at the store for an hour and are looking around in back when the two arrive. The store manager is standing alone at the cash register. Unaware of the man's identity, Barney arrests the manager.

Captain Dewhurst releases the manager and sends Barney across the street to "get five coffees." While Barney is away, Dewhurst tells Andy that it's a rough case. He notes, "We're up against a gang that knows every move we make. Now, if we could only figure out a way to learn their moves." Andy thinks the situation over carefully.

The next day, Andy decides to "set up" the Parkers by sharing with them some "inside" information. He tells them that according to Captain Dewhurst, it was a good thing the robbers hit the night before because Saturday is a big shopping day. There will be more money involved, and the money will have to stay in the supermarket the whole weekend because the banks will be closed. Andy adds that the police have noticed that "the gang" never hits twice in the same area, so Captain Dewhurst does not plan to stake out the supermarket that was just robbed.

That evening, Andy suggests that he and Barney "go over to that supermarket that was knocked off last night and just kind of look around." Barney feels it would be a waste of time but agrees to stake out the store.

The Parkers decide to follow Andy's lead and are caught robbing the supermarket by Andy and Barney.

In the epilogue, Barney receives credit for "cracking the case." Thanks to Andy, Barney's status in the bureau is restored, and his job, at least for a while, is secure.

"I had received an offer to write for *The Smothers Brothers Show* around the time this script was written," says Sam. "Bill also had received various offers. I went on to do *The Smothers Brothers Show*, and 'A Visit to Barney Fife' became my final TAGS script.

"I enjoyed writing for the Smothers Brothers, but I missed writing for Andy and Don. They were a fabulous team. I always enjoyed writing for them. After Don left, however, some of the magic disappeared. It did not seem to be as much fun without him. So, maybe it was the right time for me to move on to something else."

INDEX

Greenbaum, Deane, 57, 185

Greenbaum, Everett: biographical information, 72, 77, 93, 136, 160, 206, 317, 368, 400; changes from original script, 180, 219, 272, 320, 322, 370; character's influence on script, 80, 92, 108-9, 135, 136, 137, 235, 236, 244, 248, 270, 271, 298, 305, 307-8, 339, 343, 367, 368, 381, 399; comments about actors & crew, 72, 75, 78, 90, 98, 199, 238, 243, 276, 296, 297, 322, 338, 365, 398; comments about characters, 7, 47-48, 55, 57, 74, 109, 137, 208, 210, 239, 341; comments about writing, 3, 8, 58, 100, 125, 130, 174, 176, 201, 224, 241-42, 244, 246; consistency with other episodes, 101, 463; didn't like parts of episode, 45-46, 70, 178, 307, 370; ideas from own experiences, 56, 91, 100, 109, 110, 119, 123, 135, 163, 221, 233, 235, 269, 270, 271, 272, 273, 274, 296, 306, 321, 368; influenced by movies, 97, 110-11, 188, 250; influences from family and friends, 5, 57, 92, 93, 96, 97, 121, 122, 161, 245, 248, 249, 270, 295, 308, 321, 341, 366, 398; quotes, 45, 55, 77, 80, 90, 108, 146, 179, 199, 219, 241, 247, 267, 269, 278, 300, 395, 401; script changes by others, 135, 247, 273; script ideas for the Darlings, 146-47, 151, 200, 203, 317-19, 395-97; script ideas for Ernest T. Bass, 185, 220-21, 222, 223, 276-77, 279, 281, 378-82; script ideas for Floyd, 82, 369; script ideas for Gomer, 91, 163, 205-6, 241, 246, 252, 307; script ideas for Opie, 94, 135, 208, 251, 340, 386, 397; script ideas for Otis, 173-74, 250; script ideas from Jim Fritzell, 74, 92, 136, 221, 223, 340; writing credits, 3, 45, 55, 71, 77, 90, 96, 108, 119, 133, 146, 160, 173, 179, 199, 205, 219, 232, 241, 247, 267, 275, 295, 305, 316, 338, 365, 378, 395

Greenbaum's Galley, 340

Greer, Dabbs, 406

Gribble, Bobby, 417

Griffith, Andy: contributions in writing sessions, 65, 225, 241, 488; his reaction to departure of cast, 442, 456; his reaction to scripts, 283, 343; how Andy set the tone for cast and crew, 153, 185, 204, 440, 449, 460, 476; how others viewed Andy, 79, 291, 304, 330-31, 393, 408; musical additions, 18, 71, 93, 147, 200, 247, 322; photos, 38, 73, 115, 120, 124, 128, 148, 175, 186, 215, 228, 285, 318, 412, 424, 437, 485; rapport between Andy & Don Knotts, 108, 161, 188, 317, 383, 387-88, 398, 493; reaction to early reviews, 491; role in choosing cast & crew, 4-5, 141, 146, 159, 220, 297, 428, 457; with the Dillards, 146, 151, 182; writing contributions, 23, 28, 62, 94, 187, 219, 238, 311, 382, 413, 429, 444, 484

Griffith, Barbara Edwards, 297

Grigsby, Harold and Sue, 423, 425

"Guitar Player, The," 71

Gurney, Cecil, 219

Hagen, Earle, 19, 31, 67-68, 74, 111-12, 159, 174, 298, 302, 385

Hanover, Roger, 371-77

Hanson brothers, 141, 143

Hanson, Protho, 144-45

Harmes, Vickie, 167

on camping trip, 351-56; photo, 99; quote, 338; scenes with Barney, 98, 100, 163-64; "shazzam," 143; soloist, 297-98; upset about giveaway, 260-61; with Hanson brothers, 140-44; withThelma Lou, 345-49; writing for Gomer's character, 395, 402, 439, 491

Pyle, Goober: as a mechanic, 92-94, 468, 470-71; compared to Gomer, 439, 491; feud between Floyd & Mr. Foley, 418-19; Gomer tells stories about, 257-58, 401; in Evie Joy episode, 474-78; in Old Sam episode, 483-84, 486-88; "running like a scalded dog," 411; watching sheriff's office, 413-15; with Andy & Helen, 402-5; with Newton Monroe, 429-30; with Warren, 442-43, 457-58

"Quiet Sam," 45

Quincey, Mr., 104, 106-7

Quincey, Steve, 103-6

Rafkin, Alan, 295, 378, 442, 447, 461, 467, 473, 477

Raft, George, 283-84

Randall, Tony, 279

Randolph, Isabel, 130

Reagan, Maureen, 252

Real McCoys, The, 3, 242

Red-crested, web-footed lake loon, 350, 355-56

Reluctant Astronaut, The, 7

Remington, Fred, 122

Riccardi, Richard, 297

Rickles, Don, 428

"Ridin' That New River Train," 130

Rimshaw house, 211, 213-16

Robinson, Edward G., 250

Rodenback, Jack, 100

Rodenback, Mrs., 100

Roger (Ollie and Nora's son) 367

Romero, Caesar, 448

Roosevelt, Franklin, 216

Ross, Bob, 435, 440-41, 442-44, 456-57, 461, 468, 477-78, 488, 489

Ruben, Aaron: after he left show, 435, 441, 442; aspects of his job, 33, 66, 107, 114, 130, 201, 213, 216-17, 225; assigning scripts, 12, 221-22, 27, 38, 156, 173, 199, 220, 241, 323-24, 365, 416; comments about episodes, 11, 20, 85, 93, 94, 164, 176-77, 226, 227, 244-45, 256, 280, 281, 291; comments from others about Aaron, 4-5, 16, 304, 330, 351, 386; his comments about cast, crew, & writers, 53, 62, 74, 75, 82, 359-60; in writing sessions, 49, 102, 241-42; JFK's death, 281-82; quotes, 65, 71, 173, 241, 283; role in casting and character development, 36, 40-41, 46-47, 61, 78-79, 91, 126, 146-47, 246, 275-76, 297, 310, 356, 428, 474; script consultation & changes, 18, 28, 29, 36, 50, 84, 96, 103, 135, 219, 253, 272, 328, 350, 373, 382, 413, 429, 468; similar plots, 90, 293, 404; working with writers, 3, 12, 224, 299-300

"Rumor, The," 404

Rush, Dennis, 325 (photo)

Ruskin, Coby, 267, 297, 330, 331, 338, 344, 350, 383, 416, 421, 428

Saberton, 392

Sally (a convict at large), 78-81

"Salty Dog," 151

Sam. *See* Old Sam

Sam (Floyd's dog), 22-23

Sandrich, Jay, 192-93, 271